Portland Community College Libraries

WITHDRAWN

D1019979

The Rebellious Slave

The
REBELLIOUS
SLAVE

NAT TURNER
IN AMERICAN MEMORY

Scot French

HOUGHTON MIFFLIN COMPANY

Boston   New York

2004

Copyright © 2004 by Scot French

All rights reserved

For information about permission to reproduce selections from
this book, write to Permissions, Houghton Mifflin Company,
215 Park Avenue South, New York, New York 10003.

Visit our Web site: www.houghtonmifflinbooks.com.

Library of Congress Cataloging-in-Publication Data
French, Scot.
The rebellious slave : Nat Turner in American
memory / Scot French.
p.   cm.
Includes bibliographical references and index.
ISBN 0-618-10448-8
1. Southampton Insurrection, 1831.   2. Turner, Nat, 1800?–1831.
3. Slaves — Virginia — Southampton County — Biography.
4. Turner, Nat, 1800?–1831 — Public opinion.   5. Southampton
Insurrection, 1831 — Public opinion.   6. Public opinion —
United States.   7. Memory — Social aspects — United States.
8. Slavery — United States — History.   I. Title.

F232.S7F74 2004   975.5'5503'092 — dc22
[B]   2003056895

Book design by Melissa Lotfy
Typefaces: Adobe Caslon and Filosofia

Printed in the United States of America

MP 10 9 8 7 6 5 4 3 2 1

Portions of Chapter 5 were previously published as "Mau-Mauing the
Filmmakers: Should Black Power Take the Rap for Killing *Nat
Turner,* the Movie?" In *Media, Culture, and the Modern African-
American Freedom Struggle,* ed. Brian Ward (Gainesville: University
Press of Florida, 2001), pp. 233–54. Reprinted with permission of the
University Press of Florida.

FOR CHRIS AND GIDEON

❖

Contents

Acknowledgments

This book, which evolved out of my Ph.D. dissertation in History at the University of Virginia, has been ten long years in the making. I would like to thank my family, friends, and colleagues for their patience and support throughout. A few individuals deserve special mention.

My thesis advisor, Edward L. Ayers, and the other members of my dissertation committee — Reginald D. Butler, Peter S. Onuf, Richard Handler, and Alon Confino — contributed enormously to my intellectual development and offered a wealth of suggestions on revising this manuscript for publication. Professors Gail Bederman, William Van Deburg, Waldo E. Martin, Jr., Nell Irvin Painter, Alan Trachtenberg, Michael West, and the late Armstead L. Robinson offered insightful commentary on various conference papers drawn from this study.

My fellow graduate students at the University of Virginia commented on early drafts and offered valuable input at various stages of the project. Thanks to Michael Ackerman, Alan Berolzheimer, Steve Camarota, Alice Carter, Barry Cushman, Colleen Doody, Rebecca Edwards, Amy Feely, Jeff Fleisher, Bruce Fort, Charles Irons, Peter Kastor, Gregg Kimball, Juliette Landphair, Bruce Larson, Matt Lassiter, Andy Lewis, Lisa Lindquist-Dorr, Gregg Michel, Andy Morris, Jen Moon, Amy Murrell, Andy Myers, Scott Rohrer, Josh Rothman, Anne Rubin, Scott Stephenson, Will Thomas, Phil Troutman, Drew VandeCreek, Andy Webster, and Rob Weise.

A two-year predoctoral research fellowship from the University of Virginia's Carter G. Woodson Institute for African-American and African Studies introduced me to a community of scholars that has never ceased to stimulate and sustain me. Of the many fine people I have come to know during my tenure at the institute, none have been greater friends and supporters than Reginald Butler, Gertrude Fraser, Michele Mitchell, Daryl Scott, Corey Walker, and Brian Ward.

My editor, Anton Mueller, has guided and encouraged me throughout this project. It was his great vision that made this book possible. Erica Avery, Alison Kerr Miller, and Rhiannon Agosti lent stalwart assistance in the final phases of publication.

I owe a heartfelt thanks to Tony Horwitz for featuring my work in his 1999 *New Yorker* article "Untrue Confessions: Is Most of What We Know About the Rebel Slave Nat Turner Wrong?" His enthusiastic reading of several chapters from my unfinished dissertation persuaded me to reach for an audience beyond the academy.

I am indebted to William Styron, Louise Meriwether, and the late Gilbert Francis for opening their doors to me and making their private papers available without restriction. Their generosity allowed me to mine a rich vein of previously unpublished source materials. Rick Francis and Kitty Futrell graciously served as my Southampton County tour guides and called my attention to several key documents in the local archives.

Several friends and family members deserve special mention for their unstinting faith in me and their unflagging support of this project: Ruben, Ruth, and Monika Madrid; Jeff and Jesse French; the Agundez, French, Helton, Gellert, Madrid, Lussier, and Robinson families; Barry and Karen Bogosian; Ruhi Grover; Nancy Pick; Gina Haney and Glenn Foulds; Peter and Lynn Hedlund; Chris and Patricia Jessee; Sonoma Kaur; Will Rourk and Jessica Primm; Michael and Colleen Tuite; Janene and Tom Fontaine; Victoria and Erich Young; Paul and Helene McCarthy; Chuck and Julie Badlato; Sally Henninger; Rikki Farber and (my best man) Aaron Zitner.

Most of all, I thank my parents, Norman and Margot, for encouraging me to reach for worlds beyond my own. I thank my son, Gideon, for reminding me that rocks and trees are interesting too. And I thank my wife, Chris, for giving me the strength to see this project through to the finish. I could not have done it without her.

The Rebellious Slave

INTRODUCTION

T HIS WILL BE a very noted day in Virginia," Governor John
Floyd wrote in his diary entry for the twenty-third day of August, 1831. "At daylight this morning the Mayor of the City
put into my hands a notice to the public, written by James Trezvant
of Southampton County, stating that an insurrection of the slaves in
that county had taken place, that several families had been massacred
and that it would take a considerable military force to put them
down." Eyewitness reports from the scene of "massacre and devastation" defied belief. Mutilated corpses — men, women, and children,
blacks and whites, slaves and masters — littered the landscape. "Like
the head of Medusa," wrote one awestruck observer, "it can scarcely be
looked on without converting the spectacle into marble."[1]

First the white people fell. "Between eighty and a hundred of the
whites have already been butchered — their heads severed from their
bodies," read one hastily written dispatch from a military encamp-
ment in neighboring Greensville County. "We saw several children
whose brains were knocked out," a mounted volunteer from Norfolk
reported. "Whole families, father, mother, daughters, sons, sucking
babes, and school children, butchered, thrown into heaps, and left to
be devoured by dogs and hogs, or to putrify on the spot," observed a
member of a Richmond cavalry troop. At one house, a military officer
found the bodies of "an old lady and six others" strewn about the yard,
"chopped to pieces with axes, the tree fences and house top covered
with buzzards preying on the carcasses." Horrified, he could not bring

himself to visit other nearby houses, "altho' there were several other families in sight, in the same situation."[2]

Then the black people fell. "From the best information," a North Carolina newspaper reported, "32 dead bodies [negroes] have been seen, besides a number are supposed to have died in the woods of their wounds." The senior editor of the *Richmond Whig*, who traveled to Southampton County as a member of a cavalry troop, deplored "the slaughter of many blacks, without trial, and under circumstances of great barbarity." He estimated the number killed in that manner — "generally by decapitation or shooting" — at forty, perhaps higher. The *Lynchburg Virginian* reported that "troops under the command of Gen. Broadnax, had slain upwards of 90 blacks, taken the leader in that section prisoner, shot him, cut off his head and limbs, and hung them in different sections, to inspire a salutary terror among the slaves." The *Raleigh Register* reported that "two leaders were shot and their heads placed upon stakes in the public road."[3]

White civil and military authorities, anxious to restore order, sought to minimize the extent of the rebellion and the threat of renewed attack. Geographically, they confined the trouble to a single "neighborhood" or "infected district" within Southampton County. Chronologically, they represented the uprising as a brief, spontaneous act, with little planning and no clear motive behind it. Militarily, they insisted that all but a few of the insurgents had been captured or killed. Early reports of four hundred armed insurgents gave way to revised estimates of no more than forty or fifty at best, many of them young boys coerced into joining. The confessions of prisoners and the interrogation of eyewitnesses pointed to an even smaller cadre of ringleaders — "the celebrated Nelson, called by the blacks, 'Gen. Nelson,'" "Will Artist, a free man of color," and "General Nat Turner (a preacher and a slave)," chief among them.[4]

As the other suspected ringleaders fell, the stature of Nat Turner rose. It was he, the Richmond newspapers reported, who had masterminded the whole affair.

> A fanatic preacher by the name of Nat Turner (Gen. Nat Turner) who had been taught to read and write, and permitted to go about preaching in the country, was at the bottom of this infernal brigandage. He was artful, impudent and vindictive, without any cause or provocation that could be assigned. (*Richmond Enquirer*, August 30, 1831)

This Nat seems to be a bold fellow, of the deepest cunning, who for years has been endeavoring to acquire an influence over the minds of those deluded wretches. He reads and writes with ease, it is said, and has long been a preacher. Superstitious himself, his object has been to operate upon the superstitious hopes and fears of others; and the late singular phenomenon of the Sun, enabled him to fill their minds with the most anxious forebodings, regarding it as an omen from Heaven, that their cause would result prosperously. (*Richmond Compiler*, September 3, 1831)

Thus, within two weeks of the uprising, an image of the rebel leader as a "fanatic preacher" with extraordinary powers of persuasion had already begun to take form. Turner's ability to elude capture despite a massive manhunt only added to his mystique. "Who is this Nat Turner?" the editors of the *Richmond Enquirer* asked. "Where is he from?"[5]

Turner eluded capture for more than two months, finally surrendering to a poor white farmer who found him hiding in a makeshift cave. A local lawyer, Thomas R. Gray, interviewed Turner in his jail cell, recorded his purported "Confessions," and published them as a pamphlet shortly after Turner was executed. The Virginia General Assembly, responding to public outcry in the immediate aftermath of the rebellion, debated plans for the gradual abolition of slavery and the removal of all free persons of color from the Commonwealth. In the end, state legislators decided by a slim majority to defer action on such sweeping reforms and instead passed measures aimed at tightening control over the slave population. Memories of "Old Nat's War," preserved in officially sanctioned histories and submerged oral traditions, stirred emotions and spurred debate for generations to come.

What follows is neither a traditional biography of Nat Turner nor a definitive account of Nat Turner's Rebellion. This is a book about America's search for transcendent meaning in its troubled past, with a focus on the larger-than-life figure of the rebellious slave. The stories told here, spanning two centuries, illuminate a multicultural discourse on race, slavery, and revolutionary violence rooted in common claims to America's founding myths, symbols, and traditions.

Part I examines the evolving image of the rebellious slave in American thought from the period of the American Revolution through the cataclysmic events of 1831. The jeremiads of Thomas Jefferson, David Walker, and William Lloyd Garrison anticipated the appearance of a black Spartacus and warned of a coming race war should Americans fail to eradicate slavery. Part II focuses on the official inquiry into Turner's Rebellion and the making of a master narrative designed to tranquilize an agitated public and facilitate the restoration of order throughout the region. The declarations of key participant observers — a Richmond newspaper editor, a Southampton County slave girl, the governor of Virginia — reveal the deadly uncertainties that prevailed before the publication of Nat Turner's so-called "Confessions" put rumors of a wider conspiracy to rest. Part III charts the evolving image of Turner as an American icon — alternately revered and reviled, embraced and distanced — through the eras of slavery and emancipation, civil war and reconstruction, Jim Crow and civil rights. Slaveholders, abolitionists, advocates of black uplift, defenders of white supremacy, New Negroes, New Dealers, civil rights pacifists, Black Power militants — all enlisted Turner, at one time or another, as hero or villain. The literary-historical controversy surrounding William Styron's 1967 novel, *The Confessions of Nat Turner*, commands extended treatment, as it remains the single most influential work on the subject, overshadowing even the original "Confessions" in public consciousness today.

The concept of *social* or *collective memory* undergirds this study. Historical in focus, it asks: How have various individuals and social groups within American society imagined themselves and their relationship to one another by reference to the event known as "Nat Turner's Rebellion"? How has the image of Turner, as depicted in American history, literature, and folklore, responded to the changing needs of society and shifting currents in American thought?[6]

Scholars have long recognized that history — "the memory of things said and done" — represents society's ongoing search for a useable past. As Carl Becker wrote more than seventy years ago, "every generation, our own included, will, must inevitably, understand the past and anticipate the future in the light of its own restricted experience, must inevitably play on the dead whatever tricks it finds necessary for its own peace of mind." The historian Merrill D. Peterson applied this insight to his classic study *The Jefferson Image in the American Mind* (1960), which charted the postmortem career of Thomas Jefferson as a popular cultural icon. "This is not a book on the history Thomas Jefferson made," Peterson explained in the preface, "but a book on what history made of Thomas Jefferson." More recently, historians have employed the concept of social or collective memory "to explore how a social group, be it a family, a class, or a nation, constructs a past through a process of invention and appropriation and what it means to the relationship of power within society." Much of this scholarly literature, Alon Confino writes in *The Nation As Local Metaphor* (1997), has focused on conflicts within and between dominant and subordinate groups over "who wants whom to remember what, and why." Yet memory, he notes, can also illuminate the broad planes of consensus that hold nations and other "imagined communities" together.

My long-standing interest in conflicting perceptions of the past, piqued by the controversy over Styron's fictionalized representation of Turner, led me first to the study of another historical figure associated with race and slavery: Thomas Jefferson. In 1992 my friend and colleague Edward L. Ayers invited me to coauthor an article for a volume of essays titled *Jeffersonian Legacies,* a retrospective look at the slaveholding statesman on the two hundred and fiftieth anniversary of his birth. The article surveyed changing American attitudes toward Jefferson from 1943 to 1993, picking up where Merrill Peterson left off in his classic study. Ayers and I were struck by the diminishing cultural authority of professional historians in shaping perceptions of the American past. Jefferson's rumored sexual liaisons with his slave mistress Sally Hemings, long dismissed as a groundless slander by his biographers yet preserved as fact in black oral tradition, became the focal point of public debates over Jefferson's character and the nation's willingness to accept a counternarrative at odds with the official portrait. Jefferson's biographers found their claims to scholarly objectivity increasingly challenged by popular writers who embraced black oral tradition and the emerging image of Jefferson as the all-too-human father of a mixed-race country. The "tricks" that all parties to the debate played on the past shook my faith in objectivity as an oft-stated principle of historical inquiry. I came away convinced that the lines between history, a scholarly discipline based on rules of evidence, and memory, its popular but unruly cousin, were far blurrier than commonly believed.[7]

The *Jeffersonian Legacies* article revealed cracks and fissures in America's heroic self-image, which I probe more deeply in this study of Nat Turner's Rebellion in history and memory. Turner himself plays a critical role as the reputed leader and mastermind of the rebellion, yet the focus is less on him than on those who lay claim to his story. As Turner recedes into history, various people, both famous and obscure, assume key roles as guardians of his memory. The stories they tell — recorded and preserved in public records, private letters, books and articles, visual imagery and dramatic reenactments — reveal intense struggles for social power and cultural authority in a socially stratified, culturally diverse nation.

While my work is informed by a growing body of scholarship on the subject of Turner's Rebellion in history and memory, it draws inspiration from sources outside the academy as well. Like *Rashomon*, the 1950 murder-mystery by Japanese filmmaker Akira Kurosawa, my study offers no single accounting of the incident in question, but rather a series of prophecies and flashbacks in which expert witnesses with varying degrees of cultural authority imagine and reimagine the scene. It offers no clear resolution to the problem of misleading or conflicting testimony, leaving readers with a nagging sense of insecurity about what can be known with any certainty about the past. I found another muse in the Tom Stoppard play *Rosencrantz and Guildenstern Are Dead,* which puts the spotlight on two minor characters from Shakespeare's *Hamlet.* In like fashion, my study of Nat Turner shifts the spotlight from the center to the periphery, from the well-established protagonist to other, relatively minor characters with varying degrees of proximity to the "main event." It analyzes the public testimony offered by these bit players for insights into the worlds in which they lived. It follows them offstage, whenever possible, and eavesdrops on their conversations with others. Finally, *The Return of Martin Guerre,* a French film based on a legendary case of stolen identity, provided me with a historical analogy. A small village must decide whether a man claiming to be the long-lost Martin Guerre is who he says he is. I see the "return" of Martin Guerre as something of a metaphor for the reappearance of Nat Turner, in various literary-historical guises, over the course of two centuries. With each celebrated "return," the public must ask: Is this the real Nat Turner — or a clever imposter?[8]

Turner was neither the first nor the last American slave to conspire against his would-be masters, yet he stands alone in American thought as the epitome of the rebellious slave, a black messiah whose words and deeds challenged the slaveholding South and awakened a slumbering nation. A maker of history in his own day, Turner has been made to serve the most pressing needs of every generation since. In remembering Nat Turner, we are forced to confront — or deftly evade, at our peril — the intertwined legacies of slavery and racial oppression in a nation founded on revolutionary ideals of freedom and equality.

1

PROPHECY

THE REBELLIOUS SLAVE figured prominently in American thought long before Nat Turner and his followers left their bloody mark on history. The antislavery jeremiads, or political sermons, of Thomas Jefferson (*Notes on the State of Virginia,* 1787), David Walker (*Appeal to the Coloured Citizens of the World,* 1829–30), and William Lloyd Garrison (*Liberator,* 1831) included frightful prophecies of bloody slave uprisings and apocalyptic race wars as a spur to national repentance and reform. These writers agreed that slavery corrupted the manners and morals of white people, oppressed and degraded black people, and incurred the wrath of a vengeful God. They disagreed, however, as to the most practical and principled means of dispensing freedom and averting a racial Armageddon. Jefferson proposed the gradual emancipation of all slaves born after a certain date, conditioned upon their removal and resettlement beyond the limits of the United States. Walker, a free man of color, demanded the immediate, unconditional emancipation of his enslaved brethren and the extension of equal rights to all "coloured citizens" of the United States. He counseled resistance to tyrants, by force of arms if necessary. Garrison urged the oppressed black masses to await their deliverance in "God's time." Better that freedom should come by "moral force" on the part of the nation, he advised, than by "physical force" on the part of the slaves.

The jeremiad — named for the Old Testament prophet Jeremiah — provided the ideal vehicle for these antislavery writers and orators to express their love of country (*amor patriae*) even as they lamented the sins of the nation and the failings of their countrymen. Historians have traced this form of public address from its development in early modern England to its transformation by New England Puritan orators into "America's first distinctive literary genre." The Puritans conceived of themselves as a chosen people, sent by God on an "errand into the wilderness" to establish a model church-state. So long as they honored their sacred covenant with God, their ministers proclaimed, they would enjoy peace and prosperity unparalleled in world history. Should they forget the errand, however, a host of worldly afflictions would descend upon them. God's special dispensation to the Puritans became, like British common law, the birthright of all Anglo-Americans who traced their lineage to the Puritan exodus from England. When British imperial authorities began tightening administrative control over the North American colonies in the mid-eighteenth century, opposition writers fused the moralistic language of classical republicanism (civic virtue versus corruption) with the self-anointing rhetoric of the Puritan jeremiad (Americans as a "chosen people") to build the case for civil disobedience, armed resistance, and, ultimately, independence.[1]

African-American writers and orators adapted the jeremiad to their own purposes. Comparing themselves to the ancient Israelites, they awaited the arrival of a messiah who would lead them out of bondage and into the Promised Land. Like their white counterparts, these "black Jeremiahs" saw themselves as "scribes of a chosen people who were working out an independent destiny." That destiny, by and large, lay not in the establishment of a black nation outside the boundaries of the United States, but within a reformed American society purged of slavery and committed to the revolutionary principles set forth in the Declaration of Independence.[2]

The antislavery jeremiads of Jefferson, Walker, and Garrison, read in correspondence with one another, illuminate a spirited discourse on race, slavery, and national belonging that spanned the first fifty years of the American republic. Their open sympathies with the rebellious slave stand in sharp contrast to the views of white civil and military authorities charged with investigating Nat Turner's Rebellion and ensuring that such an event would never happen again.

As the leading spokesman for American independence and master architect of the new republic, Jefferson distinguished himself as an antislavery Jeremiah of the first order. Born in 1743 on the frontiers of English settlement in colonial Virginia, Jefferson enjoyed the privileges reserved to his race, class, and gender. His earliest recollection, according to one nineteenth-century biographer, was of "his being handed up and carried on a pillow by a mounted slave." When his father died in 1757, fourteen-year-old Jefferson inherited a large estate; at age twenty-one, he took possession of five thousand acres and twenty-two slaves. His marriage in 1772 doubled his landholdings and brought an additional one hundred and thirty-five slaves into his possession. Monticello, the neoclassical mansion that Jefferson built for himself and his growing family, towered over a sprawling plantation complex, the economic viability of which depended on a massive force of enslaved black laborers.[3]

Jefferson took his first public stand against slavery as a young colonial Virginia legislator. In 1769, as a newly elected member of the Virginia House of Burgesses, he supported measures that would have made it easier for slaveholders to manumit slaves by will or by deed. Jefferson prevailed upon Colonel Richard Bland, "one of the oldest, ablest, & most respected members" of the colonial legislature, to introduce his bill. "I seconded his motion," Jefferson later recalled, "and as a younger member, was more spared in the debate; but he was denounced as an enemy of his country, & treated with the grossest indecorum."[4]

The British imperial crisis heightened Jefferson's awareness of black aspirations to freedom. In stating the case for American independence, Jefferson began to think of enslaved blacks as a people without a country, a "captive nation" with its own God-given destiny. British despotism, in his view, had created two nations, one subjugated, the other enslaved, and placed them at war with each other. Jefferson saw the independence of both nations as the prerequisite for peace and mutual security. As soon as he and his fellow patriots had secured their own liberties through independence, he would turn his intellectual energies to the gradual emancipation of the slaves and their resettlement as "a free and independent people" somewhere outside of Virginia.[5]

By 1775, as Jefferson and other British American colonists shouted themselves hoarse in defense of their Anglo-Saxon liberties, Virginia and other slaveholding colonies of the mid-Atlantic and lower South had become virtual police states. A system of patrols and passes regulated the movement of slaves and free persons of color; spe-

cial courts of oyer and terminer, established "for the more speedy prosecution of slaves conmitting Capitall Crimes," meted out punish-
ments "without the solemnitie of the jurie." A rigid censorship of
news related to slave unrest effectively silenced the opposition from
within.[6]

The outbreak of the Revolutionary War tested the loyalties of the
slaves and raised the insurrection anxieties of Virginia slaveholders to
a fever pitch. Lord Dunmore, the royal governor of Virginia, offered
freedom to those slaves willing to bear arms against the rebellious
American colonists. Colonial propagandists reminded the enslaved
black masses of continued British support for the international slave
trade and spelled out the limitations of Dunmore's Proclamation. The
royal governor had promised freedom to none but able-bodied men
willing to cross enemy lines and take up arms against their former
masters. What would his proclamation do for women and children,
the aged and infirm, who could not — or would not — risk their lives
for an uncertain future under British rule? Virginia slaves were urged
to cast their lot with their masters, "who pity their condition, who
wish in general to make it as easy and comfortable as possible, and
who would willingly, if it were in their power, or were they permitted,
not only prevent any more negroes from losing their freedom, but restore it to such as have already lost it." Despite threats of capital punishment and the heightened vigilance of slave patrols and colonial militia, some three to four hundred runaways managed to reach British
lines and enlist in "Lord Dunmore's Ethiopian Regiment." Outfitted
in military uniforms bearing the revolutionary slogan "Liberty to
Slaves," they fought in one major battle and served with Dunmore until his retreat from the Chesapeake Bay in August 1776.[7]

Lord Dunmore's willingness to arm slaves against their masters
buttressed Jefferson's case for a British conspiracy to establish "an absolute tyranny over these states." In his original draft of the Declaration of Independence, Jefferson asked a "candid world" to consider the
last and perhaps most damning charge against the king: that he had
"waged cruel war against human nature itself, violating its most sacred
rights of life & liberty in the persons of a distant people who never offended him, captivating and carrying them into slavery in another
hemisphere, or to incur miserable death in their transportation
thither," and that he was "now exciting those very people to rise in
arms among us, and to purchase that liberty of which *he* . . . deprived

them." To Jefferson's chagrin, the Continental Congress voted to delete all but the most oblique references to slavery from the final draft of the Declaration, bowing to the objections of South Carolina and Georgia. Congress amended the final version to state that the king had "excited domestic insurrections amongst us," leaving future generations to ponder just who had been "excited" to rise against whom.[8]

American independence from Great Britain and the transformation of Virginia from colony to self-governed state presented Jefferson and his fellow revolutionaries with an opportunity to address the future of slavery — and the legal status of free blacks and mulattoes — without fear of the "royal negative." At its first session, the Commonwealth of Virginia's newly constituted General Assembly appointed Jefferson to a three-member committee charged with revising the state's code of laws to eliminate any vestiges of monarchy. Among the "most remarkable" recommendations of the committee, Jefferson later recalled, was a proposal "to emancipate all slaves born after passing the act." Authored by Jefferson, the plan called for those freed by statute to "continue with their parents to a certain age, then be brought up, at the public expense, to tillage, arts or sciences, according to their geniuses, till the females should be eighteen, and the males twenty-one years of age, when they should be colonized to such place as the circumstances of the time should render most proper." To replace its ever-diminishing black labor force, the Commonwealth of Virginia would "send vessels at the same time to other parts of the world for an equal number of white inhabitants," with special inducements to encourage voluntary migration.[9]

Jefferson gave this embryonic emancipation/colonization plan wide circulation in *Notes on the State of Virginia.* He first drafted *Notes* in 1781 in response to queries from the secretary of the French legation, the Marquis de Barbé-Marbois, and continued to expand and revise the manuscript over the next three years. Besieged with requests from friends, he arranged for the private printing of some two hundred copies. Publication of an unauthorized French translation forced Jefferson to issue an authorized version in 1787; the first American edition appeared the following year, followed by piecemeal publication in American newspapers.[10]

In "Query XIV: Laws," Jefferson expounded on the racial anxieties that led him to insist on the colonization of blacks and mulattoes outside the United States as a condition of their emancipation.

It will probably be asked, Why not retain and incorporate the blacks into the state, and thus save the expence of supplying, by importation of white settlers, the vacancies they will leave? Deep rooted prejudices entertained by the whites; ten thousand recollections, by the blacks, of the injuries they have sustained; new provocations; the real distinctions which nature has made; and many other circumstances, will divide us into parties, and produce convulsions which will probably never end but in the extirmination of the one or the other race.

To these "political" considerations, Jefferson added "physical" and "moral" ones as well. Emancipation without deportation would leave the former slaves free to "mix" with their former masters, thus blurring "real distinctions" between the races. An unabashed racial chauvinist, Jefferson considered whites superior to black people in beauty, reason, and imagination. "This unfortunate difference of colour, and perhaps of faculty," he wrote, "is a powerful obstacle to the emancipation of these people." Colonization would remove this obstacle, he suggested, by placing the slave, when freed, "beyond the reach of mixture." Jefferson's long-standing anxieties over race-mixing, stated as a general philosophy in *Notes on the State of Virginia,* assumed an intensely personal and overtly political dimension when it was reported, during his presidency some fifteen years later, that he had fathered as many as five children by his slave mistress, Sally Hemings.[11]

In "Query XVIII: Manners," Jefferson put on his frock coat and ascended to his literary pulpit as an American Jeremiah. He reminded his fellow slaveholders that "the liberties of a nation" were "the gift of God" and that they risked what they had so recently won by denying such liberties to others.

Indeed, I tremble for my country when I reflect that God is just; that his justice cannot sleep for ever: that considering numbers, nature and natural means only, a revolution of the wheel of fortune, an exchange of situation, is among possible events; that it may become probable by supernatural interference! The Almighty has no attribute that can take sides with us in such a contest.

Jefferson held out hope that his fellow Americans might act, in time, to avert such a calamity. "The spirit of the master is abating, that of the slave rising from the dust, his condition mollifying, the way I hope preparing, under the auspices of heaven, for a total emancipation, and that this is disposed, in the order of events, to be with the consent of the masters, rather than by their extirpation."[12]

Jefferson's views on black inferiority — the suspicion that under-girded his insistence on expatriation as a condition of emancipation — did not go unchallenged by African Americans. In 1791, Benjamin Banneker, a surveyor and astronomer from Maryland, sent Jefferson a copy of an almanac he had compiled, along with a letter protesting the continued enslavement and oppression of the "African race" in the United States. Banneker reminded Jefferson of the special dispensa-tion that God had made to the British American colonists in bestow-ing the blessings of liberty upon them. Surely Jefferson, of all people, understood that the founders of the new nation risked God's wrath in depriving African Americans of those same God-given blessings.

> Look back, I entreat you, on the variety of dangers to which you were exposed; reflect on that time, in which every human aid ap-peared unavailable, and in which even hope and fortitude wore the aspect of inability to the conflict, and you cannot but be led to a se-rious and grateful sense of your miraculous and providential pres-ervation; you cannot but acknowledge, that the present freedom and tranquility which you enjoy you have mercifully received, and that is the peculiar blessing of Heaven.

For Banneker, the Declaration of Independence represented a sacred covenant with God. He chided Jefferson and his fellow American pa-triots for violating the spirit, if not the letter, of that covenant "in de-taining by fraud and violence so numerous a part of my brethren, un-der groaning captivity and cruel oppression." Banneker offered no legislative remedies, issued no dire prophecies. Instead, he advised Jef-ferson and his compatriots to "wean" themselves from their "narrow prejudices" toward African Americans and to, "as Job proposed to his friends, 'put your soul in their souls' stead.'" In viewing the problem of slavery from the vantage point of the slave, they would need no direc-tion "in what manner to proceed."[13]

Jefferson endorsed revolutionary violence in pursuit of liberty even as he fretted over the prospect of slave rebellion at home. From Paris, where he served as a diplomat from 1784 to 1789, he wrote to his friend and fellow American revolutionary James Madison:

> I hold it that a little rebellion now and then is a good thing, & as necessary in the political world as storms in the physical. Unsuccessful rebellions indeed generally establish the encroachments on the rights of the people which have produced them. An observation of this truth should render honest republican governors so mild in their punishment of rebellions, as not to discourage them too much. It is a medicine necessary for the sound health of government.

The French Revolution, fought under the banner of "Liberty, Equality, and Fraternity," fueled his zeal. While Jefferson deplored the execution, without trial, of "many guilty" and "some innocent" persons at the hands of the French Jacobins, he insisted that the cost in human lives was small when compared to the benefits reaped by mankind. To his secretary William Short, he wrote: "The liberty of the whole earth was depending on the issue of the contest, and was ever such a prize won with so little innocent blood?" To François D'Ivernois he added: "It is unfortunate, that the efforts of mankind to recover the freedom of which they have been so long deprived, will be accompanied with violence, with errors, & even with crimes. But while we weep over the means, we must pray for the end."[14]

Jefferson said no such prayers on behalf of the "black Jacobins" who rebelled against the white planter class in the French West Indian colony of Saint Domingue. As U.S. secretary of state, Jefferson lent a sympathetic ear to requests from the embattled white rulers of the island for assistance in putting down "the insurrection of their negroes." By July 1793, Jefferson was extending his condolences to the deposed white planters, thousands of whom had taken refuge in the United States. Their situation, he wrote to James Monroe, "calls aloud for pity & charity. Never was so deep a tragedy presented to the feelings of man." Jefferson feared that the bloody scenes of Saint Domingue foreshadowed the violent breaking of slavery's shackles throughout the hemisphere. "I become daily more & more convinced that all the West India islands will remain in the hands of the people of colour, & a total expulsion of the whites sooner or later take place. It is high time we should foresee the bloody scenes which our children certainly, and

possibly ourselves (south of the Potomac,) have to wade through, &
try to avert them."[15]

For Jefferson, the violent expulsion of whites from Saint Domingue represented the "first chapter" in an unfolding history of slavery's demise in the New World. Whether the white people of Virginia
were destined to fall at the hands of rebellious slaves remained to be
seen. Ever the optimist, Jefferson expressed hope that Virginia's General Assembly — inspired by events in Saint Domingue — would find
"a peaceable accommodation between justice, policy & necessity" and
adopt a plan of gradual emancipation and removal. "The sooner we
put some plan underway," he wrote to St. George Tucker in 1797, "the
greater hope there is that it may be permitted to proceed peaceably to
it's [sic] ultimate effect. But if something is not done, & soon done, we
shall be the murderers of our own children."[16]

What Jefferson feared in the abstract assumed a very real countenance with the discovery in August 1800 of an extensive conspiracy
among blacks in Richmond and across eastern Virginia. Jefferson received a detailed account of the conspiracy from James Thomson
Callender, a Republican Party polemicist and scandalmonger then
languishing in a Richmond jail on a Federalist charge of sedition.
Callender attributed much of his information to his jailer, William
Rose, whom he identified as an "old acquaintance and protégé" of
Jefferson's.

> Nothing is talked of here but the great conspiracy of the negroes.
> One Thomas Prosser, a young man who had fallen heir, some time
> ago, to a habitation within six miles of the city, had behaved with
> great barbarity to his slaves. One of them, named Gabriel, a fellow
> of courage and intellect above his rank in life, laid a plan of re-
> venge. Immense numbers immediately entered into it, and it has
> been kept with incredible secrecy for several months. A number of
> swords were made in a clumsy enough manner out of rough iron,
> others by breaking the blade of a scythe in the middle, which thus
> made two swords of a most formidable kind. There were fastened
> in proper handles, and would have cut off a man's limb at a single
> blow.
>
> The conspirators were to have met in a wood near Prosser's
> house, upon Saturday before last, after it was dark. Upon that day,
> or some very short time before it, notice was received from a fel-

low, who being invited, somewhat unguardedly, to go to the rendezvous, refused, and immediately informed his master's overseer. No ostensible preparations were, however, made until the afternoon preceding the night of the rendezvous; and as the militia are in a state of the most contemptible disorganization, as the blacks are numerous, robust and desperate, there must have been bloody work. But upon that very evening just about sunset, there came on the most terrible thunderstorm, accompanied with enormous rain, that I ever witnessed in this state. Between Prosser's and Richmond, there is a place called Brook Swamp, which runs across the high road, and over which there was a bridge. By this, the Africans were of needs to pass, and the rain had made passage impracticable. Beside, they were deprived of the junction and assistance of their good friends in this city, who could not go out to join them. They were to have attacked the Capitol and penitentiary. They could hardly have failed of success; for after all, we only could muster four or five hundred men, of whom not more than thirty had muskets.

From his jail cell, Callender witnessed the arrival and departure of black prisoners. He described the purgatorial scene in a subsequent letter to Jefferson: "In one end of the lower story, the blacks are singing psalms. In the other, a boy, who has gone crazy, is shrieking in lunacy, the sailors laughing." Callender concluded with a Latin phrase that Jefferson, classically educated in the Southern planter tradition, most surely understood: *"Sic transit mundus!"* Thus passes the world![17]

To interrogate the suspects and establish the full extent of the conspiracy, white civil authorities convened special courts of oyer and terminer. The "gentleman justices" who presided over these courts, without a jury, assigned counsel, heard evidence, issued verdicts, and pronounced sentences. The testimony of black witnesses — generally viewed by white authorities as untrustworthy and thus prohibited by law — was deemed admissible in these courts, perhaps because the cases against suspected black conspirators so often turned on the eyewitness testimony of one or more black informants. The trials confirmed, by and large, what white officials had suspected. "It is unquestionably the most serious and formidable conspiracy we have ever known of the kind," the Virginia governor James Monroe reported to Jefferson in mid-September. Jefferson believed the worst was yet to come. In a letter to his friend Dr. Benjamin Rush of Philadelphia, he wrote: "You will hear an account of an attempt at insurrection in this state. I am looking with anxiety to see what will be its effect on our State. We are truly to be pitied."[18]

Gabriel, the reputed leader of the conspiracy, used the promise of a confession to secure his safe transport from Norfolk, where he was captured, to Richmond, where he would stand trial for conspiracy and insurrection. The prisoner informed his captors that he would give "full information" to Governor Monroe and would "confess to no else." Once granted his audience with the governor, however, Gabriel refused to make a confession and denied having promised to do so. Monroe was somewhat perplexed by this turn of events, as he explained in a testy note to the mayor of Norfolk: "By your letter, it appeared he had promised a full confession, but on his arrival here he denied making it. From what he said to me, he seemed to have made up his mind to die, and to have resolved to say but little on the subject of the conspiracy." Gabriel was no more forthcoming in jail. Three men appointed to take his confession informed the executive council that the prisoner "appeared to make no confession worth reporting." In declining to make a confession, Gabriel missed the opportunity to state his case to the world and burnish his own legend, yet ensured that his words would not be twisted to the nefarious purposes of his enemies.[19]

Jefferson urged Monroe to stay the executions of dozens of slaves convicted of conspiring with Gabriel to rebel. "The other states & the world at large will forever condemn us if we indulge a principle of revenge, or go one step beyond absolute necessity," he wrote. "They cannot lose sight of the rights of the two parties, & the object of the unsuccessful one." Still, the question remained: What was to be done with those spared death? As Monroe observed, "it is hardly to be presumed, a rebel who avows it was his intention to assassinate his master, if pardoned, will now become a useful servant." Jefferson concurred. "Our situation is indeed a difficult one, for I doubt whether these people can ever be allowed to go at large among us safely." Jefferson urged Monroe to reprieve the condemned prisoners and confine them to a "fort or garrison of the state or of the Union" until the next meeting of the Virginia General Assembly in December. "Surely the legislature would pass a law for their exportation," Jefferson wrote, "the proper measure on this & all similar occasions."[20]

In December 1800, Monroe delivered a special report on the "proposed insurrection" to the Virginia General Assembly. "It belongs to the Legislature to weigh with profound attention, this unpleasant incident in our history," Monroe said. "What has happened may occur again at any time, with more fatal consequences, unless suitable measures be taken to prevent it." The General Assembly instructed Monroe to correspond with newly elected President Jefferson "on the subject of purchasing land without the limits of this State, whither persons obnoxious to the laws, or dangerous to the peace of society may be removed." In January 1802, Monroe coupled a report on yet another "threatened insurrection" — this one involving slaves in Nottoway County — with a pointed reminder that "the public danger proceeding from this description of persons is daily increasing." He cited, among the causes, "the contrast in the condition of the free negroes and the slaves" and "the growing sentiment of liberty existing in the minds of the latter." The following month, Monroe informed Jefferson that the legislature had reiterated its interest in colonization as a safety valve designed to draw off the most dangerous elements of the "negro" population.[21]

Jefferson welcomed the opportunity to advise Monroe and the state legislature on the matter. He recommended that Virginia send its black exiles to a remote locale, "inhabited already by a people of their own race & color" and "insulated from the other descriptions of men." He singled out the French colony of Saint Domingue, then under the control of the black revolutionary leader Toussaint L'Ouverture, as the "most promising" destination for blacks in the western hemisphere. Jefferson speculated that Toussaint "might be willing, on many considerations, to receive even those exiled for acts deemed criminal by us, but meritorious, perhaps, by him." If no place could be found for Virginia's black exiles in the western hemisphere, Jefferson looked to Africa as "a last and undoubted resort."[22]

Jefferson expressed genuine dismay that slaves found guilty of participation in Gabriel's conspiracy "fell victim" to a law that condemned them to death. He had no qualms about sending slaves found "guilty of insurgency" to join a colony of free blacks established by the English Sierra Leone Company on the coast of West Africa. "They are such as will be a valuable acquisition to the settlement already existing there, and well calculated to cooperate in the plan of civilization," he assured the British ambassador in June 1802. Monroe was less sanguine about the idea of granting freedom to rebellious slaves as a condition of their removal. He could not imagine that the General Assembly, in commuting the death sentences of black insurgents to banishment, intended to "put culprits in a better condition than the deserving part of those people [the slaves]."[23]

Throughout his two-term presidency (1801–1809), Jefferson foreswore any public comment on the subject of emancipation. Yet he continued to fret privately that the slaves would liberate themselves, on their own bloody terms, in the absence of "any early provision for the extinguishment of slavery among us." In an 1805 letter to William A. Burwell, Jefferson expressed optimism that economic self-interest — and perhaps a measure of fear — might prompt recalcitrant slaveholders to support a plan of gradual emancipation and removal. "The value of the slave is every day lessening; his burden on his master daily increasing," Jefferson declared. "Interest is therefore preparing the disposition to be just; and this will be goaded from time to time by the insurrectionary spirit of the slaves." Jefferson warned against overconfidence on the part of the white population; rebellion could erupt anywhere at any time. A local uprising might be "easily quelled in it's [sic] first efforts; but from being local it will become general, and whenever it does it will rise more formidable after every defeat, until we shall be forced, after dreadful scenes & sufferings to release them in their own way, which, without such sufferings we might now model after our own convenience." Nearly a decade later, in the midst of the War of 1812, Jefferson was still heralding the approach of an avenging angel. "The hour of emancipation is advancing, in the march of time," he proclaimed. "It will come; and whether brought on by the generous energy of our own minds; or by the bloody process of St. Domingo . . . is a leaf of our history not yet turned over."[24]

The changing social and political geography of the United States heightened Jefferson's late-life fears for the survival of the new republic. By the 1810s, slavery was well on its way to extinction in the North, where wage labor proved cheap and plentiful and free blacks posed no significant threat to white supremacy. Antislavery sentiment, fueled by evangelical Christianity, flourished in such a climate. In the South, by contrast, slavery was becoming more deeply entrenched, migrating southwestward from the older seaboard states of Maryland, Virginia, the Carolinas, and Georgia to the newly admitted states of Louisiana, Mississippi, and Alabama. Powerful interests, both social and economic, converged in defense of the "peculiar institution."

Jefferson watched with increasing anxiety as congressional debates over slavery's extension into the western states escalated into the first full-blown sectional crisis since the framing of the U.S. Constitution. When the Missouri territorial assembly applied for statehood in 1819, U.S. Representative James Tallmadge of New York introduced an amendment prohibiting the transportation of slaves into the state and mandating the adoption of measures aimed at gradual emancipation; incensed, Southern partisans charged that the Tallmadge amendment violated state sovereignty and threatened the delicate balance of power between slave states and free states in the U.S. Senate. The Missouri Compromise, brokered by Henry Clay, maintained the balance of power in the U.S. Senate by admitting Maine as a free state and Missouri as a slave state; more significant, it prohibited slavery in the remaining Louisiana territory north of 36°30′ north latitude (the southern boundary of Missouri), with the exception of Missouri. The sharp line of demarcation between the free-soil North and slave-holding South symbolized the growing sectional divide over slavery's future.

Jefferson's refusal to speak out on the subject of emancipation, even in retirement, rendered him increasingly irrelevant to policy-making at the state and national levels. He reserved his jeremiads for the ears of young disciples, such as Edward Coles, his Albemarle County neighbor. In an 1814 letter, Coles implored the "Sage of Monticello" to assert his influence on behalf of the flagging antislavery movement in Virginia. The seventy-one-year-old Jefferson begged off, saying that he had done his best, as a young man, to abolish slavery, and that it was time for others to lead the way. "This enterprise is for the young; for those who can follow it up, and bear it through to its consummation," he wrote. "It shall have all my prayers, & these are the only weapons of an old man." Coles begged to differ; it would take more than prayers, he argued, to sway public opinion on such a weighty matter. "To effect so great and difficult an object great and extensive powers both of mind and influence are required, which can never be possessed in so great a degree by the young as by the old." Coles reminded Jefferson that the venerable Benjamin Franklin — "to whom, by the way, Pennsylvania owes her early riddance of the evils of slavery" — remained as active in his autumn years as in the spring of his life.[25]

Throughout his long career as an American statesman-prophet,

Jefferson maintained a remarkable consistency on the subject of emancipation. He was for black freedom on his terms, and his terms only. Jefferson never found a more "practicable" plan for the eradication of slavery than the one he set forth in *Notes on the State of Virginia.* "My sentiments have been 40 years before the public," he wrote in May 1826, six weeks before his death at the age of eighty-three. "Had I repeated them 40 times, they would only have become the more stale and threadbare. Altho I shall not live to see their consummation, they will not die with me; but living or dying, they will ever be in my most fervent prayers."[26]

With a grand patriotic flourish, Jefferson died on July 4, 1826, fifty years to the day after the signing of the Declaration of Independence. In his last will and testament, he arranged for the manumission of five trusted servants — all of them products of mixed-race unions at Monticello, all of them literate and highly skilled, not one of them, by his lofty standards, likely to become a burden on American society. Jefferson made no such provisions for the vast majority of those who, in his oft-quoted words, labored for his happiness. Shortly after his death, the executors of Jefferson's estate advertised some "130 valuable negroes" for sale, "the most valuable for their number ever offered at one time in the State of Virginia." Proceeds went toward the liquidation of Jefferson's massive debts, which he bequeathed to the next generation.[27]

David Walker's Appeal

> Here let me ask Mr. Jefferson, (but he is gone to answer at the bar of God, for the deeds done in his body while living,) I therefore ask the whole American people, had I not rather die, or be put to death, than to be a slave to any tyrant, who takes not only my own, but my wife and children's lives by the inches? Yea, would I meet death with avidity far ! far ! ! in preference to such *servile submission* to the murderous hands of tyrants.[28]
>
> —David Walker,
> *Appeal to the Coloured Citizens of the World* (1829)

One of the most perceptive and damning critiques of Jefferson's position on race and slavery came from the pen of David Walker, a free black antislavery and civil rights activist from Boston. Walker refused to accept Jefferson's characterization of blacks as inferior to whites and unworthy of citizenship in American society. "This country is as much ours as it is the whites," Walker wrote. "Whether they will admit it now or not, they will see and believe it by and by." Walker placed white Americans on notice that they — like Jefferson — would soon "answer at the bar of God" for the persecution and oppression of black people. Their only hope of salvation lay in the immediate and total abolition of slavery and the recognition of former slaves as fellow citizens.[29]

Walker was born to an enslaved father and a free mother in the vicinity of Wilmington, North Carolina, sometime around 1796 or 1797. His legal status as a free person of color allowed him to leave Wilmington and travel around the United States, settling for a time in Charleston, South Carolina. Walker may have been living in Charleston in July 1822 when a free man of color named Denmark Vesey and one hundred and thirty-one suspected co-conspirators, all of them slaves, were arrested, largely on the testimony of informants. Of the forty-nine slaves convicted of conspiracy and sentenced to die, twelve had their sentences commuted to sale and transportation out of state; all the rest, with Vesey, were hanged. Though Walker did not mention the Charleston conspiracy in his *Appeal*, he surely knew of the event from firsthand experience or secondhand reports. His harsh condemnation of slave informants and other "coloured men, who are in league with tyrants" may have drawn upon this famous example.[30]

Sometime around 1825, Walker moved to Boston, where he opened a used clothing shop and served as one of two Boston agents for the New York–based *Freedom's Journal*, the first African-American newspaper. In 1828, Walker delivered an address before the newly established Massachusetts General Colored Association, a group devoted to uniting "the colored population" of the United States. "It is indispensably our duty," Walker declared, "to try every scheme we think will have a tendency to facilitate our salvation, and leave the final result to that God, who holds the destinies of people in the hollow of his hand, and who ever has, and will, repay every nation according to its works." That the colored citizens of the world were God's chosen people, Walker had no doubt. "I verily believe that God has something in reserve for us," he declared, "which when he shall have poured it out upon us, will repay us for all our suffering and miseries."[31]

Walker published the first edition of his *Appeal* in September 1829. "It is expected," he wrote in the foreword to the third edition, "that all coloured men, women, and children, of every nation, language, and tongue under heaven, will try to procure a copy of this *Appeal* and read it, or get someone to read it to them, for it is designed more particularly for them." Walker proceeded to lament the depths to which his people had fallen, the sins they had committed even as they suffered under the most oppressive slave regime the world had ever known. "Ignorance and treachery one against the other — a grovelling servile and abject submission to the lash of tyrants, we see plainly, my brethren, are not the natural elements of the blacks, as the Americans try to make us believe; but these are misfortunes which God has suffered our fathers to be enveloped in for many ages, no doubt in consequence of their disobedience to their Maker." One need only travel through the southern and western states, Walker noted, to witness the full force of such ignorance — "fathers beating their sons, mothers their daughters, and all to pacify the passions of unrelenting tyrants." Yoked together by oppression, demoralized and divided among themselves, the colored people of the United States could muster little, if any, resistance to their enslavement and persecution.[32]

Walker lashed out at those misguided wretches who allied themselves with their white overlords when the moment of liberation was at hand. He cited the example of a slave trader who had been overpowered by sixty rebellious captives and left for dead, only to be assisted in his escape by a colored woman. "Brethren, what do you think of this?" Walker asked. "For my own part, I cannot think it was any thing but servile deceit, combined with the most gross ignorance; for we must remember that *humanity, kindness* and the *fear of the Lord,* does not consist in protecting *devils.*" Walker considered it the duty of every black man and woman to "kill or be killed" once the shackles had been broken and the battle had been joined. "The man who would not fight under our Lord and Master Jesus Christ, in the glorious and heavenly cause of freedom and of God — to be delivered from the most wretched, abject and servile slavery, that ever a people was afflicted with since the foundation of the world, to the present day — ought to be kept with all of his children or family, in slavery, or in chains, to be butchered by his *cruel enemies.*"[33]

Walker exhorted his colored brethren to prepare themselves for the day when God's plan would reveal itself and a black "Hannibal" would lead them to victory over their white oppressors:

> If you commence, make sure work — do not trifle, for they will not
> trifle with you — they want us for their slaves, and think nothing

of murdering us in order to subject us to that wretched condition
— therefore, if there is an *attempt* made by us, kill or be killed.

Look upon your mother, wife and children, and answer God
Almighty; and believe this, that it is no more harm for you to kill a
man, who is trying to kill you, than it is for you to take a drink of
water when thirsty; in fact, the man who will stand still and let another man murder him, is worse than an infidel, and, if he has
common sense, ought not to be pitied.

Walker insisted that white Americans bore full responsibility for raising the "armies of heaven" that would one day destroy them. "No
doubt some may say that I write with a bad spirit, that I being a black,
wish these things to occur," he wrote. "Whether I write with a bad or a
good spirit, I say if these things do not occur in their proper time, it is
because the world in which we live does not exist, and we are deceived
with regard to its existence." If God was just — "and I know it,"
Walker said, "for he has convinced me to my satisfaction" — he would
not allow the perpetrators of slavery to go unpunished.[34]

As his philosophical and ideological foil, Walker chose Jefferson,
the great American statesman renowned worldwide for his enlightened views. Walker charged that Jefferson's racial theorizing in *Notes
on the State of Virginia* had provided white Americans with a rationale
for the continued enslavement and subjugation of black people. Walker
singled out Jefferson's suggestion that nature had formed blacks as "a
distinct race," inferior to whites in body and mind, as particularly
harmful. "See this, my brethren! !" Walker exclaimed. "Do you believe
that this assertion is swallowed by millions of whites? Do you know
that Mr. Jefferson was one of as great characters as ever lived among
the whites? See his writings for the world, and public labours for the
United States of America? Do you believe that the assertions of such a
man will pass away into oblivion unobserved by this people and the
world?" Walker used Jefferson's *Notes* — which perpetuated the "in-
supportable insult" of black inferiority — to prick the consciences and
stir the pride of his "suffering brethren." He called on every colored
citizen "with the spirit of a man" to buy a copy of Jefferson's pamphlet
"and put it in the hand of his son. For let no one suppose that the refu-
tations that have been written by our white friends are enough — they
are *whites* — we are *blacks*. We, and the world wish to see the charges
of Mr. Jefferson refuted by the blacks *themselves*, according to their

chance." Only by their actions, Walker maintained, could the colored citizens of the world refute such charges. Only by standing tall and refusing to submit would they prove themselves men.[35]

Walker managed to deliver hundreds of copies of his *Appeal* to various parts of the slaveholding South. In Savannah, Georgia, police confiscated sixty copies of Walker's *Appeal* on a Boston brig from a white steward who had been instructed to deliver the pamphlets to a free black Baptist preacher. Twenty copies of Walker's *Appeal* found their way to Elijah Burritt, the editor of a newspaper in Milledgeville, Georgia, who reprinted lengthy excerpts from the pamphlet. Arrested twice for circulating insurrectionary literature, released twice on technicalities, Burritt wisely fled for his life. Two northern white missionaries working among the Cherokees in Georgia "were maltreated and imprisoned in 1829 or 1830, for having one of Walker's pamphlets, as well as for admitting some colored children into their Indian school." In Wilmington, North Carolina, a "well disposed free person of color" informed local authorities that copies of Walker's *Appeal* were circulating in the area; a subsequent investigation led to the arrest of Walker's agent, a slave "who had received this book with instructions to distribute them through the State particularly in Newbern, Fayette[ville] and Elizabeth [City]." Somehow Walker managed to deliver two hundred copies of his pamphlet to Jacob Cowan, an enslaved tavern keeper who — unbeknownst to his "very indulgent master" — distributed them among the local population. In Charleston, South Carolina, a white steward on a Boston brig was charged with "distributing some pamphlets of a very seditious & inflammatory character among the Slaves & persons of color of said City." The steward, Edward Smith, admitted that he brought three copies of Walker's *Appeal* with him from Boston to Charleston at the request of a stranger — "a colored man of decent appearance & very genteely dressed" — but insisted that he "did not know or Enquire what the pamphlets were about" when he agreed to do so. He was fined $1,000 and sentenced to a year in prison for his unwitting role in fomenting rebellion.[36]

The circulation of Walker's pamphlet prompted the Virginia General Assembly to introduce a bill aimed at preventing "incendiary literature" from circulating among the colored masses. Section I established harsh new penalties for "any white person, free negro, mulatto or slave" who played any role in the writing, printing, or circulating of "any paper, pamphlet, or book advising insurrection or rebellion amongst the slaves." Section II banned "all meetings of free negroes or mulattoes, at any school house, church, or meeting house, or other place, for teaching them reading or writing, either in the day or night under whatsoever pretext." Section III forbade "any white person or persons" to teach "free negroes or mulattoes" to read or write. Section IV made it a high misdemeanor for the "owner or occupier of any plantation or tenement" to allow the establishment of a school on the premises "for the purpose of teaching his or her slaves, or those of another person to read or write." In early April 1831 — less than five months before the uprising in Southampton County — the Virginia General Assembly passed a revised bill, omitting the ban on incendiary literature while retaining provisions against the teaching of slaves and free blacks or mulattoes to read or write. Any white person caught teaching free blacks or mulattoes could be fined up to fifty dollars and imprisoned for up to two months; any white person caught teaching slaves for pay or compensation, or contracting with another white person to teach slaves for pay or compensation, could be fined up to one hundred dollars. The bill also stepped up surveillance of free blacks and mulattoes suspected of failing to leave the state within twelve months of their manumission.[37]

Walker scorned the efforts of white legislators in Virginia and other states to silence him. "Why do the Slave-holders or Tyrants of America and their advocates fight so hard to keep my brethren from receiving and reading my Book of Appeal to them?" he asked in a footnote to the third and final edition of his pamphlet. "Is it because they treat us so well? Is it because we are satisfied to rest in slavery to them and their children? Is it because they are treating us like men, by compensating us all over this free country!! for our labours?" If so, Walker concluded, white Americans would have nothing to fear from the colored citizens of the United States. Perhaps, he mused, they feared the extension of their own republican doctrines to the oppressed colored citizens of the United States. "Perhaps the Americans do their very best to keep my Brethren from receiving and reading my 'Appeal' for fear they will find in it an extract which I made from the Declaration of Independence, which says, 'we hold these truths to be self-evident, that all men are created equal,' &c. &c. &c."[38]

Walker did not live to see the deliverance of his people by "heaven's armies." He died in August 1830 at the age of thirty-three. The coroner's report listed the official cause of death as consumption, an affliction common to city-dwellers of the day. Yet rumors abounded among black Bostonians that "southern planters" had placed a bounty on Walker's head. If true, the assassins acted too late, for Walker's *Appeal* continued to circulate in the South long after his death.[39]

Garrison's Liberator

> Knowing that vengeance belongs to God, and he will certainly re-pay it where it is due; believing all this, and the Almighty will deliver the oppressed in a way which they know not, we deprecate the spirit and tendency of this Appeal. Nevertheless, it is not for the American people, as a nation, to denounce it as bloody or monstrous. Mr. Walker but pays them in their own coin, but follows their own creed, but adopts their own language.
>
> —William Lloyd Garrison,
> review of Walker's *Appeal* in the *Liberator* (1831)

The uniformly hostile response to Walker's *Appeal* among white Americans, particularly in the slaveholding South, struck the abolitionist editor William Lloyd Garrison as hypocritical, given the revolutionary rhetoric of American independence and widespread support for revolutionary movements in Europe. Garrison accused his "guilty countrymen" of putting "arguments into the mouths, and swords into the hands of the slaves. Every sentence that they write — every word that they speak — every resistance that they make, against foreign oppression, is a call upon the slaves to destroy them." Like Walker and Jefferson before him, Garrison warned of "terrible calamities" should the national "sin of slavery" continue unabated. He alone among the three lived to witness the bloody warfare so long predicted.[40]

Born into an evangelical Protestant household in Newburyport, Massachusetts, Garrison came of age during the era of spiritual revival and social reform known as the Second Great Awakening. His seven years as an apprentice to the editor of the *Newburyport Herald* introduced him to the printing press as one of "the great instrumentalities" for change. At the age of twenty-one, he began editing his own newspaper, *The Free Press,* and made his first "slight allusions" to the antislavery cause. Yet Garrison opened the pages of his first newspaper to proslavery views as well. As his own children noted in their loving yet unflinching account of these early years: "He copied, without editorial comment or reprobation, in his second number, that portion of Ed-

ward Everett's speech in Congress wherein the Massachusetts clergyman declared, that there was no cause in which he would sooner
buckle a knapsack to his back, and put a musket to his shoulder, than
the suppression of a servile insurrection at the South." Several years
would pass before Garrison himself became active in the antislavery
crusade.[41]

The Fourth of July provided an ideal occasion for Garrison to perfect his antislavery jeremiad. In 1826, as Americans prepared to mark
the fiftieth anniversary of the signing of the Declaration of Independence, Garrison urged Fourth of July orators to dwell on one theme:
"till our whole country is free of the curse — it is SLAVERY." In his
own 1829 Fourth of July address, delivered at the Park Street Church
in Boston, Garrison delivered a tub-thumping jeremiad titled "Dangers to the Nation." He warned of dire consequences should the
American people fail to "conquer the monster" of slavery.

> The nation will be shaken as if by a mighty earthquake. A cry of
> horror, a cry of revenge, will go up to heaven in the darkness of
> midnight, and re-echo from every cloud. Blood will flow like wa-
> ter — the blood of guilty men, and of innocent women and chil-
> dren. Then will be heard lamentations and weeping, such as will
> blot out the remembrance of the horrors of St. Domingo. The ter-
> rible judgments of an incensed God will complete the catastrophe
> of republican America.

Fortunately, it was well within the power of the American people
to avert such a catastrophe, Garrison proclaimed. They must rededi-
cate themselves to the unfulfilled American creed of liberty and equality and commit themselves to the long, arduous task of emancipation.
"There must be a beginning," he said, "and now is a propitious time —
perhaps the last opportunity that will be granted us by a long-suffering
God."[42]

Like most white antislavery activists of the 1820s, Garrison subscribed to the doctrine of gradualism and looked favorably on various
colonization schemes. "The emancipation of all the slaves of this generation is most assuredly out of the question," he declared in his Park
Street Church oration. "The fabric, which now towers above the Alps,
must be taken away brick by brick, and foot by foot, till it is reduced so
low that it may be overturned without burying the nation." Garrison

came to regret those words. Ten days after his Park Street Church address, he attended a "freedom jubilee" sponsored by the African Abolition Freehold Society of Boston. A white clergyman who spoke on the occasion angered the crowd by taking the position that neither the slaves nor the nation were ready for unconditional emancipation. The reaction of the black audience impressed Garrison. "I felt as if, were I a black, I too would growl my disapprobation," he wrote. "It was the language of nature — the unbending spirit of liberty; and it gave me a higher opinion of this body of men." Unlike their white counterparts in the antislavery movement, African Americans viewed emancipation as "a simple question of right, not expediency."[43]

David Walker's *Appeal* may have influenced Garrison's conversion from colonizationist to abolitionist as well. Garrison first took note of the pamphlet — he did not say how he procured a copy — while editing *The Genius of Universal Emancipation* in Baltimore. "We have had this pamphlet on our table for some time past," he wrote in January 1830, "and are not surprised at its effects upon our sensitive southern brethren. It is written by a colored Bostonian, and breathes the most impassioned and determined spirit. We deprecate its circulation, though we cannot but wonder at the bravery and intelligence of its author." Brief references to the pamphlet appeared in several subsequent issues of the newspaper. In February 1830, Garrison attributed the "astounding legislation" in Virginia — prohibiting the instruction of free blacks, mulattoes, and slaves — to "the circulation of a stirring pamphlet, addressed to all colored people, by David Walker of Boston." Garrison refused to condemn the pamphlet, calling it "a most injudicious publication, yet warranted by the creed of an independent people." The arrest of a Georgia editor who published extracts from Walker's *Appeal* prompted this comment from Garrison in March 1830: "The circulation of this 'seditious pamphlet' has proven one thing conclusively — that the boasted security of the slave states, by their orators and writers, is mere affectation, or something worse."[44]

Two months after his famous Park Street Church oration, Garrison publicly renounced gradualism and embraced the doctrine of total, immediate, and universal emancipation. "Since the delivery of my address in Boston relative to this subject," he wrote, "I am convinced, on mature reflection, that no valid excuse can be given for the continuance of the evil a single hour." Garrison rested his doctrine of immediate, unconditional emancipation on four planks:

1. That the slaves are entitled to immediate and complete emancipation: consequently, to hold them longer in bondage is both tyrannical and unnecessary.
2. That the question of expediency has nothing to do with that of right; and it is not for those who tyrannise to say when they may safely break the chains of their subjects.
3. That, on the ground of expediency, it would be wiser to set all the slaves free to-day than to-morrow — or next week, than next year.
4. That, as a very large portion of our coloured population were born on American soil, they are at liberty to choose their own dwelling place; and we possess no right to use coercive measures in their removal.

Garrison sought to counter the argument advanced by Jefferson and others that emancipation without colonization would jeopardize public safety and perhaps lead to race war. He maintained that immediate emancipation would remove "every inducement to revolt" and hasten the transformation of slaves into "peaceable citizens." As he saw it, "one million of degraded slaves are more dangerous to the welfare of the country, than would be two million of degraded freemen." The sooner the religious and secular instruction of the black masses began, he argued, "the better for them and us."[45]

In the fall of 1830, Garrison announced plans to establish a new journal, the *Liberator*, dedicated to "the abolition of slavery, and the moral and intellectual elevation of our colored population." He chose Boston — "the birthplace of liberty" — as the place where he would "lift up the standard of emancipation in the eyes of the nation." In his inaugural editorial, Garrison compared slavery to a burning house; he would not raise a "moderate alarm" but would shout with all the moral force he could muster. "I will not equivocate — I will not excuse — I will not retreat a single inch — AND I WILL BE HEARD." Garrison's harsh, uncompromising language, his ringing denunciations of "Southern oppressors" and "Northern apologists," his stirring jeremiads, became the hallmark of the *Liberator*.[46]

Those who viewed Garrison as an incendiary determined to fan the flames of rebellion among the slaves in the South would find no public endorsement of antislavery violence in the *Liberator*. Garrison took the position that the slaves, like all good Christians, "ought to suffer, as did our Lord and his apostles, unresistingly, knowing that the Almighty will deliver the oppressed in a way which they know not." If the slaves rebelled, Garrison noted, it would be God's will, not his.

> *We* do not preach rebellion — no, but submission and peace. Our enemies may accuse us of striving to stir up the slaves to revenge; but their accusations are false, and made only to excite the prejudices of the whites, and to destroy our influence. We say that the possibility of a bloody insurrection at the south fills us with dismay; and we avow, too, as plainly, that if any people were ever justified in throwing off the yoke of their tyrants, the slaves are that people.[47]

Though Garrison wielded the threat of slave rebellion like a sword of Damocles over the heads of his white countrymen, he held out the promise of divine dispensation should the nation atone for the sin of slavery. To one pessimistic editorial writer who declared that "an immediate and general emancipation of the southern black population, without bloodshed, is utterly impracticable," Garrison responded: "We believe otherwise; at least, our countrymen had better make the experiment, because you acknowledge that blood must be eventually shed if the slaves are not liberated." There were, he added, "only two ways to break up the slave system — either by moral force of the nation, or physical force on the part of the slaves." God forbid, he exclaimed, that the latter should come to pass.[48]

But come to pass it did. On September 3, 1831, the *Liberator* heralded news of the "Insurrection in Virginia."

> What we have long predicted, at the peril of being stigmatized as an alarmist and declaimer — has commenced its fulfillment. . . . Read the account of the insurrection in Virginia, and say whether our prophecy be not fulfilled. What was poetry — imagination — in January, is now a bloody reality.

In his efforts to wake the nation from its "detestable complacency" on the issue of slavery, Garrison had fared no better than the antislavery Jeremiahs who preceded him. He recognized as much after eight lonely months as editor of the *Liberator*.

We have warned our countrymen of the danger of persisting in their unrighteous conduct. We have preached to the slaves the pacific precepts of Jesus Christ. We have appealed to christians, philanthropists and patriots, for their assistance to accomplish the great work of national redemption through the agency of moral power — of public opinion — of individual duty. How have we been received? We have been threatened, proscribed, vilified and imprisoned — a laughing stock and a reproach.

It took the bloody spectacle of insurrection in Virginia — the very "calamity" he had hoped to avert — to make himself heard.[49]

2

INQUISITIONS

THE OFFICIAL INVESTIGATION into the Southampton insurrection, which began with the interrogation of prisoners in late August 1831 and ended with the trial and execution of Nat Turner some two and a half months later, involved far more than establishing the guilt or innocence of suspected rebels. It entailed the drafting of a historical narrative that would satisfy public curiosity, restore public confidence, and make possible the reconciliation of blacks and whites, slaves and masters, throughout the region.

White civil and military authorities, aided by a self-censoring press, quickly assured the public that the insurrection had been thoroughly suppressed and that all of the guilty parties had been captured or killed, with the exception of the reputed ringleader, Nat Turner. Yet rumors of a wider conspiracy involving slaves and free blacks throughout the region, buttressed by arrests and convictions in counties far and near, kept the white populace on edge. Everyone, it seemed, had a different story to tell, with little regard for the social and political consequences. The stubborn persistence of rumors at variance with the official narrative posed a rebellion, of sorts, against efforts to restore order.

The public statements and private musings of the Richmond newspaper editor John Hampden Pleasants, a Southampton County slave named Beck, and the Virginia governor John Floyd reveal the deadly uncertainties that prevailed in the months before Nat Turner's capture. Their stories highlight the willingness of the slaveholding

South to acknowledge, if only for a moment, that slaves throughout the region had joined in a massive conspiracy to kill their masters and liberate themselves. Thomas R. Gray, an enterprising young lawyer, published "The Confessions of Nat Turner" in November 1831 to remove such "doubts and conjectures" from the public mind. Perhaps, in retrospect, he succeeded too well.

John Hampden Pleasants

John Hampden Pleasants, the senior editor of the *Constitutional Whig* and an influential figure in Virginia politics, understood the power of the press in shaping perceptions of reality. He lashed out at his fellow editors in the aftermath of the insurrection for reporting unsubstantiated rumors of a slave conspiracy extending far beyond the locality where the uprising took place. Pleasants sought to restore public confidence through the drafting of a narrative that clearly identified the culprits and exonerated the great mass of slaves who had no hand in the uprising. His dispatches from Southampton, based on information gleaned from local sources, helped to establish Nat Turner as the reputed leader and mastermind of the insurrection months before Turner's capture and "confession."[1]

Pleasants was born in 1797 at "Contention," his father's plantation in Goochland County, Virginia. As a youth, he "enjoyed in preeminent degree the advantages of a rural training in the educated circle which characterized the Virginia country gentleman." His father served four terms in the U.S. House of Representatives and half a term in the U.S. Senate before resigning to become governor of Virginia. At the age of eighteen, Pleasants entered the College of William and Mary, the most prestigious school in the South and a finishing school for Virginia gentlemen. A lawyer by training, he soon "discovered in himself a fear of public speaking, which not only hampered his legal activities, but shattered his hopes of following in his father's political footsteps." Abandoning his law practice, Pleasants "drifted into newspaper work." In August 1822, he and Joseph Butler founded the *Lynchburg Virginian;* fifteen months later, they sold the paper and moved to Richmond to establish the *Whig.*[2]

Doubling as a soldier and a war correspondent, Pleasants traveled to the scene of the insurrection with the Richmond Light Dragoons, an elite cavalry troop. His first dispatch, dated Thursday evening, August 25, described the chaos and confusion that prevailed among the inhabitants of the region. "On the road we met a thousand different reports, no two agreeing, and leaving it impossible to make a plausible guess at the truth." Upon his arrival in the Southampton County village of Jerusalem, Pleasants found a considerable force of federal troops and state militia and some three to four hundred "ladies from the adjacent country" who had taken refuge there. He began gathering information from local sources and drafted his first sketchy account of the uprising. "Rumor had infinitely exaggerated" the "extent of the insurrection," he wrote, "swelling the numbers of negroes to a thousand or 1200 men, and representing its ramifications as embracing several of the adjacent counties, particularly Isle of Wight and Greensville. . . . The numbers engaged are not supposed to have exceeded 60 — one account says a hundred — another not so many as 40." A second dispatch, dated Saturday, August 27, offered more telling details. Pleasants speculated that the insurgents "acted under the influence of their leader Nat, a preacher and prophet among them," who was "misled by some hallucination of his imagined spirit of prophecy." A final dispatch, dated Sunday, August 28, reported that the insurgents were "all taken or killed, except Mr. Turner the leader, after whom there is pursuit."[3]

Pleasants minimized the extent of the conspiracy by focusing on the charismatic leadership of Nat Turner. Only those slaves who fell directly under Turner's spell were involved in the Southampton affair; only by his "example and exhortations" were they moved to commit such blood-curdling atrocities. "He is represented as a shrewd fellow, reads, writes, and preaches; and by various artifices had acquired great influence over the minds of the wretched beings whom he has led into destruction," Pleasants reported. "It is supposed that he induced them to believe that there were only 80,000 whites in the country, who, being exterminated, the blacks might take possession. In establishing Turner as the mastermind, Pleasants limited the extent of the conspiracy to the reach of his voice.[4]

While Pleasants expressed his horror at "the atrocities" perpetrated by Turner and his followers, his dispatches from Southampton were more remarkable for their harsh condemnation of marauding white lynch mobs. "At the Cross Keys," he wrote, "summary justice in the form of decapitation has been executed on one or more prisoners.

The people are naturally enough, wound up to a high pitch of rage, and precaution is even necessary to protect the lives of the captives." Pleasants opened his second dispatch with more details of prisoners being killed by "the enraged inhabitants" of Southampton County: "Some of these scenes are hardly inferior in barbarity to the atrocities of the insurgents; and it is to be feared that a spirit of vindictive ferocity has been excited, which may be productive of farther outrage, and prove discreditable to the country." Upon his return to Richmond, Pleasants apologized to "the people of Southampton" for the unsympathetic tone of his earlier remarks. "Not having witnessed the horrors committed by the blacks, or seen the unburied and disfigured remains of their wives and children, we were unprepared to understand their feelings, and could not at first admit of their extenuation, which a closer observation of the atrocities of the insurgents suggested." Still, Pleasants left no doubt that he deplored the vigilantism that he and his fellow soldiers had witnessed. He referred, once again, to the "slaughter of many blacks, without trial, and under circumstances of great barbarity." Pleasants estimated that between twenty-five and forty suspects, "possibly a yet larger number," had been executed by the vigilantes, "generally by decapitation or shooting." Only the presence of troops from Richmond and Norfolk "prevented the retaliation from being carried much farther."[5]

Pleasants had little tolerance for the circulation of "false, absurd, and idle rumors" that undermined the confidence of whites and fueled the kind of panic and hysteria he had witnessed in Southampton. "Editors seem to have applied themselves to the task of alarming the public mind as much as possible by persuading the slaves to entertain a high opinion of their strength and consequences," he wrote. Pleasants repeated one of the most popular conspiracy theories of the day, only to dismiss it out of hand. The theory held that slaves throughout the region intended to rise on the fourth Sunday in August; the slaves in Southampton County, owing to some miscalculation, supposedly rose a week too soon. "This is the popular impression," Pleasants wrote, "founded upon confessions, upon the indication of the negroes in Nansemond and other places to unite, and upon the allegation that Gen. Nat extended his preaching excursions to Petersburg and this city; allegations which we, however, disbelieve." Pleasants did not elaborate on his reasons for rejecting the theory; he simply expressed his disbelief and awaited further developments.[6] Pleasants looked to the trials in Southampton and other counties to "develop all the truth" about the extent of the conspiracy, yet he made his own editorial bias clear. "We suspect the truth will turn out to be that the conspiracy was confined to Southampton," he wrote, "and that the idea of its extensiveness originated in the panic which seized upon the South East of Virginia."[7]

The skeptical comments of a Richmond newspaper editor could hardly contain the spread of a popular conspiracy theory that had circulated widely by private letter and word of mouth. Robert E. Lee, then a second lieutenant stationed at Fortress Monroe in Norfolk, heard the "fourth Sunday" theory from his superior officer, Colonel William Worth, the commander of federal troops sent to reinforce the volunteers in Southampton; Lee repeated the high-level military intelligence in a letter to his mother: "Colonel Worth says that from all he can learn he is satisfied that the plot was widely extended, and that the Negroes in S.H. by anticipating the time of the rising by one week (mistaking the 3rd Sunday for the last in the month) defeated the whole scheme & prevented much mischief." S. B. Emmons of Waltham, Massachusetts, heard the "fourth Sunday" theory on a stagecoach from Richmond to Fredericksburg, Virginia. A man named Smith, "direct from the seat of the insurrection," shared the details with Emmons, who repeated what he heard in a letter to the editor of the *Liberator*. "The stage passenger alluded to, mentioned that the slaves commenced an attack a week too soon, owing to some miscalculation. This circumstance I have seen corroborated by other accounts." Military intelligence or idle gossip, the theory made an impression on the "public mind" that would not be easily erased.[8]

Beck

The most unsettling narrative to emerge from the trials came from a Southampton County slave girl named Beck. Her testimony implicated fifteen slaves in two counties — four from Southampton, eleven from neighboring Sussex — in a plot to kill the white people. By her reckoning, the slaves had been planning the rebellion for more than a year. Beck claimed to have seen them with her own eyes, heard them with her own ears. She named names and gave specific dates. Her master vouched for her veracity. Accurate or not, her story posed a direct challenge to the emerging master narrative of "Nat Turner's Rebellion." Not once in the trial record did Beck mention Turner by name or indicate that the "fanatical preacher" described by Pleasants and others had any involvement in the plot she described.[9]

Beck belonged to Solomon D. Parker, a slaveholder whose Southampton County plantation straddled the Sussex County line. Court records officially identified her as a "negro girl slave." One defense lawyer who cross-examined her in Southampton County later remembered her as "a small black girl of from twelve to fifteen years," while another correspondent thought she was older, perhaps "sixteen or seventeen." Beck identified herself as a "house servant" who was "seldom in the outhouses" where the majority of the slaves lived. Beck's close proximity to her master and mistress may have been the most significant factor in determining her loyalties. She accompanied her mistress on extended visits to Sussex County, sometimes staying with friends of the Parker family for two or three weeks at a time. There, Beck and her mistress attended the Raccoon Swamp Antioch Baptist Church, which counted some forty whites and more than a hundred blacks as members. As the older black men gathered outside the church, Beck listened to their conversations and tried to make sense of the ungodly things they were saying about the white people.[10]

In testimony elicited by white lawyers and recorded by various "gentleman justices" from Southampton and Sussex Counties, Beck described a series of incidents that led her to believe that more than a dozen "negro men slaves" had conspired "to murder the white people" of Virginia. By her calculation, slaves in the area were conspiring to rebel as early as the spring of 1830, more than eighteen months before the uprising. Beck did not elaborate on what she heard in those early conversations; nor did she identify any of the alleged conspirators by name. Still, from the perspective of the white people in the courtroom, her testimony had to be unnerving.[11]

Beck recalled in great detail a conversation between a "party of negroes" at the "last May meeting" of the Raccoon Swamp church in Sussex County three months before the uprising. She singled out six of the suspects by name — Solomon, Frank, Boson, Nicholas, Booker, and Bob; she added that "there were several other negroes present whom she did not know." Beck testified that she heard Nicholas and Booker "say that they would join the negroes to murder the white people." She quoted Solomon as saying that "he would join too, for

God damn the white people they had been reigning long enough." Beck apparently made her presence known to the conspirators, for they warned her not to repeat what she had heard. Mrs. Parker's Bob reportedly "told her if she told of it the white people would shoot her like a squirrel and would not bury her"; she said she was later "told the same thing by all the others."[12]

Beck overheard another discussion "among the negroes about rising" on "the Saturday night before and the Monday night of the last Southampton elections." The trial records do not indicate whether Beck identified the suspects by name. She did, however, give very specific dates. "On both those nights, she was called in by her mistress and slept in the House. On Friday night she went out and stayed so late that she was not suffered to go in." Her master, Solomon Parker, verified that "on some night" he had refused to allow her into the house.[13]

On Monday, August 22, the first full day of the insurrection, Beck eavesdropped on a conversation among several slaves at "a black persons house" on Solomon Parker's plantation. Frank, a slave owned by Parker, reportedly told the others that "his master had croped him and he would be croped before the end of the year." Beck testified that she "had heard three other slaves make use of the same declaration some time previously in the neighborhood." Jim and Isaac, two slaves from neighboring Sussex County, were also present during the conversation; they allegedly told Beck that what she had heard "was a secret and if she told the white people would shoot her."[14]

Beck heard more conspiratorial talk among the slaves in Sussex County, where she and her mistress stayed with family friends for the next several days. On Tuesday, August 23, Beck heard a slave named Shadrack tell Mrs. Key's Jenny that he would join "the negroes" if they came that way. Later that day, Beck heard a slave named Squire state that "the white people" of Southampton County should not come to Sussex County "for they were not safe" there; she also heard Squire say that he intended to join the insurgents if the opportunity arose.[15]

By her own admission, Beck knew about the conspiracy for months in advance but did not report what she knew until the third day of the uprising. At one point, she testified that she did not take what she had heard seriously. At another, she recalled that several of the conspirators had threatened her with punishment if she told. At still another, she explained that "the reason of her not telling before was that she did not understand it." All of these explanations are plausible. Before the uprising, Beck could have dismissed what she had heard as idle threats or boastful talk. She had no compelling reason to draw a connection between the comments she heard outside the Raccoon Swamp meetinghouse in Sussex County and the comments she heard later during the Southampton County elections. It was only in the larger context of the uprising that these events appeared related.[16]

From the moment she took the stand, Beck herself was on trial. Defense lawyers challenged her credibility by suggesting that she had changed her story between the first set of trials in Southampton County on September 8 and the second set of trials in Sussex County on September 12 and 13. More specifically, they accused her of fabricating the incident at the May meeting of the Raccoon Swamp church. The Sussex County prosecutor countered by calling two men who had been present when Beck was first interviewed by Sussex County authorities. Their testimony indicated that Beck had not changed her story, that her testimony about the incident at the Raccoon Swamp church was perfectly consistent with her earlier statements.[17]

Several of the defendants challenged Beck's credibility by denying that they knew her. They may not have remembered her. Three months had passed since their meeting outside the Raccoon Swamp church; Beck lived in another county and may not have seen the men since. Moreover, as a young girl eavesdropping on the conversations of older men, she may not have made much of an impression on them at the time. The court record indicates that at least one of the Sussex County suspects did know Beck despite his initial denials. According to a witness who was present when the prisoners were examined and committed to jail, "The prisoner Solomon denied that he knew the witness Beck but on her telling him that he was her uncle and reminding him of having seen him at the funeral of her father who was his brother he acknowledged it."[18]

Beck's master, Solomon Parker, took the stand several times during the Sussex County trials to defend her character. At the trial of Frank, he told the court that her testimony "correspond[ed] to the best of his recollection with evidence she ha[d] given on a former occasion, and that he ha[d] no reason to doubt that she [was] a person of truth." At the trial of Solomon, he qualified his assessment, saying he believed Beck was "disposed to tell the truth" but adding that he thought it might be "probable in some cases where she might be interested she might not tell the truth."[19]

The "gentleman justices" who presided over the county courts were divided over Beck's credibility. In Southampton County, three slaves implicated by Beck were acquitted. Less than a week later, however, justices in the Sussex County convicted five of the slaves accused of conspiring outside the Raccoon Swamp church and two of the slaves accused of making threats after the uprising broke out. The cases of three other slaves were referred back to Southampton County, where the crimes allegedly took place; there, the court convicted two of the suspects and a third from Southampton.[20]

In their ambivalent response to Beck's testimony, the courts failed to provide any clear guidance on the question of a larger conspiracy. The limited scope of their inquiries and the widely diffused nature of their deliberations produced a series of vignettes rather than a coherent narrative that linked events in one locale to events in another. One Southampton County resident, writing in the *Richmond Enquirer*, conveyed the sense of confusion produced by acquittals in Southampton one day, convictions in Sussex the next.

> There has been very little variation in the evidence submitted to the [Southampton] Court, in the course of the trials for the late insurrection, and with the exception of one witness, a woman belonging to Mr. Solomon Parker, there has been nothing elicited, which goes to prove a concert, beyond the day before the execution broke out. . . . Several were tried six or eight days ago in this county, upon her unsupported testimony, and were all acquitted upon the same testimony: whilst in Sussex, five or six were convicted upon the same testimony. She is again to be introduced here, on the trial of three or four others, and may, perhaps, obtain more credit with the Court.

The next day, the Southampton County court found Beck's testimony sufficient to convict three slaves — one from Southampton, two from Sussex. The correspondent revealed the unsettling effect of the latest court rulings: "There have been three convictions since the date of my letter, upon the evidence of the girl of Solomon Parker, who had previously been repudiated by the Court. If her tale was true, the plot was more extensive than we had previously believed."[21]

Despite occasional moments of doubt, white civil and military authorities continued to insist that the conspiracy was local. On September 26, the *Whig* published a long letter from a well-informed "gentleman" of Southampton County, ridiculing the idea of a region-wide slave conspiracy. "We hear of twenty-five stand of arms being found at Brandon — many more at this, that, and the other place — positive evidence of a previous knowledge of insurrection in all the adjoining counties — Nat preaching in Petersburg, Brunswick, and Richmond — not one word of which, am I able to believe, though I have sought to have it corroborated, from every respectable source." The author chastised the courts, in particular, for failing to put rumors of a larger conspiracy to rest. "In remote counties, I cannot conceive how an isolated conviction can take place for insurrection, unless the Court believe the prisoner to have had some knowledge of the affair here." The evidence presented at the trials, he asserted, had fallen far short of that standard.[22]

To set the record straight, the author offered a detailed narrative of the uprising, from its inception in the fanatical mind of Nat Turner to its bloody conclusion. "General Nat" was not a preacher but rather "an exhorter" who had "acquired the character of a prophet" by playing on the superstitions of his fellow slaves. His influence, though "immense" among his closest confidants, extended no further than his own neighborhood. Turner apparently fixed upon the idea of "freeing himself and his race from bondage" several years before the uprising, "saying that the blacks ought to be free, and that they would be free one day or other." He interpreted the "singular appearance of the sun in August" as a sign from the Holy Spirit to "execute his purpose." He shared his plans with six confidants on the Sunday afternoon before the Monday uprising — a claim the author based on "the declaration of several negroes" and "collateral circumstances." The author marshaled circumstantial evidence "in support of this momentary procedure." First, the insurgents began their attack "without a single firelock, and without the least particle of ammunition"; surely they would have been better prepared, the author argued, "if the design had been thought of for the least length of time." Second, they failed to make "one dozen efficient recruits, along their whole route of slaughter"; most of the slaves who joined them did so under duress and fled at the first opportunity.[23]

In their efforts to calm fears and restore order, civic-minded editors needed more than just detailed narrations of the facts and carefully reasoned arguments against a larger conspiracy. They needed the testimony of Nat Turner himself. His unknown whereabouts contributed to rumors of a larger conspiracy or, worse, an impending attack. Reported sightings of the rebel leader as far north as Baltimore and as far west as the New River, which passes through southwestern Virginia, lent credibility to rumors of his extended preaching expeditions before the rebellion. So long as Nat Turner remained a fugitive, the rebellion remained an unfinished story.[24]

State officials wanted Turner captured alive so that he could be put on trial and made to answer for his crimes. In mid-September, Governor John Floyd issued a proclamation offering a five-hundred-dollar reward to "any person, or persons" who would "apprehend and convey to the Jail of Southampton County, the said slave NAT." Southampton County resident Wm. C. Parker — quite possibly the same Wm. C. Parker who later served as Turner's court-appointed lawyer — provided the governor with a physical description of the rebel leader, "supervised and corrected by persons acquainted with him from his infancy." The description included some telling biographical details: a rough guess of Turner's age, a classification of his racial identity, and a brief history of the scars and knots on Turner's body:

> He is between 30 & 35 years old — 5 feet six or 8 inches high — weighs between 150 & 160 rather bright complexion but not a mulatto — broad-shouldered — large flat nose — large eyes — broad flat feet rather knock kneed — walk brisk and active — hair on the top of head very thin — no beard except on the upper lip and the tip of the chin. A scar on one of his temples produced by the kick of a mule — also one on the back of his neck by a bite — a large knot on one of the bones of his right arm near the wrist produced by a blow —

The physical description of Turner attached to the governor's proclamation duplicated the one provided by Parker in all but one significant regard: it omitted reference to the cause of the scars on Turner's body. This seemingly small omission would have rather large consequences in the court of public opinion.[25]

Turner's body served, in effect, as a parchment on which slavery's critics and apologists could inscribe their views of the peculiar institution. From his editorial desk at the *Liberator,* William Lloyd Garrison interpreted the scars on Turner's body as proof positive that the rebellious slave had been goaded to violence by an abusive owner. "Nat is represented to have 'a scar on one of his temples, also one on the back of his neck, and a large knot on one of the bones of his right arm, near the wrist, produced by a blow.' Why should we wonder at his determined efforts to revenge his wrongs and obtain his liberty? Such treatment as he received at the hands of his tyrannical owner was calculated to feed his wrath and bring a dreadful retaliation." The editors of the *Richmond Enquirer* denounced Garrison's accusations as "odious libels" against the slaveholding South. "These wounds are, of course, ascribed to the ill treatment of the 'Slavists' as they are now courteously called by the New York Sentinel! But what is the fact? That the letter from Southampton county, which gave the authentic description of his person, expressly says, that the scar on his temple came from the kick of a mule; that on the back of the neck from the bite of one of his own companions; and the knot on the elbow from another fray in which he had engaged." In fact, the letter from Southampton did not say that the bite on the back of Turner's neck came from "one of his own companions," nor did it identify the source of the blow that created the knot on his right arm.[26]

False sightings of Turner throughout the region kept whites on edge throughout the months of September and October 1831. The editor of the *Edenton Gazette* marveled at the brief, spectacular careers of such reports. A "dreadful insurrection" in Delaware, widely heralded by the press, amounted to little more than a housebreak by "a ruffian of a negro," who quickly retreated without harming anyone. Frantic reports from the eastern shore of Maryland that "the negroes were murdering the whites and shooting at others" were followed by two weeks of conspicuous silence. "And so it is," the editor concluded, with a gentle jab at a jittery white populace, "that we have been kept on tip-toe for a month past, to keep our readers informed of facts, and in the meantime to prevent the too frequent occurrence (in these squally times) of fits and faintings among our old women, and hysterics and ennui among the young maidens."[27]

White patrollers and bounty-hunters continued to search for Turner in the swamps, woods, and fields of Southampton County. "It is said he is still in the neighbourhood and occasionally visits his home," a county resident reported. On Saturday, October 15, a slave named Nelson reportedly informed local authorities that "on that day he had seen Nat Turner in the woods, who hailed him, but that he, Nelson, seeing Nat armed, was afraid and ran from the villain." News of the sighting "caused much sensation among the inhabitants; and in a short time five or six hundred persons were in pursuit." By October 21, Turner's "place of concealment (a cave, not far from the scene of his atrocities) had been discovered, and some arms, provisions, &c. found." On October 29, "Mr. Francis, of Southampton County, came upon *Nat* suddenly, started him from a fodder stack last Thursday morning, in the vicinity of his late butcheries, and fired at him with a horseman's pistol, but he made his escape into the woods." Finally on October 30, "a Mr. Phipps surprised him in a thicket in the neighborhood where he had been seen on Thursday. Mr. P. levelled his gun at him and demanded his surrender; Nat finding death inevitable, if he resisted or fled, surrendered, and was conducted to the jail at Jerusalem."[28]

The capture of Nat Turner gave Southampton County authorities their first opportunity to interrogate the "contriver and leader of the late insurrection." Several people who witnessed the magistrates' examination of Turner provided the Virginia newspapers with summaries of his initial "confessions." They generally confirmed what the newspapers had been saying for months — that the uprising was local and that Nat Turner was the mastermind. Several took the opportunity to denounce Turner as a coward who never left the area during his two months in hiding and put up no fight when captured. One went even further, stating that Turner was "now convinced that he [had] done wrong, and [advised] all other Negroes not to follow his example." These early "confessions," widely reported in the press, reinforced the image of the rebel leader as a "fanatic" with no legitimate grievance against his masters and no significant following among the slaves. Yet they lacked the authority of officially sanctioned records. History demanded a more public accounting certified as accurate and authentic by the appropriate authorities — including Turner himself.[29]

Thomas R. Gray and "The Confessions of Nat Turner"

The task of recording Turner's "Confessions" for posterity fell to Thomas Ruffin Gray, a slaveholding planter-turned-lawyer from

Southampton County. Gray set out to replace "a thousand idle, exaggerated and mischievous reports" with a single definitive account of the conspiracy that would remove all "doubts and conjectures from the public mind." The "Confessions" put Turner on record as saying that he alone conceived of the plan, sharing it only with a few close confidants, and that he knew nothing of any wider conspiracy involving slaves from neighboring counties and states. More important, the pamphlet created a powerful, enduring image of Nat Turner narrating his own story. Gray portrayed himself as awestruck in the presence of the man: "The calm, deliberate composure with which he spoke of his late deeds and intentions, the expression of his fiendlike face when excited by the enthusiasm, still bearing the blood of helpless innocence about him; clothed with rags and covered with chains; yet daring to raise his manacled hands to heaven, with a spirit soaring above the attributes of man; I looked on him and my blood curdled in my veins."[30]

Gray belonged to a wealthy family with deep roots in Southampton County and powerful connections in local, state, and federal politics. His father, Captain Thomas Gray, was a major planter and an officer in the state militia. His grandfather, Colonel Edwin Gray, served in the colonial Virginia House of Burgesses, the Virginia constitutional conventions of 1774–76, and the Virginia General Assembly. His uncle, Edwin Gray, represented the Southampton district in Congress. With the help of his father, Gray acquired extensive holdings in land and slaves. Then, in 1830, he sold his farmland and most of his slaves, moved to the county seat of Jerusalem, and embarked on a career in law.[31]

The insurrection gave the young lawyer an opportunity to practice; it also put him in a position to interview suspects and compile relevant information. He served as defense counsel for five Southampton County slaves suspected of involvement: Davy, Sam, Jack, Nathan, and Moses. The trial records give no indication that Gray put up a spirited defense; all five suspects were found guilty and sentenced to hang. Gray may have pleaded for leniency on behalf of his clients; the justices recommended that the governor commute the sentences of Nathan and Moses to sale and transportation out of state. Gray probably attended other trials as well; the Southampton County court held as many as five trials a day in early September.[32]

Gray apparently took it upon himself to meet with Turner on the day of his arrest and imprisonment in the Southampton County jail.

"Since his confinement, by permission of the jailor, I have had ready access to him," Gray wrote in his introduction to "The Confessions," "and finding that he was willing to make a full and free confession of the origin, progress, and consummation of the insurrectory movements of the slaves of which he was the contriver and head, I determined for the gratification of public curiosity to commit his statements to writing and publish them, with little or no variation, from his own words." Gray's plans to record and publish Turner's "confessions" were well known to others. One anonymous Southampton County correspondent — one of the magistrates who first interviewed Turner — told the *Richmond Compiler:* "I had intended to enter into further particulars, and indeed to have given you a detailed statement of his confessions, but I understand a gentleman is engaged in taking them down verbatim from his own lips, with a view of gratifying public curiosity. I will not therefore forestall him." The magistrate's summary, as published in the *Compiler,* suggests that the style — if not the content — of Turner's "confessions" might have differed dramatically had another author taken them down.[33]

Gray interviewed Turner on November 1, introduced "The Confessions" as evidence at Turner's trial on November 5, and secured a copyright for the manuscript on November 10, the day before Turner's execution. Virginia newspapers announced that Gray intended to print fifty thousand copies of the pamphlet, featuring "an accurate likeness" of the rebel leader as rendered by Norfolk portrait painter John Crawley and lithographed by Endicott & Swett of Baltimore. Unable to find a printer in Richmond, Gray arranged to have his manuscript printed in Baltimore. Judging by the first appearance of newspaper advertisements, copies of "The Confessions" went on sale sometime in mid- to late November 1831, two weeks after Turner's execution. The pamphlet sold for twenty-five cents in Petersburg and Richmond bookstores; a Baltimore bookseller advertised the pamphlet at a reduced price of twelve and a half cents. Gray apparently sold out the initial run; a second printing was made in Richmond in 1832.[34]

The twenty-three-page pamphlet included a brief address, "To the Public," signed by Gray; a copy of an affidavit signed by six members of the Southampton County court, stating that the "confessions of Nat, to Thomas R. Gray" were read to Turner in their presence, and that Turner acknowledged them to be "full free and voluntary"; a "faithful record" of Turner's first-person narrative, framed by Gray's introductory remarks and closing comments; an unofficial transcript of Turner's trial, as reported by Gray; a "list of persons murdered in the insurrection"; and a "list of negroes brought before the Court of Southampton, with their owner's names, and sentence."

Gray depicted Turner as an exceptional figure, distinguished from his followers by his honesty, his commanding intelligence, and his firm belief in the righteousness of his cause. Like a defense attorney arguing on behalf of a client, Gray attested to the high moral character and intellect of the rebel leader. To those who considered Turner a fraud and a trickster, Gray replied: "He makes no attempt (as all the other insurgents who were examined did,) to exculpate himself, but frankly acknowledges his full participation in all the guilt of the transaction." To those who thought Turner "ignorant," Gray responded: "He certainly never had the advantages of education, but he can read and write, (it was taught to him by his parents,) and for natural intelligence and quickness of apprehension, is surpassed by few men I have seen." To the suggestion that Turner acted "cowardly" in surrendering without a fight, Gray countered that the rebel leader chose to live and fight another day: "He said he knew it was impossible for him to escape as the woods were full of men; he therefore thought it was better to surrender, and trust to fortune for his escape." Gray disputed any suggestion that Turner acted out of base motives, "that his object was to murder and rob for the purpose of obtaining money to make his escape. It is notorious, that he was never known to have a dollar in his life; to swear an oath; or drink a drop of spirits." Nor was Turner motivated by "revenge or sudden anger." Gray attributed the insurrection to religious enthusiasm and fanaticism of a mind "warped and perverted by the influence of early impressions." That Turner was every bit the madman he appeared to be, Gray had little doubt. "He is a complete fanatic, or plays his part most admirably."

Gray presented Turner's "own account of the conspiracy" to the public as a cautionary tale with social and political ramifications. Well-meaning white evangelists who disseminated their egalitarian doctrines among the slaves could see how such materials became combustible in the "dark, bewildered, and overwrought mind" of a "gloomy fanatic" like Nat Turner. Ordinary citizens and local authorities who allowed unsupervised gatherings of slaves to take place under the cloak of religion could see the mischief and misery that resulted. Gray called for vigilance, not vengeance. "Each particular community should look to its own safety, whilst the general guardians of the laws, keep a watchful eye over all."[35]

"The Confessions" offered a sharp rebuttal to conspiracy theorists, particularly those who believed that Turner traveled widely and re-cruited followers throughout the region. Turner told Gray that he shared his plans with a few close confidants — Henry, Hark, Nelson, and Sam — in February 1831; they were joined by just two others, Will and Jack, at a meeting in the woods on the afternoon before the insurrection broke out. Asked by Gray "if he knew of any extensive or concerted plan" among the slaves to rise against the white people, Turner answered that he knew of no such plot. Pressing, Gray asked Turner if he knew of a conspiracy in North Carolina at about the same time as the Southampton uprising. Turner denied any knowledge of it. Gray searched the face of the prisoner for signs of deception. "I see, Sir, you doubt my word," Turner reportedly stated, "but can you not think the same ideas, and strange appearances about this time in the heaven's might prompt others, as well as myself, to this undertaking?" Gray spelled out the implications for his readers: "If Nat's statements can be relied on, the insurrection in this county was entirely local, and his designs confided but to a few, and these in his immediate vicinity." Gray added, pointedly, that all of the conspirators had been captured and punished for their crimes: "Not one that was known to be con-cerned has escaped."[36]

Gray annexed his own account of Turner's trial — featuring the in-troduction of the "Confessions" as state's evidence — to the pamphlet. Turner appeared before the Southampton County Court of Oyer and Terminer on Saturday, November 5, 1831, and entered a plea of not guilty, "saying to his counsel [William C. Parker], that he did not feel so." Only one witness testified for the prosecution; his version of events, Gray noted, comported with "Nat's own Confession." Turner, according to Gray, offered no defense, apparently believing that God had sanctioned his deeds. "I have made a full confession to Mr. Gray, and have nothing more to say." (The official trial transcript omitted any reference to Gray or the reading of the "Confessions" in Turner's presence.) The court found Turner guilty and sentenced him "to be hanged by the neck until dead." His value, for the purposes of reim-bursement, was set at three hundred and seventy dollars.[37]

Gray had already completed his manuscript and set off to have it published when the execution of Turner took place on Friday, November 11. Two sharply divergent accounts of the event — one disdainful of Turner, the other respectful — appeared in the Virginia press:

> This wretched culprit expiated his crimes (crimes at the bare mention of which the blood runs cold) on Friday last. He betrayed no emotion, but appeared to be utterly reckless of the awful fate that awaited him, and even hurried the executioner in the performance of his duty! . . . Precisely at 12 o'clock he was launched into eternity. There were but a few people to see him hanged. (*Norfolk Herald*, November 14, 1831)

> We learn by a gentleman from Southampton, that the fanatical murderer, *Nat Turner*, was executed according to sentence, at Jerusalem, on Friday last, about 1 o'clock. He exhibited the utmost composure throughout the whole ceremony; and although assured that he might, if he thought proper, address the immense crowd assembled on the occasion, declined availing himself of the privilege, and told the Sheriff in a firm voice, that he was ready. Not a limb nor a muscle was observed to move. (*Petersburg Intelligencer*, November 15, 1831)

The public would long argue whether Turner left the world a hero or a villain. Turner, for his part, had said all he had to say.[38]

Virginia newspapers helped to publicize "The Confessions of Nat Turner" even as they called the veracity of Gray's transcription into question. Declaring the pamphlet "deeply interesting," the editors of the *Richmond Enquirer* nevertheless questioned the accuracy of Gray's transcription. The "eloquently and classically expressed" confession attributed to Turner appeared to be "calculated to cast some doubt over the authenticity of the narrative, and to give the Bandit a character for intelligence which he does not deserve, and ought not to have received." Still, the *Enquirer* saw the pamphlet as a useful weapon against Northern abolitionists. "It ought to teach Garrison and the other fanatics of the North how they meddle with these weak wretches."[39]

Garrison read "The Confessions" as a testimonial to the heroic stature of Nat Turner. Gray's pamphlet, he wrote, would "only serve to rouse up other black leaders and cause other insurrections, by creating among blacks admiration for the character Nat, and a deep undying sympathy for his cause." Under indictment in several slave states for circulating incendiary literature among the slaves, Garrison facetiously identified Thomas R. Gray as a co-conspirator. "We advise the Grand Juries in the several slave States to indict Mr. Gray and the printers of the pamphlet forthwith; and the legislative bodies at the south to offer a large reward for their apprehension." He added, in a postscript, that the text of the "Confessions" gave no indication that Turner had ever seen "a copy of the infernal 'Liberator' or 'Walker's Pamphlet.'"[40]

The narrative contained in "The Confessions of Nat Turner" appealed to diverse constituencies with a wide range of social and political agendas. It gave slaveholders and their sympathizers a plausible explanation for the uprising, one that ruled out mistreatment or generalized discontent as primary causes. It gave local whites a convenient scapegoat, a figure to blame for the rebellion. It gave Northern abolitionists a black hero and a martyr for the burgeoning movement. And it presented historians with a definitive account of the event, attributable to the rebel leader himself.[41]

Where Beck told of ordinary slaves cursing their masters and threatening to kill their white oppressors, Thomas Gray told a more lurid tale, a history of the fanatical mind behind "Nat Turner's Rebellion" straight from the lips of the Bandit himself. In the court of public opinion, it was no contest.[42]

Governor John Floyd and the Virginia Legislature

The trial of Nat Turner and the publication of his "Confessions" did little to persuade the Virginia governor John Floyd that the conspiracy was, in the words of Thomas R. Gray, "entirely local." If anything, Floyd became more adamant and effusive in expressing his opinion that the uprising sprang from sources beyond the county, state, and region. In the three months between the Southampton uprising in late August and his address to the state legislature in early December, Floyd assembled a collection of documents that would underscore his suspicions of a larger conspiracy and buttress his case for legislative reforms. The documents fell into three broad categories: incriminating letters written by suspected conspirators, warnings from concerned white citizens, and "incendiary" literature.

Floyd came into possession of an incriminating letter from "Williamson Mann" of Chesterfield, Virginia, to "Ben Lee" of Richmond, dated August 29, 1831, seven days after the outbreak in Southampton. Somewhat difficult to decipher, the letter appears to sketch the broad outlines of a conspiracy among poor whites, slaves, and free persons of color. The author presents himself as a poor white man who has coached the slaves of Richmond on "how they must act in getting of their liberation. They must set fire to the city beginning at Shockoe hill then going through east west north south set fire to the bridges." Slaves in other counties, if all went as planned, would follow suit. "They are about to break out in Goochland & in Meclenburg Cy. & several other counties very shortly." The author appears to be motivated by class resentments. "I do wish they may succeed," he writes, "by so doing we poor whites can get work as well as the slaves or collard." How this letter came into the hands of the governor and what he thought of its contents are not readily apparent from the document. Floyd made no comments in the margins.[43]

A "gentleman from Richmond" furnished Floyd with another incriminating letter — this one "found in the road six or seven miles below the city." Unlike "Williamson Mann," the author of this letter took pains to avoid detection, sending the letter by private messenger rather than the post office: "Dear brother I send you this by brother billy who can tel you more than I can rite you must be shore to rememer the day, for al dependes on that for you now tis the last Sunday in October, we are al ready down belo you must not be faint harted all depends on you if you deceve us we are al lost for ever your affecionat brother Joe do burn this as soon as yo read it." Floyd identified the source of the document but gave no indication of his reaction in the margins.[44]

Several letter writers warned Floyd that Northern abolitionists were circulating incendiary literature among the slaves and free blacks of Virginia. John C. Harris, the postmaster of Orange County, Virginia, told Floyd that a "free coloured man" from his village had subscribed to *The Liberator* during a recent visit to Washington, D.C., "not knowing as he states the incendiary character of the paper." When the issue arrived, Harris passed it around to members of the community, then forwarded it — "much soiled and mutilated" — to the governor for his perusal. "I know that our Laws, happily, do, and that they ought to protect the rights of the Press, yet in times like these, such seditious *incentives* to insurrection and murder, ought, with sound discretion, to be prohibited." L.N.Q. of Philadelphia told Floyd that black ministers in that city were preaching insurrectionary doctrines to their congregations, "urged on by the editor of the *Liberator* and his murderous companions." He warned of similar activities in Virginia. "Depend upon it, Sir, that much mischief is hatching here and in spite of all the salutary laws you can pass pamphlets and papers will be circulated among your slaves. Why do not the Southern States hold a convention and demand of the State of Massachusetts to silence these dangerous men?" Floyd read these letters as evidence of an extensive conspiracy, stretching from Massachusetts to Virginia. He wrote back to L.N.Q. and asked for permission to submit his letter to the General Assembly. "That body will soon be here and the Southampton affair will doubtless occupy their attention."[45]

Floyd assembled a thick file of "incendiary" literature. Various correspondents sent him copies of the *Liberator*, including several duplicates. Chief Justice John Marshall sent him the "Minutes and Proceedings of the First Annual Convention of the People of Colour," held in Philadelphia earlier that year. Colonel John Rutherford, a state legislator from Richmond, sent him a copy of the *Genius of Universal Emancipation*, dated January 8, 1827. Thomas Ritchie, the editor of the *Richmond Enquirer*, presented him with a copy of the *African Sentinel and Journal of Liberty*, dated October 1, 1831. Several Virginia postmasters sent copies of a broadside published by Sherlock S. Gregory of Albany, who pledged to use "all honorable means to sever the iron bonds that united the slaves to their masters." Other documents in the collection included "An Address Delivered Before the Free People of Color in Philadelphia, New York, and other Cities," by William Lloyd Garrison; a three-page circular from the American Colonization Society; an "African Hymn," composed by the Reverend Shadrack Bassett ("Ever since Jehovah took the field, I determined not to yield, I will wield the sword with pleasure"); and David Walker's notorious "Appeal to the Colored Citizens of the World."[46]

In a letter dated November 19, one week after Turner's execution, Floyd shared his evolving conspiracy theory with the South Carolina governor James Hamilton. Floyd traced the "spirit of insubordination which has, and still manifests itself in Virginia" to "the Yankee population," particularly "the Yankee pedlars and traders." They "began first" by making the slaves religious, "telling the blacks, God was no respecter of persons; the black man as good as the white; that all men were born free and equal; that they can not serve two masters; that the white people rebelled against England to obtain freedom; so have the blacks a right to do." At the same time, "without any purpose of this kind," Northern and Southern preachers began to evangelize among the population at large, creating a climate of enthusiasm and a spirit of religious revival. The lethargy of state and local officials contributed to the growing danger. "Our magistrates and laws became more inactive; large assemblies of negroes were suffered to take place for religious purposes." Black preachers — tutored in Yankee doctrines of religious equality, taught to read and write by their white mistresses, encouraged by their pious white masters to evangelize among the slaves — began to prepare the black masses for the bloody work of insurrection. From the pulpit they would read "the incendiary publications of Walker, Garrison and Knapp of Boston; these too with songs and hymns of a similar character were circulated, read and commented upon." And through it all "we" — the white men entrusted with safeguarding the commonwealth of Virginia — "[were] resting in apathetic security until the Southampton affair."[47]

Floyd concluded that "the extent of this insurrection" was "greater than will ever appear." While the actual killing "commenced with Nat and nine others," many more undoubtedly knew of the plan. "From all that has come to my knowledge during and since this affair," Floyd confided to Hamilton,

> I am fully convinced that every black preacher, in the whole country east of the Blue Ridge, was in on the secret, that the plans as published by those northern prints were adopted and acted upon by them, that their congregations, as they were called knew nothing of this intended rebellion, except a few leading, intelligent men, who may have been head men in the church. I am informed that they had settled on the form of government to be that of the white people, whom they intended to cut off to a man, with this difference that the preachers were to be their governors, generals and judges.

This was hardly a spontaneous eruption confined to a single neighborhood of Southampton County, the work of a gloomy fanatic and a handful of deluded followers. This was an organized rebellion, a mass movement led by black preachers devoted to black liberation and the establishment of a black principality. Floyd expressed a measure of respect, if not admiration, for the slaves who took up arms in Southampton. "All died bravely," he wrote, "indicating no reluctance to lose their life in such a cause."[48]

In his December 1831 message to the Virginia General Assembly, Governor John Floyd detailed what he saw as the growing insurrectionary threat posed by the free people of color in the Commonwealth. Many free blacks, he argued, had become converts to the revolutionary doctrines of racial equality espoused by William Lloyd Garrison and other outside agitators. Through the circulation of "incendiary pamphlets and papers" in the South, the abolitionists had "opened enlarged views" among the free blacks and incited them to "the achievement of a higher destiny, by means for the present less violent, but not differing in the end from those presented to the slaves." Floyd depicted free blacks as ready agents of Northern abolitionist agitation among the slaves. "If the slave is confined by law to the estate of his master, as it is advisable he should be, the free people of color may nevertheless convey all the incendiary pamphlets and papers with which we are sought to be inundated." Floyd concluded that it was "indispensably necessary" for the free black population "to withdraw from this community." He proposed, "as the last benefit which we can confer upon them," that the Legislature "appropriate annually a sum of money to aid in their removal from this Commonwealth." Governor Floyd's message disappointed those who hoped he would recommend "some provision for the gradual emancipation of slavery"; the removal of free blacks seemed hardly adequate as a response to the "Southampton Tragedy." Privately, however, Floyd noted that he viewed the removal of free blacks as "preparatory, or rather as the first step to emancipation." In the weeks ahead, he urged his "friends in the Assembly" to raise "the question of gradual abolition."[49]

Meanwhile, groups of white citizens from across the state petitioned the General Assembly to address the threat to peace and public safety posed by the "curse" of slavery and the unfettered growth of the black population in Virginia. A circular signed by fifteen slaveholders from Hanover County quoted census figures showing that the white population, once a substantial majority, had been "overtaken by the blacks" in the slaveholding regions of Virginia east of the Blue Ridge Mountains. "Will you wait until the land shall be deluged in blood and look alone to the fatal catastrophe, of the extinction of the black races by force as the only remedy? Or rather will you begin the great and good work by kin, gentle, gradual and sure means?" A memorial from citizens of Loudoun County called upon the legislature to take "energetic but prudent measures" that would lead to "the removal of a race irreconcilably antagonistic to ours." Petitioners from Buckingham County encouraged the legislature to consider the plan of gradual emancipation and colonization "suggested by Mr. Jefferson." Prince William County residents made a similar plea: "Now is the time we should profit from the warning hint of the immortal Jefferson and cast it from us ere it is too late."[50]

The 1831–32 session of the Virginia General Assembly became a referendum on various schemes to gradually reduce and eventually eliminate the black population of Virginia. Efforts to forestall a public debate on slavery and emancipation failed when the House of Delegates voted overwhelmingly to refer a Quaker memorial to a special committee on slaves, free Negroes, and mulattoes. The *Richmond Whig* hailed the vote as a momentous occasion for Virginia and the nation. "We do not know that yesterday, will not be celebrated by posterity, as a day entitled to be associated with the Fourth of July, by the benefits which may flow to Virginia from the step taken."[51]

The special committee charged with hearing antislavery petitions divided sharply over the propriety of discussing emancipation so soon after the Southampton uprising. "We debate it — the Press debates it — everybody debates it . . . as if the slaves around us had neither eyes nor ears," declared Delegate James H. Gholson of Brunswick County. Delegate William O. Goode of Mecklenburg, anxious to dispose of the issue, introduced a resolution that the committee be "discharged from the further consideration of all petitions, memorials and resolutions which have for their object, the manumission of persons held in servitude under existing laws of this Commonwealth." Delegate Thomas Jefferson Randolph of Albemarle, representing the abolitionist faction, countered with an amendment directing the Special Committee to take up his plan for the uncompensated post-nati emancipation and colonization of slaves. Randolph's amendment passed. Thus began an extraordinary public debate on the future of slavery in Virginia, occasioned by "the melancholy occurrences growing out of the tragical massacre in Southampton."[52]

In staking out their ideological positions — conservative, moderate, abolitionist — Virginia lawmakers placed a corresponding spin on the events associated with Nat Turner's Rebellion. Conservatives, who favored no legislative action, dismissed the insurrection as a "petty affair" blown dangerously out of proportion by alarmists and extremists. John E. Shell, a representative from Brunswick County, made light of the recent "war" in Southampton, citing the ease with which "this mighty general" Nat Turner and his "formidable army" of black troops had been routed by armed white citizens and their loyal slaves.

> Mr. Speaker, I was a soldier in this war — not a hero — mark that — not a hero. It is not impossible that I might have acquired renown, but for the unfortunate intervention of one of those accidental incidental casualties which so frequently impede the march of fame, and check the aspirations of ambition. My prospect to win a laurel, was blighted by the smallest imaginable circumstance. Sir, dreadful as it is, I must tell you that, just before we reached the scene of action, three men and two boys encountered this mighty general, and his formidable army, and literally demolished them — defeated them "horse, foot and dragoons" — and scattered death and confusion among them.

Abolitionists countered that the relative strength of the black and white forces was hardly at issue. The constant threat of slave rebellion, they argued, produced an almost unbearable anxiety in the white population and contributed to a steady out-migration. James McDowell, a delegate from the Shenandoah Valley county of Rockbridge, reminded his colleagues of the panic and hysteria that gripped the region in the immediate aftermath of the uprising. Reading aloud from official documents attesting to the general alarm, McDowell asked:

> Was it the fear of Nat Turner and his deluded and drunken handful of followers which produced or could produce such effects? Was it this that induced distant counties where the very name of Southampton was strange, to arm and equip for a struggle? No, sir, it was the suspicion eternally attached to the slave himself, the suspicion that a Nat Turner might be in every family, that the same bloody deed could be acted over at any time in any place, that the materials for it were spread through the land and always ready for a like explosion.[53]

Moderates took the position that race war was hardly imminent but that "something must be done," without infringing on property rights, to reduce the danger posed by a growing black population. General William H. Broadnax of Dinwiddie County, who advocated state-funded colonization of free blacks, represented this position:

> It is true there has been great excitement, and much unpleasant apprehension of danger. I am happy to have learned that all this is to a considerable extent subsiding. It demonstrates certainly, however, the propriety, the necessity of our adopting some measure to re-assure public confidence: and prevent as far as practicable the recurrence of scenes similar to those so often alluded to.

After three weeks of debate, the House of Delegates ruled, by a vote of sixty-five to fifty-eight, that it was "inexpedient" to act on various schemes for the abolition of slavery in the 1831–32 session. The legislators resolved instead to support state-subsidized colonization of free blacks and newly manumitted slaves, "believing that this effort . . . will absorb all our present means, and that a further action for the removal of the slaves should await a more definite development of public opinion."[54]

Having dispatched with the question of abolition, the Virginia General Assembly took up a bill for the "Removal of Free Negroes." The bill called for "all persons of colour within the Commonwealth, who are now free, or who may hereafter become free therein," to be "removed" — it did not specify how — "from this State to Liberia, or such other place or places on the western coast of Africa," as designated by a Central Board of Commissioners. Much of the debate on the bill, as reported in the *Richmond Enquirer*, turned on the question of force. Should the law compel free persons of color to leave? Or should it rely on the disposition of free blacks to leave voluntarily?

Delegate William Broadnax, whose Southside county of Dinwiddie counted close to a thousand free blacks among its fifteen thousand inhabitants, doubted "the willingness of the free negroes generally to move." He noted that free persons of color to the north had adopted resolutions declaring colonization "injurious" to their interests, and, from what he had heard, opposition ran high among free blacks in Virginia as well. If the legislature intended to remove more than the "very few" free persons of color who left voluntarily,

Broadnax concluded, "it would be absolutely necessary to resort to force." Though a warm proponent of colonization, Broadnax saw nothing "voluntary" in the mass exodus of free blacks from Southampton County.

> Who does not know that when a free negro, by crime or otherwise, has rendered himself obnoxious to a neighborhood, how easy it is for a party to visit him one night, take him from his bed and family, and apply to him the gentle admonition of a severe flagellation, to induce him to *consent* to go away. In a few nights, the dose can be completed, perhaps increased, until, in the language of physicians, *quantum stuff* has been administered to produce the desired operation; and the fellow then becomes *perfectly willing* to move away.
>
> I have certainly heard, if incorrectly, the gentleman from Southampton will put me right, that of the large cargo of emigrants lately transported from that county to Liberia, all of whom *professed* to be *willing* to go, were rendered so by some such severe ministrations as I have described. A Lynch club — a committee of vigilance — could easily exercise a kind of inquisitorial *surveillance* over any neighborhood, and convert any desired number, I have no doubt, into a willingness to be removed. But who really prefers such means as these to the course proposed in the bill?

Broadnax maintained that any scheme of legislated removal would involve "force of some kind or other, direct or indirect, moral or physical, legal or illegal." He favored "legal force" over "private or indirect compulsion," he explained, "because, it will be more general and uniform in its application — because it will be more just and impartial in its operation — because it will be *known* beforehand, and can be provided for — because it is more consistent with open dealing and public faith — because the other will be harsh, arbitrary, capricious, unequal, unexpected, unjust, and cruel."[55]

After considerable debate, the House passed a bill for the voluntary removal of free blacks and mulattoes, which included appropriations of $90,000 for 1832 and $35,000 for 1833. The seventy-nine to forty-one vote marked a resounding victory for the colonizationists and their allies in the General Assembly. Yet the bill did not fare as well in the Senate, where amendments reduced the first-year appropriation to $50,000 and eliminated the provision for removing newly manumitted slaves. Shorn of its abolitionist provisions, the revised removal bill died quietly on an eighteen to fourteen vote for indefinite postponement.[56]

Under intense pressure to do something in response to Nat Turner's Rebellion, the Virginia General Assembly passed a law imposing harsh new restrictions on slaves and free blacks. The first two sections — clearly written with Turner in mind — banned blacks from preaching or attending unsupervised religious gatherings. The rigid enforcement of these and other black codes by white patrollers in the aftermath of Turner's Rebellion would be long remembered by slaves and ex-slaves alike.[57]

Aftermath

Thomas R. Gray could give voice to the damned, but he could not bring back the dead. And he could not erase the memories of those whose worlds had been turned upside down by Beck's testimony and upset by persisting rumors of a region-wide slave conspiracy. Church records for the Raccoon Swamp meetinghouse in Sussex County — where Beck overheard numerous black parishioners whispering rebellion — reveal a deepening schism between the black and white congregations in the months after Nat Turner's acts. In October 1831, the church expelled William Archer, "having been committed to gaol as one concerned in the Horrid Insurrection." Church leaders cited the "present perplexed situation" as justification for appointing committees to examine the possible involvement of two others, Williamson's Isaac and Wyche's Pompey. The leaders of the congregation went even further by November, openly acknowledging their suspicion of all black members by investigating the "general course pursued" by the colored brethren "in time of the Horrid Insurrection and the character they supported as professors of Godlyness." The inquisition continued all through the winter and spring. In March 1832, church leaders "called over the list of coloured Brethren, made some corrections," and awaited "further enquiry." In April, the church "reexamined list of Coloured Brethn" and "made all corrections." Some sort of evidence was offered, but the church record said nothing more about it.[58]

By May 1832, the church reported just forty-two white members, with no communication from the black members at all. The

Portsmouth Baptist Association took note of the church's troubles in its annual report. "The Church at Rackoon Swamp has been in a very dissatisfied condition on account of their coloured members," the report stated. "They express an entire loss of confidence in their religious feeling, and from the department of their community make no report to the Association." Other churches reported similar problems. The Baptist Association responded by advising its churches to expel those blacks who "refused the instruction and government of the Church" and to "refuse license to coloured persons to preach, and to interdict their holding meetings."[59]

Whatever the source of their dissatisfaction, the black members did not sever their ties with the church. In May 1833, the church reported 141 members. There was no mention of either a mass resignation or a mass expulsion of black members during the preceding year. By 1834, church membership had risen to 148, just two shy of the total in May 1831. Church leaders exulted over the rapid increase in black membership. In their annual report to the Portsmouth Baptist Association, they stated, "Ethiopia is stretching out her hand to God, as an evidence of which we have just received 13 colored persons by baptism." By 1835, the reconciliation between the black and white congregations of the church was complete. Church leaders reported "good tidings," including thirteen new members, and concluded, "The set time to favour our church has come."[60]

The reconciliation between blacks and whites in Sussex involved more than just the salving of wounds within the church. It also involved the official repudiation of Beck's testimony and an apology, of sorts, to the slaves who suffered as a result. On February 21, 1835, more than three years after Turner's execution, a court hearing in Sussex County revived local memories of the uprising and its aftermath. Boson, a slave who had escaped from the Sussex County jail after his conviction on the basis of Beck's testimony, had been captured in Norfolk and returned for identification and execution. Five members of the county court (four of whom had participated in the original trials) agreed that the prisoner was indeed Boson and ordered that his original sentence of death be carried out. They set March 27 as the date for the hanging. And then, in a stunning display of humility and self-condemnation, they unanimously recommended that the governor pardon Boson and commute his sentence to sale and transportation out of state.[61]

The justices were not alone in beseeching the governor to pardon

Boson. Eighteen residents of Sussex County signed a petition asking the governor to heed the recommendation of the court. The first signature belonged to George Blow, a prominent Sussex County planter and a member of the county court at the time of the original trials. The second signature belonged to Boson's owner, William Peters, an elder in the Raccoon Swamp church and a justice of the peace. In their letter to the governor, the petitioners argued that their personal experience of the uprising, their personal stake in the outcome of the events, made them best suited to judge their own error. "We know the circumstances; we encountered the danger; we suffered all the inconveniences of that most appalling period, being in the immediate vicinity of the scene of blood, and WE, yes! We, who may consider ourselves as a part of the intended victims of that massacre, do intercede for the life of the condemned." The petitioners confessed that the circumstances under which they heard Beck's testimony prejudiced them against those slaves suspected of involvement in the uprising. "Time has mellowed our feeling, and given full exercise to our reason," they wrote. "We can now view the event freed from that exasperation, which blinded our unbiased judgments."[62]

The petitioners proceeded to attack the credibility of Beck — or "Parker's Negro Woman," as they called her. "On her evidence alone," they wrote, "nearly all the condemnations in Sussex were made — and very many of those in Southampton. Now we declare to you that many of the good citizens of both those counties have strong doubts as to the correctness of her testimony." The petitioners introduced new evidence designed to cast doubt upon Beck's memory of the incident at the Raccoon Swamp meetinghouse. Mr. and Mrs. Laine, a white couple who did not testify at the original trials, now claimed that Solomon — whom Beck placed at the Raccoon Swamp Church with the other conspirators — was at their plantation all day long and never went near the meetinghouse.[63]

The petitioners asked the governor to consider the relative stature of the witnesses as he weighed the new evidence against the old. "Here then you have the evidence of two white witnesses — persons of intelligence — of unblemished reputation, and standing as fair in our Society, as any other members of it — who prove to you that the girl of Parkers was certainly mistaken *in all* she deposed and said about Solomon." If Beck lied about Solomon, the petitioners reasoned, she may have lied about Boson as well. "Can you consent to the sacrifice of another victim," they asked the governor, "on that identical testimony?"

In the eyes of the petitioners, the slaves convicted of conspiracy were themselves unfortunate victims of the uprising. To clinch their argument, the petitioners noted that Beck's testimony conflicted with the judgment of history. How could the court find Boson guilty of conspiracy in Sussex County when everyone agreed that "the insurrection had its *origin,* and was confined exclusively, to a *neighbourhood* in Southampton"? How could the court find Boson guilty of planning the uprising in May 1831 when "all the evidence at the trials in Southampton left the mind *convinced* that it was not an affair of premeditation but *suddenly* gotten up by a fanatic, who had to use religious delusion and force, to induce *a very few desperadoes* to *commence* it with him"?

James S. French, the lawyer who defended Boson and several other slaves implicated by Beck, urged the governor to commute Boson's sentence to sale and transportation out of state. French noted that the climate of opinion in Sussex County had changed dramatically since the court found Boson guilty. "Indeed," French wrote, "I believe there are many of those who were at the time most exasperated against him, who now agree with me in opinion." Like the Sussex County petitioners, French attacked the credibility of Beck. He noted that twelve of the slaves implicated by her testimony lived in Sussex County, "fully twenty five miles from the scenes of violence." The court heard no evidence that the slaves were absent during the August uprising, no evidence that they committed an overt act of insurrection, no evidence that they engaged in a single disorderly act. And yet eleven of the twelve were convicted, French noted, "upon a naked charge, unsupported by corroborating circumstances, and preferred by a single witness — and that witness a slave." French based his appeal on legal grounds: "Can a single slave by his or her evidence legally deprive another slave of life?"[64]

Boson apparently pleaded his own case with local white authorities before turning himself in. Since his escape, French noted, he had "remained in the same neighbourhood until the present time," had "frequently been seen, sought several conversations with respectable gentlemen, protested his innocence, and professed himself ready to deliver himself up at any time that he could be assured he would not be hung." That Boson could negotiate his own surrender under terms acceptable to him is a remarkable testament to changing public perceptions of the events that had led to his conviction.[65]

On February 27, 1835, the Executive Council advised the governor to commute Boson's death sentence to sale and transportation out of state. On March 2, Governor Littleton W. Tazewell approved the order. History, as recorded by Thomas R. Gray in "The Confessions of Nat Turner," and memory, as detailed in the "confessions" of the white petitioners from Sussex, were officially reconciled.[66]

3

APOTHEOSIS

PUBLICATION OF "The Confessions of Nat Turner" in November
1831 prompted a defiant William Lloyd Garrison to predict
that Thomas R. Gray's pamphlet would "rouse up other black
leaders and cause other insurrections, by creating among blacks admiration for the character Nat, and a deep undying sympathy for his
cause." Yet the much-anticipated rising never came. Slaves throughout the South labored under stringent new codes that banned unsupervised gatherings and kept would-be Nat Turners from preaching
the gospel of armed rebellion. Free persons of color, faced with intense persecution, adopted resolutions denying any involvement in
the "insurrectionary movements" and pledging their loyalty to the
state. Abolitionists had little use for the rebellious slave as an icon of
their fledgling movement. Members of the newly founded American
Antislavery Society, led by Garrison, repudiated "physical violence" as
a means of resistance and urged the slaves to await their deliverance by
peaceful means.[1]

Dissatisfaction with the Garrisonian doctrine of nonresistance, fueled by mob violence against abolitionists, gave rise to more militant
voices within the antislavery movement and elevated the stature of
Nat Turner in the 1840s. Black abolitionists, meeting independently,
debated whether to publicly affirm the right and duty of the slaves to
rebel. By the end of the decade even Frederick Douglass, who favored
moral suasion over physical force, welcomed the prospect of slave rebellion and routinely paid tribute to the heroic figure of Nat Turner.

White militants seized upon Turner's Rebellion as evidence that the enslaved black masses possessed the "physical courage" necessary to mount a successful rebellion. Among Nat Turner's staunchest admirers were John Brown and Thomas Wentworth Higginson, who conspired with others to attack the federal arsenal at Harpers Ferry, Virginia, arm the slaves with pikes, and "run them off" to freedom.

Fiction writers, responding to the sectional crisis of the 1850s, used Turner's Rebellion as a dramatic backdrop for literary-historical excursions into the debate over slavery and abolition. G.P.R. James (*The Old Dominion; or, The Southampton Massacre*) and Harriet Beecher Stowe (*Dred: A Tale of the Great Dismal Swamp*) popularized Thomas R. Gray's image of Turner as a gloomy prophet of doom and destruction who conjured a devout following from among the enslaved masses. The messianic Turner joined Stowe's long-suffering Christian martyr, "Uncle Tom," as an archetypal slave personality in the American literary imagination. African-American folk traditions surrounding Turner's Rebellion found literary expression in the ex-slave narratives of Charity Bowery, Harriet Jacobs, and Henry Box Brown. Their stories shifted the focus from the violent acts of Turner and his followers to the unmanly panic of the slaveholders and the reign of terror unleashed upon the black community.

The secession of the slaveholding states under the rebel flag of the Confederacy and the outbreak of the Civil War in 1861 yoked the fate of two warring powers to the aspirations of some four million slaves. Fears of anarchy and insurrection on the Southern home front prompted Confederate leaders to pass the so-called Twenty Negro Law in October 1862, exempting from military service the owners or overseers of twenty or more slaves. When Lincoln issued his preliminary Emancipation Proclamation in September 1862, an editorial writer for a Richmond newspaper accused him of "fomenting, like Nat Turner, a slave uprising in which men, women, and children were to be killed in their beds at night." Lincoln agonized over the prospect of inciting a race war; his official Emancipation Proclamation, issued in January 1863, urged slaves to "abstain from all violence unless in necessary self-defence." Ultimately, however, Lincoln viewed the emancipation of the slaves as both a military necessity and a moral imperative. The enlistment of 186,000 emancipated slaves and free persons of color in the Union army — half of them from the Confederate states, another quarter from the slaveholding border states — gave African Americans a hand in the Union victory and a strong claim to citizenship after the war. Frederick Douglass, a tireless recruiter, portrayed the black Union soldier as the spiritual descendant of Nat Turner and other black men who had fought and died for the freedom of the race and the spiritual redemption of the nation. Once an outcast, Turner could be recast — in the black abolitionist tradition — as an American patriot who "struck the first blow for freedom."[2]

The apotheosis of Nat Turner within the abolitionist movement took place against a national backdrop of social upheaval and political violence. As slavery expanded into the cotton-rich states of the Gulf region, the South moved to protect the "peculiar institution" from internal criticism and outside interference. The Southern antislavery movement, once vibrant, withered and died. The case for slavery as a positive good became orthodoxy for a new generation of proslavery ideologues and demagogues. Increasingly, white Northerners came to see their own civil liberties threatened by a despotic "slave power conspiracy," aided and abetted by proslavery presidents and Supreme Court justices.

American expansionism under the doctrine of Manifest Destiny widened the sectional divide over slavery in the 1840s and 1850s. The annexation of Texas thrust the United States into war with Mexico and aroused abolitionist suspicions of a plot to expand the South's slaveholding empire across the continent. "Free Soilers," who saw slavery's expansion into the western territories as a threat to the rights of free white laborers, added a powerful new voice to the antislavery movement. At war's end, a defeated Mexico ceded its vast western holdings to the United States, reopening a debate over slavery's borders that had been quelled since the Missouri Compromise. When newly acquired California bypassed the formation of a territorial government and applied for admission as a free state, the two major political parties fractured along sectional lines. The Compromise of 1850, negotiated by Henry Clay, included a mix of antislavery and proslavery legislation designed to appease the Northern and Southern factions in each party. Under the terms of the compromise, California would be admitted as a free state, while the Utah and New Mexico territories would be organized with no explicit ban on slavery; slave trading would be abolished in the District of Columbia, while slave hunting would be encouraged under a new fugitive slave law. Militant abolitionists vowed to prevent the kidnapping and return of fugitive slaves through acts of civil disobedience and, if necessary, mob violence. Despite several well-publicized rescues, more than three hundred alleged fugitives were hauled into federal courts and forcibly reenslaved.

Tensions escalated with passage of the Kansas-Nebraska Act, which erased the geographical line between free states and slave states established under the Missouri Compromise. The act, sponsored by Democratic presidential hopeful Stephen A. Douglas, provided for the establishment of territorial governments on the basis of "popular sovereignty," leaving "all questions pertaining to slavery" to the inhabitants of the territories. A small-scale civil war ensued as proslavery forces, aided by "border ruffians" from Missouri, and antislavery forces, joined by gun-toting abolitionists from New England, vied for control of the new territorial government in Kansas. Rival governments were established, guerrilla warfare broke out, and "Bleeding Kansas" became a symbol of the nation's open wound. The violence spread to the halls of Congress, where South Carolina congressman Preston Brooks brutally caned Massachusetts senator Charles Sumner over remarks Sumner had made in a speech denouncing "The Crime Against Kansas." The political fallout from the Kansas-Nebraska Act doomed the Whig Party, split the Democratic Party along sectional lines, and gave rise in the North to the Republican Party, firmly opposed to slavery's extension into the territories.

By the late 1850s, the nation had become, in the words of Abraham Lincoln, a "house divided" — politically and culturally — along sectional lines. The Supreme Court's *Dred Scott* decision, which denied U.S. citizenship to all persons of African descent and invalidated the Missouri Compromise, left abolitionists and Republicans convinced that the "slave power conspiracy" extended to the highest court in the land. Likewise, John Brown's 1859 raid on Harpers Ferry, Virginia, gave Southern partisans ample evidence of a Republican-abolitionist conspiracy to foment insurrection among the slaves. Lincoln insisted that his party had nothing to do with John Brown's raid and no intention of interfering with the institution of slavery where it already existed. Nevertheless, his election as president in 1860 prompted the secession of seven Deep South states and pushed the nation to the brink of civil war.

Throughout the antebellum period, antislavery activists debated the moral legitimacy and political efficacy of violence as a means of se-curing freedom and independence. America's revolutionary heritage complicated the question. In a nation founded on armed rebellion, how could black people demonstrate their fitness for citizenship, their "manhood," if they were not — like Nat Turner — willing to fight and die for their freedom?

The Rebellious Slave As Outcast

The public exoneration of free persons of color by civil and mili-tary authorities in the immediate aftermath of Nat Turner's Rebel-lion did little to discourage white mobs from venting their rage upon a class long feared and despised for its presence in a slave society. In meetings up and down the eastern seaboard, "colored citizens" of the United States professed themselves innocent of any insur-rectionary intent. A "numerous and respectable meeting of persons of color" in Baltimore, Maryland, took exception to "evil reports" circulating against them: "We have been too long in the land of bi-bles, and temples, and ministers, to look upon blood and carnage with complacency. . . . We have been too long in this enlightened metropolis, to think of amelioration of our condition, in any other way than that sanctioned by the Gospel of Peace." The free people of color in Anne Arundel County, Maryland, "expressed their entire confidence in the white people, and pledged themselves, should there be any attempt to excite rebellion among the blacks, to make it known immediately to the white people in the neighborhood." From the free people of color in Trenton, New Jersey, came this statement: "Re-solved, Whereas we have lived peaceably and quietly in these United States, of which we are natives, and have never been the cause of any insurrectionary or tumultuous movements as a body, that we do view every measure taken by any associated bodies to remove us to other climes, anti-christian and hostile to our peace, and a violation of the laws of humanity." Among the resolutions passed at a "respect-able meeting of the colored citizens" of Lyme, Connecticut, was one stating, "We are not for insurrection, but for peace, freedom and equality."[3]

Turner's Rebellion cast a long shadow over the proceedings of the Second Annual Convention for the Improvement of the Free People of Color in the United States, held in Philadelphia in June 1832. Efforts to expel free blacks from Virginia and other states in the aftermath of the uprising had revived interest in the establishment of an "asylum" for black refugees in Upper Canada. (The First Convention had been called in response to a similar crisis — the expulsion of free blacks from Ohio after a "race riot" in 1829.) A committee report on the Canada settlement conveyed the suffering endured by free blacks since the uprising.

> The recent occurrences at the South have swelled the tide of prejudice until it has almost revolutionized public sentiment, which has given birth to severe legislative enactments in some of the States, and almost ruined our interests and prospects in others, in which, in the opinion of your Committee, our situation is more precarious than it has been at any other period since the Declaration of Independence.

While generally opposed to colonization, committee members acknowledged that "the rigid oppression abroad in the land is such, that a *part* of our suffering brethren cannot live under it." Delegates to the convention resolved, at the urging of the committee, to establish an agent in Upper Canada "for the purpose of purchasing lands and contributing to the wants of our people generally who may be, by oppressive legislative enactments, obliged to flee from these United States and take up residence within her borders."[4]

William Lloyd Garrison congratulated the free black delegates to the Philadelphia convention for embracing the philosophy of "non-resistance" and distancing themselves from the deeds of the rebellious slave.

> Most proudly do I bear testimony that on no occasion have I heard the utterance of a single threat against the owners of slaves at the south, or the proposal of any measure for their injury. On the contrary, I have seen a scrupulous, rigid, and unanimous determination to give no countenance to violence of any kind, and not to intermeddle with the slave population. Gentlemen, this is to you a crown of honor; and it furnishes your friends a weapon with which to cut down all the slanders of your enemies.

Garrison observed that the "colored citizens" had "stronger reasons for dreading a southern insurrection than the whites themselves," given the persecution they suffered as a result.[5]

Most abolitionists, black and white, followed the lead of Garrison on the question of antislavery violence. In December 1833, representatives of the major abolitionist groups — the New England Antislavery Society, led by Garrison; the New York City Antislavery Society, led by Arthur and Lewis Tappan; and the Society of Friends, or Quakers — met in Philadelphia to form a new national organization, the American Antislavery Society. The delegates adopted a Declaration of Sentiments, written by Garrison, that endorsed the revolutionary doctrine of human rights in the Declaration of Independence while rejecting the revolutionary violence employed by the Founding Fathers.

> Their principles led them to wage war against their oppressors, and to spill human blood like water, in order to be free. Ours forbid the doing of evil that good may come, and lead us to reject, and to entreat the oppressed to reject, the use of all carnal weapons for deliverance from bondage; relying solely on those which are spiritual, and mighty through God to the pulling down of strong holds.
>
> Their measures were physical resistance — the marshalling in arms — the hostile array — the mortal encounter. Ours shall be such only as the opposition of moral purity to moral corruption — the destruction of error by the potency of truth — the overthrow of prejudice by the power of love — and the abolition of slavery by the spirit of repentance.

The new group went on to declare every slaveholder a "man-stealer" and every law upholding the right of slavery "utterly null and void" in the eyes of God. It reminded "the people of the free States" that they were "living under a pledge of their tremendous physical force, to fasten the galling fetters of tyranny upon the limbs of millions in the Southern states," and urged them "to remove slavery by moral and political action, as prescribed in the Constitution of the United States."[6]

In debating the question of antislavery violence, abolitionists looked to the Bible for guidance. A "highly respectable audience of ladies and gentlemen" filled the Boston Anti-Slavery Hall in April 1835

to hear a debate on the following question: "Would Christian principles justify the slaves of this country in resorting to physical violence
to obtain their freedom?" George Thompson, the British abolitionist,
took the Garrisonian position that "if anyone in the universe of God
would be justified in resorting to physical violence to free himself from
unjust restraints, that human being was the American slave." Thompson insisted, however, that the Bible sanctioned only "peaceful and
moral warfare" against evil.

> He [Thompson] would say to the enslaved, "Hurt not a hair on
> your master's head. *It is not consistent with the will of your God, that
> you should do evil that good may come.* In that book in which your
> God and Savior has revealed his will, it is written — LOVE your
> enemies, BLESS THEM that CURSE you, DO GOOD by those
> that *hate* you, and PRAY FOR THEM which despitefully use you
> and persecute you; that ye may be the children of your Father
> which is in heaven."

A Mr. Weeks countered that the rebellious slaves could find ample
justification for a "resort to arms" in the Bible, "the Old Testament as
well as the New."

> He [Weeks] could not believe that his Maker had implanted a
> spirit of freedom within him, and yet made it criminal to protect
> himself from oppression. He was aware that he should be referred
> to the text, "He that taketh the coat," &c. But the bible could be
> made to prove anything. Christ drove out the money-changers.
> Peter carried a sword. Christ did not denounce the Roman sol-
> diery.

A member of the audience asked Weeks "whether he had forgotten
the sixth commandment, 'Though shalt not kill'?"[7]
    The open discussion of slavery and slave revolt in Boston con-
trasted with the closing of debate in the South. Abolitionist efforts
to flood the Southern mails with antislavery tracts and pamphlets
prompted calls for federal intervention. In his December 1835 message to Congress, President Andrew Jackson urged passage of a law
that would "prohibit, under severe penalties, the circulation in the
Southern states, through the mails, of incendiary publications, *intended to instigate the slaves to insurrection.*" Meanwhile, states through-

out the South passed laws that gave postmasters and justices of the peace broad new "inquisitorial powers" over the mails. Such measures, justified in the name of security, had a chilling effect on freedom of thought in the slaveholding South. As the American Antislavery Society observed in an appeal to President Jackson: "Certain writings of one of your predecessors, President Jefferson, would undoubtedly be regarded, in some places, so insurrectionary as to expose to popular violence whoever should presume to circulate them."[8]

By the late 1830s, as mob violence against abolitionists increased, some antislavery activists openly questioned the Garrisonian doctrine of nonresistance. In Alton, Illinois, the abolitionist newspaper editor Elijah Lovejoy declared that he would arm himself to ward off mobs that had menaced his family and destroyed three of his presses. "I have had inexpressible reluctance to resort to this method of defense," he explained in a letter to the *Liberator*. "But dear-bought experience has taught me that there is at present no safety for me, and no defense in this place, either in the laws or the protecting aegis of public sentiment." When Lovejoy, gun in hand, was shot and killed while confronting a mob, many abolitionists — to the dismay of Garrison — hailed him as a Christian martyr. Others found Garrison's "peace principles," which rejected participation in all activities of the government (including voting and office-holding), too extreme. The schism within the American Antislavery Society led to the establishment of the rival American and Foreign Antislavery Society in 1840. It also revitalized a black abolitionist convention movement that welcomed the return of Nat Turner.[9]

Henry Highland Garnet and Frederick Douglass

The rising spirit of militancy within the abolitionist movement elevated the stature of the rebellious slave in the 1840s. Once deferential to white sensibilities, black abolitionists declared their independence of thought and action through their public endorsement of slave rebellion and their public tributes to Nat Turner and other black rebel leaders. Two high-profile mutinies aboard slave ships — the *Amistad*, off the coast of northern Cuba in 1839, and the *Creole*, en route from Hampton Roads, Virginia, to New Orleans, in 1841 — added the names of Joseph Cinqué and Madison Washington to the list of "heroic slaves" deemed worthy of public commemoration. By 1850, black abolitionists had transformed the rebellious slave of history into a powerful symbol of black manhood and slave discontent.[10]

Henry Highland Garnet set the tone for the new militancy among black abolitionists when he endorsed the right of slaves to revolt in his famous "Address to the Slaves of the United States of America" at the National Convention of Colored Citizens in 1843. Born into slavery in 1815, Garnet became a free person at the age of nine when he and his family escaped from an estate in Kent County, Maryland, and headed north to freedom. After stops in Wilmington, Delaware, and Pennsylvania, the family eventually settled in New York City. There Garnet attended the New York African Free School along with some three hundred African-American students, several of whom also rose to prominence as writers, orators, and activists. As a grammar school student, Garnet formed a club whose members vowed not to celebrate the Fourth of July so long as slavery continued. "The other resolve which was made," fellow student Alexander Crummell recalled, "was, that when we had educated ourselves we would go South, start an insurrection, and free our brethren in bondage." Garnet subsequently came under the influence of the Reverend Theodore S. Wright, a Presbyterian minister from New York City, who introduced him to the antislavery movement.[11]

As a young man, Garnet hewed the Garrisonian line, eschewing violence and political action in favor of moral suasion. In 1834, he served as secretary of the Garrison Literary and Benevolent Association, a youth club for blacks in New York City. By the late 1830s, however, Garnet and other black activists had begun moving "toward militancy and greater independence from white abolitionists." In 1840, he broke with the Garrisonians and became "the first colored man" to join the Liberty Party. Like other party leaders, Garnet openly endorsed the right of the slaves to rebel, but counseled against it on the grounds of expediency. "Ah, sir," he said in a speech at the 1842 Liberty Party Convention, "those heaving fires that formerly burst forth like the lava of a burning volcano, upon the inhabitants of Southampton and elsewhere, when the colored man rose and asserted *his rights to humanity and liberty,* are kept in check only by the abolitionists. They hold open the safety valve of the nation; and these *enemies of the country,* as they are called, are the very men, sir, that prevent a general insurrection of the slaves from spreading carnage and devastation throughout the entire South." Such claims rested on the proposition that the slaves heard — and heeded — the advice of their abolitionist friends to the North.[12]

Garnet signaled a growing willingness among black abolitionists to endorse slave revolt in his "Address to the Slaves of the United States" at the 1843 National Convention of Colored Citizens in Buffalo. More than seventy delegates listened as Garnet, the twenty-eight-year-old pastor of a Presbyterian church in Troy, New York, delivered his fire-and-brimstone sermon. It was "sinful in the extreme," he declared, to voluntarily submit to the degradation of slavery. "Neither God, nor angels, or just men command you to suffer for a single moment. Therefore it is your solemn and imperative duty to use every means, both moral, intellectual, and physical, that promise success." The time had come, Garnet said, for the slaves to stand up for themselves. "You can plead your own cause, and do the work of emancipation, better than any other." The prospect of punishment and death should not dissuade them from demanding freedom, Garnet advised the slaves. "However much you and all of us may desire it, there is not much hope of Redemption without shedding blood. If you must bleed, let it all come at once — rather, *die freemen, than live to be slaves.*" Garnet stopped short of advocating armed rebellion, saying it was "inexpedient" under the present circumstances. "Your numbers are too small, and moreover the rising spirit of the age, and the spirit of the Gospel, are opposed to war and bloodshed." Instead, he urged the slaves to initiate a general strike by simply refusing to work. "Let every slave throughout the land do this," he declared, "and the days of slavery are numbered."[13]

Garnet gave a short history of American slave conspiracies and rebellions executed by courageous black men. The roll call of heroes began with Denmark Vesey of South Carolina, who "formed a plan for the liberation of his fellow men" in 1822. "In the whole history of human efforts to overthrow slavery," Garnet said, "a more complicated and tremendous plan was never formed. He was betrayed by the treachery of his own people, and died a martyr to freedom." Next came "the patriotic" Nathaniel Turner, who was "goaded to desperation by wrong and injustice. By Despotism, his name has been recorded on the list of infamy, but future generations will number him upon the noble and brave." The "immortal" Joseph Cinqué, leader of the *Amistad* mutiny of 1839, followed in the footsteps of his black American brethren. "He was a native African, and by the help of God he emancipated a whole ship-load of his fellow men on the high seas." Finally there was "that bright star of freedom" Madison Washington, the leader of the *Creole* uprising of 1841. "He was a slave on board the brig Creole, of Richmond, bound for New Orleans, that great slave mart, with a hundred and four others. Nineteen struck for Liberty or death. But one life was taken, and the whole were emancipated, and the vessel was carried into Nassau, New Providence." Garnet downplayed the violence of these insurrections, stressing instead the courage and nobility of their leaders. He offered the acknowledgment of history as the reward for such noble self-sacrifice. "Those who have fallen in freedom's conflict, their memories will be cherished by the true hearted, and the God-fearing, in all future generations; those who are living, their names are surrounded by a halo of glory."[14]

The minutes of the 1843 convention provide a glimpse of the controversy stirred by the address. "Perceiving some points in it that might in print appear objectionable," Charles B. Ray of New York moved that the speech be referred to a select committee so that it might "pass through a close and critical examination" and be "somewhat modified" before publication. Garnet objected, saying the address should be adopted by the convention and "sent out with its sanction." For nearly an hour and a half, Garnet waxed eloquent on the need to take a more militant stand.

> He reviewed the abominable system of slavery, showed its mighty workings, its deeds of darkness and death — how it robbed parents of children, and children of parents, and husbands of wives; how it prostituted the daughters of the slaves; how it murdered the colored man. He referred to the fate of Denmark Vesey and his accomplices — of Nat Turner; to the burning of McIntosh, to the case of Madison Washington, as well as to many other cases — to what had been done to move the slaveholders to let go their grasp, and asked what more could be done — if we have not waited long enough — if it were not time to speak louder and longer — to take higher ground and other steps.

The speech moved many of the delegates to tears. As Garnet concluded his "masterly" oration, the convention hall erupted in applause.[15]

Frederick Douglass, a twenty-five-year-old delegate from Boston, led the opposition to the militant position staked out by Garnet. Born on the eastern shore of Maryland, the son of an enslaved black mother and a white father whom he never knew, Douglass experienced the hardships and violence of slavery (which he recounted in his three autobiographies) for twenty years before his successful escape to New York in September 1838. There he married Anna Murray, a free woman of color, moved to the city of New Bedford, Massachusetts, and worked an assortment of odd jobs for three years before becoming, in his words, "known to the anti-slavery world." Shortly after his arrival in New Bedford, Douglass began to read the *Liberator.* "The paper became my meat and drink," he later recalled. "My soul was set all on fire."[16]

Douglass became a regular participant in local antislavery meetings; his comments at one such meeting caught the attention of William C. Coffin, a white abolitionist, who arranged for him to make his first public speech at the Massachusetts Antislavery Society meeting on the island of Nantucket in 1841. After hearing Douglass speak, an exuberant William Lloyd Garrison rose and engaged the audience in a spontaneous call and response. "Have we been listening to a thing, a chattel personal, or a man?" he asked. "A man! a man!" came the reply. "Shall such a man be held a slave in a Christian land?" he asked. "No! No!" the audience roared. Douglass agreed to become an agent of the Massachusetts Antislavery Society and quickly established a reputation as a stirring speaker and an ardent defender of Garrisonian principles.[17]

The 1843 Convention of Colored Citizens in Buffalo showcased the ideological differences between Douglass and Garnet and their emerging rivalry for leadership of the movement.[18] Douglass told his fellow delegates that "there was too much physical force, both in the address and in the remarks" of the militant Garnet. Should the address reach the slaves and should they follow its advice, Douglass argued, "it might not lead the slaves to rise in insurrection for liberty," but it "would, nevertheless, and necessarily be the occasion for an insurrection, and that was what he wished in no way to have any agency in bringing about." Douglass told the convention that he "was for trying the moral means a little longer." Garnet replied that the address simply "advised the slaves to go to their masters and tell them they wanted their liberty, and had come to ask for it; and if the master refused it, to tell them, then we shall take it, let the consequence be what it may."

Douglass countered that such a policy, though nonviolent in theory, "would lead to an insurrection" and urged his fellow delegates to "avoid such a catastrophe. He wanted emancipation in a better way, as he expected to have it." The debate stretched out over the course of several days. A. M. Sumner argued that adoption of Garnet's address would be "fatal to the safety of the free people of color of the slave States, but especially so to those who lived on the borders of the free States; and living in Cincinnati as he did, he thought he was fully prepared to anticipate very properly what might be the result thereabouts, and he felt bound on behalf of himself and his constituents, to oppose its passage." After final arguments by Garnet and Douglass, the matter was put to a vote. Eighteen delegates supported adoption of the address; nineteen opposed it. The nays carried the day by one vote.[19]

The Garrisonian press applauded the vote to reject publication of Garnet's militant pamphlet. "It is a matter of thankfulness," wrote Maria W. Chapman, editor pro tem of the *Liberator,* "whenever the spirit of freedom and of good, — of love, forgiveness, and magnanimity prevails, even in a single heart, over evil, force, revenge, and littleness." Chapman described Garnet as a tool of white apostates who had abandoned the Garrison-led American Antislavery Society. "We say emphatically to the man of color, trust not the counsels that lead you to the shedding of blood. That man knows nothing of nature, human or Divine, — of character, — good or evil, who imagines that a civil and servile war would ultimately promote American freedom." Chapman urged adherence to the nonviolent principles espoused in the constitution of the American Antislavery Society. "'Stay the beginnings' is our earnest warning to all who are beginning to *talk* about insurrection."[20]

Garnet responded by asserting his right to pursue his own course as an abolitionist. "You say that I 'have received bad counsel.' You are not the only person who has told your humble servant that his humble productions have been produced by 'counsel' of some Anglo-Saxon. I have expected no more from ignorant slave-holders and their apologists, but I really expected better things from Mrs. Maria W. Chapman, an anti-slavery poetess, and editor *pro-tem* of the Boston *Liberator.*" Rest assured, Garnet concluded, "There is one black American who dares speak boldly on the subject of universal liberty."[21]

Garnet continued to press his case for slave revolt as a legitimate means of self-liberation. He delivered his "Address to the Slaves" at the next National Convention of Colored People, held in Troy, New York, in October 1847, but advocates of moral suasion again held sway. The Committee on Abolition, led by Frederick Douglass, expressed its "entire disapprobation of any plan of emancipation involving a resort to bloodshed," casting its argument in both moral and practical terms.

> Your Committee regard any counsel of this sort as the perfect folly, suicidal in the extreme, and abominably wicked. We should utterly frown down and wholly discountenance any attempt to lead our people to confide in brute force as a reformatory instrumentality. All argument put forth in favor of insurrection and bloodshed, however well intended, is either the result of unpardonable impatience or an aesthetic want of faith in the power of truth as a means of regenerating and reforming the worlds.

Undaunted, Garnet published his "Address to the Slaves," along with David Walker's "Appeal to the Colored Citizens of the World," several months after the convention.[22]

The public debate over Garnet's address obscured the degree to which Douglass himself viewed antislavery violence as both a legitimate expression of black manhood and powerful evidence of slave discontent. In his 1845 autobiography, Douglass described the significance of his fight with an overseer who had physically and verbally abused him.

> This battle with Mr. Covey was the turning point in my career as a slave. It rekindled the few expiring embers of freedom, and revived within me a sense of my own manhood. . . . My long-crushed spirit rose, cowardice departed, bold defiance took its place; and I now resolved that, however long I might remain a slave in form, the day had passed forever when I could be a slave in fact. I did not hesitate to let it be known of me, that the white man who expected to succeed in whipping, must also succeed in killing me.

Douglass routinely presented Nat Turner as a symbol of the rebellious spirit that dwelled within every slave. In a May 1848 speech before the New England Antislavery Society in Boston, he urged white Northerners to sever their military pact with the slaveholders and give the slaves a fighting chance. "Would you but do this, oh, men of the North, I know there is a spirit among the slaves which would not much longer brook their degradation and their bondage. There are many Madison Washingtons and Nathaniel Turners in the South, who would assert their rights to liberty, if you would take your feet from their necks, and your sympathy and aid from their oppressors." Douglass depicted Turner as a heroic figure — "a noble, brave, and generous soul — patient, disinterested, and fearless of suffering" — in the tradition of the American Founding Fathers. "How was he treated, for endeavoring to gain his own liberty, and that of his enslaved brethren, by the self-same means which the Revolutionary fathers employed? When taken by his enemies, he was stripped naked, and compelled to walk barefooted, some thirty yards, over burning coals, and, when he reached the end, he fell, pierced by a hundred American bullets." Actually, Turner was led to the gallows and hanged by the neck until dead, but Douglass was uninterested in the finer points of history. He sought to rouse his Northern audience to righteous indignation by implicating the federal government — and not just the Southern states — in the crime of slavery. "I say to you, get out of this position of bodyguard to slavery. Cease from any longer rendering aid and comfort to the tyrant-master!"[23]

Douglass used the story of Madison Washington, the Virginia slave who led the mutiny aboard the *Creole,* to remind the nation that its revolutionary traditions and ideals of freedom and independence belonged to black Americans as well as white. In "The Heroic Slave," a fictional narrative published in his Rochester, New York, newspaper, Douglass memorialized the rebel leader as *"one* of the truest, manliest, and bravest" of all the great men produced by the state of Virginia. "Let those account for it who can," he wrote, "but there stands the fact, that a man who loved liberty as well as did Patrick Henry, — who deserved it as much as Thomas Jefferson, — and who fought for it with a valor as high, an arm as strong, and against odds as great, as he who led all the armies of the American colonies through the great war for freedom and independence, lives now only in the chattel records of his native State." Denied recognition by proslavery historians, the heroic figure of Madison Washington remained "enveloped in darkness." Douglass proposed to enlighten his readers with a narrative based on little more than "marks, traces, possibles, and probabilities." Merging fact (names, dates, and selected details from journalistic accounts) and fiction (invented scenes, characters, and dialogue), Douglass transformed the little-known rebel leader into a figure of "Herculean" proportions, the perfect embodiment of slave discontent and black manhood.[24]

Douglass attributed his radical turn on the question of antislavery violence to his 1847 meeting with the militant white abolitionist John Brown, then a "respectable merchant" in Springfield, Massachusetts. Well aware of Douglass's moderate views, Brown shared his own thoughts on means and ends: "He denounced slavery in look and language fierce and bitter, thought that slaveholders had forfeited their right to live, that the slaves had the right to gain their liberty in any way they could, did not believe that moral suasion would ever liberate the slave, or that political action would abolish the system." Brown proceeded to outline his evolving plan for the liberation of the slaves. His words had a profound effect on Douglass. "My utterances became more and more tinted by the color of this man's strong impressions." Slavery, he declared, "could only be destroyed by blood-shed."[25]

The Slave's Narrative

The ex-slave narratives of Charity Bowery and Harriet Jacobs, midwifed by the white abolitionist editor Lydia Maria Child, made abolitionist heroes and martyrs of those who suffered at the hands of white vigilantes in the immediate aftermath of Nat Turner's Rebellion. Both Bowery and Jacobs hailed from Edenton, North Carolina, about fifty miles southeast of the epicenter of the uprising in Southampton County. In their narratives, published more than two decades apart, they made only passing mention of Nat Turner and made no judgment about his bloody deeds. Rather, they emphasized the cruelty and moral depravity of the white vigilantes and patrollers who vented their wrath on "innocent men, women, and children" and celebrated the fortitude of those black people who survived the ordeal.

Lydia Maria Child exemplified the rise of women to positions of prominence within the Garrisonian wing of the abolitionist movement. A successful romance novelist in the 1820s, she redirected her literary skills in the 1830s to the publication of abolitionist literature. In 1833, she wrote *An Appeal in Favor of That Class of Americans Called Africans,* a widely read antislavery tract that made converts of Charles

Sumner, Wendell Phillips, and Thomas Wentworth Higginson. The following year, she encouraged James R. Bradley, an ex-slave attending Lane Seminary in Cincinnati, to write down his narrative for publication in an edited volume. A leading member of the Boston Female Antislavery Society, Child was named to the executive committee of the American Antislavery Society in 1840 after the Garrisonians seized control of the group and opened its leadership positions to women. The following year she moved to New York, where she edited the society's weekly newspaper, the *National Anti-Slavery Standard.*

Charity Bowery's story, as recorded by Child, appeared in the *Liberty Bell* magazine (1839) and, later, Frederick Douglass's newspaper, the *North Star* (1848).[26] Child based the narrative on her conversations with Bowery, whom she described as "an aged colored woman" living in New York: "I shall endeavor to relate it precisely in her own words, so oft-repeated that they are tolerably well impressed on my memory. Some confusion of names, date, and incidents, I may very naturally make. I profess only to give 'the pith and marrow' of Charity's story, deprived of the highly dramatic effect it received from her swelling emotions, earnest looks, and changing tones." Much of the story that followed depicted Bowery as the "archetype of outraged motherhood," a phrase coined by literary critic Joanne Braxton in her study of black women's autobiography within the slave narrative genre.[27] Freed in her master's will, Bowery set out to buy freedom for some of her sixteen children with money she earned from selling oysters and crackers, but her "divil" mistress refused to set them free. "One after another — one after another — she sold 'em away from me." With no hope of reuniting her family, Bowery left for the Free States, where she earned a "comfortable living" washing clothes but pined for her lost children.

Child attached Bowery's recollections of Nat Turner's Rebellion as an appendix, of sorts, to the narrative. "In the course of my conversations with this interesting woman," Child noted, "she told me much about the patrols, who, armed with arbitrary power, and frequently intoxicated, break into the houses of the colored people and subject them to all manner of outrages." Such patrols were a common, everyday form of violence, familiar to all slaves.

> But nothing seemed to have excited her imagination so much as the insurrection of Nat Turner. The panic that prevailed throughout the Slave States on that occasion reached her ear in repeated

echoes, and the reasons are obvious why it should have awakened intense interest. It was in fact a sort of Hegira to her mind, from which she was prone to date all important events in the history of her limited world.

Unfortunately Child recorded but a scant few of Bowery's comments "in her own words." Bowery recalled the climate of fear produced by the patrols looking to punish anyone who might fit the profile of a rebellious slave. "The best and the brightest men were killed in Nat's time," she told Child. "Such one's are always suspected." Bowery painted a picture of heroic slaves being hounded by white mobs yet refusing to obey harsh new rules against reading and writing. "On Sundays," she said, "I have seen the negroes up in the country going away under large oaks, and in secret places, sitting in the woods with spelling books." Slave religion went underground as well:

> All the colored folks were afraid to pray in the time of the old prophet Nat. There was no law about it; but the whites reported it round among themselves that, if a note was heard, we should have some dreadful punishment; and after that, the low whites would fall upon any slaves they heard praying, or singing a hymn, and often killed them before their masters or mistresses could get to them.

Bowery expressed no bitterness toward Turner for having unleashed the furies of the white mob. The name she used to describe him, "old prophet Nat," suggested a benign figure, a wise man or a communal elder, old beyond his thirty-one years.[28]

Child encouraged Harriet Jacobs to include far more expansive recollections of the Turner backlash in her autobiography, *Incidents in the Life of a Slave Girl*. Born into slavery in 1813, Jacobs was about eighteen at the time of the rebellion. By then she had learned to read, spell, and sew. She had also been sexually harassed by her master and had given birth to a son by a white neighbor. More than twenty years passed before she recorded her recollections of life as a slave in the perilous months after the uprising but before Nat Turner's capture. Jacobs escaped to the North in 1842, began writing her autobiography in 1853, and completed the manuscript in 1858. At the request of her Boston publisher (who subsequently went bankrupt), she prevailed upon Lydia Maria Child to write the preface. Child, who considered the account "unusually interesting," became her agent and editor as well.[29]

Child was particularly intrigued by a brief passage in Jacobs's manuscript on the persecution of blacks in the immediate aftermath of Nat Turner's rebellion. Jacobs had written: "Those who never witnessed such scenes can hardly believe what I know was inflicted at this time on innocent men, women, and children, against whom there was not the slightest ground for suspicion." Child asked Jacobs to elaborate, in writing, on what she had witnessed of "the outrages committed on the colored people, in Nat Turner's time": "You say the reader would not believe what you saw 'inflicted on men, women, and children, without the slightest ground of suspicion against them.' What *were* those inflictions? Were any tortured to make them confess? And how? Were any killed? Please write down some of the most striking particulars, and let me have them to insert."[30]

The narrative, as published, included enough scenes of mayhem and torture to please even the most bloodthirsty editor:

> Colored people and slaves who lived in remote parts of town suffered in an especial manner. In some cases the searchers scattered powder and shot among their clothes, and then sent other parties to find them, and bring them forward as proof that they were plotting insurrection. Every where men, women, and children were whipped till the blood stood in puddles at their feet. Some received five hundred lashes; others were tied hands and feet, and tortured with a bucking paddle, which blisters the skin terribly.
>
> Every day for a fortnight, if I looked out, I saw horsemen with some poor panting negro tied to their saddles, and compelled by the lash to keep up with their speed, till they arrived at the jail yard. Those who had been whipped too unmercifully to walk were washed with brine, tossed into a cart, and carried to jail.

Some of those interrogated by the whites broke under the strain.

> One black man, who had not the fortitude to endure scourging, promised to give information about the conspiracy. But it turned out that he knew nothing at all. He had not even heard the name

Nat Turner. The poor fellow had, however, made up a story, which augmented his own sufferings and those of the colored people.

African-American men were as helpless as women before the rampaging whites. "If any of the fathers or husbands told of these outrages, they were tied up to the whipping post, and cruelly scourged for telling lies about white men." Jacobs had to prevail upon a "white gentleman" to protect her family during the search of her house.[31]

A more martial spirit pervaded the slave narrative of Henry "Box" Brown, who recalled the paralyzing fear that Turner's Rebellion inspired in slaveholding whites. Brown, a fugitive slave who escaped to freedom by mailing himself north in a box, recalled witnessing a series of "strange events" while living in Richmond in 1831. "I did not then know precisely what was the cause of these scenes," he wrote in his autobiography, published eighteen years after the uprising, "for I could not get any very satisfactory information concerning the matter from my master, only that some of the slaves had undertaken to kill their owners; but I have since learned that it was the famous Nat Turner's insurrection that caused all the excitement I witnessed." Brown recalled that "the whole city was in the utmost confusion; and a dark cloud of terrific blackness, seemed to hang over the heads of the whites." Given their overwhelming military advantage, the whites should have remained calm, yet they panicked just the same. "So true is it," Brown wrote, "that 'the wicked flee when no man pursueth.'" With biting sarcasm, Brown lampooned the Southern slaveholder who lived in "constant fear" of a slave uprising. "The rustling of 'the lightest leaf, that quivers in the breeze,' fills his timid soul with visions of flowing blood and burning dwellings; and as the loud thunder of heaven rolls over his head, and the vivid lightning flashes across his pale face, straightaway his imagination conjures up terrible scenes of the loud roaring of the enemy's cannon, and the fierce yells of an infuriated slave population, rushing to vengeance."[32]

Brown described in detail the atrocities committed by white vigilantes, including the half-hanging, "a refined species of cruelty, peculiar to slavery." Yet he also described the resistance of African Americans to laws that forbade them to congregate or preach in the aftermath of the insurrection. He told of a "colored preacher" who "refused to obey the imperial mandate, and was severely whipped; but his religion was too deeply rooted to be thus driven from him, and no promise could be extorted from his resolute soul, that he would not proclaim what he considered the glad tidings of the gospel." Brown offered the resistance of the colored preacher as evidence of black manhood in the face of overwhelming oppression. "Query: How many white preachers would continue their employment, if they were served in the same way?"[33]

The Novels of Harriet Beecher Stowe and G.P.R. James

As the sectional crisis intensified in the early to mid-1850s, two internationally acclaimed fiction writers used fictionalized accounts of Nat Turner and the Southampton uprising as a vehicle for social commentary on slavery and abolition. Harriet Beecher Stowe's *Dred: A Tale of the Great Dismal Swamp* and G.P.R. James's *The Old Dominion; or, The Southampton Massacre* drew heavily on the "Confessions of Nat Turner" in their fictional portrayals of the rebel leader, yet the two literary productions diverged dramatically on the righteousness of the antislavery cause.

Stowe was born in Litchfield, Connecticut, making her a New Englander by birth if not by temperament. Her father, Lyman Beecher, was a Protestant minister who became a renowned evangelist and theologian of the Second Great Awakening; her mother, Roxana, died at an early age, exhausted by the birth of seven children. Harriet grew up in a highly literate, highly ambitious household, where family members encouraged one another to pursue professional careers. Several of her siblings became famous in their own right. Catharine Beecher founded the Hartford Female Seminary, which developed a national reputation for its emphasis on the "practical" education of women. Henry Ward Beecher became a minister, immortalized for his role in shipping rifles ("Beecher's Bibles") to antislavery settlers during the bloody battles over popular sovereignty in Kansas. When Harriet was thirteen, she experienced her rebirth in Christ, which one biographer called "the capstone of a Beecher family education." That same year, she enrolled in her sister's school, where she developed the rhetorical skills for a career in public speaking and writing. After graduation, she followed her sister's lead and became a teacher at the seminary. She was twenty years old and living in Hartford, far removed from the world of slaves and slaveholders, at the time of the Southampton uprising.[34]

Harriet Beecher ventured into antislavery politics in 1836 with a letter to the editor of a Cincinnati newspaper, written under a male pseudonym, decrying the actions of a mob that destroyed the presses of abolitionist editor James G. Birney. For the most part, however, she remained aloof from the antislavery movement during her eighteen-year residence in Cincinnati. Married to a theology professor named Stowe, she became a writer of stories and sketches for such magazines as *Godey's Lady's Book, Western Literary Magazine,* and the *New-York Evangelist.* One sketch, published in 1845, foreshadowed her antislavery novels of later years. Entitled "Immediate Emancipation," it told the "true story" of a slave from Kentucky who ran away with the help of a Quaker; when the owner came looking for his slave in Cincinnati, the Quaker persuaded him to abandon the search and emancipate the slave instead.

The passage of the Fugitive Slave Law politicized Stowe. A series of highly publicized kidnappings and forcible reenslavements, conducted under the cloak of federal law, appalled her. In February 1851, while living in Maine (her husband had accepted a teaching position at Bowdoin College), she asked her brother Henry to furnish her with "suggestions and materials for some graphic sketches that shall have some bearing on the slave power & principle — something to make slavery a *picture* instead of a political idea."[35] The following month she informed the editor of the *National Era* that she had begun work on a "series of sketches" that would convey the "light and shadows" of slavery. "Up to this year," she told the editor, "I have always felt that I had no particular call to meddle with this subject, and I dreaded to expose even my own mind to the full force of its exciting power. But I feel now that the time has come when even a woman or a child who can speak a word for freedom and humanity is bound to speak." Stowe stressed the literary realism of her work. "My vocation is simply that of a painter, and my object will be to hold in the most lifelike and graphic manner possible Slavery, its reverses, changes, and the negro character, which I have had ample opportunities for studying. There is no arguing with pictures, and everybody is impressed with them, whether they mean to be or not."[36]

The hero and title character of *Uncle Tom's Cabin* (1852) is the very antithesis of the rebellious slave. A devout Christian, Tom resists the impulse to lash out at his tormentors, even under the most extreme provocation. His creed is that of the Garrisonians: "LOVE your enemies, BLESS THEM that CURSE you, DO GOOD by those that *hate* you, and PRAY FOR THEM which despitefully use you and persecute you; that ye may be the children of your Father which is in heaven." When Tom's financially strapped master rewards his years of faithful service by selling him down the river, Tom rejects the advice of others to run off. "Mas'r always found me on the spot — he always will. I never have broke trust, nor used my pass no ways contrary to my word, and I never will." Tom has the welfare of the slaves in mind as well. To run away, he reasons, would only place others in jeopardy of sale. "If I must be sold, or all the people on the place, and everything go to rack, why let me be sold. I s'pose I can b'ar it as well as any of 'em." Tom scolds his wife and children when they wish God's vengeance upon the slave traders. "Pray for them that spitefully use you, the good book says." Even as Tom's misfortunes and sufferings mount, his faith in God's plan endures.[37]

For all of her sentimental tributes to faithful Uncle Tom, Stowe warned her readers that the brutalizing, dehumanizing effect of slavery might turn the humblest, most obedient slave into a desperado. To address the prospect of slave rebellion in the United States, she contrived an extended dialogue between twin brothers Augustine (the indulgent master) and Alfred (the disciplinarian) St. Clare:

> *Alfred:* Of course, they must be kept down, consistently, steadily, as I *should.*
> *Augustine:* It makes a terrible slip when they get up — in St. Domingo, for instance.
> *Alfred:* Poh! We'll take care of that, in this country. We must set our face against all this educating, elevating talk, that is getting about now; the lower class must not be educated.
> *Augustine:* That is past praying for; educated they will be, and we have only to say how. Our system is educating them in barbarism and brutality. We are breaking all humanizing ties, and making them brute beasts; and, if they get the upper hand, such we shall find them.
> *Alfred:* They shall never get the upper hand!
> *Augustine:* That's right, put on the steam, fasten down the escape-valve, and sit on it, and see where you'll land.
> *Alfred:* Well, we will see. I'm not afraid to sit on the escape-valve, as long as the boilers are strong and the machinery works.
> *Augustine:* The nobles in Louis XVI's time thought just so; and

Austria and Pius IX think so now; and some pleasant morning, you may be caught up to meet each other in the air, *when the boilers burst.*

Alfred: Dies declarabit.

Augustine: I tell you, if there is anything that is revealed with the strength of a divine law in our times, it is that the masses are to rise, and the under class become the upper one.

Alfred: That's one of your red republican humbugs, Augustine. Why didn't you ever take to the stump; — you'd make a famous stump orator! Well, I hope I'll be dead before this millennium of your greasy masses comes on.

Augustine: Greasy or not greasy, they will govern *you*, when their time comes, and they will be just such rulers as you make them. . . . The people of Hayti —

Alfred: O, come, Augustine! As if we hadn't had enough of that abominable, contemptible Hayti! The Haytiens were not Anglo Saxons; if they had been, there would have been another story. The Anglo Saxon is the dominant race of the world, and *is to be so.*

Augustine: Well, there is a pretty fair infusion of Anglo Saxon blood among our slaves, now. There are plenty among them who had only enough of the African to give a sort of tropical warmth and fervor to our calculating firmness and foresight. If ever the St. Domingo hour comes, Anglo Saxon blood will lead on the day. Sons of white fathers, with all our haughty feelings burning in their veins, will not always be bought and sold and traded. They will rise, and raise with them their mother's race.

Sure enough, the spirit of rebellion (in Stowe's literary imagination) burned brightest in the "talented young mulatto" George Harris and the "quadroon" Cassy. Removed from his job at a bagging factory, sentenced to the drudgery of farm labor, denied permission to see his wife on a neighboring plantation, George expresses nothing but rage toward his master. "My master! Who made him my master?" His wife, Eliza — like Uncle Tom, a devout Christian — urges George to await his deliverance in God's time. "I have been careful, and I have been patient," he says, "but it's growing worse and worse; flesh and blood can't bear it much longer . . . I *won't* bear it. No, I *won't!*" George sets off for

Canada, a fugitive slave on the verge of rebellion. "I'll be free, or I'll die!" Time and again George declares his willingness to resort to physical violence, if necessary. "I'll fight for my liberty to the last breath I breathe," he declares to his former employer. "You say your fathers did it; if it was right for them, it is right for me!" Cassy, the much-abused ex-concubine of Simon Legree, actually plots his murder as an act of liberation: "Would it be a sin to rid the world of such a wretch?" She tries to recruit Uncle Tom to strike the fatal blow. "Not for ten thousand worlds, Misse!" he responds. "Then I shall do it," she says. "O, Misse Cassy! for the dear Lord's sake that died for ye, don't sell your soul to the devil, that way! Nothing but evil will come of it! The Lord hasn't called us to wrath. We must suffer, and wait his time." In the end, Tom's message of love and forbearance prevails; Cassy resolves not to kill her master and runs away instead.[38]

Hailed by leaders of the antislavery movement, mocked and vilified by Southern critics, *Uncle Tom's Cabin* established Stowe as the literary voice of the abolitionist movement. Stowe began work on her second antislavery novel, *Dred: A Tale of the Great Dismal Swamp*, in February 1856. The violent clash of proslavery and antislavery forces in Kansas and the widening sectional conflict provided the extraliterary context for her novel. Several dramatic events impinged on her creative consciousness as she wrote the book, including the sacking of the "Free Soil" town of Lawrence, Kansas, and the caning of Massachusetts senator Charles Sumner by South Carolina representative Preston Brooks. "The book is written under the impulse of our stormy times," she told a friend in England: "how insignificant yet how undaunted we are — how the blood & insults of Sumner and the sack of Lawrence burn within us." Stowe made no attempt to disguise her pointed commentary on current events; she recalled the caning of Sumner in her preface to the British edition of *Dred*. "The chivalry of South Carolina presented the ruffian with a cane, bearing the inscription, 'Hit him again.' After this who will doubt what the treatment of the slaves has been?"[39]

Stowe summoned the memory of Nat Turner in creating the title character for her new novel. She cited the source of her fictional representation in an appendix, a documentary technique modeled after her *Key to Uncle Tom's Cabin*, published in 1854. "As an illustration of the character and views of Dred," she noted, "we make a few extracts from the Confessions of Nat Turner, as published by T. R. Gray, Esq., of

Southampton, Virginia, in November 1831. One of the principal conspirators in this affair was named Dred." Stowe incorporated various
biographical details from "The Confessions" into her narrative. In one
excerpt, for example, the narrator describes the charismatic leadership
of Dred in a rough paraphrase of "The Confessions": "The perfectness
of his own religious enthusiasm, his absolute certainty that he was inspired by God, as a leader and deliverer, gave him ascendancy over the
minds of those who followed him, which nothing but religious enthusiasm can ever give. And this was further confirmed by the rigid austerity of his life." Elsewhere, Stowe translated key phrases and passages from "The Confessions" into dialogue, as when Dred describes
his apocalyptic visions to a fellow slave: "Behold, I saw white spirits
and black spirits, that contended in the air; and the thunder rolled, and
the blood flowed, and the voice said, 'Come rough, come smooth!
Such is the decree. Ye must surely bear it.'" Readers could turn to Appendix I of the novel and find the original source of the passage in the
original "Confessions."[40]

Stowe used real historical events and characters to give the rebellious slave of her own creation a royal pedigree. She made Dred the
son of Denmark Vesey, a "free colored man from Charleston" who had
"conceived the hopeless project of imitating the example set by the
American race, and achieving independence for the blacks." Stowe
mocked the naiveté of the "historians" who had prepared the official
report on Vesey's conspiracy. They could not fathom what motivated
"a free colored man" to join a slave conspiracy, despite Vesey's testimony that he had "several children who were slaves" and "wished he
could set them free." But Vesey's enslaved son, the fourteen-year-old
Dred, understood, having borne silent witness to his father's martyrdom. "He could not be admitted to his father's prison, but he was a
witness of the undaunted aspect with which he and the other conspirators met their doom. The memory dropped into the depths of his
soul, as a stone drops into the desolate depths of a dark mountain
lake." Stowe suggested that memories of black resistance and rebellion
passed, in like fashion, from generation to generation of slaves, thus
subverting the official histories produced by white authorities.[41]

Critics greeted Dred — Mrs. Stowe's latest "negro-slave story" —
with "extravagant commendations and almost unqualified contempt."
The commendations came from Stowe's admirers and fellow travelers
in the antislavery press. "'Dred,'" read one such review, "is yet another

and striking picture of the evils of negro slavery, with this difference, that, while 'Uncle Tom' represents these horrors suffered by the slave, 'Dred' delineates the moral degradation, the bad feeling, the state of alarm and of civil conflict, the poverty and the misery of the master." The unqualified contempt came from Stowe's detractors south of the Mason-Dixon Line. The editors of the *Southern Literary Messenger* dismissed the book as "that dismal story of the Dismal Swamp, which Mrs. Stowe gave to the world . . . and which, aimed as it was, against the people of the Southern States, like the terrible boomerang, came back upon her and destroyed her reputation."[42] Likewise, *DeBow's Review* declared: "This is another exhibition of abolition spite and spleen, which, as it is productive of the cent and dollar, make very good charity, religion, and philanthropy in that quarter." The *Review* closed with this ominous note: "When the full fruition of all this falsehood, calumny, and bitterness, is likely to be realized, the South will know how to protect herself and her rights. A temporary truce exists at present. None of us are deceived by it."[43]

Several reviewers singled out the character of "Dred" — inspired by Stowe's reading of the 1831 "Confessions of Nat Turner" — for sharp commentary, among them the *Christian Examiner and Religious Miscellany:*

This nightmare monstrosity is an offence to us, a humbug, a most unnatural, impossible, unnecessary, and unavailable being, or what not? What could have possessed the eminent and able authoress to conjure up or to invent such a creature, is a problem past our skill in explanations. He answers to no reality, and unless he is taken as a sort of impersonation of the Nemesis, the avenging ogre of Slavery, he has nothing to do with the story. If Mrs. Stowe had put her quotations from the old prophets into the beak of a harsh-croaking crow perched on a scathed pine-tree over a camp-meeting, she would have been even more likely to have carried our interest with her than she does by a single thing said by her about "Dred," or by him for himself.[44]

Littell's Living Age also denounced the character:

Dred himself had been generally thought a failure, and we are not inclined to disturb the verdict. In some of his rhapsodies he crosses the narrow line which separates the sublime from the ridiculous. In others, he passes the broad one which distinguished sense from nonsense. . . . What he does is as disappointing as what he says. He receives in his lurking-place in the Dismal Swamp the fugitives whom Mrs. Stowe, having no other means of providing for them, sends to Canada; he starts up opportunely whenever a wanderer is to be guided or a murderer to be interrupted. He traverses the forest on foot, or, springing bough to bough, announces, in the strange language of which we have given specimens, wrath and woe and destruction; and, when he last appears, is seen dying of a wound received in some undescribed combat.[45]

Stowe anticipated brisk sales of her novel. "If 'Dred' has as good a sale in America as it is likely to have in England, we shall do well," she wrote to her husband. "There is such a demand that they had to placard the shop windows in London with, — 'To prevent disappointment, "Dred" not to be had till,' etc. Everybody is after it, and the prospect is an enormous sale." Stowe kept close tabs on British sales figures. September 15, 1856: "'Dred' is selling over here wonderfully. Low says with all means at his command, he has not been able to meet the demand. He sold fifty thousand in two weeks, and probably will sell as many more." September 25: "The last I heard from Low, he had sold sixty thousand of 'Dred,' and it was still selling well." October 10: "One hundred thousand copies of 'Dred' sold in four weeks! After that who cares what the critics say?"[46] Yet Stowe did care what the critics had to say. She commented on the reviews in the British press. "It is very bitterly attacked, both from a literary and a religious point of view," Stowe told her husband. "The 'Record' is down upon it with a cartload of solemnity; the 'Athenaeum' with waspish spite; the 'Edinburgh' goes out of its way to say that the author knows nothing of the society she describes; but yet it goes everywhere, is read everywhere, and Mr. Low says that he puts the hundred and twenty-fifth thousand to press confidently."[47]

Defenders of slavery found their own literary advocate in G.P.R. James, the British author of *The Old Dominion; or The Southampton Massacre*. Born in London in 1801, James grew up in "comfortable circumstances," thanks in part to the profits from James's Powder, a popular patent medicine invented by his grandfather. As a boy, he enjoyed reading historical novels and travelogues. After a stint in the British army, he became a "well-to-do wanderer." Encouraged by two famous friends, Washington Irving and Sir Walter Scott, he embarked on a career as a writer, churning out more than seventy novels "and a score of other works" during his lifetime. James favored historical themes. His three-volume study *Richelieu* (1829) was "popular and immediately successful"; his history *Edward, the Black Prince* (1836) led to his appointment as historiographer royal to King William IV. After a financial setback, James and his family moved to the United States, "where his books were well known and where he intended to make a comfortable living once again through lectures and writing."[48]

James arrived in the United States on July 4, 1850, at the height of a national uproar over the Fugitive Slave Law. He socialized with some of the most prominent figures in the abolitionist movement, dining on one occasion with Senator Charles Sumner at the home of the poet Henry Wadsworth Longfellow. Yet James deftly avoided taking a public stand on slavery. An English author with a loyal transatlantic following, James could ill afford to alienate his American sponsors. As the *National Era* noted upon his arrival in July 1850: "This author has many friends in America, and he is scarcely the man to forfeit this sort of half-personal regard, by supercilious and unjust criticisms on our manners and institutions, and a false estimate of our national character."[49]

A brief literary skirmish over an antislavery poem and anti-American sentiments attributed to James did nothing to slow sales of his books in the United States. In 1852, the English novelist William Makepeace Thackeray asked New York publisher James Harper to name the best-selling author in the United States. Harper pulled down a ledger, opened it to the letter "J," and declared: "George Payne Rainsford James heads the list, far ahead of any other author as you can judge for yourself by glancing at the number of his books sold. He turns out a novel every six months, and the success is always the same and tremendous." Thackeray — whose parody of James had appeared in the literary magazine *Punch* just a few years earlier — asked Harper to explain the "immense hold" that James seemed to have over the American reading public. "The main reason," Harper explained, "is that his romances can always be safely placed upon the family table, with the certainty that no page will sully, or call the blush to, the cheek of any member of the household."[50]

In 1852, exhausted from his "excessive literary labours," James accepted a British consular post in Norfolk, Virginia. Despite his best efforts to remain neutral on the "slavery question," James incurred the wrath of the slave traders who operated out of Norfolk. He described their assaults against him in a letter to his friend Charles Ollier:

> The slave dealers have got up a sort of outcry against me — I believe because, under Lord Clarendon's own orders, I have successfully prosecuted several cases of kidnapping negroes from the West Indies — and the consequence is that not a fortnight passes but an attempt is made to burn my house down. The respectable inhabitants of Norfolk are indignant at this treatment of a stranger, and the authorities have offered a reward for the apprehension of the offenders; but nothing has proved successful. This outcry is altogether unjust and unreasonable; for I have been perfectly silent on the question of slavery since I have been here, judging that I had no business to meddle with the institutions of a foreign country in any way. But I will not suffer any men, when I can prevent or punish it, to reduce to slavery British subjects without chastisement.

James, it seems, had no strong objection to the continued enslavement of non-British subjects. Only a keen sense of diplomatic propriety kept him from purchasing a slave during his stay in Norfolk. "It was not easy to manage without employing slave labour," his son Charles recalled in his own autobiography, "but my father did not consider that his official position . . . would allow of that. My mother, however, with her own money, hired a black cook who was a slave." The family grew attached to the enslaved woman — "Aunt Kitty in southern parlance." As the "poor old soul" lay in her deathbed with yellow fever, "nothing would keep up her courage but having 'Massa' talk to her" — "Massa" being none other than G.P.R. James.[51]

James found inspiration for *The Old Dominion* in his own experience as a British diplomat living in a slaveholding city not far from the scene of the Southampton uprising. The novel follows the adventures of Sir Richard Conway, a twenty-seven-year-old Englishman who travels to Virginia to clear title to lands bequeathed him by his late Aunt Bab. In a series of letters to his sister, written upon his arrival in Norfolk, Conway reveals his growing ambivalence on the slavery question. "I hear you exclaim, my dear Kate, 'You will of course emancipate the slaves!' And you will be horrified when I reply, 'I do not know.'" Conway has begun to question whether emancipation is in the best interest of the slaves; his "preconceived opinions" have been "very much shaken" by what he has seen during his brief stay in the United States. The Negro in the free states, he concludes, may be worse off than the Negro in the slaveholding states. "In the former, he is a decidedly sad, gloomy, ay, an ill treated man, subject to more of the painful restrictions of caste than I could have conceived possible. Here, he appears to be a cheerful, light-hearted, guileless, childlike creature, treated with perfect familiarity, and as far as I have seen, with kindness." Conway finds evidence of a general contentment among the slaves in the "violent peals of negro laughter" that fill the streets of Norfolk. "Yes, my dear sister!" he writes to his English relative. "Whatever you may think, these poor unhappy people, as we are taught to believe them, laugh all day long with such merry and joyous peals, that it is impossible to believe that the iron of which we are told, is pressing very deeply into their souls."[52]

Nat Turner makes his appearance before long. While walking through the Southampton County woods, Conway encounters a solitary "negro" fishing by the side of a stream. "When I came near, I perceived he was one of the finest-formed men I had ever beheld, tall and powerful, with very little of the usual deformity of his race. He had, indeed, the thick lips, the nose flattened, — though not very much, — and the wooly hair of his race; but there was no bowed shins or large hands and feet; yet, as far as I could judge from his color, he was of unmixed African blood." Conway asks the man if he has caught any fish; the elevated manner and tone of the reply catches him by surprise. "I shall catch when the appointed time comes. Nothing happens, master, but at its appointed time, whether it be great or small." Conway suspects that he is in the presence of an extraordinary black man, with "powers of mind" equal to those of any white man. "In fact, this man's words were the first attempt at anything like a grasp of a wide and comprehensive idea which I had ever met with in his race, and it excited my curiosity greatly." Conway attempts to learn more about this rare bird — who gives his name as Nathaniel Turner — but his prey is far too elusive. Only once, when Conway alludes to the emancipation of the slaves in the West Indies, does "a sort of eager light break forth from his eyes." Still, Turner betrays no insurrectionary intent of his own. "I have been a slave all my life, and I have had very good masters.

I doubt not it will all be brought right in the end; and perhaps we niggers are placed in the situation proper for us. At all events, it is God's will, and so we ought to be content." Turner emphasizes, somewhat ominously, that he will remain content *"so long as it is God's will I should be so."* Conway asks how, "in the complication of this world's affairs," one might distinguish between God's will and man's. "Whatever is, is God's will," Turner replies. "His will will always be revealed in good time." The novel builds toward the climactic uprising, with loyal slaves and their kind masters emerging as heroes, abolitionists and slave traders as villains, and a repentant Turner acknowledging his folly.[53]

Southern literary critics applauded the representation of history in *The Old Dominion*. The Virginia-based *Southern Literary Messenger* declared that the 1831 "Southampton Massacre," led by the messianic Turner, provided an ideal backdrop for adventure and romance. "The incident on which the story hinges is a painfully tragic one, and closely connected with the habits and nature of the negro slave; this supplies the novelist with material for a stirring narrative and nice delineation of character." Still, the work was not without its flaws and faux pas. James had "managed the delicate matter of slavery as a social institution with considerable skill," yet his depiction of the slaves was a bit ham-handed. "We think he has somewhat overdrawn the hero of the rebellion — Nat Turner — and has not entirely caught the modes of thought and manner of speaking of the black race." Moreover, "in dealing with the white race in Virginia, Mr. James has not done complete justice to our native population." Nevertheless, the editors found "a very many scenes in the book" to be "singularly truthful" and encouraged the English author to "push his labours in the rich field of Virginia history yet farther."[54]

By contrast, an anonymous critic ("P.") writing in the *Philadelphia Bulletin* lampooned the novel as a rehash of "the same familiar story" that James had been churning out for thirty years. The typical James novel opened with a solitary horseman.

> But this novel's novel features
> Are those of the sable creatures,
> Slaves of old Virginia masters,
> Who regard as worst disasters
> All the plans of abolition

> To change them or their condition.
> And he shows us, too, some others,
> Whom his countrymen call "brothers,"
> Who get up an insurrection,
> And, but for their prompt detection,
> Would have filled the State with slaughter,
> Making blood to flow like water.

Here the author alluded to the 1846 antislavery poem attributed to James and published in the *Dublin University Magazine:*

> Now, G.P.R. James, in former
> Times, was known to be much warmer
> In his love for sable creatures,
> For their mind and for their features;
> And long since he wrote a poem
> For his English friends, to show 'em
> How our Yankee starry banner
> Was a satire, in a manner,
> With a keen allusion knowing
> To the "stripes" upon it showing.
>
> But of late the Queen of Britain,
> As reward for what he'd written,
> Or to drive from her dominions
> All his tales and stale opinions,
> Made him Consul down at Norfolk,
> That he might not show before folk
> Any more of the old twaddle
> That's engendered in his noddle.
>
> Well, in Norfolk he's residing,
> Where he finds excuse for hiding
> Every abolition notion
> That he had across the ocean,
> And he flatters each Virginian
> Of the courtly old Dominion;
> For a suit of tar and feathers
> Isn't pleasant in all weathers.[55]

James, for his part, reveled in the critical response to his book. "It has found favour in the South and is powerfully abused in the North, both of which circumstances tend to increase the sale, so that it has been wonderfully well read."[56] When James died in 1860, the *Southern Literary Messenger* defended his literary corpus against the sneering of "so-called realistic" critics who found his historical costume dramas hopelessly out of fashion. James, ever the gentleman, had never lowered himself to respond. "He pursued his occupation, unchecked by ridicule, unterrified by criticism, sure of his purpose, confident of the purity of his motives; his only boast, (and who can deny its justice?) that no line of his would ever call a blush to the cheek of the most sensitive woman."[57]

Martin Delany's Blake

African-American folk traditions surrounding Nat Turner's Rebellion found literary expression in Martin R. Delany's *Blake; The Cabins of America*, seven installments of which appeared in the *Anglo-American Magazine* from January to July 1859. Delany was born in 1812 to a free black mother and a slave father in Charlestown, Virginia. Harassment by white neighbors forced Pati Delany and her children to migrate north when Martin was ten years old; soon afterward Samuel Delany bought his freedom and joined the rest of the family in Chambersburg, Pennsylvania.

In 1831, the year of the Southampton uprising, Martin traveled on foot to Pittsburgh, where he made his home for the next twenty-five years. There he attended a school run by a Methodist minister, the Reverend Lewis Woodson, a delegate to several early black national conventions. Delany supported himself as a barber. In 1839, he toured the Southwest, traveling through Texas, Mississippi, Louisiana, and Arkansas; his firsthand observations of slave life informed his later writings on the subject. Delany became active in the abolitionist movement in the 1840s. He edited the *Mystery*, one of the few black newspapers in the United States, for nearly four years; from late 1847 to the middle of 1849, he coedited the *North Star* with Frederick Douglass. His views in this period, according to Floyd J. Miller, "were not unlike those of many other black abolitionists." Delany decried "the stridency of Northern prejudice against free blacks," stressed "the necessity for black communities to develop their own sense of pride and community awareness," insisted on "moral rectitude" and "personal righteousness" among members of the race. Delany made a decisive break with the black abolitionist mainstream in 1852, when he published his manifesto, *The Condition, Elevation, Emigration, and Destiny of the Colored People of the United States, Politically Considered.* The book called for black emigration to Central America and the establishment of an independent "nation."[58]

Blake tells the story of Henry Blake, a fugitive slave who travels throughout the South organizing a general insurrection. During his travels, he meets survivors of earlier rebellions, who welcome him as the next Messiah. His bold plan of action stirs memories, particularly among the older slaves, of Nat Turner and other black rebels of history and folklore. In South Carolina, Henry makes a brief visit to the dwelling of "an old black family on the suburb, one of the remaining confidentials and adherents of the memorable South Carolina insurrection." As Henry confides the details of his "fearful scheme" to the couple, they begin to shed tears of joy. "Ah!" says the old man. "Dis many a day I been prayin' dat de Laud sen' a nudder Denmark 'mong us. De Laud now anseh my prar in dis young man!" Moving northward into the Dismal Swamp region of North Carolina and Virginia, Henry meets "a number of the old confederates of Nat Turner," who welcome "the daring young runaway as the harbinger of better days." Their leader is Ghamby Gholar, "a noted high conjurer and compeer of Nat Turner," who has secluded himself in the Swamp for more than thirty years. "I been lookin' fah yeh dis many years," he tells Henry, "an' been tellin' on 'em that you 'ood come long, but da 'ooden' heah dat. Now da see!" The living memory of slave conspiracies and black rebellion, preserved in religious prophecy and oral tradition, has prepared the slaves in these parts for the arrival of a black leader who will deliver them from bondage.[59]

Henry discovers that the Dismal Swamp, long a haven for rebels and runaways, is fertile ground for his insurrectionary plans. There "the names of Nat Turner, Denmark Veezie, and General Gabriel" are held "in sacred reverence" by "some of Virginia and North Carolina's boldest black rebels." Henry listens politely as his hosts, aging veterans of race wars, regale him with stories of past glories and "pretended deeds." One old man, "having the appearance of a centennarian," informs Henry that he fought with "Gennel Gabel" in the American Revolution. "Ah, chile, dat 'e did fit in de Molution wah, Gabel so, an' 'e fit like a mad dog! Wen 'e sturt, child da can't stop 'im; da may as well let 'im go long, da can't do nuffin' wid 'im." Henry flatters the ancient warrior, saying he and Gabriel were "the kind of fighting men they then needed among the blacks." Moving on to Richmond, the young firebrand rekindles the memory of Southampton among the city-dwelling slaves. "Southampton — the name of Southampton to them was like an electric shock."[60]

The novels of Stowe, James, and Delany represented three distinctive cultural perspectives on Nat Turner's Rebellion, drawing heavily on African-American and white Southern oral traditions. These widely circulated works of fiction introduced the historical subject of Nat Turner's Rebellion to readers with no direct access to such oral traditions, thus nationalizing and internationalizing his memory on the eve of the Civil War.

"The Black John Brown": Remembering Nat Turner After Harpers Ferry

John Brown's 1859 raid on Harpers Ferry whetted the public appetite for histories of American slave conspiracies and servile insurrections. Despite Brown's insistence that he had never intended "a general rising of the slaves," newspapers in at least five major cities — San Francisco, Louisville, Philadelphia, New York, and Boston — drew parallels between the Harpers Ferry raid and the Southampton insurrection of nearly three decades before.[61] Some writers sought to calm public fears of an impending slave revolt, stressing the relative infrequency of servile insurrections and the overwhelming obstacles that faced would-be conspirators; others warned that the slaveholders sat on a powder keg of slave discontent that could explode at any time.

Brown had been contemplating the liberation of slaves in Virginia for at least a dozen years before leading the raid on Harpers Ferry. As early as 1847, he confided his evolving plan of attack to Frederick Douglass, who later recorded the details of their conversation in his autobiography. The plan, as Brown explained it to Douglass, did not "contemplate a general rising among the slaves, and a general slaughter of the slavemasters: an insurrection, he thought, would only defeat the object." It did, however, "contemplate the creating of an armed force which should act in the very heart of the South." Brown elaborated, in his conversations with Douglass, on the theory of manhood that undergirded his plan of attack. He "was not averse to the shedding of blood, and thought the practice of carrying guns would be a good one for colored people to adopt, as it would give them a sense of their manhood. No people, he said, could have self-respect, or be respected, who would not fight for their freedom."[62]

As the sectional crisis intensified in the 1850s, Brown expressed an increasing willingness to use violence, if necessary, to fight the so-called Slave Power. When the Kansas-Nebraska Act of 1854 repealed the Missouri Compromise and put the issue of slavery to a popular vote in the newly organized territories, Brown and his sons joined antislavery forces in Kansas and participated in the "civil war" that followed. Proslavery and free-state forces set up rival governments, and bloody guerrilla warfare ensued. The "sack" of Lawrence, the free-state capital, by proslavery forces in 1856 led to violent reprisals by Brown and his followers, who were accused of murdering five proslavery settlers in cold blood. Brown's paramilitary experience in Kansas may have shaped his plans for a raid on Virginia. In 1858, he told an acquaintance that "the only way to abolish slavery was to post a company of men somewhere in the mountains of the slave States to assist the slaves in escaping, and thus make the system of slavery insecure." Brown decried the "do-nothing policy" of the Garrisonian nonresistants and the "no account" platform of the free-soil Republicans. "He said his doctrine was to free the slaves by the sword."[63]

Brown began revealing his great plan "little by little to his armed followers." By February 1858 he had secured the support of six prominent abolitionists — Thomas Wentworth Higginson, Dr. Samuel Gridley Howe, Theodore Parker, Franklin Sanborn, Gerrit Smith, and George Luther Stearns — who later became known as "The Secret Six."[64] In May 1858, Brown visited Chatham, Canada West, where he met with black abolitionists and unveiled his "Provisional Constitution" for the soon-to-be-occupied territories of the slave states. Six months later, in something of a dress rehearsal, Brown led a raid on several plantations in southern Missouri, "running off" a small number of slaves and leading them to safety in Canada. Brown began final preparations for his raid on Virginia in the spring and summer of 1859. In July, he rented a two-story farmhouse in southern Maryland, seven miles from the Virginia border; there, he gathered his recruits together and informed them of his final plan. They would attack Harpers Ferry, seize weapons from the federal arsenal, gather recruits from among "dissident whites" and "mutinous slaves," and then move on through the Southern states as a liberation army. "If I could conquer Virginia," Brown later explained, "the balance of the Southern states would nearly conquer themselves, there being such a large number of slaves in them."[65]

Several of Brown's supporters — including Frederick Douglass — considered an attack on Harpers Ferry suicidal. "To me," Douglass wrote in his autobiography, "such a measure would be fatal to running off slaves (as was the original plan), and fatal to all engaged in doing so. It would be an attack upon the federal government, and would array the whole country against us." Douglass urged Brown to return to his original plan, in which the raiders made strategic strikes from the mountains and drew off slaves "gradually and unaccountably." Brown listened respectfully to Douglass but refused to budge. "Come with me Douglass," he said. "I will defend you with my life. I want you for a special purpose. When I strike, the bees will begin to swarm, and I shall want you to help hive them." Douglass refused, but pledged his continued support.[66]

Twenty-one men — sixteen whites and five free blacks — volunteered for the raid on Harpers Ferry. Late in the evening of October 16, 1859, the main force descended upon the town and proceeded to capture the armory, the arsenal, and the rifle works. A small detachment scoured the countryside and returned with ten slaves and three slaveholders in their custody; Brown armed the slaves with pikes and ordered them to guard the slaveholders as hostages. The first casualty of the raid was a free black baggage master named Heyward Shepherd, shot by one of Brown's men when he refused a command to halt. Word of the "insurrection" spread quickly; armed civilians and militiamen converged on the scene and opened fire on Brown and his men, who barricaded themselves in the rifle works and fire-engine house of the armory. Despite the desperate pleas of his lieutenants, Brown refused to retreat, perhaps waiting for reinforcements that never came. Dangerfield Newby, a free black volunteer, was the first of Brown's men to die, shot in the throat by a sniper. Two others, including Brown's son Watson, were shot while carrying a flag of truce. Several more were killed as they tried to escape. By the following morning, only Brown and four surviving raiders remained in the engine house with the hostages. A company of U.S. marines, commanded by Brevet Colonel Robert E. Lee, surrounded the building. Lieutenant J.E.B.

Stuart approached the engine house under a flag of truce and handed Brown a note, demanding his unconditional surrender. When Brown refused, the marines stormed the building. Brown and two of his men were captured and taken into custody; two others were killed. Of the twenty-one men who volunteered for the Harpers Ferry raid, ten were killed or fatally wounded in the battle, five were captured, and six managed to escape.[67]

A hastily convened grand jury indicted Brown on charges of murder, treason, and conspiracy. Brown repeatedly — and emphatically — denied the charges. In an interview shortly after his capture, he was asked if he expected "a general rising of the slaves" in the event of his success. "No, sir," he replied, "nor did I wish it. I expected to gather them up, from time to time and set them free." When a bystander interjected that "to set them free would sacrifice the life of every man in this community," Brown responded haughtily, "I do not think so."[68]

At the trial, prosecutor Andrew Hunter argued that Brown had advised the slaves, by his actions if not his words, to rebel. "When you put pikes in the hands of slaves, and have their master captive, that is advice to the slaves to rebel, and is punishable by death."[69] The jury convicted Brown of all charges and sentenced him to death. Brown reiterated his innocence at his sentencing.

> I deny everything but what I have already admitted: of a design on my part to free the slaves. I intended certainly to have made a clean thing of that matter, as I did last winter, when I went into Missouri and there took slaves without the snapping of a gun on either side, moving them through the country, and finally leaving them in Canada. I designed to have done the same thing on a larger scale. That was all I intended. I never did intend to murder, or treason, or the destruction of property, or to excite or incite the slaves to rebellion, or to make insurrection.[70]

Brown later clarified this statement, saying he did not intend to run the slaves out of Virginia, as he had in Missouri, but rather to place them "in a condition to defend their liberties, if they would, without any bloodshed."[71]

White Southerners, by and large, found such denials disingenuous. To them, Brown "was a fanatic who sought not only to steal cherished property, but to establish anarchy, to reenact the Nat Turner horrors, to make the terrible scenes of the Haytian negro revolt insignificant beside the atrocities he would set on foot."[72] As they had in the aftermath of the Southampton insurrection, white Southerners reassured themselves with stories recounting the faithfulness of their slaves. "And this is the only consolation I have to offer you in this disgrace," Governor Henry A. Wise told the Virginia legislature in December 1859, "that the faithful slaves refused to take up arms against their masters; and those who were taken by force from their happy homes deserted their liberators as soon as they could dare to make the attempt. Not a slave around was found faithless."[73] Others concurred, declaring Brown's mission a failure.

John Brown made no mention of Nat Turner or the Southampton uprising in his public comments on the Harpers Ferry raid; if anything he sought to avoid any association with slave conspiracies, past or present. Nor did he mention Turner by name in his private correspondence. Yet close friends and associates confirmed, after his death, that Brown was well aware of the Southampton uprising and that he considered Nat Turner one of his heroes. In *The Public Life of Capt. John Brown,* published in 1860, James Redpath wrote that Brown "was a great admirer of Oliver Cromwell. Of colored heroes, Nat Turner and [Cinqué] stood first in his esteem."[74] In an 1881 speech at Harpers Ferry, Frederick Douglass recalled that Brown made reference to Turner in their first meeting: "He held that there was need of something startling; that slavery had come near to being abolished in Virginia by the Nat. Turner insurrection, and he thought his method would speedily put an end to it, both in Maryland and Virginia."[75] In a 1909 biography of Brown, based largely on secondary sources, W.E.B. Du Bois expanded the list of slave conspiracies and insurrections that may have inspired Brown in planning his raid on Harpers Ferry. "He learned of Isaac, Denmark Vesey, Nat Turner and the Cumberland region insurrections in South Carolina, Virginia and Tennessee; he knew of the organized resistance to slave-catchers in Pennsylvania, and the history of Hayti and Jamaica."[76]

If John Brown felt compelled to distinguish his deeds from those of Nat Turner in the aftermath of Harpers Ferry, Republican presidential candidate Abraham Lincoln felt compelled to distance himself from Brown and Turner alike. In February 1860, four months after the Harpers Ferry raid, Lincoln addressed himself to "the Southern people" in a campaign speech at the Cooper Institute in New York City.

"You charge that we stir up insurrections among your slaves. We deny it; and what is your proof? Harper's Ferry! John Brown!! John Brown was no Republican; and you have failed to implicate a single Republican in his Harper's Ferry enterprise." Lincoln appealed to history for vindication. "Slave insurrections are no more common now than they were before the Republican party was organized," he observed. "What induced the Southampton insurrection, twenty-eight years ago, in which, at least, three times as many lives were lost as at Harper's Ferry? You can scarcely stretch your very elastic fancy to the conclusion that Southampton was 'got up by Black Republicanism.'" Lincoln noted that the Republican Party had abjured "any interference whatever" with slavery in the slaveholding states of the South. Like Jefferson and the Founding Fathers, the Republicans believed that slavery was wrong, but, Lincoln insisted, "The slaves do not hear us declare even this. For anything we say or do, the slaves would scarcely know there is a Republican party." It was the slanders of Southern politicians, competing for advantage among themselves, he said, that had turned "Black Republicanism" into a rallying cry for "insurrection, blood and thunder among the slaves."[77]

Lincoln downplayed the threat of "a general, or even a very extensive slave insurrection" in the United States. First, he noted that the slaves had "no means of rapid communication" so necessary for concerted action. Second, he considered the efforts of "incendiary freemen, black or white" inadequate to the task. "The explosive materials are everywhere in parcels; but there neither are, nor can be supplied, the indispensable connecting trains." Third, he acknowledged the "affection of the slaves for their masters and mistresses" as a mitigating factor. "A plot for an uprising could scarcely be devised and communicated to twenty individuals before some one of them, to save the life of a favorite master or mistress, would divulge it." Lincoln noted that the betrayal of large slave conspiracies was the "rule," adding that "the slave revolution in Hayti was not an exception to it, but a case occurring under special circumstances." In short, the insurrection anxieties of the Southern people were unfounded. "Occasional poisonings from the kitchen, and open or stealthy assassinations in the field, and local revolts extending to a score or so, will continue to occur as the natural results of slavery; but no general insurrection of the slaves, as I think, can happen in this country for a long time. Whoever much fears, or much hopes for such an event, will likely be disappointed." In delivering this history lesson, Lincoln portrayed the imminent return of Nat Turner as an apparition, produced by the overheated imaginations of his Southern critics.[78]

The Harpers Ferry raid was not a slave insurrection, Lincoln argued, in that it failed to secure the support of the slaves. "It was an attempt by white men to get up a revolt among the slaves, in which the slaves refused to participate. In fact, it was so absurd that the slaves, with all their ignorance, saw plainly enough that it could not succeed." Lincoln described the raid as the "peculiar" effort of a brooding fanatic and a few deluded followers, neither the work of the Republican Party nor the fault of New England. He chastised Southern politicians for using the memory of Harpers Ferry to "break up" the Republican Party, saying that the demise of party politics would bring far more bloodshed than the failed raid. "There is a judgment and a feeling against slavery in this nation, which cast at least a million and a half of votes," he said. "You cannot destroy that judgment and feeling — that sentiment — by breaking up the political organization which rallies around it. You can scarcely scatter and disperse an army which has been formed into order in the face of your heaviest fire; but if you could, how much would you gain by forcing the sentiment which created it out of the peaceful channel of the ballot-box, into some other channel? What would that other channel probably be? Would the number of John Browns" — or Nat Turners, for that matter — "be lessened or enlarged by the operation?"[79]

Black abolitionists, by contrast, sought to heighten the anxieties of slaveholders by reminding them of previous slave uprisings and warning of more to come. Thomas Hamilton, the publisher and editor of the New York–based *Weekly Anglo-African,* used the occasion of the Harpers Ferry raid to remind his readers of the "most remarkable episode in the history of human slavery" — the Southampton insurrection. He reprinted "The Confessions of Nat Turner" in its entirety and editorialized on the enduring significance of the event. Hamilton found many similarities between Nat Turner and John Brown; both were idealists, both looked to the Bible for guidance, both sought the "pure and simple emancipation of their fellow men." Yet Hamilton drew a sharp contrast between Turner's revolutionary ideology of black nationalism and Brown's egalitarian vision of a Christian brotherhood. "Nat Turner's terrible logic could only see the enfranchisement of one race, encompassed by the extirpation of the other, and he followed his gory syllogism with rude exactitude," he wrote. "John Brown . . . is moved with compassion for tyrants as well as slaves, and seeks to extirpate this formidable cancer, without spilling one drop of christian blood." Hamilton concluded that "these two narratives" presented "a fearful choice" to Southern slaveholders and the nation as a whole. "Which of the two modes of emancipation shall take place? The method of Nat Turner or the method of John Brown?"[80]

Black abolitionist orators embellished the legend of Nat Turner in the immediate aftermath of the Harpers Ferry raid. In early November 1859, the Reverend J. Sella Martin delivered a lecture on "the Hero Mr. Turner" at the Shiloh Church in Boston. A reporter who covered the event estimated that "the audience of six to eight hundred, did not contain more than twenty or thirty white persons, the others being of all shades of color."

Martin offered a biographical sketch of Turner that differed, in several key respects, from "The Confessions of Nat Turner." First, he claimed that Turner did not believe he was "possessed of supernatural powers," but gave that impression so as "to hold the slaves to his purpose." Second, he claimed that Turner had heard about the "insurrectionary movement" of Denmark Vesey in Charleston, "and it is probable this acted as a powerful stimulus to Turner's latent plans." Third, and perhaps most interesting, he claimed that Turner "cultivated the friendship of the poor whites, who thought much of him." Martin related several anecdotes about how Turner, caught in the act of conspiracy, used his native intelligence and his good relations with white people to ward off suspicion. Whether these undocumented anecdotes reflected the active imagination of Martin or a rich folk tradition among African Americans is an open question. Martin "briefly traced the history" of the uprising, "which spread terror throughout the South." He ranked the efforts of its leader "among the bravest and best in history." As for John Brown, "the next insurrectionary hero," he was "about to offer up his life as Turner had done before him." Martin "hoped the next attempt, by whomsoever made, would be more successful."[81]

In March 1860 another black abolitionist, Dr. John S. Rock, used the ninetieth anniversary of the Boston Massacre as an occasion to pay tribute to both Nat Turner and John Brown and to question the adulation bestowed on Crispus Attucks and other "colored patriots" of the American Revolution. Rock argued that the concept of "American liberty," so closely associated with the Boston Massacre, was meaningless to a race of people who had never experienced it. "The only events in the history of this country which I think deserve to be commemorated," he said to applause from the gathering, "are the organization of the Anti-Slavery Society and the insurrections of Nat Turner and John Brown." Rock expressed his support for antislavery violence. "I believe in insurrections — and especially those of the pen and the sword." William Lloyd Garrison was "the perfect embodiment of the moral insurrection of thought," John Brown "the representative of that potent power, the sword." Rock said nothing more of Nat Turner, but left no doubt that he endorsed the methods employed by the insurrectionaries at Southampton and Harpers Ferry.[82]

Newspapers across the nation, responding to intense public interest in the subject, placed the Harpers Ferry raid within a historical tradition of slave conspiracies and servile insurrections — all of them, by their reckoning, doomed to failure. The *Louisville Journal* set the general tone with this editorial remark, introducing a brief item on Denmark Vesey and the Charleston plot of 1822: "The late Harper's Ferry affair has revived the recollection of previous plots to produce insurrection among the slaves in Southern states. These plots, however, have been easily crushed."[83] For those who hoped or feared that the slaves might one day rise and liberate themselves, the history of slave conspiracies — as reported in the newspapers of the day — suggested otherwise.

The "late movement at Harper's Ferry" inspired the *California Press* to publish an editorial called "Servile Insurrections" that recounted the horrors of Southampton and reaffirmed the "duties of American citizens in every quarter of the Republic" to defend "the lives and property of the citizens of the whole Republic." The editors stressed the relative infrequency of servile insurrections in the slaveholding states and the "utter impossibility" of a "successful insurrection on an extensive scale." Their brief history of servile insurrections omitted the well-known conspiracies led by Gabriel and Denmark Vesey but included the bloody uprising led by Nat Turner. "In 1831," they wrote, "an insurrection broke out in the county of Southampton, on the southern borders of Virginia, of which an account will be found in another portion of this paper. It occasioned greater loss of life among the whites, and greater consternation than any other insurrectionary movement among the negroes ever made in this country." Several pages later, the editors published a contemporary account of the Southampton insurrection that appeared in the

Norfolk Herald; the anonymous correspondent, quoting civil and military authorities, assured readers that the uprising had been quickly suppressed by state and federal troops dispatched to the scene.

The editors of the *Press* offered similar reassurances to their readers in the aftermath of Harpers Ferry. So long as federal and state forces worked in unison, so long as "the national sentiment of America" remained "impressed with the horrors of servile insurrection," so long as American citizens recognized their "duties" to one another, no serious threat of a major servile insurrection existed.[84]

Similarly, the *New York Journal of Commerce* devoted two columns to previous "Insurrections at the South," stressing the inevitable failure of such attempts. "From the nature of the case," the editors noted, "these outbreaks must ever be impotent to effect the object aimed at. The organizations of the land are too strong, and the resources of insurgents too feeble, ever to command success. Besides, conspirators have some conscience left, and cannot always be reliable. Their dreadful secret cannot be kept long." The *Journal* recalled the Charleston plot led by Denmark Vesey, "a free mulatto," in 1822. A conscience-stricken slave divulged the plot, and after a "long and full trial" some thirty or forty slaves were condemned to death. "We have never heard of any subsequent attempt in that quarter to repeat this style of self-emancipation," the editors observed.

The article went on to describe "a more successful attempt" at self-emancipation. In August 1831, Nat Turner, an "ignorant and fanatical" slave from Southampton County, Virginia, "succeeded in persuading a gang of his fellow slaves to rise upon their owners and perpetrate an indiscriminate massacre." The *Journal* quoted liberally from "The Confessions of Nat Turner"; its only original observations lay in comparisons between the 1831 slave insurrection and the recent Harpers Ferry raid. The Southampton insurrection was the much bloodier of the two, the newspaper noted. "Guns, axes, and swords were the weapons used in this murderous work, — compared with the destruction wrought by which, the scene at Harper's Ferry was one of mercy." The *Journal* blamed the misguided efforts of white abolitionists for checking the "benevolent efforts" of Southern emancipationists in the aftermath of the Southampton insurrection. The "fanaticism of Garrison and his crew" and the "violent doctrines of Seward and his compeers" served only to rivet the bonds of slavery more tightly and postpone "the day of relief."[85]

Readers occasionally responded to these historical accounts with

editorial comments of their own. A reference to "the Tennessee insurrection of 1857" as "probably of equal consequence with Nat. Turner's"
drew ridicule from a reader of the *Evening Post*. The Tennessee insurrection, he wrote, "was no insurrection at all — only a little rumpus
kicked up among some negro laborers in the iron mines." Some idle
talk among the slaves, related to the 1856 election campaign, had
aroused suspicions of an impending revolt; local whites, fearing the
worst, came down on the suspected conspirators with great ferocity,
whipping several to death and committing "many atrocities." The
same man who led the whites in crushing the insurrection later became convinced "that there had been no attempt at rebellion." Yet the
truth of the matter never came out because "the editors, and the colo-
nels, and planters, and magistrates, and great dignitaries of Tennessee
and Kentucky" refused to acknowledge their folly. "We know the truth
of this old cry of negro revolt," the letter writer declared. "There is no
danger of it. The slaves have no extended means of concert. They cannot read, and they are utterly without discipline. The negro is a coward
against the white man. He is a child — lacking every moral element of
what we call Saxon courage." So what of Nat Turner, then? What of
the fifty-five white men, women, and children killed by the black insurgents in the Southampton uprising? The writer was unimpressed:
"The 'Virginia Insurrection' is not respectable enough, even to be
made a political hinge of. Such an *emeute* in any northern state would
have been classed with engine fights, and Dead-rabbit skylarks."[86]

Inspired by the Harpers Ferry raid, abolitionist newspapers expressed interest in chronicling the history of American slave conspiracies and insurrections. The *National Anti-Slavery Standard* devoted
half a page to brief items on slave insurrections, culled from other
newspapers. "They are, of course, very incomplete, and probably in
many respects quite inaccurate," the editors noted. "The reader should
remember that the accounts of these insurrections which generally obtain currency are not those given by the slaves, but by the masters,
and therefore to be received with caution. Every circumstance of cruelty on the part of the slaves in such cases is painted in glowing colors,
while the atrocious provocations so long borne by them are entirely
ignored." The editors concluded with an appeal for more accurate
information.

We wish some person qualified for the work would write a history
of Slave Insurrections in the United States. Such a work, carefully

and conscientiously compiled from authentic sources, and imbued with the spirit of impartial liberty, would be exceedingly valuable. Let us hope that no one may undertake such a task who has not the patience to perform it well. A hotch-potch of crude and hastily gathered materials, made to cohere by the aid of scissors and paste, would not meet the public want.

The time had come, in short, for a well-documented, scholarly account of American slave insurrections.[87]

Joshua Coffin

The first historian to take up the call was Joshua Coffin, a sixty-eight-year-old retired schoolteacher from Newbury, Massachusetts. Coffin began researching the history of slave insurrections in 1833 after hearing a series of antislavery lectures by Amos A. Phelps, pastor of the Pine-Street Church in Boston. To demonstrate that slavery was neither "highly advantageous" nor "perfectly safe," Coffin listed a series of scares, plots, and insurrections, starting with reports of mischief and insolence among the "negroes" in South Carolina in 1711 and ending with a general insurrection of the slaves in Jamaica in 1832. He devoted just two lines to the Southampton uprising in Virginia: "In August, 1831, an insurrection took place among the slaves in Southampton Co, Va., headed by Nat Turner, a slave. Before they were quelled, they had murdered 64 persons, men, women, and children." Phelps thanked Coffin for the "collection of facts" and attached the entire letter as an appendix to his *Lectures on Slavery and Its Remedy*, published by the New England Antislavery Society in 1834.[88]

Renewed public interest in slave insurrections aroused by the Harpers Ferry raid prompted Coffin to update and revise his earlier work on the subject. In a letter to the *National Anti-Slavery Standard*, Coffin complained that a recent article on "The Virginia Plot" of 1800 gave "a very false account of General Gabriel and his intended insurrection." Coffin trumpeted his own forthcoming work as a more accurate source of information. "As I intend to publish, in a few days, in pamphlet form, a short account of some of the insurrections that have been attempted in this country from 1638 to the present time, I will only add that Gabriel was never a *free* negro. He was the *slave* of Thomas Prosser, of Richmond, Va." The editors of the *Anti-Slavery*

Standard praised Coffin for his scholarly work and affirmed his authority to speak on the subject. "Thanks to our old friend, long 'out of sight' but not 'out of mind,' for his note, which not only assures us of his unabated interest in everything relating to slavery, but conveys the gratifying information that he is about to give the world the benefit of at least some portion of his researches in a field with which he is doubtless more familiar than any living man." While the editors awaited "with interest the appearance of his pamphlet," they expressed the hope that Coffin could be "induced to prepare a thorough history of Slave Insurrections in this country from its earliest settlement to this day."[89]

The American Antislavery Society of New York published Coffin's updated pamphlet in 1860 under a long and portentous title: *An Account of Some of the Principal Slave Insurrections and Others, Which Have Occurred, Or Been Attempted, in the United States and Elsewhere, During the Last Two Centuries. With Various Remarks. Collected from Various Sources by Joshua Coffin.* In the introduction, Coffin referred to current events that had stimulated public interest in the subject. "The late invasion of Virginia by Capt. John Brown and his company has, with all its concomitant circumstances, excited more attention and aroused a more thorough spirit of inquiry on the subject of slavery, than was ever before known." To remain silent "on a question of so momentous importance" would be a crime, Coffin argued. "It demands and will have a thorough investigation, and all attempts to stifle discussion will only accelerate the cause they were designed to crush." The American Antislavery Society distributed copies of the pamphlet through its offices in New York, Boston, and Philadelphia.[90]

In preparing the pamphlet, Coffin drew heavily on his 1833 letter to Phelps, repeating the theological arguments verbatim. Yet he expanded the chronological scope of his study to include several incidents from the seventeenth century and several more recent events, including the *Amistad* mutiny of 1839, the *Creole* mutiny of 1841, and the Santa Cruz rebellion of 1846. He also added more detail about the leaders of the uprisings. In 1833, Coffin did not mention the name of Gabriel in connection with the "insurrection" that took place in Richmond; in 1860, he devoted several pages to the conspiracy and its leader, quoting several primary and secondary sources. In 1833, Coffin did not mention the name of Denmark Vesey in connection with "an alleged conspiracy" that took place in Charleston, South Carolina; in 1860, he named Vesey as one of six ringleaders. In

1833, Coffin devoted just two lines to Nat Turner and the South-ampton uprising; in 1860, he quoted "The Confessions," the *Richmond Whig*, and two Virginia legislators who came out against slavery in the aftermath of the insurrection. The personalization of these slave conspiracies and revolt marked a significant shift toward "great man" histories, perhaps linked to the public commemoration of heroes and martyrs.[91]

Thomas Wentworth Higginson

Thomas Wentworth Higginson, one of the "Secret Six" who con-spired with John Brown on the Harpers Ferry raid, wrote the first ex-tended history of Nat Turner based on extensive research in primary sources.[92] Higginson was seven years old at the time of the South-ampton uprising, thirty-seven when his article "Nat Turner's Insurrec-tion" appeared in the *Atlantic Monthly*. His family background was somewhat less genteel than his Brahmin name and Harvard pedigree might suggest. His father, once a wealthy Boston shipping merchant with a fashionable home on Beacon Hill, had been "ruined financially" during the war of 1812; the family was rescued from more humbling circumstances when Harvard College appointed Stephen Higginson as its steward in 1818 and provided his family with a large house on college-owned land. Young "Wentworth," as he was known, grew up in this privileged atmosphere, attending private schools with chil-dren of the "best" families. At the age of thirteen he was admitted to Harvard, where he studied French literature and language under Henry Wadsworth Longfellow, rhetoric and oratory under Edward Tyrell Channing. To save money — his father died when he was ten — Higginson lived at home with his mother; he later moved out so that his mother could take in students as paying boarders. After gradua-tion, he worked as a teacher and a private tutor, then returned to Har-vard as a nonmatriculated scholar. He enrolled in Harvard Divinity School and, after some hesitation, resolved on a career as a Unitarian minister. Under the influence of Theodore Parker and James Freeman Clarke, he found himself "gravitating toward what was then called the 'liberal' ministry." For more than a decade, he would use his "secular-ized" pulpit as a public platform from which to promote various social reforms.[93]

Higginson was attracted, at first, to the Garrisonian brand of abolitionism, with its emphasis on moral suasion and its repudiation of violence. The Compromise of 1850, with its provisions for the return of fugitive slaves, pushed Higginson away from Garrisonian nonresistance and into the political wing of the antislavery movement. As a Free Soil Party candidate for Congress, Higginson called for the halting of the expansion of slavery, abolishing slavery in the District of Columbia, repealing the Compromise Bill, and repealing the three-fifths clause of the Constitution. His suggestion that the men of Massachusetts obey "a higher law" than the Fugitive Slave Law led a Democratic newspaper to charge that Higginson "openly advocates the nullification of the laws of the land, when they do not correspond with his individual opinions." Soundly defeated at the polls, Higginson continued to push for social reforms through political action, banking on the "secret souls" of men who publicly supported the Fugitive Slave Law and other repulsive measures.

Higginson began to flirt with more militant strands of abolitionism, edging toward support for mob action, guerrilla warfare, and slave insurrections. He publicly endorsed the daring rescue of a fugitive slave named Shadrach, facing trial in a Massachusetts courthouse, by a group of "colored" men from Boston. Higginson and several other abolitionists plotted the rescue of another fugitive slave, Thomas Sims, but failed to follow through on their plans. The arrest of a fugitive slave named Anthony Burns in Boston persuaded Higginson that the time had come for more direct action. He led an armed assault on the federal courthouse that resulted in the killing of a guard and the beating of several would-be rescuers but failed to secure the freedom of Burns. Higginson was arrested for inciting a riot, but a grand jury refused to indict him.

When passage of the Kansas-Nebraska Act turned the extension of slavery into a battle over "popular sovereignty," Higginson joined with other New England abolitionists in recruiting men and raising money for armed expeditions to Kansas. During an expedition to Kansas on behalf of the Massachusetts Aid Committee, he met John Brown and discovered the ennobling influence of war. The "virtue of courage," he discovered, "had not died out in the Anglo-American race." In an 1858 essay for the *Atlantic Monthly*, Higginson distinguished between three types of "physical courage" — the courage of "heroic races," such as the Highlanders and the Afghans, the courage of "habit," developed by experience and training, and the courage "created by desperate emergencies." African Americans exemplified the third kind of courage. "Suppled by long slavery, softened by mixture of blood, the black man seems to pass at one bound, as women do, from cowering pusillanimity to the topmost height of daring. The giddy laugh vanishes, the idle chatter is hushed, and the buffoon becomes a hero."

Higginson revealed a burgeoning interest in slave rebellions that dovetailed with his romantic racialism and antislavery principles. "Nothing in history surpasses the bravery of the Maroons of Surinam, as described by Stedman, or those of Jamaica, as delineated by Dallas," he declared. The courage of whites paled — literally — in comparison. "What are we pale faces, that we should claim a rival capacity with theirs for heroic deeds? What matter, if none, below the throne of God, can now identify that nameless negro in the Tennessee iron-works, who, during the last insurrection, said 'he knew all about the plot but would die before he would tell? *He received seven hundred and fifty lashes and died.*' Yet where, amid the mausoleums of the world, is there carved an epitaph like that?" Higginson made it his task to write just such an epitaph.[94]

Higginson sought to link the "insurrection" at Harpers Ferry to a historical tradition of black rebellion. On October 27, 1859, Higginson wrote to James Russell Lowell, editor of the *Atlantic Monthly*, and proposed a pair of sketches on the Maroons of Surinam and Jamaica — a topic "suggested by the late Virginia Affair." Higginson envisioned his articles as part of a larger series on black rebellion to be bound and sold as a single volume. "These are to be two chapters in a History of Slave Insurrections, or Series of Sketches rather, which I am at work on, for Thayer & Eldridge to publish next autumn," he told his mother. "It is a good subject & can be made useful & somewhat lucrative."[95] The first article in the series, "The Maroons of Jamaica," appeared in February 1860; it described the guerrilla warfare of "black mountaineers" who rebelled against English rule in the seventeenth century. Higginson noted that the history of the Jamaican Maroons, once the subject of parliamentary debates in Great Britain, had "vanished from popular memory" since the abolition of slavery in British America. "Their record still retains its interest, however, as that of one of the heroic races of the world; and all the more because it is with their kindred that this nation has to deal in solving the tremendous problem of incorporating their liberties with our own.

We must remember the story of the Maroons, because we cannot afford to ignore a single historic fact which bears upon a question so momentous."⁹⁶ The second article, "The Maroons of Surinam," appeared in May 1860. Once again, Higginson stressed the "martial virtues" of the "rebel negroes." They fought valiantly against the mighty forces of the United Provinces. Not one "ever turned traitor or informer, ever flinched in battle or under torture, ever violated a treaty or even a private promise."⁹⁷

The outbreak of the Civil War in April 1861 inspired Higginson to reflect on the likelihood of a slave insurrection and the threat that a Denmark Vesey or a Nat Turner posed to the Confederacy and the doctrine of white supremacy. Southern slaveholders exhibited a "mad inconsistency," Higginson argued, in portraying slaves as contented Uncle Toms in one breath and fanatical, hate-filled Nat Turners in another. "A slave population is either contented and safe, or discontented and unsafe," he wrote; "it cannot at the same time be friendly and hostile, blissful and desperate." Higginson suggested that a slave insurrection, like war itself, might prove a blessing in disguise by elevating the character of blacks in the eyes of whites. "No doubt insurrection is a terrible thing," he wrote, "but so is all war, and every man of humanity approaches either with a shudder. But if the truth were told, it would be that the Anglo-Saxon habitually despises the negro because he is not an insurgent, for the Anglo-Saxon would certainly be one in his place. Our race does not take naturally to non-resistance, and has far more sympathy with Nat Turner than with Uncle Tom." Higginson clearly recognized the symbolic value of slave rebellions in the African-American struggle for racial equality.⁹⁸

"Denmark Vesey," the third in Higginson's series of *Atlantic Monthly* sketches on slave insurrections, appeared in June 1861; public response to the essay, which was reprinted in its entirety by the *New York Tribune*, convinced Higginson that a similar treatment of Nat Turner might "be a marketable article after all." Higginson told his editor that the Turner piece would be far superior to the Vesey piece, outlining his reasons: "(1) Nat Turner's name is much more famous & has always inspired much curiosity (2) this is the first authentic narrative ever written & has cost great labor (3) this was a tragedy fulfilled & not merely organized & (4) it occurred in the very region fr. which slaves are now flocking in to Fort Monroe." Higginson reminded his editor that such topical material could only boost the circulation of the magazine. "For myself I think the only way to keep up the strength of the *Atlantic* during these absorbing excitements is to make the excitement itself feed it, by having articles of current interest." In pitching the article this way, Higginson revealed an acute awareness of the market for popular histories, built around compelling figures and events from the American past.[99]

"Nat Turner's Insurrection" appeared in the August 1861 issue of the *Atlantic Monthly*. Once again, John Brown played the moderate, merciful foil to the revolutionary, cold-blooded Turner. "John Brown invaded Virginia with nineteen men, and with the avowed resolution to take no life but in self-defence. Nat Turner attacked Virginia from within, with six men, and with the determination to spare no life until his power was established. John Brown intended to pass rapidly through Virginia, and then retreat to the mountains. Nat Turner intended to 'conquer Southampton County as the white men did in the Revolution, and then retreat, if necessary, to the Dismal Swamp.'" Higginson highlighted the courage of the slaves; in the crucible of war, Uncle Tom became Nat Turner. "Those dusky slaves, so obsequious to their master the day before, so prompt to sing and dance before his Northern visitors, were all swift to transform themselves into fiends of retribution now; show them sword or musket, and they grasped it, as though it were an heirloom of Washington himself." Higginson did not describe the killings — "we must pass over the details of the horror" — yet he did note that the black rebels were more humane than whites or Indians in battle. "There was no gratuitous outrage beyond the death-blow itself, no insult, no mutilation."[100]

Higginson found great significance in the fact, reported by "the Virginia newspapers," that Nat Turner had a wife who belonged to a different master. From this biographical detail Higginson extrapolated a more general picture of slave life and its discontents. "For this is equivalent to saying, that, by day or by night, her husband had no more power to protect her than the man who lies bound to a plundered vessel's deck has power to protect his wife on board the private schooner disappearing in the horizon. She may be well treated, she may be outraged; it is in the powerlessness that the agony lies." Despite such grievances, Higginson wrote, Nat Turner and his men did not exact their revenge by taking liberties with white women.

> These negroes had been systematically brutalized from childhood;
> they had been allowed no legalized or permanent marriage; they

had beheld around them an habitual licentiousness, such as can easily exist under slavery; some of them had seen their wives and sisters habitually polluted by the husbands and brothers of these fair women who were now absolutely in their power. Yet I have looked through the Virginia newspapers of that time in vain for one charge of an indecent outrage on a woman against these triumphant and terrible slaves.

Turner and his men, in short, fought bravely and honorably in the heat of battle, proving themselves — and their race — worthy of admiration.[101]

Higginson placed the "memory" of Nat Turner's insurrection within a stream of historical consciousness — presumably shared by slaves and slaveholders alike — that stretched back to 1800. "The insurrection revived in one agonizing reminiscence all the distresses of Gabriel's Revolt, thirty years before; and its memory endures still fresh now that thirty added years have brought the more formidable presence of General Butler." Here, Higginson alluded to Benjamin Butler, the Union general who declared fugitive slaves "contrabands of war" and refused to return them to their owners. Higginson suggested that the slaves of Southside, Virginia, who were fleeing to Union lines at the first opportunity were the spiritual — if not the lineal — descendants of Nat Turner and his followers. "It is by no means impossible," he wrote, "that the very children or even confederates of Nat Turner may be included at this moment among the contraband articles at Fort Monroe." Higginson concluded his commemoration of Turner with a rhetorical flourish. While the much-celebrated Polish revolutionaries of 1831 were long forgotten, "this poor negro — who did not even possess a name, beyond one abrupt monosyllable, — for even the name of Turner was the master's property, — still lives a memory of terror and a symbol of retribution triumphant."[102]

"Gabriel's Defeat," the last article in Higginson's *Atlantic* series, appeared in September 1862. Higginson reflected on cycles of history that raised one figure — a Gabriel, a Denmark Vesey, a Nat Turner — to prominence while recalling the deeds of those who came before. "John Brown revived the story of Nat Turner, as in his day Nat Turner recalled the vaster schemes of Gabriel." Higginson declared the rapidly "vanishing" records of these remarkable events "worth preserving" for future generations. "I have never been able to see why American historians should be driven to foreign lands for subjects," he mused, "when our own nation has furnished tyrannies more terrible than that of Philip of Spain, and heroes more silent than William of Orange." Perhaps, he astutely observed, it was because "those most qualified to record the romance of slave-institutions have been thus far too busy in dealing with the reality."[103]

The Rebellious Slave and the Dime Novel

Two of the most widely circulated accounts of Nat Turner's Rebellion written during the Civil War era came from the pens of Orville J. Victor and Metta V. Victor, a literary couple associated with New York City publishing houses that specialized in the production of so-called dime novels and popular works of history and biography. Metta Victor wrote *Maum Guinea and Her Plantation Children* (1861), a historical romance that included a sixteen-page account of the Southampton uprising as recalled by the widow of one of its leaders, Nelson; Orville Victor edited *Maum Guinea* and penned his own *History of American Conspiracies* (1863), a collection of nonfiction essays that included a chapter called "Nat Turner's Slave Insurrection." Through their collaboration on *Maum Guinea*, the Victors reached more than one hundred thousand readers, including (it is said) President Lincoln, prominent abolitionists in the United States and England, and countless Civil War soldiers.[104]

Metta Victor (*nee* Fuller) was born near Erie, Pennsylvania, in 1831, the same year as the Southampton uprising. Her family moved to Wooster, Ohio, where she entered a female seminary and developed into something of a prodigy. At the age of fifteen she had already had her sentimental poems and stories published in Boston and New York. By 1851 she had moved to Michigan with her sister; five years later she was married to Orville Victor, the editor of the Sandusky, Ohio, *Daily Register* and the associate editor of the *Cosmopolitan Art Journal*, published in New York City. A native of Sandusky, Orville Victor had attended the public schools there, graduated from the Seminary and Theological Institute of Norwalk, Ohio, and read law for a time before embarking on a career in journalism and publishing.[105]

In 1858, the Victors moved from Ohio to New York City, where they became associated with the publishing house of Beadle and Adams, the progenitor of the "dime novel" genre. Charles S. Harvey, who recalled the phenomenon for *Atlantic Monthly* readers some fifty years later, claimed that "many Americans who were old enough to read at the time" remembered the year 1860 better for the publication of Beadle's first dime novel than for the election of Lincoln or the secession of South Carolina.

What boy of the sixties can ever forget Beadle's novels! To the average youngster of that time the advent of each of those books seemed to be an event of world consequence. The day which gave him his first glimpse of each of them set itself apart from the roll of common days. How the boys swarmed into and through stores and news-stands to buy copies as they came hot from the press! And the fortunate ones who got there before the supply gave out — how triumphantly they carried them off to the rendezvous, where eager groups awaited their arrival. These little books ranged from 25,000 to 30,000 words, or about a third of the average bound novel of today. Conveniently shaped for the pocket, they promptly became an inseparable part of the outfit of the boy (and to some extent of the girl also) of the period. Their paper covers were salmon-colored. And they were just as free from yellowness on the inside as they were on the outside.[106]

Of the eight stories that Metta Victor eventually wrote for Beadle's dime novel series, none sold more copies than *Maum Guinea and Her Plantation Children*. It was published in December 1861 as a double number, priced at twenty cents. "Its sales exceeded 100,000 copies, and it was translated into several languages," Harvey wrote. "The New York *Tribune*, the New York *Evening Post*, and other prominent papers in that day of large deeds, when newspaper space was valuable, gave some space to Mrs. Victor's story."[107]

Readers of *Maum Guinea* first encountered a reference to "Nat Turner's insurrection" in the preface to the book, where the author insisted that her fictionalized account of the historical event had been "drawn from the most reliable authorities." Victor did not reveal the names of her authorities, but a reference within her novel to Nat Turner's wife being made to "give up her husband's papers" suggests that she relied on Thomas Wentworth Higginson's recently published essay in the *Atlantic Monthly* for at least some of her factual details.

The story of "Nat Turner's insurrection" is presented within the novel as the truthful — and excruciatingly painful — recollection of a slave named Sophy who shares her life story during a holiday evening gathering of the slaves on the Louisiana plantation. Sophy was born on a "tobacky farm" in Southampton County, Virginia, where she worked as "a kitchen-girl" for her master and mistress. At the age of fifteen she married a slave named Nelson, who was good to her; they had a cabin of their own and "lived together berry comfortable." Yet Sophy described a series of incidents that drove Nelson to rebel. First, the overseer — a "mighty cross man" who was "allers knocking niggers about" — gave Nelson "an awful whipping," then poured salt-brine on his wounds. Nelson was filled with rage, but Sophy persuaded him not to do anything to "aggrawate" the overseer. Sophy and Nelson had a two-year-old son named Sam, who helped Nelson forget his troubles with the overseer. Then, one day while Nelson was working in the fields, "Massa" took little Sam away and sold him for five hundred dollars. Nelson changed after that. "He was so silent and stubborn, I was almost 'fraid of him," Sophy recalled. Nelson and Sophy had a second child named Dan'l; when he reached the age of six, "Massa" sold him too. Nelson began going out late at night; sometimes he did not return home until the next morning. When Sophy asked him where he had been, he made up stories about hunting coons or fishing.

Here Sophy's story intersected with the more famous account of slave conspiracy and rebellion recorded by Thomas R. Gray in "The Confessions of Nat Turner." One Sunday afternoon Nelson attended a barbecue in the woods with some of the hands from a neighboring plantation; when he returned early the following morning he told Sophy to get dressed "and be ready, 'for mighty things are to be done in de land.'" Nelson was joined by six men, armed with "guns and big knives." When Sophy began to cry and pray, she was hushed by the leader of the band, Nat Turner, a slave from a neighboring plantation who "all de brack folks t'ought was a prophet." As Turner described his spiritual visions and outlined the earthly mission that lay ahead, his words varied considerably from those attributed to him by Gray. A clear motive of vengeance, conspicuously absent from the "Confessions," characterized this fictionalized slave memoir. "Cheer up, woman," Turner told Sophy. "Your chil'ren shall no longer be sold from your bosom, nor your husband lashed at the whipping post. I am come to repay." Sophy pleaded with Nelson to spare the life of Katie, the ten-year-old daughter of their mistress and master. But Turner decreed that every white man, woman, and child in Southampton County had to die.

Sophy recalled her moral confusion as she viewed the corpses of white people, young and old, innocent and guilty, killed by Turner and his men. A desire for revenge against "cruel" masters and overseers competed with feelings of compassion and pity for their "innocent" wives and children. Sophy reminded herself — and her audience — of the wrongs suffered by the slaves.

> I t'ought over how I felt when I found my husband, almost killed with whipping, and de salt brine on his bleeding back — w'en I heard de stage-coach rumble away over de hill wid my little Sam — w'en Dan'l was tood away — w'en I was flogged myself — I t'ought of all our wrongs and hardships, and I couldn't blame my husband — I knew he b'lieved he was doin' de Lord's work — but I wish dey had spared dear Katie.

Sophy interrupted her story and turned to the slaves gathered around her. "Do you t'ink it was right, my friends?" she asked. The question elicited conflicting replies from a young couple, Hyperion and Rose, whose desire to marry had been thwarted by a selfish master, not unlike Sophy's master in Southampton. "Yes," said Hyperion. "No," said Rose. "Well, de most of e'em t'ought it was right, w'edder it were, or not," Sophy replied. "Liberty is sweet, even to poor brack slave — and in Virginny dar's plenty of white blood mixed wid ours, you all know."

Sophy went on to recount the "awful days" that followed the Southampton slave uprising — the fear and uncertainty of the slave women as they waited for word of victory or defeat, the scattering of the rebel forces, the indiscriminate arrest and killing of black men suspected of involvement, and, most horrifying, the "burning" of Nelson by an angry mob. Sophy became "kind o' crazy-like for a w'ile," then something lifted her out of her misery. Suspecting that Nat Turner was hiding nearby, she found him close to starvation and smuggled him food for two or three weeks. Eventually Turner was flushed from his hiding place, captured, tried, convicted, and hanged. "He died like a man,"

Sophy recalled. "Oh he was a prophet, sure 'nuff, Nat Turner was; but he couldn' overcome dis yere wicked worl' — de time wasn't ripe." Sophy concluded her story by explaining how she came to tell the tale during holiday week on the Louisiana plantation. Unable to hire herself out in Southampton County, Sophy ran away and hid in the Great Dismal Swamp until she was captured and sold at an auction. She eventually found herself on the Fairfax plantation in Louisiana, where she brooded over her lost children and dreamed of the day when she would reunite with her husband in heaven.

In the preface to the novel, Metta Victor denied any attempt "to subserve any special social or political purpose"; hers was simply a "pleasing" tale of slave life in the plantation South. "The several slave-stories given are veritable historical transcripts," she wrote. "That of Nat Turner's insurrection is drawn from the most reliable authorities. The various descriptions of barbecues, negro-weddings, night dances, hungs, alligator adventures, slave sales, are simply reproductions of what is familiar to every Southerner." Victor left it to others to draw out the political implications of the book. "If the moralist or the economist should find in it anything to challenge his or her attention, it will be for the reason that the book is a picture of slave-life as it is in its natural as well as in some of its exceptional phases." In abjuring any overt "social or political purpose," Victor veiled her own antislavery sentiments and projected the authority of a historian rather than a propagandist.[108]

The similarities in style and content between *Maum Guinea* and the more famous *Uncle Tom's Cabin* were not lost on readers, reviewers, or historians. Abraham Lincoln was said to have found *Maum Guinea* "as absorbing as *Uncle Tom's Cabin*."[109] William Everett, writing in the *North American Review*, described *Maum Guinea* as "one of the thousands of stories of Negro life which owe their style, character, and very existence to *Uncle Tom's Cabin*."[110] More recently, historian George Frederickson found affinities between these two "romantic racialist novels" in their characterization of "docile blacks and restive browns." In *Maum Guinea*, Frederickson noted, "all the characters with real sufferings and sensibilities are described as light-skinned mulattoes, while the pure-blooded Negroes are simple souls who can endure anything with a smile."[111] Indeed, the novel suggests that Nat Turner himself was a mulatto when Sophy describes Turner's wife as "a purty cre'tur, young and bright, wid good white blood in her too."[112]

If the story of Nat Turner's insurrection was — as Victor's characters in *Maum Guinea* suggested — a "secret" held closely by slaves in the plantation South, Victor helped to circulate it widely among white readers, Northern and Southern. The literary historian Edmund Pearson notes that the Civil War opened huge new markets for the publishers of dime novels.

> Their books went to the soldiers by the million. I think that a generous number of these were given by the publishers, but there were also enormous sales. The little books were sent to the camps in bales, like firewood. They were shipped on freight cars, wagons, and canal boats. When bundles of them arrived in camp, the sutler had to distribute them quickly, or else they would be torn from them. Among the commodities which the Union and Confederate pickets exchanged between the lines the Beadle novels were in great demand. Pathetic stories are told of blood-stained copies of dime novels found on dead men on the battlefield and of great numbers of soldiers who were buried with the novels in their pockets.[113]

Historians can only speculate on the impact of *Maum Guinea* on American audiences in the Civil War era. Did white Northerners who read the novel feel more sympathy toward the slave population of the South? Were white Southerners as infuriated by *Maum Guinea*, with its sentimental characterization of slave life and its moralistic tone, as they were by its famous predecessor, *Uncle Tom's Cabin*? Harvey claimed that the London edition of *Maum Guinea*, which "circulated by the tens of thousands in England, had a powerful influence in aid of the Union cause at a time when a large part of the people of that country favored the recognition of the independence of the Southern Confederacy."[114] More recently, Michael K. Simmons argued that *Maum Guinea* constituted "a significant social statement" by its publishers "and quite likely was utilized as a propagandistic tool to further the abolitionist cause."[115]

Orville Victor raised the public profile of Nat Turner once again in 1863 with the publication of his *History of American Conspiracies: A Record of Treason, Insurrection, Rebellion, &c. in the United States of America, from 1760 to 1860*. The six-hundred-page book did not fit within the "dime book" genre favored by the Beadle publishing

house; James D. Torrey of New York published it instead. Victor devoted two of the twenty chapters to slave conspiracies, one led by
Denmark Vesey, the other by Nat Turner. He acknowledged the im-
port of Gabriel's Rebellion but said the record was too "meagre and
indefinite" for a full narrative treatment. Victor placed "these exciting
episodes of Southern history" alongside other conspiratorial moments
in American history, such as "Pontiac's (Indian) Conspiracy," "Benedict Arnold's Conspiracy," "Shay's Rebellion," "Aaron Burr's Conspiracy," "New England Discontents and the Hartford Convention Conspiracy," "Georgia Indian Difficulties," "South Carolina Nullification
Insurrection," "Kansas Nebraska Troubles," and "John Brown's Conspiracy."[116] A lithograph of "Nat Turner & His Confederates in Conference" accompanied Victor's essay, introducing a visual icon to the
growing store of cultural artifacts associated with the uprising. The
lithograph, signed by F.O.C. Darley and J. Rogers, portrayed Nat
Turner and his followers in a sympathetic light, their strength, courage, and determination etched in both posture and countenance.[117]

Victor cited Thomas Wentworth Higginson's 1861 articles in the
Atlantic Monthly as his primary source of information on the Vesey
and Turner conspiracies. "It has been the policy of the slave-holding
States," he wrote, "not only to suppress, with a relentless hand, every
appearance of disaffection among their slaves, but also to keep from
the light all testimony regarding the occasional slave uprisings which
have not failed to occur." Of the eight to ten extended conspiracies
among "the negro bondsmen of the South," he noted, "only the faint-
est records are in existence, as if the slave masters themselves feared to
read the story." Fortunately Higginson — a "painstaking inquirer" —
had managed to "regather, from public and private sources, incidents
and circumstances enough to render the record historically accurate."[118]

Victor established his antislavery sympathies in the preface to *History of American Conspiracies*. "The Negro Insurrections of Denmark
Vesey and Nat Turner are painful chapters to peruse," he wrote, "yet
they possess a profound interest for all who care to understand the
workings of the American slave system. In spite of studious suppression of testimony by the authorities and the press, enough has tran-
spired to show that the institution of involuntary servitude has rested
upon the bosom of a volcano." Though Victor drew heavily on the historical "data" presented by Higginson, he offered a decidedly less san-

guine interpretation of slave insurrection and its impact on the black freedom struggle. "The insurrection of Turner only served to fasten the chains more firmly upon the negro race; it deprived him of the confidence of the whites; it restricted his little liberties and privileges; it made the master more willing to treat his slave merely as property, and to sell him as he would have sold an animal: it was a disaster to the black, from which flowed only misery to himself and his children." Such comments did not necessarily distance Victor from the mainstream of antislavery thought in the North; many writers and orators condemned slave rebellions even as they sympathized with the plight of the slaves.[119]

William Wells Brown

African-American writers contributed their own accounts of Nat Turner's Rebellion to the growing literature on slave rebellion. William Wells Brown, an ex-slave who had long espoused "the slave's right to obtain his freedom, if necessary, by revolution," included a lengthy discourse on Nat Turner in *The Black Man: His Antecedents, His Genius, and His Achievements* (1863). Brown made no attempt to soften the image of Turner; his account of the insurrection included the slaying of women and children. Brown wanted to show how the harsh conditions of slavery had created Nat Turner, inducing racial hatred and fanaticism in a man denied his full manhood. He also sought to fuel the insurrection anxieties of slaveholders.[120]

Though Brown relied heavily on "The Confessions" for biographical details, he also reproduced several anecdotes of unknown origin from Turner's childhood. Brown used these anecdotes to show how slavery had turned the "kind and docile feeling" of a slave child "into the most intense hatred of the white race." In the first incident, two district patrollers severely flogged young Nat for being absent from his master's plantation without a pass. Young Nat, in turn, plotted his revenge. With the help of two boys from a neighboring plantation, he strung a clothesline across a dark road and gave his enemies a "high fall" from their horses. "The patrolers were left on the field of battle, crying, swearing, and calling for help." In the second incident, a gang of white boys pelted young Nat with snowballs. "The slave boy knew the lads, and determined upon revenge. Waiting till night, he filled his pockets with rocks, and went into the street. Very soon the same gang of boys were at his heels, and pelting him. Concealing his face so as not to be known, Nat discharged his rocks in every direction, until his enemies had all taken to their heels." These and other incidents left Nat "gloomy and melancholy"; he retreated into his own world, avoiding intercourse with other slaves and brooding over visions of "white spirits and black spirits engaged in battle."[121]

Brown made no attempt to present Turner as a colored American patriot in the tradition of George Washington. His Turner was a thoroughgoing black nationalist who envisioned "the overthrow of the whites, and the establishing of the blacks in their stead." Brown echoed the threat that had been voiced by abolitionists, black and white, ever since Turner's Rebellion: "In every Southern household there may be a Nat Turner, in whose soul God has lighted a torch of liberty that cannot be extinguished by the hand of man." Southern slaveholders could no longer look to the North for help in putting down a slave uprising; public opinion in the nonslaveholding states, which condemned the insurrection in 1831, now applauded this action. "This is a new era," Brown concluded, "and we are in the midst of the most important crisis that our country has ever witnessed. And in this crisis the negro is an important item. Every eye is now turned towards the south, looking for another Nat Turner."[122]

The Emancipation Proclamation and the Black Soldier

The politics of "insurrection anxiety" intensified with Lincoln's preliminary Emancipation Proclamation, which ordered the emancipation of all slaves in those states or parts of states still in rebellion against the United States as of January 1, 1863. For Lincoln and some of his harshest critics, Nat Turner's insurrection provided a common reference point, a worst-case scenario in which newly emancipated black men — drunk with freedom and hungry for vengeance — rose against their former masters and slaughtered innocent white women and children.

That Lincoln knew about the Southampton insurrection is documented in his campaign speech of 1860; that he had Nat Turner in mind as he drafted the preliminary proclamation in 1862 is documented by his biographers: "George Bancroft, the historian, at the White House found the President 'turning in his thoughts the question of a slave insurrection.' What should be his course if suddenly there came news of scores or hundreds of Southern masters, their women and children, slaughtered in their beds and their houses burned, in the style of the Nat Turner rebellion?"[123] Lincoln clearly agonized over the prospect of inciting rebellion. In a draft of the proclamation, he wrote: "I hereby enjoin upon the people so declared to be free to abstain from all violence, unless in necessary self-defence; and I recommend to them that, in all cases when allowed, they labor faithfully for reasonable wages."[124]

While Northern critics questioned the constitutionality and practicality of the proclamation, Southern critics raised the specter of insurrection. It was cowardly, the *Richmond Enquirer* declared, for Lincoln to incite a servile war as a surrogate for military battle; it was fiendish for him to use "the negro" as his agent. "A servile war is necessarily one of extermination, and the peculiar character of the negro adds to its horrors. Released from authority, he is at once a savage; and the very ignorance which drives him to his own destruction, stimulates him to the dark excesses."[125] The editors illustrated their point with a lesson from history. "How was it in Southampton in 1831," they asked, "when Nat. Turner engaged in the work to which Lincoln now invites? Not satisfied with murdering the few men who fell into their power, they massacred even the babe in the cradle." Turner and his followers displayed an indiscriminate brutality that placed them beyond the pale of civilization. First, they "exterminated the family of Mr. Travis, Turner's kind and indulgent master. Next Mrs. Waller and her ten children were slain and piled up in a heap on the floor. Near by, a school of little girls was captured, and all massacred except one, who escaped. The family of Mrs. Vaughan was next destroyed. In this manner, between Sunday night and Monday noon, they had murdered fifty-five persons, nearly all of whom were women and children." Surely no civilized person could approve of a presidential proclamation that, in effect, encouraged slaves to rise and slay innocent women and children.[126]

Should the slaves emancipated by Lincoln foolishly decide to take their freedom by force, the editors warned, they would surely suffer the same fate as Nat Turner and his followers.

How was it in the long hatched Southampton case, to which we have already referred? Sunday night the insurrectionists began their work. Monday at noon they were in full flight, and hiding in the swamps. It needs scarcely to be asked how they fared. They suffered terrible retribution. They were hunted like wild beasts, as they were, and were at first killed wherever they were found. Several of these murderers of women and children were taken to Cross Keys, and their heads cut off on the spot; afterwards captives were tried and hung — among them Nat Turner.

Lincoln, they concluded, "would simply drive . . . slaves to their own destruction. Cheerful and happy now, he plots their death."[127]

The prediction that the Emancipation Proclamation would unleash servile insurrections reminiscent of Turner's Rebellion caught the attention of the Northern press. "The news of President Lincoln's emancipation proclamation," the *New York Herald* reported, "has fallen like a firebrande into rebeldom." As evidence, the editors pointed to the *Richmond Enquirer*'s "rabid, frothy editorial" on the subject. "It says that document, 'ordaining servile insurrection, has not been for a moment misunderstood North or South.' It styles President Lincoln 'a savage, and the very ignorance which drives him to his own destruction stimulates him to the darkest excesses.' It then compares the scenes to be enacted under the proclamation with the Nat Turner massacre in 1831. The Enquirer says: 'It is one of the means which the most callous highwayman should shudder to employ.'" The editors of the *Herald* offered no further comment on the editorial, letting the item speak for itself.[128]

When Lincoln issued the Emancipation Proclamation on January 1, 1863, the editors of the *Herald* made their own position plain. They saw nothing good coming of the proclamation, whether the slaves rose "after the fashion of Nat. Turner" or not. They pointed out that the proclamation did not apply to slaves in areas under federal control and did nothing to free those in areas under rebel control. Even as a war measure, the proclamation was "unnecessary, unwise and ill-timed." By needlessly heightening insurrection anxieties — as indicated by the editorial in the *Richmond Enquirer* — the proclamation united "the whites of the South" as never before in opposition to the Union. The slaves, for their part, were subjected to "a more rigid surveillance and discipline" by local authorities, thus neutralizing any military advantage their emancipation might bring the federal armies. "No signs of disaffection among them will be permitted beyond the lines of our armies; or should they, hap-hazard, break out into revolts and massacres, after the fashion of Nat. Turner, in his Southampton slaughter, the desired pleas will be furnished for armed European intervention to put an end to what then may be properly called this inhuman war." The editors highlighted the insurrection anxieties of the president himself. "President Lincoln evidently has some misgivings upon this point, or he would not enjoin the slaves concerned to 'abstain from all violence unless in necessary self-defence.' He seems to realize the danger that in sowing the wind he may reap the whirl wind." The editors called on Lincoln to abandon the "abolitionist programme" and respect the "predominant public opinion in the North." The war must be fought, they argued, "not for negro emancipation, but for the restoration of the Union and the constitution in their integrity."[129]

For black abolitionists, the Emancipation Proclamation officially transformed the war from a struggle to preserve the Union to a struggle for freedom in which black soldiers played a significant part. Frederick Douglass, a longtime advocate of wartime emancipation and the enlistment of black soldiers in the Union army, invoked the names of Nat Turner and other "glorious martyrs in the cause of the slave" to help recruit black volunteers for the first colored regiment from the North. "Liberty won by white men would lose half its luster," he wrote. Here was a "golden opportunity" to demonstrate the willingness of black men to fight and die for their own freedom. "Let us win for ourselves the gratitude of our country, and the best blessings of our posterity through all time."[130]

From the outset of the war in April 1861, Douglass had urged Lincoln to enlist "slaves and free colored people" in the prosecution of the war. In a May 1861 editorial titled "How to End the War," Douglass wrote: "Let the slaves and free colored people be called into service, and formed into a liberating army, to march South and raise the banner of Emancipation among the slaves."[131] That same month, Douglass urged black men to "drink as deeply into the martial spirit of the times as possible; organize themselves into societies and companies, purchase arms for themselves, and learn how to use them." The day would soon come, he predicted, "when a few black regiments will be absolutely necessary."[132] In a September 1861 editorial titled "Fighting Rebels with Only One Hand," Douglass addressed the "blind, unreasoning prejudice" that motivated federal policy. "Why does the Government reject the Negro? Is he not a man? Can he not wield a sword, fire a gun, march and countermarch, and obey orders like any other? Is there the least reason to believe that a regiment of well-drilled Negroes would deport themselves less soldier-like on the battlefield than the raw troops gathered up generally from the town and cities of the State of New York?"[133]

In making his case for the enlistment of black troops, Douglass recalled the deeds of Nat Turner and several other "Negro heroes" who had fought for freedom against the most formidable odds. He told the story of William Tillman, a "colored" steward who worked on a schooner that had been recently seized by pirates on its way from New York to Montevideo. The pirates released the captain and mate but took Tillman and several others hostage; from their conversations Tillman learned "that the vessel was to be taken to Charleston, and that he himself was to be sold as a slave." Vowing not to be taken alive, Tillman plotted with a fellow prisoner to recapture the vessel. When the pirates fell asleep, Tillman "began his fearful work — killing the pirate captain, mate and second mate, and thus making himself master of the ship with no other weapon than a common hatchet." The liberated captives managed to pilot the ship back to New York, where the *New York Tribune* declared Tillman a hero and the nation "indebted to him for the first vindication of its honor on the sea." Douglass linked the heroic deeds of Tillman — "an obscure Negro" — to those of his more famous black forebears. "Love of liberty inspired him and supported him, as it had inspired Denmark Vesey, Nathaniel Turner, Toussaint L'Ouverture, Shields Green, Copeland, and other Negro heroes." In telling this story, Douglass offered a powerful rebuke to those who "peremptorily and insultingly declined . . . the assistance of colored citizens in suppressing the slaveholders' rebellion."[134]

President Lincoln explicitly authorized the raising of black troops in his Emancipation Proclamation of January 1863. After declaring slaves in designated areas of the rebellious states to be free, Lincoln wrote: "And I further declare and make known that such persons of suitable condition will be received into the armed service of the United States to garrison forts, positions, stations, and other places, and to man vessels in all sorts of said service."[135] Congress quickly affirmed the president's authority "to enroll, arm, equip and receive into the land and naval service of the United States such number of volunteers as he may deem useful to suppress the current rebellion." Just three weeks after the Emancipation Proclamation was issued, the War Department authorized Massachusetts governor John A. Andrew to enlist volunteers, including "persons of African descent, organized into separate corps." Andrew immediately announced the formation of the Fifty-fourth Massachusetts Regiment, open to volunteers from any state; Douglass and other black leaders enthusiastically agreed to serve as recruiting agents.

Douglass deployed the memory of Nat Turner and other "glorious martyrs" in a March 1863 editorial urging black men to volunteer for a "colored regiment" forming in Massachusetts. Writing in his Rochester newspaper, Douglass stressed the "ties of blood and identity" that linked "men of color" in New York and Massachusetts with those in Louisiana and South Carolina. His choice of abolitionist icons reflected the sacrifices that "brave black men" — North and South, free and enslaved — had made for each other in the past. "Remember Denmark Vesey of Charleston; remember Nathaniel Turner of Southampton, remember Shield Green and Copeland, who followed noble John Brown, and fell as glorious martyrs for the cause of the slave." Douglass did not elaborate on the specific deeds of these martyrs; that they had fought and died to free the slaves was enough.[136]

Douglass appealed to the race loyalty of black men with little or no love for the Union. Free black men owed it to themselves, he argued, to fight for the freedom of the slaves. "There are weak and cowardly men in all nations," he wrote. "We have them amongst us. They tell you this is the 'white man's war'; that you will be no 'better off after than before the war'; that the getting of you into the army is to 'sacrifice you on the first opportunity.' Believe them not; cowards themselves, they do not wish to have their cowardice shamed by your brave example." Douglass promised that black soldiers would receive "the same wages, the same rations, the same equipments, the same protection, the same treatment, and the same bounty, secured to the white soldiers." More important, they could earn a place for themselves in the pantheon of heroes that included Turner, Vesey, and the brave black men who died at Harpers Ferry. [137]

The impending collapse of the Confederacy inspired Harriet Beecher Stowe to reflect on the "prophetic visions of Nat Turner" and the terrible punishment exacted on the nation for the sin of slavery. In the January 1865 issue of the *Atlantic Monthly*, Stowe contemplated the great wartime sacrifices and sufferings of her fellow citizens from the warmth and tranquility of her New England home. Was there no consolation, she asked, for the fathers, mothers, wives, and sisters of the Union dead? Could they not find solace in the salvation of their country, the liberation of their fellow man?[138] Stowe counseled her bereaved countrymen to take pride in knowing that their loved ones had died for the noblest of causes. God had subjected the slaveholding republic to a "purifying chastening," Stowe wrote, "that shall make us clean from dross and bring us forth to a higher national life."[139]

Stowe surveyed the desolated landscape of the South and concluded that God had reserved his harshest rebuke for Virginia, "the land where the family of the slave was first annihilated, and the negro, with all the loves and hopes of a man, was proclaimed a beast to be bred and sold in market with the horses and the swine." There, Stowe solemnly observed, "the prophetic visions of Nat Turner, who saw the leaves drop blood and the land darkened, have been fulfilled. The work of justice which he predicted is being executed to the uttermost."[140] With a literary flourish, Stowe transformed the bloody race war prophesied by Turner into a divinely sanctioned civil war that would purge the nation of slavery's sin and hasten the dawn of a new millennium in America. She reassures her readers, North and South, that "when this strange work of judgment and justice is consummated, when our country through a thousand battles and ten thousands of precious deaths, shall have come forth from this long agony, redeemed and regenerated, then God Himself shall return and dwell with us, and the Lord God shall wipe away all tears from all faces, and the rebuke of His people shall He utterly take away."[141]

4

SIGNPOSTS

I N 1860, there were four million slaves in the United States. By December 1865, there were none. The abolition of slavery, secured by federal armies on the Civil War battlefield and formalized in the Thirteenth Amendment, made both slavery and slave rebellions relics of the past. Yet the rebellious slave, as a symbol of black aspirations to freedom and equality, remained a formidable presence on the social and cultural landscape of the nation long after slavery's destruction. Emancipation without deportation — Jefferson's worst nightmare — precipitated a prolonged, frequently violent struggle over the limits of black freedom in American society. As African Americans exercised the rights formally extended to them under Reconstruction, their fellow citizens devised new mechanisms of control to maintain white mastery over black bodies and white sovereignty over public affairs. The continued subjugation of African Americans, codified in discriminatory laws and practices sanctioned by the highest court in the land, kept the threat of "Negro risings" alive long after the death of slavery.

The changing image of Nat Turner mirrored the shifting ideologies of black and white Americans as they grappled with the social revolution wrought by emancipation. Conservative black leaders of the post-Reconstruction era, who assigned themselves the task of "uplifting the race," emphasized the education and high moral character of "Old Prophet Nat" rather than the violent acts of murder and mayhem that characterized the rebellion itself. They depicted the rebel leader as an American patriot and a Christian martyr. More radical black leaders, rising to the fore at the turn of the century, adopted Turner as a symbol of "New Negro" assertiveness in the face of white racism and mob violence. White Southerners, with a few noteworthy exceptions, adopted the hostile view of the old master class toward the rebellious slave. Dismissing Turner and his followers as bloodthirsty fanatics, they made heroes instead of the "faithful slaves" who had stood by their mistresses and masters in the midst of servile insurrection and the Civil War.

These competing images of the rebellious slave rarely came into open conflict in the political and cultural apartheid of the Jim Crow South. The overthrow of Reconstruction, the resubjugation of blacks, and the restoration of native white rule legitimized the "Lost Cause" mythology of the Old South as a virtual paradise for slaves and masters. Abolitionist tributes to Nat Turner, John Brown, and other antislavery heroes and martyrs were all but banned south of the Mason-Dixon Line. African Americans retreated into a "public sphere" of their own making — the black church, the black press, the black fraternal order, and the black academic society — where they could express themselves freely on issues of concern and invoke the past in the service of the present. The segregation of public life by law and custom perpetuated the segregation of historical consciousness and permeated popular culture.

The first stirrings of an open assault on white Southern depictions of the slave as docile, childlike, and submissive accompanied the rise of the more assertive "New Negro" and black radical leadership in the early twentieth century. By the mid-1930s, a small cadre of revisionist scholars, writers, artists, and activists was mass-producing counterimages of Nat Turner as black American patriot and working-class hero. Their work anticipated the emergence of a mass movement against Jim Crow after World War II and the "Negro Revolt" of the 1960s.[1]

The Rebellious Slave Under Reconstruction

The military defeat of the Confederate army, sealed by General Robert E. Lee's surrender at Appomattox Courthouse, brought the thorny questions of Reconstruction to the fore. Under what conditions would the Southern states be readmitted to the Union? Should former rebel leaders be allowed to hold public office? And what of the freed slaves, tens of thousands of whom absconded to Union lines and labored or fought for the Union army? Would they be granted "forty acres and a mule" and full civil and political rights under the patronage of the Republican Party? Or would they be left to fend for themselves as landless, laboring masses?

In January 1865, Secretary of War Edwin M. Stanton and General William T. Sherman met with African-American church leaders in Savannah, Georgia, to discuss strategies to ease the transition from slavery to freedom. The ex-slaves made clear that they saw landownership as crucial to their survival in the postwar South. Four days later, Sherman issued an order to set aside lands in coastal South Carolina and Georgia, extending thirty miles inland, for exclusive settlement by black refugees. Under this directive, each family would get forty acres and the use of an army mule as a head start toward financial freedom.

In March 1865, as military victories by Union forces extended the reach of the Emancipation Proclamation deep into the Confederacy, the Republican-controlled Congress established the Bureau of Refugees, Freedmen, and Abandoned Lands, better known as the Freedmen's Bureau, to govern the transition to free labor in the South. Congress empowered the bureau to assign abandoned or confiscated lands to the black freedmen and white refugees who had remained loyal to the Union. Though bureau agents leased some forty-acre parcels to African Americans in Louisiana, South Carolina, Georgia, and Florida, the effort was halfhearted and short-lived. Few Republicans, radical or moderate, supported the confiscation of lands owned by disloyal planters for redistribution among the freedmen. The *New York Times,* which spoke for moderate Republicans in the North, wrote: "An attempt to justify the confiscation of Southern land under the pretense of doing justice to the freedmen strikes at the root of all property rights in both sections. It concerns Massachusetts quite as much as Mississippi." Others worried that giving the ex-slaves land or reparations of any kind would "ruin the freedmen" by leading them to believe they could acquire land "without working for it." In September 1865, President Andrew Johnson rescinded the policy of land confiscation and redistribution and ordered that lands abandoned by Confederate planters during the war be restored to their former owners.[2]

African Americans held fast to the promise of "forty acres and a mule," hoping against hope that they might receive compensation for their enforced servitude. The vast majority believed that the federal government planned to divide the great plantations among them in January, and they did not want to commit themselves to work for another if they might soon labor for themselves instead. Their reluctance and outright refusal to sign labor contracts with their former masters represented a formidable challenge to the authority of the white planters and generated rumors of impending insurrection throughout the South.

In October 1865, a special correspondent for the *Nation* examined the growing tension between ex-slaves and ex-masters over issues of land and labor. The writer had visited the "negro-quarters" on a large plantation near the village of Marion, South Carolina, and found the freedmen there — like others throughout the district — reluctant to sign contracts to grow cotton on shares. The correspondent asked the owner of a nearby cotton plantation about rumors, prevalent among whites, of a pending "negro insurrection."

> "It is a general fear," said Mr. B. "The negroes have made up their mind that land is to be given them at New Year's, and of course it will be a great disappointment to them when they find that that time has gone by and nothing has been done for them. Our negroes here are more intelligent than those thirty miles below us, and we have more white men among them, but I think there will be a rising on the coast. Of course it couldn't extend far, but some families will be murdered and some property destroyed, and a deplorable example will be set to both white and black. It will begin the work of extirmination."[3]

Such rumors circulated widely throughout the South. Some whites feared that the former slaves planned to "murder the white race [and] the old slave holders to get their land and houses." Others worried that freedmen would rise, en masse, sometime around Christmas Day 1865, once they realized that they would not be getting the "forty acres and a mule" they had been promised. "We are living in such times," declared a white woman from Orangeburg, South Carolina, "worst than all I dread a general uprising of the blacks in January when they find no land is for them."[4]

White vigilantes, citing the threat of an impending rebellion, waged preemptive nighttime raids on black settlements throughout the South, disarming, looting, and generally terrorizing the inhabitants. Some Freedmen's Bureau agents and Union army officers, finding no evidence of a conspiracy, suspected that the Christmas Day scare was nothing more than "a pretext so that the whites may disarm the colored population and thus control and manage them without danger of resistance." The much-anticipated Negro uprising, like so many insurrection scares of the post-emancipation era, never materialized. The great mass of ex-slaves, threatened with arrest for "vagrancy" and lease as convict laborers if they refused, signed their contracts and returned to work in the fields, much as they had before emancipation.[5]

The assassination of President Lincoln just five days after the war's end left the task of rebuilding the nation in the hands of his successor, Andrew Johnson, a staunch Unionist Democrat from Tennessee. With the Republican-controlled Congress in recess, Johnson announced his Reconstruction policy for the seven Southern states without restored Unionist governments: Alabama, Florida, Georgia, Mississippi, North Carolina, South Carolina, and Texas. Under Johnson's plan, those ex-Confederates who signed a loyalty oath or received a presidential pardon would be allowed to vote and hold office. African Americans, declared ineligible for U.S. citizenship in the Supreme Court's 1857 *Dred Scott* decision, would remain a disfranchised peasantry, laboring under conditions that differed little from slavery.

Outraged by the restoration of ex-Confederates to political power and the passage of "black codes" that returned the freed men and women to virtual slavery, congressional Republicans seized control of the Reconstruction process from President Johnson and wrote black freedom into law. In 1866, they passed, over Johnson's veto, an act extending full civil rights to African Americans. They also passed the Fourteenth Amendment, which conferred citizenship on all persons born or naturalized in the United States, punished those states that denied black men the right to vote, and disqualified from state and national office all ex-Confederates who had held office before the war. To ensure ratification of the amendment, Congress passed the Reconstruction Act of 1867, which placed the South under military rule until new state governments — committed to the protection of black voting rights — could be formed. Black men would be allowed to par-

ticipate in the election of delegates to state constitutional conventions; white men who were disqualified from office-holding under the
Fourteenth Amendment would be banned from participation in the
state constitutional conventions as well. Once a state adopted a new
constitution that guaranteed black suffrage and ratified the Fourteenth Amendment, it could apply for readmission to the Union.

The extension of civil and political rights to African Americans
under the protective arm of the federal government and the patronage
of the Republican Party emboldened black Baptist church leaders in
Virginia to pay tribute to Nat Turner as a hero of emancipation — a
radical challenge to the dominant white image of Turner as a fanatical
mass murderer. Their brief remarks, as reported in the press, set off a
rare public debate over the place of the rebel leader — whether Nat
Turner or Jefferson Davis — in the pantheon of American heroes.

Nearly one hundred delegates to the Third Annual Meeting of the
Colored Shiloh Regular Baptist Association in August 1867 listened
as letters from the forty-five member churches were read aloud.
"When the Association came to vote on the letter from the Cold
Spring church, Southampton County, Elder Williams requested the
delegates to arise, stating that 'this church was located where Nat
Turner first struck for freedom.' After reading the letters, the Modera-
tor requested the delegates to come to the stand, when he extended
to them the right-hand of fellowship, the ceremony being very impressive." The impromptu tribute to Turner spoke volumes about the
revolutionary changes in social relations and political power that had
taken place under congressional Reconstruction.[6] The black church,
an "invisible institution" under slavery, had emerged as a center of
political activity for newly liberated African Americans. The black
church leaders in Virginia expressed no lingering hostility toward the
people who had enslaved them; for them, emancipation marked a glorious new day for race and nation. Determined to assimilate into
mainstream society, they resolved to strike the name "African" from
their churches: "We are not Africans, but Americans." Delegates to
the Colored Baptist convention made no secret of their Republican
Party sympathies. They resolved that "thanks be tendered to the Forti-
eth Congress of the United States for enfranchising us as citizens and
giving us protection in the exercise of all our rights and privileges and
we earnestly advise all our brethren and friends to vote for righteous
men to be put into authority."[7]

The Colored Baptist tribute to Turner might have passed without comment if not for the intense political struggles then raging for control of the newly ascendant Republican Party in Virginia. On August 1, 1867, just one week before the Colored Baptist Association meeting, several hundred delegates to the Virginia Republican Party convention crowded into the African Church of Richmond to debate whether to accept native white Virginians — ex-Confederates willing to endorse the national party platform — into the fold. Radicals argued that cooperation with former Confederates might dilute the party's agenda and drive the freedmen from the party; moderates, who urged cooperation, were shouted down.[8]

The editors of the *Richmond Dispatch* heard echoes of the radical Republican platform in the Colored Baptist Association tribute to Nat Turner.

> We regretted to see that, in the Association of the Shiloh district of colored Baptists, held in Manchester a few days since, the horrid massacre set on foot by Nat. Turner in Southampton in 1830 was alluded to with the appearance of much *eclat* and parade. The delegates from that county . . . were marched forward, and there was much shaking of hands and general felicitation upon the occasion. Now this was all very bad and very much out of place.

The editors offered their own version of Turner's Rebellion, stressing the savagery of the attack and the killing blow it dealt to the antislavery cause.

> Nat. Turner's massacre was the most barbarous and brutal of all the human butcheries of the century. Studying the moon more than he did the Bible and the fantastical shapes in the clouds more than the principles and sentiments of justice and humanity, the poor monomaniac Turner set on foot the bloody and savage massacre, in which men, and women, and innocent girls, and even helpless babes, were slaughtered by insensate followers. It was a horror of horrors, a brutal and phrensied shedding of human blood, such as has never been exceeded in its unprovoked and brutal character.

The insurrection did not advance the antislavery cause, the editors argued, but in fact "reversed the tide of sentiment" in the Virginia legislature and swept away all hopes of gradual emancipation. "'First blow for freedom,' indeed! It was the deadliest blow to kind feeling for the blacks and to the growing sentiment in favor of abolition which could have been inflicted."[9]

The *Dispatch* proceeded to accuse the church elder who feted the Southampton delegation of fomenting antiwhite sentiment among blacks.

> The Rev. Mr. Williams would better subserve the cause of Chris-
> tianity — would much better advance the interests of the colored
> people and inculcate the kind and conciliatory feeling which is
> indispensable to peaceful and prosperous relations between the
> blacks and the whites — if he would refrain from reviving such
> bloody and revolting recollections. But to revive them and endorse
> them is an act of hostility. It can receive no other interpretation.

The editors alluded to other orators — presumably outside agita-
tors — who had been dredging up the past in order to discourage the reconciliation of former slaves and former masters.

> The bad teachers of the blacks of Virginia, who find it to their in-
> terest to separate them from the great body of the people for party
> purposes, are weaving in with their orations such reminiscences as
> may accomplish their objects; all of which tend to foment bad feel-
> ing and suggest distrust in the minds of the freedmen amongst
> whom they live, and upon whom they must depend for employ-
> ment — the people with whose welfare theirs is clearly identified.

Though dismayed by the incident at the Colored Baptist meeting, the editors of the *Dispatch* predicted that such troubles would soon "pass away." Black Virginians would awaken to their own best interests and "curse the day when they listened to the cunning and heartless stories of the hypocrites now misleading them."[10]

The editorial condemnation of the Colored Baptist tribute to Nat Turner provoked a satirical response from a correspondent for the *New Nation*, a Richmond weekly that espoused the radical Republican platform of "Union, freedom, and equal rights." Drawing a series of parallels between Turner and Confederate president Jefferson Davis, "Equal Justice" asked the editors of the *Dispatch* to explain why they disapproved of memorializing one rebel leader and not the other.

Turner "sacrificed the lives of a few of his enemies and friends" in his failed attempt "to overthrow a government which denied him and his race a reckoning among 'sentient' beings, but classed them with things to be bought and sold at pleasure." Davis "sacrificed the lives of hundreds of thousands" in his failed attempt "to overthrow a government which protected him in the assumed right to own Nat and his wife and his children." The letter writer accused the *Dispatch* of employing a double standard — one for black rebels, who fought for freedom, and one for white rebels, who fought for the right to own slaves. "Now, I say go ahead, both parties, and keep up the storm, or *let both parties stop,* and let the name of every rebel, (impenitent and persistent,) be forever denied all honorable remembrance."[11]

The alliance of newly enfranchised blacks, white Northerners ("carpetbaggers"), and native white Southerners ("scalawags") gave the Republican Party control of state governments across the South. Yet opposition to the Republicans and the tax-funded measures they favored, such as public education, remained strong. The election of blacks to state legislatures throughout the South — though hardly proportional to the number of blacks in the total population — raised charges that radical Republicans had placed the South under "Negro rule." Black politicians were routinely portrayed as ignorant and corrupt. Violence against Republican Party organizers, black and white, mounted. Chapters of the Ku Klux Klan, a secret fraternal order, spread throughout the South; its hooded campaign of racially and politically motivated terror prompted Congress to pass a series of Enforcement Acts giving the federal government broad new powers to intervene in state and local affairs.

In Nat Turner's Southampton County, where a former slave defeated a white planter in the campaign for delegate to the 1867 constitutional convention, embittered white moderates warned that "negro government" under radical Republican rule would produce nothing but "bloodshed, crime, vice, and ignorance." The following year, a Freedmen's Bureau agent reported the appearance of a Ku Klux Klan chapter in Southampton County, established by whites to "intimidate the freedmen and keep them from the polls, thus defeating the new Constitution." The agent heard rumors that local whites were arming themselves in anticipation of a "Nigger insurrection," a prospect "about as probable as water running up the side of a mountain." In April 1869, a Virginia newspaper reported on "a serious riot" between "the white people and the negroes" of Southampton County. "Armed bodies of negroes paraded the streets and a good deal of firing was done. A party of fifteen whites, at last got together and dispersed the negroes under the threat of firing on them. No one was killed, and two negroes wounded."[12]

As an undeclared war raged on in Southampton County and other localities throughout the South, editorial spats over the memory of Turner's Rebellion flared up periodically in the Virginia press. In 1869, an editorial writer for the *Cincinnati Commercial* struck a nerve by suggesting that fate had robbed Nat Turner of the glory he deserved. "If the rebellion had been successful, *as it deserved,* failing by no fault of his, to free his oppressed race, his monument today would not be unfinished as Washington's." When a Richmond newspaper reprinted the item from the Cincinnati newspaper without comment, the editors of the *Petersburg Index* excoriated the editors of both. "Is the *Commercial* destitute of shame that it gives utterance to such sentiments? And what should be said of a Virginia journal which publishes such matters without a word of condemnation?" Summoning their own personal recollections of the 1831 "massacre," the editors expressed amazement that anyone could find anything heroic in the deeds of Nat Turner and his followers. "Times have wonderfully changed since its occurrence and man must have changed with them, when the schemes of an incarnate fiend, which could only have been accomplished by indiscriminately killing men, women, and children, are commended and applauded."[13]

The end of Reconstruction marked the end of any sustained public controversy over the memory of Nat Turner in Virginia. In 1869, having adopted a new constitution that guaranteed equal rights to African Americans, the state was readmitted to the Union with full representation in Congress. The Richmond newspaper that published the biting satire "Equal Justice" and championed the radical Republican cause folded in 1870, leaving African Americans without an editorial voice in the state's capital. In Southampton County and other localities throughout the state, extralegal forms of intimidation and coercion helped crush the brief political insurgency of African-American voters. Those who admired Nat Turner as a hero and martyr might say so in the privacy of their own home, but they placed themselves and their loved ones at considerable risk if they said so within earshot of their vigilant — and well-armed — white neighbors.

As Northern whites wearied of sectional conflict and Southern whites "redeemed" state governments from "Negro rule," the era of Reconstruction sputtered to an end. Passage of a watered-down Civil Rights Act of 1875 marked the last hurrah of the radical Republicans. Sponsored by Senator Charles Sumner of Massachusetts, it guaranteed all citizens equal access to public accommodations, common carriers, public schools, churches, cemeteries, and jury service. In the South, support for Republican state governments evaporated as the Democratic-Conservative opposition, marching under the banner of states' rights and white supremacy, succeeded in bringing white voters to the polls and keeping black voters away. The readmission of the eleven former states of the Confederacy and the removal of the last federal troops from the South in 1877, with the blessing of Republican president Rutherford B. Hayes, marked the official end of the Reconstruction era and the return of the South to "home rule."

The Southampton Insurrection Scare of 1883

Much to the dismay of white conservatives, African Americans continued to vote and hold office in Virginia for more than two decades after Reconstruction. Dozens of African Americans won elective office on Republican or "fusion" tickets. Economic issues provided the basis for an interracial political alliance known as the Readjuster Movement, which enjoyed stunning electoral success in the early 1880s. The Readjusters favored partial repudiation of the state debt in order to fund public education and reduce taxation. The "Funders," by contrast, argued that fiscal responsibility — and Southern honor — demanded full funding of the debt. General William Mahone, who began organizing the Readjuster Party of Virginia in 1877, reached out to potential supporters "without distinction of color." Though African Americans remained loyal, by and large, to the Republican Party, they emerged as a crucial swing vote that would hand control of the Virginia General Assembly to a coalition of Republicans and Readjusters in 1880.[14]

The prospect of "Negro rule" under a Readjuster-controlled state government stirred the insurrection anxieties of white voters. Shortly before the elections of 1883, the Funders issued the so-called Danville Circular, which grossly exaggerated the number of black office-holders in Danville, Virginia, and raised racial tensions in the city to a fever pitch. When a white man stumbled over the foot of a black man on a public sidewalk three days before the election, an antiblack "riot" ensued in which four black men and one white man were killed and another ten people were injured. Threats of violence kept most black voters home on election day; as a result, the Democrats defeated the Readjuster-Republican coalition and secured control of the state government for decades to come.[15]

After the election, a Readjuster newspaper accused the Funders of circulating a patently false version of the Danville Riot "in which the negroes were represented as in armed insurrection." In precincts throughout the state, the *Richmond Whig* charged, Funders "of the baser sort" spread such rumors to enflame white voters, intimidate black voters, and, thus, steal the election from the Readjusters. "It is nonsense," the editors wrote, "for anybody in or out of this State to say that the Danville Circular and the bait of alleged 'negro risings' had not reached the remotest portions of the State on or before election day. . . . The sentiment and passion of a war of races had been industriously cultivated all over the Commonwealth, and there were few, if any points, where the people were not frightened or misled by the Danville frauds, supplemented by murder."[16]

On November 9, 1883, one week after the Danville Riot, the *Norfolk Virginian* informed its readers of a "Rumored Uprising of the Negroes of Southampton County." Norfolk officials had received a telegram from the village of Newsoms the previous evening, stating that once again "the citizens of that town, and in fact of the whole county, were very much excited over the rumors that the negroes were making arrangements for a general uprising for the purpose of massacring the whites and the destruction of property." The telegram stated that the white people of Southampton "were making preparations to defend themselves." White volunteers from Norfolk and surrounding areas responded quickly to the alarm. Several military officers "assembled at the railroad telegraph office with a number of citizens who volunteered to go to the assistance of the people of Southampton if telegraphed for." A subsequent dispatch, published the next day, noted that the excitement "was greatly enhanced by the fact that the colored people could not be found in their usual habitations." The black men who worked around the railroad depot had not been seen for several days. The scouts sent out to check on the rumors "reported finding a squad of 25 colored men, which confirmed the report that something was wrong."[17]

News of the "rumored uprising" in Southampton County, scene of Turner's Rebellion some fifty years earlier, spread quickly by telegraph. The *New York Times* and the *New York World* published wire service reports the next day. The editors of the *New York Herald* blamed the scare on the overheated political rhetoric of the recent election campaign in Virginia. They suggested that the "negro laborers" missing from their posts in Southampton may have "taken to the woods" in the mistaken belief that the Democrats intended to massacre them. "But however that is," they added, "and whether this Southampton business proves to be a mere 'scare' or a genuine alarm, there is more need of discreteness among both whites and blacks in Virginia at this moment, with regard to the antipathies and antagonisms of race, than at any time since the civil war." The editors warned that continued race-baiting by white politicians in Virginia would "revive the old 'race issue' in the coming national election."[18]

For all the commotion, the rumored "insurrection" never materialized. The *Norfolk Landmark* concluded that the reports out of Southampton "were utterly groundless." The newspaper quoted several eyewitnesses who confirmed that "no movement had been discovered among the blacks." The owner of a Branchville sawmill reported that "his negroes" were back at work as usual; John Cloyd, the suspected leader of the conspiracy and "a well known darkey of Southampton," had been at the fair on the day the Negroes were supposed to attack. A final dispatch from the scene stated that "no hostile organization of the negroes could be discovered in Southampton, and all alarm and anxiety had subsided among the white people."[19]

The Rebellious Slave As "Race Hero"

The restoration of white rule in the South and the steady erosion of black civil and political rights after Reconstruction forced African Americans into a strategic retreat. They turned to black-controlled institutions — the family, the church, the press, the fraternal order — for support and sustenance as they regrouped and reconsidered their options. A growing number of black leaders embraced the conservative ideology of "racial uplift" as the key to economic mobility and the eradication of antiblack prejudice. They hailed the rise of an educated, respectable black middle class as evidence of "race progress" and appointed themselves agents of civilization among the poor, illiterate black masses. Through their tributes "Eminent Negro Men and Women" and "Negro Stars in All Ages of the World," they sought to inspire race pride and redeem the reputation of the Negro in the eyes of the world.[20]

The changing depiction of Nat Turner in the post-emancipation writings of William Wells Brown illustrates the conservative shift in black political thought. In *The Black Man: His Antecedents, His Genius, and His Achievements* (1863), Brown depicted Turner as a bold avenger "in whose soul God has lighted a torch of liberty that cannot be extinguished by the hand of man." His sixteen-page sketch of Turner's rebellion concluded with a Civil War–era call to arms: "The right of man to the enjoyment of freedom is a settled point; and where he is deprived of this, without any criminal act of his own, it is his duty to regain his liberty at every cost. If the oppressor is struck down in the contest, his fall will be a just one, and all the world will applaud the act." Brown dropped the militant coda from a rewritten sketch of Turner's Rebellion in his Reconstruction-era history, *The Negro in the American Rebellion* (1867). Brown looked to the Republicans in Congress, not the rise of "another Nat Turner," for deliverance from de facto slavery. In the waning days of Reconstruction, Brown incorporated Turner's Rebellion into an uplifting narrative of racial progress in *The Rising Son; or, The Antecedents and Advancement of the Colored Race* (1874). With the "negro's political equality" firmly established under Republican Party rule, Brown turned his attention to the moral and intellectual development of the race. "Education is what we now need and education we must have, at all hazards," he wrote. He presented Nat Turner as a sober, pious, educated man of the cloth and a model of middle-class comportment.[21]

In his final work, *My Southern Home; or, The South and Its People* (1882), published after the withdrawal of federal troops from the South, a jaded Brown depicted Nat Turner as a madman with no significant following. Frustrated with the "lethargy" of his people, Brown delivered a jeremiad in which he lamented the lack of an effective or sustained black protest tradition in the South.

> The efforts made by oppressed nations or communities to throw off their chains, entitles them to, and gains for them the respect of

mankind. This, the blacks never made, or what they did, was so feeble as scarcely to call for comment. The planning of Denmark Vesey for an insurrection in South Carolina, was noble, and deserved a better fate; but he was betrayed by the race that he was attempting to serve. Nat Turner's strike for liberty was the outburst of an insane man, — made so by slavery.

An advocate of emigration to the West, Brown urged the black freedmen to follow the path that he had followed as a runaway slave — not the path that Nat Turner followed to an early grave. He believed that emigration to other regions would bring black people into contact with "educated and enterprising whites" and hasten the moral, social, and intellectual development of the race. Brown reminded his fellow African Americans that the great heroes and martyrs of the antebellum era would not lead them into battle or shield them from the scorn of their enemies. "The great struggle for elevation is now with ourselves. We may talk of Hannibal, Euclid, Phyllis Wheatly, Benjamin Banneker, Toussaint L'Ouverture, but the world will ask us for our men and women of the day. We cannot live upon the past; we must hew out a reputation that will stand the test, one that we have a legitimate right to."[22]

The iconoclastic views of Brown notwithstanding, most advocates of racial uplift viewed the commemoration of great black men and women — slavery's heroes and martyrs included — as crucial to the advancement of the race. The 1880s saw the emergence of a new literary genre, "Negro race history," which incorporated slavery and emancipation into uplifting narratives of black spiritual and moral progress while challenging proslavery arguments and racist imagery so prevalent in American popular culture and mainstream academic scholarship. Early race historians, many of them Protestant clergymen, portrayed rebellious slaves as Christian soldiers, saints, and martyrs. The figure of "Old Prophet Nat," preserved in the oral traditions of ex-slaves and their descendants, fit neatly into this religious framework.[23]

George Washington Williams, a Baptist clergyman and self-trained historian, gave the rebellious slave a prominent place in his two-volume *History of the Negro Race in America* (1880). Williams was born in 1849, the son of freeborn, mixed-race parents. He spent most of his formative years in Massachusetts. In 1863, at the age of fourteen, he ran away from home and enlisted in the Union army, where he rose to the rank of sergeant major. Williams was honorably discharged after suffering a serious wound but later reenlisted and served on the staff of a Union general in Texas. After the war, he enlisted in the cavalry of the U.S. Army, "serving in the Comanche campaign of 1867 with conspicuous bravery." He left the military in 1868, "having been convinced as a Christian that killing people in time of peace as a profession was not the noblest life a man could live."[24]

Williams decided to write a comprehensive history of "the American Negro" after preparing a Fourth of July oration on the subject for the centennial of the United States in 1876. He retired from the Ohio state legislature, gave up his law practice, and began working full-time on the book. He visited libraries and archives in Ohio, New York, and Washington, D.C., and, by his own estimate, consulted "over twelve thousand volumes" and "thousands of pamphlets." After three years of "wide and careful reading," he devised a plan for the book that divided the history of the Negro race into nine parts spanning two volumes. The first volume covered the period from antiquity to the American Revolution; the second covered the years between the founding of the American republic and the end of Reconstruction.[25]

Williams presented his chapter "Negro Insurrections" as a direct challenge to those proslavery writers who depicted enslaved blacks as docile and submissive by nature. "The question was often asked: Why don't the Negroes rise at the South and exterminate their enslavers?" Williams answered that the enslaved black masses did not accept their enslavement — "as has been stated, they sought the North and their freedom through the Underground Railroad" — but simply lacked effective leadership. That the slaves "did rise on several different occasions" despite "this great disadvantage" was a testament to their "real character." Williams emphasized the elaborate planning that went into the conspiracies of Gabriel and Denmark Vesey, the large numbers of slaves involved, the careful exclusion of those who could not be trusted. These "bold," "well-conceived" plots failed, he noted, but not for lack of courage or commitment on the part of the rebel leaders or their followers.[26]

The Protestant Christian ethos that suffused "race histories" of this era is most evident in the segment devoted to Nat Turner, who, Williams wrote, "combined the lamb and the lion. He was a Christian and a *man*." Williams drew heavily on "The Confessions of Nat Turner" in establishing the religious training and high moral character of the "Prophet," but he also embellished his narrative with biographical details and anecdotes of unknown origin.

Young "Nat." was born of slave parents, and carried to his grave many of the superstitions and traits of his father and mother. The former was a preacher; the latter a "mother in Israel." Both were unlettered, but, nevertheless, very pious people. The mother began when Nat. was quite young to teach him that he was born, like Moses, to be the deliverer of his race. She would sing to him snatches of wild, rapturous songs, and repeat portions of prophecy she had learned from the preachers of those times. Nat. listened with reverence and awe, and believed everything his mother said. He imbibed the deep religious character of his parents, and soon manifested a desire to preach.

Williams drew pointed analogies between Turner and other Bible-study heroes who rejected earthly authorities and answered only to God.

Like Moses, he lived in the solitudes of the mountains and brooded over the condition of his people.

. . .

Like John the Baptist, when he had delivered his message, he would retire to the fastness of the mountain, or seek the desert, where he could meditate upon his great work.

. . .

Like Joan of Arc, he "heard the spirits," the "voices," and believed that God had "sent him to free his people."

Williams left his readers to wonder whether the remarkable prophecies attributed to Nat Turner were of natural or supernatural origin. Yet he left no doubt that Turner's brave spirit of resistance to oppression, his unwavering faith in God, lived on in the souls of black folk. "No stone marks the resting place of this martyr to freedom, this Black John Brown," he wrote. "And yet he has a prouder and more durable monument than was ever erected of stone or brass. The image of Nat. Turner is carved on the fleshy tablets of four million hearts."[27]

The African-American press, catering to the rising black middle class in segregated communities of the North, South, and West, served as a major venue for discussions over which figures to honor and where they ranked relative to one another in the context of black history. By the mid-1880s, African Americans boasted more than one hundred newspapers scattered across the nation. The editors of these newspapers wielded great influence as "race leaders" and appeared frequently alongside historical figures in compendiums of the "Greatest Negroes."[28]

T. Thomas Fortune of the *New York Age* invoked the martial spirit of the rebellious slave on numerous occasions as a crusading black newspaper editor. Born a slave in 1856, educated at a Freedmen's Bureau school and Howard University, Fortune dabbled in teaching and politics before settling on a career in journalism. A staunch advocate of civil rights, Fortune used his editorial columns to assail the steady erosion of legal protections for African Americans in the decade following Reconstruction. He responded to the Danville Riot by calling on African Americans to stand and fight. "If it is necessary for colored men to turn themselves into outlaws to assert their manhood and their citizenship," he wrote, "let them do it." Fortune refused to back down under a barrage of criticism from the white press. African Americans owed it to themselves, he argued, to retaliate against their white assailants. "If they run away like cowards they will be regarded as 'inferior' and worthy to be shot; but if they 'stand their ground' manfully and do their honest share of shooting they will be respected, and by so doing they will lessen the propensity of white roughs to incite to riot."[29]

Fortune looked to African-American history for examples of heroic black men who refused to submit meekly to white oppression. He summoned forth the spirit of the rebellious slave in an 1883 editorial urging "Afro-Americans" — a term he helped to popularize — to band together and agitate for reform. "Our history in this country dates from the moment that restless men among us became restless under oppression and rose against it," he wrote. "From Denmark Vesey to Nat Turner, from the flight of Frederick Douglass and Henry Highland Garnet from the bloodhounds of Maryland to the present time the voice of the race has been heard on the lecture platform and on the field of battle protesting against the injustice heaped upon the race."[30]

Turner as a brave patriot appeared once again in Fortune's 1887 call for the creation of the Afro-American League, a national organization designed to mobilize black resistance to white villainy and oppression. Fortune argued that the injustices suffered by black citizens — disfranchisement, lynch law and mob rule, the unequal distribution of school funds, segregation on common carriers, and segregation in public accommodations — justified the creation of a race-based organization for mutual protection. "We propose to accomplish our purposes by the peaceful methods of agitation, through the ballot and the courts," he wrote, "but if others use the weapons of violence to combat our peaceful arguments it is not for us to run away from violence. A man's a man, and what is worth having is worth fighting for." Fortune proceeded to recite the names of "Negro patriots" who were not afraid to die for their liberty. "Attucks, the black patriot — he was no coward! Toussaint L'Ouverture — he was no coward! Nat Turner — he was no coward! And the two hundred thousand black soldiers of the last war — they were no cowards. If we have a work to do, let us do it. And if there come violence let those who oppose our just cause 'throw the first stone'!" Fortune commemorated Turner in verse as well as prose. In 1884, the *Cleveland Gazette* published his six-stanza, forty-line poem titled, simply, "Nat. Turner." The poem, like many written by Fortune in this period, presented resistance to oppression as the measure of black manhood: "'I will be free! I will be free! Or, fighting, die a man!' cried he."[31]

An editorial by Frederick Douglass, Jr., the son of the famous black abolitionist and an associate editor of the *National Leader* in Washington, D.C., drew Fortune into a testy debate over the place of Nat Turner in the African-American pantheon of heroes. Unlike Fortune, Douglass did not espouse a militant race-consciousness, embracing instead a colorblind American nationalism. Writing in 1889, thirty years after the raid on Harpers Ferry, Douglass "wanted to know if it was not almost time that the colored people were doing something to perpetuate the memory of John Brown." Fortune, responding from his editorial desk at the *New York Age,* saw no particular reason why black people should build a monument to Brown when so many white people were working to keep his memory alive. He proposed another figure, "a fore-runner of John Brown," in greater need of recognition.

> We refer of course to Nat Turner, who was executed at Jerusalem, Southampton County, Virginia, for inciting and leading his fellow slaves to insurrection long before John Brown invaded Kansas and planned an unfortunate raid on Harper's Ferry. Nat Turner was a black hero. He preferred death to slavery. He ought to have a monument. White men care nothing for his memory. We should cherish it.

Fortune complained that black men who built monuments to white men — even "great and good" men like John Brown — perpetuated the glorification of whites over blacks. "It is quite remarkable," he wrote,

"that whenever colored men move that somebody's name be perpetuated, that somebody's name is always a white man's."[32]

Douglass accused Fortune of racial chauvinism in ranking Nat
Turner over John Brown. To criticize colored men for honoring the
memory of an indisputably great white man, as Fortune had done,
"helps to sustain the charge made against us by whites of the South,
'that it is the colored people who draw the color line.'" Worse, it privileged color over character.

> We have always been of the opinion that the character and good
> acts of a man were worthy of emulation and perpetuation, and not
> his color. But the young gentleman who edits the *Age* makes color
> the condition of action toward erecting a monument in honor of
> one who broke the chains about his neck and made him free to act
> by himself. The suggestion made by the *Leader* has led the *Age* to
> discover no good traits in Nat. Turner's character that precedes his
> being black.

Douglass suggested that Fortune's editorial smacked of opportunism
and insincerity. "Nat. Turner has been dead many years, and the editor
of the *Age* has never found time to suggest a monument for him until
now, and he only suggests it now in opposition to the one being
erected in honor of John Brown."[33]

Fortune flatly denied the charge of drawing the "color line." He insisted that his counterproposal was motivated not by racial prejudice
against whites but by racial pride in the achievements of blacks. "We
yield to none in admiration of the character and sacrifices of John
Brown," he wrote. "The character and sacrifices of Nat. Turner are
dearer to us because he was of us and exhibited in the most abject condition the heroism and race devotion which have illustrated in all
times the sort of men who are worthy to be free." Fortune argued that
the failure of African Americans to honor great men of their own race
reflected poorly on the race as a whole. "What we protest against is
Negro worship of white men and the memory of white men, to the utter exclusion of colored men equally patriotic and self-sacrificing. It is
the absence of race pride and race unity which makes white men de-
spise black men the world over."[34]

In the identification and ranking of "race heroes," Victorian-era
advocates of uplift revealed a preference for middle-class and profes-

sional elites. While Nat Turner had the requisite qualities of courage and manliness, he lacked the polish of his more refined peers. In 1890, the *Indianapolis Freeman* ("An Illustrated Colored Newspaper") asked its readers to guess "the names of the ten greatest Negroes — living or dead." A panel of "five competent judges" — including T. Thomas Fortune — would read the entries and select the winners. The editors of the *Freeman* did not supply readers with the names of great Negroes — just an uncaptioned picture of Frederick Douglass and a ballot ranked first through tenth. "We cannot specify any standard of greatness," they wrote. "The guessers and the judges must determine that." About one out of every ten readers who submitted an entry suggested Nat Turner as one of the greatest Negroes of all time. The names "N. Turner" or "Nat Turner" appeared on seventy-five of the more than seven hundred ballots published in the *Freeman* over the course of five weeks. Votes for Turner came from twenty-five states, with the greatest concentrations in Maryland, Illinois, and Kansas.[35]

After much delay, the *Freeman* announced the names of "The Ten Greatest Negroes" — all of them men — as selected by the all-male panel of judges: Frederick Douglass, "cosmopolitician, philanthropist, statesman"; Toussaint L'Ouverture, "liberator, statesman"; Blanche K. Bruce, "master of the science of government, successful lecturer, politician par excellence"; Peter H. Clark, "educator and polemic"; Bishop D. A. Payne, "theologian"; J. C. Price, "controversialist, educator, orator"; George W. Williams, "compiler and historian"; J. Milton Turner, "orator"; T. Thomas Fortune, "agitator and essayist"; and Edward A. Cooper, "journalist." Nat Turner, leader of the greatest slave uprising in American history, did not make the list. The rebel leader, disparaged by whites as a fanatic and a murderer, lacked the respectability of the "liberator-statesman" Toussaint L'Ouverture, the "cosmopolitician-statesman" Douglass, and the eight other "men of mark" on the list.[36]

Cooper, the editor of the *Freeman* and one of the "Ten Greatest Negroes," criticized the standards of "greatness" employed by the judges. "If we had boys to train for the duties of life and desired to bring them to full manhood or hoped to have them truly great," he wrote, "we could not point to these men with one or two exceptions as models." The judges chose popular men, successful men, not "great" men of extraordinary character. Where were the black Shakespeares, the black Miltons, the black George Washingtons? W. Allison Sweeney replied, on behalf of the judges, that the editor of the *Freeman* was using a "white yardstick" to measure Negro greatness. "You asked for Negroes, to Negroes we were confined, and outside the Negro race you precluded us from going, either for examples or models of comparison or adjustment." Sweeney accused Cooper of exaggerating the shortcomings of his own race while turning a blind eye to the "blemishes and mistakes" of white men such as George Washington, "a slaveholder and a gambler." In his view, the ten black men selected by the judges stood as "worthy models of emulation and examples for the Negro youth of the world."[37]

Judging from the hundreds of contest entries, many African Americans of the late nineteenth century considered the rebellious slave worthy of inclusion among the "Ten Greatest Negroes, Living or Dead." Yet the spirit of the age favored the bestowal of public honors on a rising generation of black men who distinguished themselves as race leaders — journalists, educators, theologians, politicians — in the post-emancipation era. These "men of mark" stood as symbols of race progress and models of middle-class comportment — a far cry from the bedraggled figure of Nat Turner, raising his manacled hands to the heavens.

Nat Turner amid the "Moonlight and Magnolias"

The deeds of Nat Turner and Gabriel provided darkly dramatic backdrops for the popular "moonlight and magnolias" Southern romances of the 1880s and 1890s. Authors of three texts — all white Southern women — drew heavily on the oral traditions of their Virginia upbringings, supplemented by generous excerpts from "The Confessions of Nat Turner." Two of the authors portrayed the rebellious slave in a broadly sympathetic light; the third resisted the temptation to portray Nat Turner as a black fiend who made white women his intended victims. And while their portraits of plantation society stressed the bonds of mutual affection between kindly masters and faithful slaves, all hinted at the dark undercurrents roiling beneath the surface.

Mary Spear Tiernan produced a remarkably sympathetic portrait of the rebellious slave Gabriel (modeled after Nat Turner) in her novel *Homoselle* (1881). Born in Baltimore, Tiernan grew up in Richmond, Virginia, where her father served as district attorney. During the Civil

War, she worked for the Treasury Department of the Confederacy. One of her brothers, a color bearer for a Virginia regiment, died at the second Battle of Manassas. Another brother, a sergeant of artillery, was mortally wounded in the Battle of Fayette Court House, West Virginia. In 1873 Tiernan married an elderly Baltimore merchant and settled in that city. She became active in the Women's Literary Club and contributed numerous essays and historical articles to the *Southern Review, Century,* and *Scribner's*.[38]

In *Homoselle,* a visiting English journalist named Halsey revels in the picturesque qualities of "Country Life in Virginia," only to discover that abolitionist agitation threatens to ignite a bloody race war. A free Negro, denied permission to marry a pretty mulatto house servant, conspires with a Northern white abolitionist and the black slave preacher Gabriel to incite a slave rebellion. The English journalist eavesdrops on one of their secret meetings and decides he must do something to prevent the uprising without betraying the "poor creatures" involved in the conspiracy. Using the mulatto house servant as his informant, he learns the plans of the insurgents and — on the night of the attack — swims across the James River to inform the white authorities in Richmond.

Tiernan modeled her fictional Gabriel — a relatively minor figure in the novel — after Nat Turner, drawing much of his dialogue straight from "The Confessions." Tiernan invested Gabriel with the same powers of intelligence and sense of purpose that Thomas R. Gray gave to Nat Turner. Gabriel "seemed to be one of the few Heaven-taught leaders of men who have figured in world history." She did not, however, give him the same unswerving faith in the righteousness of his cause. "Sometimes I think I was doin' the Lord's will in tryin' to free my brethren; and then agin I feel like I was wrong," Gabriel tells a white preacher who visits him shortly before his execution. "One time I believe that all I wanted was my people's freedom: and another time I am afeard I was considerin' too much 'bout Gabriel bein' thar deliverer, instead of leavin' it to the Lord to act in his own good time." The preacher leads Gabriel to "the knowledge of his transgressions" and prepares him for death as "the only means of atonement."[39]

Tiernan's narrator reflects on the sharp contrast between the heroic depiction of the rebellious slave in black oral tradition and the brief, unflattering sketches found in histories written by and for whites. In a scene at the end of the novel, as Gabriel/Turner awaits his execution, the preacher takes a long look at the rebel leader's face. "Its lineaments he never forgot," the narrator notes, "and often, in after-years, when they had mouldered in the dust, he would describe them with reverence and pity to the children of another generation." No such reverence would be accorded Gabriel/Turner by the slaveholders or their historians. "His name, and his unsuccessful attempt to liberate his fellow-slaves, are dismissed with a paragraph in the written histories of the time." Even among "his own people," the rebellious slave was fading from memory. "His figure is becoming less distinct in the full blaze of liberty achieved by other hearts and hands. It will doubtless soon lapse into the shadowland of myths."[40]

Marion Harland mined oral traditions of Nat Turner's Rebellion in her plantation romance *Judith: A Chronicle of Old Virginia* (1883). Born a year before Turner's Rebellion, Harland grew up in a small village in Amelia County, Virginia, two counties removed from Southampton. She attributed her youthful knowledge of Turner's Rebellion to an informal storytelling tradition indigenous to the Old South. "Before I was eight years old," she wrote in her memoirs, "I had heard the tale of Gabriel's projected insurrection, and of the bloodier outbreak of murderous fury led by Nat Turner, the petted favorite of a trusting master. Heard that the signal of attack in both cases was to be 'a trumpet blown loud and long.'" Once, when she was ten, the blare of a hunter's trumpet so frightened her that she went scurrying to the "deepest recesses" of a graveyard and hid there for hours. "There I lay, wet with the dews of the past night, and my face and hands scratched to bleeding, until the winding horn grew faint and fainter, and the bay of a pack of hounds told me what a fool panic had made of me." Harland relied on folklore for guidance in such moments of terror. "We always thought of the graveyard as an asylum in the event of an uprising. No negro would venture to enter it by day or night."[41]

Harland associated slave rebellion — "that worst of bugbears to a Southern woman" — with the unleashing of beastly Negro passions under the influence of religious fanaticism. "We had heard how Gabriel, a leader in prayer-meetings, and encouraged by the whites to do Christian evangelization among his own race, had deliberately meditated and written down, as sections of the code to be put into practice, when he should come into his kingdom of Lower Virginia — a plan of murder of all male whites, and a partition of the women and girl children among his followers, together with arson and tortures exceeding the deviltries of the red Indians." The much-vaunted loyalty and affection of the slaves, Harland learned, could disappear in a moment. "I am often asked why, if our family servants were really and warmly attached to us, we should have let the 'bugbear' poison our pleasures and haunt our midnight visions." The answer, she maintained, lay in the power that self-styled prophets like Nat Turner wielded over the superstitious black masses. "In every plan of rising against their masters, Religion was a potent element. The 'Mammy' who had nursed her mistress's baby at her bosom, would brain it, with the milk yet wet upon its lips, if bidden by the 'prophet' to make the sacrifice." Harland characterized such unbridled fanaticism as a racial trait, peculiar to those of African descent. "We knew them to be but children of a larger growth, passionate and unreasoning, facile and impulsive, and fanatical beyond anything conceivable by the full-blooded white."[42]

Harland incorporated the oral traditions of her Virginia youth into the plot of her novel. On the eve of Nat Turner's Rebellion, ten-year-old Judith Read listens attentively as her aunt and grandmother reminisce about Gabriel's Rebellion. Judith is shocked to learn of such flagrant disloyalty among the slaves. "I never even knew that *anybody's* servants cared so much to be free that they would kill their masters to get rid of them," she says to herself. "I shall never trust one of them again — never!" That night she awakens from a nightmare to find Mammy standing over her with a candle. "You wouldn't hurt me, would you? Mammy! Mammy!" Mammy reassures Judith, but her vague and portentous remarks indicate that she knows something bad is about to happen. On the morning after Turner's Rebellion, Grandma summons Judith to her room and tells her what happened. Grandma insists that Mammy stay in the room during the telling of the story, a bold display of confidence in her faithful servant. Mammy, in turn, attests to the loyalty and gratitude of the Summerfield slaves. "I know there ain't a colored person that ever b'longed to you or yours that wouldn't stand between Nat Turner's meat-axe any time o' day or night," Mammy declares. "Befo' a h'ar o' yo' head falls he's got to kill every man an' woman o' his own color on this plantation." Mammy acknowledges that the slaves of Summerfield would welcome their freedom if they could stay in Virginia and — presumably — labor for their old masters. "But they don' see their way clear to the Promise' Lan' over a road fenced in with babies corpses an' knee-deep in the blood o' innorcent women who have done nothin' but try to cuarry the load in the fear of the Lord that their forefathers laid 'pon them!" Her speech moves Grandma to tears. "I believe you — and I trust them!" In refusing to heed the call of the "Prophet," the black mammy — the most faithful of all faithful slaves — emerges as the heroine of Harland's novel.

The boldest challenge to the proslavery image of Nat Turner as a bloodthirsty religious fanatic who hated all whites came from the pen of Southern expatriate writer Pauline Carrington Bouvé in *Their Shadows Before: A Story of the Southampton Insurrection* (1899). Born in 1860 in Little Rock, Arkansas, the daughter of a U.S. congressman–turned–Confederate general, Bouvé considered herself a Virginian by blood and breeding. A native of Luray, Virginia, she moved as an adult to Boston, where she pursued a career as a journalist, novelist, and children's writer.[43]

Bouvé made the protagonist of her novel a young Virginia girl who, like herself, sympathized with the slaves and rebelled against the social hierarchy of the plantation South. The girl befriends Nat Turner, portrayed as a free man, educated and emancipated by his owner. He in turn protects her when she is captured by his band of rebels. For all her abolitionist sympathies, Bouvé remained loyal to the pro-Southern tradition of kindly, paternalistic masters and self-sacrificing slaves who conspired to save their white owners from harm.

Their Shadows Before follows the adventures of Penelope Winston, a spirited white girl who lives with her grandparents on a plantation in Southampton County in 1831. Penelope confesses to a sense of alienation from her white family; only in the slave quarters, with Mammy and old Uncle Isham, can she express her true feelings. She reveals her abolitionist sentiments in a probing exchange with Uncle Isham.

> *Penelope:* Did you ever hate white people?
> *Uncle Isham:* Moses an' Aaron! Who done put sech notions in you hade, honey?
> *Penelope:* Nobody. I was just thinking perhaps sometimes you couldn't help hating us a little.
> *Uncle Isham:* Dem ain't de right kinder thoughts fer er li'l lady like you an' er po' ole nigger like me.
> *Penelope:* I wouldn't blame you if you did. If I were a slave, I would hate my master. Even if he were good to me, still, I think I would hate, yes, *hate* him. I could not help it.

One day, while in the quarters, Penelope finds a "frightened" Mammy listening intently as a "strange visitor" — who turns out to be Nat Turner — issues vague prophecies. "The time is near, the time is near," he declares. "By the Sign of the Sun and the Sign of the Cross it shall come to pass!" Later that day Penelope meets Turner alone in Mammy's cabin. He touches her face with his hand and draws a circle on her forehead. "Lord Jesus, behold the mark!" Penelope learns that her grandfather has forbidden his slaves from attending Turner's religious meetings. "This negro preacher, Nat Turner, is demoralising every darky in Southampton County," he declares, "and I intend to be very strict in regard to enforcement of my orders." To protect the slaves from punishment, Penelope determines to keep Turner's presence in the quarters a secret. She listens intently as the adults — her grandfather representing the slaveholding South, her private tutor, Basil Mortimer, representing the abolitionist North — debate the prospect of slave rebellion. Grandfather: "You may rest assured that nothing of that kind will ever be attempted. A movement of that nature requires a leader, and there would be none." Mortimer: "There will arise a Gideon for every Jericho." Anxious to set the slaves free, Penelope declares herself an "abolitionist too."[44]

Bouvé placed her young protagonist in a position to witness all of the key events of the uprising, making her a co-conspirator of sorts. Penelope gets lost while taking a walk and stumbles upon Nat Turner addressing a half-dozen followers. "The end is at hand. The Sign has been given — even the Sign of Blood! — red drops on the grains of corn, red drops on oak leaves, red drops on the blades of grass! Blood, — blood, — blood! Everywhere blood!" When her rescuers arrive, she says nothing of what she has witnessed. A strange bluish appearance to the sky has the slaves in the quarters talking and singing of nothing but Judgment Day. Still she says nothing. Mammy and Isham, concerned for the safety of their white mistresses and master, devise a ruse to send them away, but Penelope — oblivious — stays behind. As the rebellious slaves close in, axes in hand, Nat Turner sweeps Penelope away to the safety of his lair. There, she listens as Turner testifies to the righteousness of his cause. "I don't think you mean to be bad," she declares. "And, anyway, you have saved my life . . . and I will never tell where you are!" Turner casts some sort of spell over Penelope that erases her memory until the moment he decides to surrender. "I know Uncle Nat killed people, women and babies," she tells her family, "but I think he thought he was born to do it, and he couldn't help doing it."

On the morning of his execution, Turner summons Penelope to his jail cell and hands her a roll of paper. "I want the white child to keep this. Let my testimony be handed down to the people of her race and mine, that, when the end is accomplished, all may know it was truly foretold by me, Nathaniel, the prophet of the Lord." From the gallows, Turner offers this final prophecy: "What the Lord begins, he shall finish. I see battles, fire, blood, — freedom!"[45]

Newspapers and magazines, detecting a growing interest in the history and folklore of slavery, published periodic articles on Turner's exploits. The authors rendered the historic scenes and characters as relics of a bygone era with little connection to the modern world of the late nineteenth century. One such article, written in 1896 by Southampton County native Martha Rochelle Tyler ("Rokela"), appeared in *Godey's* under the title "A Page of History: One of the Tragedies of the Old Slavery Day's." Tyler, the granddaughter of President John Tyler, drew heavily on her own family's oral tradition. At one point she told how "the Clerk of Courts, James Rochelle" — her maternal grandfather — "threw open his residence" to shelter the white women and children who had fled to Jerusalem. At another point she told how "the mother and sisters of George H. Thomas crouched in the bushes" as Nat Turner and his men passed them by on the path to "the old Thomas homestead." Tyler espoused none of the antiblack, proslavery rhetoric one might expect of a white woman born and raised in Southampton County during the last twenty years of slavery. She portrayed Turner as a sincere yet "fanatical" leader of a fledgling antislavery crusade. In her view, Turner was not motivated by hatred or a desire for personal revenge, but by a dissatisfaction, common among educated slaves, "with that station in life in which circumstances and State laws had placed him." That Turner was not "destined to be the great liberator of his race," as he concluded at an early age, proved only that he mistook his own will for God's.[46]

Turner's Rebellion should have shattered the myth that the "negro" loved his white master more than his own freedom, Tyler observed, but it did not. "One of the strange fallacies of the Southern whites, not only of that day but even up to the Civil War," she wrote, "was the belief that the strongest affection the negro nature was capable of feeling was love for his master. All this time they never dreamed of the danger. So confident were they of the '*affection*' of their slaves that, as I have before said, they even slept at night with unlocked doors." Tyler would restrict her comments on race to the antebellum era. The tragic events of 1831 were "a dark page in history," viewed from a safe and enlightened distance.

"Faithful Old Slaves, Degenerate Progeny"

Late-nineteenth-century Americans looked nostalgically to the Old South for relief from the racial turmoil and labor unrest of their day. A rising generation of African Americans who took pride in their collective achievements as a race and aspired to social and political equality alarmed white Southerners and threatened a persistent but tenuous status quo. Negro ambition and success posed as great a threat, in the eyes of white supremacists, as the perceived wave of "Negro crime" so widely reported in the newspapers. These allegations of crime — particularly rape — served as a pretext for white mob violence against individual suspects and retaliation against entire communities. Lynchings, which rose dramatically in the 1880s and peaked in the 1890s, represented the most extreme response to the so-called Negro problem of the late nineteenth century. Any black person accused of transgressing the social and legal boundaries established by whites risked the same treatment. Spectacle lynchings, sometimes advertised well in advance, drew large crowds from all classes of Southern white society. Press coverage and photographic postcards carried news of these events far beyond the localities in which they occurred and sent a chilling message to every black person: Stay in your place.

White Southern historians of the late nineteenth century felt no inhibition about commenting on the relevance of Nat Turner's Rebellion to the "Negro problem" of their own day. They presented slavery as an effective system of "race control" that kept a large black labor force in check and ensured the maintenance of a white-dominated social order. The refusal of most slaves to follow Turner on his murderous rampage, they argued, demonstrated the civilizing influence of slavery on the Negro masses. Slavery, in effect, trained Negroes for a permanently subordinate place in Southern society under the benevolent rule of their white superiors. Emancipation and Reconstruction, by contrast, gave blacks unrealistic aspirations to social and political equality, thus increasing the likelihood of insurrection and race war.[47]

Two Southern historians trained at Johns Hopkins University in Baltimore produced scholarly polemics on Turner's Rebellion at the turn of the century. Hopkins actively recruited native white Southerners to its program in Southern history, offering free tuition to hundreds of applicants from Maryland, Virginia, and North Carolina who showed "character and intellectual promise." By 1900 nearly half of the advanced students were from the South and a third of the faculty had "Southern origins or connections." They would contribute to a pro-Southern school of slavery, Civil War, and Reconstruction studies that dominated the white academy for the next forty years.[48]

Stephen B. Weeks, a newly minted Johns Hopkins Ph.D. from North Carolina, ruminated on the "Negro problem" and the prospect of post-emancipation race wars in his 1891 article on "The Slave Insurrection in Virginia in 1831, Known As 'Old Nat's War.'" Weeks traced the origins of the Southern white man's burden to the introduction of slavery in Virginia in 1619. "From that time to the present the negro has been with us; for two hundred and forty-six years as a slave, and now as a freedman. During all this time, whether slave or free, he has been as a thorn in the side of the white man." In recounting "Old Nat's War," Weeks relied primarily on "The Confessions of Nat Turner," supplemented by several newspaper articles and historical sketches. "No other slave insurrection gave such a shock to the South as did the uprising of Nat Turner," he observed. Weeks marveled at the "faithfulness" of the slaves, particularly during servile insurrection and Civil War. Emancipation, he lamented, had eroded the sense of loyalty that once bound black slaves to their white masters. "Since obtaining his freedom, the black man, led on by unprincipled rascals, and showing in his every action that simplicity which marks the childhood of a race, has aspired to rule the white, rich and poor, ignorant and learned alike. But the day of his domination has not yet come, and will not come while there is an Anglo-Saxon in the South to draw a sword or shoulder a musket."[49]

A no-less-militant tone pervaded the work of Johns Hopkins Ph.D. William Sidney Drewry, whose scholarly monograph *The Southampton Insurrection* (1900) included a discourse on the modern-day "Negro problem." A native of Southampton County, Drewry arrived at Johns Hopkins just as the first "systematic" course in the history of the South was being offered. As a graduate student, he had access to "the southern history room," which held one of the largest collections of materials on slavery. Yet, for all of his reading in secondary literature and all of his training in archival research, Drewry relied heavily on oral tradition in writing his book. He appended a list of more than eighty people — twelve of them black — whom he had "interviewed personally." Included were eyewitnesses to the rebellion and descendants of Nat Turner who still lived in the county.[50]

Drewry approached his local white informants with great deference. He secured their cooperation by appealing to their vanity as experts, by promising to defend the reputation of their slaveholding ancestors, and by declaring his loyalties as a "county man." In October 1898, Drewry sent a letter to "Miss Mattie" Tyler, who had recently published her article on the insurrection in *Godey's Magazine.* "Knowing you to be well posted on historical subjects &c," Drewry wrote, "I want to ask if you can tell me of any sources of information & if you know any facts relating to any of the families to whose homes Nat went." Drewry was not interested in genealogy for its own sake; he wanted to know whether any of the local families attacked by the insurgents had owned slaves transported from Haiti. Perhaps he could trace the seeds of local rebellion to the bloody revolution on that island some thirty years before. Drewry prevailed on Miss Mattie to approach other white informants on his behalf. "I know this is asking much of you, but I am sure you will pardon me when you know how much I am interested in my work & how much pleasure I have gained from seeing & writing to the very kind & obliging people of Southampton. I hope I may make the study interesting & do our county justice & defend her against the false idea that our people were cruel to their slaves."[51]

Drewry made good on his promise. As part of his proslavery thesis, he argued that the slaveholders of Virginia had perfected a system of labor management that allowed them "to dispense with the cruelties which have been mistakenly attributed to the slave system employed in the production of large tobacco and cotton crops." Because their holdings were relatively small, they did not employ white overseers but instead managed their farms themselves. "They did not consider it a disgrace to work side by side with the slaves since they did not have the legal equality of the negro continually thrust at them." The master/manager would place a Negro foreman in charge of each squad of slaves assigned to a special duty. The slaves thrived under this "class system," which vested hard-working, trustworthy individuals with responsibility and authority. "With the consciousness of being able to rise to the position of foreman, each slave was incited to interest in his own work," Drewry noted. Skilled domestic servants — hog feeders, herdsmen, stillers, cooks, nurses, foremen — became "masters" of their respective domains and took great pride in their work. The slaveholders encouraged "fealty and diligence" in their slaves by rewarding them with "crops, gardens, and other property," long breakfasts and dinners, frequent holidays, and the freedom "to choose their own employer and make their own contracts." Dozens of slaves were manumitted in return for years of faithful service. Thus, slavery in Virginia "was not such as to arouse rebellion, but was an institution which nourished the strongest affection and piety in slave and owner, as well as moral qualities worthy of any age of civilization."[52]

Drewry used the biography of Nat Turner to undermine abolitionist claims of cruelty as a motivating factor in the rebellion. Before the uprising, he wrote, Turner enjoyed a reputation as a faithful and trustworthy servant. Most of the white people in the community admired his good character. His master even made him an overseer. As a preacher, he enjoyed special privileges. "An old negro who knew Nat Turner said the latter could go away on Sunday, and if he did not return until Monday morning nothing was said to him." Drewry pointed to "The Confessions of Nat Turner" as further evidence that "cruel treatment was not a motive for the rebellion. If this had been the case, it would have been urged in mitigation of Nat's punishment. On the contrary, he stated in his testimony that he had no reason to complain of Mr. Travis, who was a kind master, and placed the greatest confidence in him." Drewry concluded that Turner "was like a spoiled child, who, having been allowed too many privileges in youth, soon thinks he ought to be master of all he surveys."[53]

Drewry cited Turner's knowledge of abolitionist activity outside Southhampton County as a source of inspiration to the rebel leader. Turner may have found inspiration in the stories told by slaves transported to Southampton County from the revolutionary island of Saint Domingue. "Nat being a preacher, freely passing from one section of the country to another, very probably had his dreams fired by the recitals of events occurring in their former homes." Antislavery rumblings among delegates to the Virginia Constitutional Convention may have influenced Turner as well. "He was undoubtedly inspired with the hope of freedom, and the mere discussion by a convention may have led him to believe that many whites would sympathize with his scheme." Finally, Drewry cited evidence that "abolition missionaries" had "secretly communicated" with the slaves. "A white man, Bradley, was known to have been very intimate with Nat Turner. This fact, together with contemporaneous circumstances, leaves no doubt but that abolition documents and agents had great influence upon the insurrection."[54]

Drewry ascribed the "failure" of the insurrection to "the refusal of the slaves in general to participate." By his calculation, "only sixty or seventy negroes were implicated, and of these only about forty were guilty, the remainder forced to participate." Fear, he acknowledged, may have induced some would-be rebels to hold back. Many more slaves living beyond the neighborhood of the uprising "would have participated had the insurgents been more successful and less readily suppressed." Still, "the greatest restraint upon the slaves," Drewry insisted, "was affection and good judgment. Their treatment and training had been such as to inspire obedience and contentment." Drewry cited countless examples of loyal slaves who had distinguished themselves as heroes in the eyes of their masters: Joe Harris, "who refused to join the band unless they promised to spare 'his white people'"; Hugh, who hid his mistress and her baby in the thicket of a graveyard and "robbed the negroes of two of their intended victims"; Mary, who warned the whites at Mr. Harris's and Mr. Porter's and "gave them time to escape"; and finally, the slaves of Dr. Samuel Blunt, who took up arms — "grubbing hoes, pitchforks, and other farm instruments" — against the rebel forces "and assisted most heartily in the repulse and taking of prisoners." Drewry declared the unstinting loyalty of these and dozens more heroic slaves "one of the most striking features of the insurrection. Even when all the whites of a family had been killed, the slaves remained faithful and gladly testified at the trials of the culprits." Far from poisoning relations between slaves and masters, Drewry concluded, the Southampton insurrection "only served to bind master and slave in tighter bonds of affection, so that upon the surrender at Appomattox, both wept at the thought of separation."[55]

The threat of Negro insurrection, Drewry concluded in a rambling discourse on the late-nineteenth-century "race problem," increased after the abolition of slavery. The Negroes, he observed, were "rapidly acquiring property which, together with the free schools, supported principally by the whites, free amusement, and cheap newspapers, enables them to give their children education equal to that of the ordinary whites. . . . But this education of the negro, which fits him for the highest office in the land, renders him a useless and discontented citizen. The whites cannot submit to negro rule and self-assertion." Drewry insisted that African Americans, if they were to remain in the United States, had to "occupy an inferior position." He called for the diffusion of the black population throughout the country or — failing that — removal. "The negro, conscious of his inferiority, and equally distributed over the country, will make a peaceful and useful citizen," he wrote. "But educated for the highest office which he can never fill, he will remain a source of disturbance and insurrection, and under such circumstances it will be best for both races that the negro be transported beyond the limits of the United States."[56]

The Southampton Insurrection answered the growing call among white Southern partisans for "Southern history" told from "the Southern point of view." Northern white historians, eager to vindicate the War of Northern Aggression as an antislavery crusade, could not be trusted to tell the truth about the Southern past. A reviewer for the *Virginia Magazine of History and Biography* praised the book as a "careful and thorough study" of a "famous subject" that had not been adequately researched. "It may be stated with confidence that the author has said the last word possible in regard to the history of an event which thrilled the whole country at the time it occurred, and was far-reaching in its consequences. He took up the subject just in time to secure the required information, and has done his work in a manner which leaves no gleanings behind." Sixty-five years would pass before another historian published a scholarly monograph on Turner's Rebellion.[57]

Professional historians who favored "the Northern point of view" largely ignored the book. Albert Bushnell Hart, a Harvard professor who identified himself as "the son and grandson of abolitionists," devoted several pages to the Nat Turner insurrection in *Slavery and Abolition, 1831–1841,* published five years after Drewry's *Southampton Insurrection.* Hart made an obligatory reference to Drewry in a footnote but incorporated none of his pro-Southern, proslavery thesis. For example, Hart dismissed the charge, lodged by Drewry and others, that abolitionist provocateurs were behind the uprising. "Garrison himself absolutely denied any relation with the insurrection, and there is neither direct proof nor indirect reference which fixes on abolitionists any share of that insurrection." Hart also challenged the picture, painted by Drewry and others, of indulgent masters and contented slaves bound by family ties and mutual affection. "The Nat Turner insurrection shook slavery to its foundations; the fact that Nat, though he bore some marks of ill-usage, had not been treated with special cruelty proved that kindness did not bring content."[58]

African-American historians, almost entirely excluded from the mainstream academy, turned to the American Negro Academy as an outlet for their race-conscious treatments of slave rebellions. Founded in 1897, the academy was the brainchild of seventy-eight-year-old Alexander Crummell, the retired rector of the St. Luke's Episcopal Church of Washington, D.C., and a longtime ambassador of American Negro civilization and culture. Crummell envisioned "an organization composed of Negro scholars, whose membership should be limited to forty and whose purpose should be to foster scholarship and culture in the Negro race and encourage Negro genius." Founding members included the poet Paul Laurence Dunbar, the sociologist W.E.B. Du Bois, the Greek scholar William Scarborough, the mathematician Kelly Miller, the theologian Francis J. Grimké, and the historian John W. Cromwell. Such men represented the great potential for intellectual development among the freedmen, given the proper training and institutional support.[59]

Several of the "Occasional Papers" produced by academy members focused on slave rebellion as a tool of liberation and a source of race pride. In "Right on the Scaffold; or, The Martyrs of 1822," author Archibald H. Grimké recalled the heroic deeds of West Indian–born Denmark Vesey but reserved his highest praise for Vesey's American-born co-conspirator, Peter Poyas. "It is no light thing," Grimké wrote, "for the Negroes of the United States to have produced such a man, such a hero and martyr. It is certainly no light heritage, the knowledge, that his brave blood flowed in their veins." Theophilus G. Steward wrote two papers on San Domingo, one detailing the role that a free black regiment from the island played in the American Revolutionary War, the other titled "The Message of San Domingo to the African Race."[60]

The historian John W. Cromwell lectured and wrote extensively on Nat Turner's Rebellion. Born in 1846 in Portsmouth, Virginia, "within fifty miles of the place of Turner's exploits," he remembered Turner as a "familiar name" in his childhood home. When he and his family left Virginia in 1851, having purchased their freedom, they carried oral traditions of Turner's Rebellion with them to their new home in Philadelphia. After the Civil War and emancipation, Cromwell returned to his native state of Virginia. In 1871, he spent a term as a public school teacher in Southampton County, where he met people who "personally knew Nat Turner and his comrades." Fifty years later, he would incorporate their stories, along with the oral traditions of his own childhood, into a scholarly account called "The Aftermath of Nat Turner's Insurrection." Unfortunately, Cromwell did not name his Southampton County informants and gave no clear indication of what they told him. He cited them just once, and then as a group, in a footnote to a paragraph describing the "reign of terror" that followed the uprising.[61]

After his brief teaching stint in Southampton County, Cromwell moved to Washington, D.C., where he edited a newspaper and lectured on Negro history. His public lecture on "the life and character of Nat Turner," delivered in July 1890, was heard "with the deepest interest and satisfaction." Alexander Crummell recorded his impressions of Cromwell's lecture, along with his own interpretation of Turner's Rebellion.

> This lecture should be read far and wide in the land, as a delineation of a grand, heroic and devoted hero; as evidence of the fact that the Negro, himself, has been a vindicator of his own rights, and assertor of his own freedom; as proof that emancipation, when it did come, came as a demand of the blacks, in the nation as well as a gift wrung from the white man. The lecture is important too as showing the weakness, the fear, and the imbecility of the slave power, in the face of a poor, illiterate degraded class.

Cromwell became a charter member of the American Negro Academy and a frequent contributor. Through the publishing arm of the academy, he issued a number of pamphlets, including a new edition of "The Confession, Trial, and Execution of Nat Turner, the Negro Insurgent" (1910). His textbook, *The Negro in American History* (1914), became a standard holding in college libraries across the country; the chapter "Slave Insurrections" featured one paragraph on Gabriel, three paragraphs on Denmark Vesey, and nearly three pages on Nat Turner.[62]

"The Lost Cause" and the Cult of the Faithful Slave

The image of the faithful slave, so affectionately drawn by William Sydney Drewry and others, found regular employment in the service of the "Lost Cause," an ideology that helped white Southerners transform military defeat on the Civil War battlefield into a moral and spiritual victory. First articulated in books and articles by ex-Confederate leaders and later expounded by organizations of loyal Sons and Daughters, the "Lost Cause" embodied a series of historical claims that, in effect, removed the stigma of rebellion from the Confederacy and recast its civil and military leaders as defenders of core American values. Advocates of the "Lost Cause" insisted that Confederate soldiers had not taken up arms in defense of slavery, an institution foisted on the South against its will; rather, the boys in gray — led by the venerable Robert E. Lee and Stonewall Jackson — had fought valiantly in defense of hearth and home and a way of life under attack from hostile outside forces. The loyal slaves confounded the abolitionists by refusing to abandon their wartime posts on the Southern home front for the false promise of freedom. A good many insisted on staying with their white families even after the war. In this whitewashed view of history, emancipation — and rebellion — brought only misery to the vast majority of former slaves who proved woefully ill equipped for the responsibilities of freedom and degenerated as a race without the moorings that slavery provided.[63]

Confederate Veteran magazine, founded in Nashville in 1893, provided a regular outlet for such ruminations. "Faithful Old Slaves, Degenerate Progeny," read the headline over one such essay, delivered at a Sons of Confederate Veterans memorial service in Port Gibson, Mississippi. The author, B. G. Humphreys, drew a sharp contrast between the "negro who has grown to manhood in freedom" and the "negro who grew to manhood in slavery." The civilizing, Christianizing influence of "Ole Massa" and "Ole Missus" — unknown to the post-emancipation generation of Southern Negroes, Humphreys lamented — was apparent in the loyalty of the slaves during the war.

> Left at home to work the field and make the crops to support our armies, the negro had it in his power at all times to strike the blow that would have brought the Confederacy to its knees. The first blaze of insurrection, the first scream of a murdered mistress,

would have dissolved the ranks of the Confederate armies, and every soldier "would have brooked the eternal devil" to make his way back to his home and loved one. Yet in all those long and bloody years never a torch was lighted, never a hand was raised.[64]

Other eulogists for the "old-time Negro" in *Confederate Veteran* marveled at the security enjoyed by white women on the old plantation, even when the white men — their "natural protectors" — were away at war. "These women were protected and never outraged," a Tennessean observed. "It was the coming of the carpetbagger, with his social equality, that caused many Negroes to become brutes."[65]

The claim that emancipation and Reconstruction produced a "degenerate" class of freedmen who posed a threat to Southern white civilization served as ideological justification for the assault on black civil and political rights and the rise of mob violence against African Americans at the turn of the century. In reality, political and economic competition from increasingly mobile, assertive, well-educated blacks posed an intolerable threat to white supremacy.

The continued participation of black voters in Republican and third-party challenges to white Democratic rule spurred a region-wide campaign of disfranchisement beginning in the 1890s. Southern progressive "reformers" argued that competition for the votes of black men forced white men to engage in systematic fraud and bribery; the elimination of the black vote, they maintained, would reduce corruption and remove a major source of friction between the races. To circumvent the Fifteenth Amendment, which banned discrimination on the basis of "race, color, or previous condition of servitude," the disfranchisers proposed various "race-neutral" mechanisms — poll taxes, literacy tests, property requirements — to sharply reduce, if not entirely eliminate, the black electorate. The disfranchisers attached special clauses to allow for the exemption of poor, illiterate whites and the disqualification of wealthy, educated blacks. The grandfather clause exempted from literacy and property tests those whose fathers or grandfathers were eligible to vote on January 1, 1867; African Americans were ineligible to vote in any Southern state until passage of the Reconstruction Act later that year. The "understanding" clause required prospective black voters to demonstrate, to the satisfaction of the white registrar, that they understood a passage from the U.S. Constitution or some other document. Such laws were devastatingly effective in reducing the black vote. The number of African-American voters in Louisiana, which passed its disfranchisement law in 1898, declined from 130,000 in 1896 to just 1,300 in 1904. By 1908, every state of the old Confederacy, with the exception of Florida, had passed laws and constitutional amendments that prevented all but a small percentage of African Americans from casting their votes.[66]

Friction between African Americans and whites in the urban spaces of the New South generated a rash of segregation laws. When Louisiana adopted a railroad segregation law in 1890, a group of mixed-race citizens from New Orleans decided to pursue a test case. They prevailed upon Homer Plessy, described as "seven-tenths white," to buy a ticket on the East Louisiana Railroad and sit in the "white" car. Railroad officials, alerted to his identity, ordered Plessy to leave, but he refused. The case of *Plessy v. Ferguson* went all the way to the U.S. Supreme Court, which issued its landmark decision in 1896. The Court ruled that Plessy was not denied equal protection of the laws under the Fourteenth Amendment, since the segregation law applied equally to both races. The plaintiffs had argued that "enforced separation of the two races stamps the colored man with the badge of inferiority. If this be so," the Court ruled, "it is not by reason of anything in the act, but solely because the colored race chooses to put that construction on it." Justice John Marshall Harlan, a former slaveowner, issued the lone dissent:

> The destinies of the two races, in this country, are indissolubly linked, and the interests of both require that the common government of all shall not permit the seeds of race hate to be planted under sanction of law. What can more certainly arouse race hate, what more certainly create and perpetuate a feeling of distrust between these races, than state enactments, which, in fact, proceed on the ground that colored citizens are so inferior and degraded that they cannot be allowed to sit in public coaches occupied by white citizens? This, as all will admit, is the real meaning of such legislation as was enacted in Louisiana.

The Plessy decision gave constitutional sanction to the passage of segregation laws governing virtually every public space. Should African Americans forget their place, the law deputized every white citizen to remind them.[67]

The "Faithful Slave" As Race Leader

The rise of Booker T. Washington to race leadership corresponded with the declining status of African Americans in the Jim Crow South. His program of industrial education and self-help resonated with the black business and professional classes, while his accommodationist rhetoric on race relations appeased the white ruling classes. To anxious white Southerners confronted with daily challenges to white supremacy, Washington offered a compromise: Grant us a role as skilled laborers in the industrial economy of the New South and we will cease to agitate for social and political equality. Washington skillfully evoked memories of the "faithful slave" even as he hailed the arrival of a "New Negro for a New Century."

Born in 1856 on a plantation in Franklin County, Virginia, Washington spent the first nine years of his life as a slave. After emancipation, he moved with his family to West Virginia, where he joined other freedmen working for wages in the salt furnaces and coal mines. In 1872, he traveled five hundred miles — much of the way on foot — to enroll at the Hampton Institute, a school for colored youth in Hampton, Virginia. In 1881, he accepted an invitation to establish a new state-chartered school for Negroes in Tuskegee, Alabama. Like the Hampton Institute, the Tuskegee Institute specialized in training Negroes for jobs in a rapidly industrializing New South economy. White Southerners found this model of vocational education acceptable because, in their eyes, it trained blacks for menial jobs and did not threaten the existing social order.[68]

Washington established himself as a race leader worthy of white Southern patronage and white Northern philanthropy with his famous address to the 1895 Cotton States and International Exposition in Atlanta, Georgia. He argued that the progress of the South depended on an alliance of black labor and white capital, rooted in the historical "friendship" between the races.

> As we have proved our loyalty to you in the past, in nursing your children, watching by the sickbed of your mothers and fathers, and often following them with tear-dimmed eyes to their graves, so in the future, in our humble way, we shall stand beside you with a devotion that no foreigner can approach, ready to lay down our lives, if need be, in defense of yours, interlacing our industrial, commer-

cial, civil, and religious life with yours in a way that shall make the interests of both races one.

Lest anyone misread his address as a plea for social equality, Washington added this disclaimer: "The wisest among my race understand that agitation of questions of social equality is the extremest folly. . . . In all things that are purely social we can be as separate as the fingers, yet one as the hand in all things essential to mutual progress."[69]

The "Atlanta Compromise," as the 1895 speech came to be known, signaled the ascendancy of a black leadership class that eschewed political agitation in favor of economic development and self-help. The death that same year of Frederick Douglass, an outspoken advocate for civil and political rights, symbolized the changing of the guard. Washington and his network of political operatives, known as the Tuskegee Machine, worked ceaselessly — and effectively — to silence radical opposition.

Washington reenacted the part of the "faithful slave" in his memoir, *Up from Slavery*. He recalled several scenes from his childhood on the Burroughs plantation in Franklin County, Virginia, in order to illustrate what he called the "strange and peculiar attachment" forged between black slaves and white masters under slavery. In one episode, he described the reaction of the slaves on learning that one of their "young masters" had been killed while fighting with the Second Virginia Cavalry at the Battle of Kelly's Ford in March 1863: "I recall the feeling of sorrow which existed among the slaves when they heard of the death of 'Mars' Billy.' It was no sham sorrow but real. Some of the slaves had nursed 'Mars' Billy'; others had played with him when he was a child. 'Mars' Billy' had begged for mercy in the case of others when the overseer or master was thrashing them. The sorrow in the slave quarter was second only to that in the 'big house.'"

Washington highlighted the "tenderness and sympathy" with which the slaves on the Burroughs plantation regarded their white mistresses, even as Northern troops approached and freedom beckoned.

In order to defend and protect the women and children who were left on the plantations when the white males went to war, the slaves would have laid down their lives. The slave who was selected to sleep in the "big house" during the absence of the males was considered to have a place of honour. Any one attempting to harm "young Mistress" or "old Mistress" during the night would have had to cross the dead body of a slave to do so.

For all of his tributes to the "fidelity" of the slaves on the Civil War home front, Washington made clear that the prayers of the bondsmen went out to Lincoln and the federal armies of liberation. "Even the most ignorant members of my race on the remote plantations felt in their hearts, with a certainty that admitted of no doubt, that the freedom of the slaves would be the one great result of the war, if the Northern armies conquered."[70]

Washington maintained that guilt-ridden whites grossly exaggerated the threat of black insurrection, past and present. His two-volume set *The Story of the Negro: The Rise of the Race from Slavery* (1909) included a chapter linking the history of slave insurrections to modern-day perceptions of the "Negro Peril." "The great slave insurrection which, during the whole period of slavery, was frequently expected and always feared, never actually took place; but the fear of such a general outbreak always haunted the South and helped to harden the hearts of the Southern people against the Negro race." Such fears persisted among whites nearly fifty years after emancipation. "Scarcely a month or a week has passed since the Negro became free that some newspaper has not expressed a fear or made a prediction that there was going to be an uprising or insurrection of the Negroes at some time in some part of the country. That uprising has never taken place." Washington claimed that "the nearest to anything like an insurrection of the Negroes" since emancipation occurred in the late 1870s when some forty thousand blacks, "as a result of real or fancied oppression," emigrated from Louisiana and Mississippi to Kansas. "The chances for another such movement, or for an uprising of any kind," he noted, "grow less every year." Washington accused white demagogues of stirring up race hatred by circulating rumors of impending race war. "If they really believe there is danger from the Negro it must be because they do not intend to give him justice. Injustice always breeds fear."[71]

Washington used Nat Turner's Rebellion as a measure of racial and regional progress since emancipation. In a chapter titled "Negro Bank and Moral Uplift," he called attention to a mutual banking association "started by fifteen farmers in the neighborhood of Courtland, Virginia, the home of Nat Turner." Here was evidence that the black masses of the South were putting the Tuskegee philosophy of racial uplift and self-help into practice. If Nat Turner symbol-ized "the efforts of Negro slaves to gain their freedom by force," the Southampton mutual banking association represented the glorious achievements of a race that had liberated itself from the moral bank-ruptcy of slavery.[72]

Washington's call for interracial cooperation, rooted in the histori-cal bond between slave and master, rang hollow as mob violence against blacks escalated in the Jim Crow South. In September 1906, in the midst of a race-baiting gubernatorial campaign and sensational press reports of Negro "outrages," white mobs went on a five-day ram-page through the black business district of Atlanta, destroying property and killing at least ten black people. While many African Americans fled the city or hid from their attackers, some took up arms and fired back. Washington portrayed the riot in Atlanta — the scene of his fa-mous Atlanta Exposition speech — as an isolated incident, unchar-acteristic of race relations in the South. "While there is disorder in one community," he declared, "there is peace and harmony in thousands of others." He called on black Atlantans "to exercise self-control and not make the fatal mistake of attempting to retaliate, but to rely upon the efforts of the proper authorities to bring order and security out of con-fusion." Other black leaders, noting the failure of white authorities to disperse the white mob, defended the right of black Atlantans to arm themselves in self-defense. As an agitated T. Thomas Fortune wrote in a private letter to Washington's secretary: "I cannot believe that the policy of non-resistance in a situation like that of Atlanta can result in anything but contempt and massacre of the race."[73]

Enter the "New Negro"

Though Washington continued to wield enormous political clout from his Tuskegee headquarters until his death in 1915, his inability to influence public policy through behind-the-scenes negotiations with white leaders and power brokers undermined his support among Afri-can Americans. Meanwhile, the steady migration of African Ameri-cans from the rural South to the urban North and Midwest and the general deterioration of race relations in the United States brought a new generation of black leaders to the fore after the turn of the cen-tury. These leaders, born and raised outside the South, openly rejected the accommodationist philosophy of Washington in favor of more militant strategies for social change. They had little use for the faithful slave of Washington's literary and historical imagination. Instead, they saw themselves as spiritual heirs of the rebellious slave, willing to take up the pen, if not the sword, in defense of their race.

Harvard-educated W.E.B. Du Bois, an early and eloquent critic of Washington's leadership, emerged as the spokesperson for a new generation of African Americans born after slavery and unwilling to accept "submission and silence" as the price of racial peace in the United States. Du Bois articulated a protest ethic that drew inspiration from the rebellious slave but rejected violence in favor of political action and public education. Though he had his greatest impact between 1900 and World War I, he remained an influential figure well into the civil rights era.

Born in 1868 to parents of mixed racial ancestry, Du Bois grew up in the predominantly white town of Great Barrington, Massachusetts. Upon graduating from high school, he accepted a scholarship from Fisk University, a black college in rural Tennessee, where he experienced systematic racial segregation for the first time. With his B.A. from Fisk in hand, Du Bois enrolled at Harvard, first as an undergraduate, then as a graduate student. In his memoir, "A Negro Student at Harvard at the End of the Nineteenth Century," Du Bois recalled that his doctoral work in history "began with a bibliography of Nat Turner and ended with a history of the suppression of the African slave trade to America; neither would need to be done again, at least in my day." With the completion of his dissertation in 1905, Du Bois became the first African American to receive the Ph.D. from Harvard.[74]

As a young scholar, Du Bois exhibited an abiding interest in "group-leadership" and the shaping of history by "great men," both black and white. In a 1901 review of Washington's *Up from Slavery*, Du Bois analyzed "The Evolution of Negro Leadership." The attitudes of an "imprisoned group," he wrote, could take three main forms: "a feeling of revolt and revenge; an attempt to adjust all thought and action to the will of the greater group; or, finally, a determined attempt at self-development, self-realization, in spite of environing discouragements and prejudice." The first attitude, revolt and revenge, dominated the period between the advent of the slave trade and 1750. The second attitude, adjustment and assimilation, emerged during the period between the late eighteenth century and the development of the cotton gin. A period of "local and spasmodic" Negro leadership followed, with Nat Turner leading the slaves of Southampton in armed revolt while free black leaders in the North pushed for assimilation. From 1840 on, a "dynasty" of national leaders, united in their resistance to white supremacy, held sway among Negro Americans. "Then came the reaction." Out of the "storm and stress" of the post-Reconstruction era arose Booker T. Washington and his "clear simple program" of accommodation. Du Bois identified two "strong currents" of opposition to Washington, both rooted in the past. A small but significant group, representing "the old ideas of revolt and revenge," favored emigration. A larger group, representing "the old ideal of self-development," favored programs and policies that would place Negroes on an equal footing with whites. Du Bois aligned himself with the latter group and, in time, would emerge as its leader.[75]

Du Bois considered Nat Turner one of the great men of American history, on a par with such Civil War icons as Abraham Lincoln, Jefferson Davis, and John Brown. He made the case for Turner's significance in correspondence with Ellis Paxson Oberholtzer, editor of the American Crisis Biographies series, a twenty-five-volume history of "the causes, the course, and the consequences" of the Civil War. Oberholtzer asked Du Bois if he would be willing to write the biography of Frederick Douglass, one of two "colored men" deemed worthy of inclusion in the series. Du Bois agreed. Two months later, Oberholtzer rescinded the offer, saying that Booker T. Washington wanted to write the Douglass biography and could not be persuaded to write about "some character illustrating a later period in the negro's development." A telling correspondence between the white editor and the black writer ensued:

> *Oberholtzer:* Now can you suggest any other name which you would be willing to take instead of Douglass? The name, while it must be worthy of a place beside the others in the series of twenty-five, will be only the rallying point for a great deal of historical knowledge of the time which I know you can glean, and for a point of view which I know you will give the reader in any study you undertake.
>
> *Du Bois:* If it falls within your scheme the best subject for me would be Nat Turner — around him would center the slave trade, foreign & internal, Negro insurrections from Toussaint

down to John Brown, the beginnings of the Underground railroad, the beginning of abolition, the movements of the free Negroes of the North & the whole plantation economy which was
changing critically in the thirties, and the general subjective
Negro point of view of the system of slavery.

Oberholtzer: Perhaps it might be possible to make Nat Turner the
central point for a description of the conditions prevailing in
the South in the early part of the Century. I confess, however,
that I am a little ignorant about the life of Turner and the importance of the movement he led. If his insurrection had any
permanent influence upon the development of the American
Crisis, as for instance, in making the Black Laws more stringent, and in altering relations between masters and slaves, as I
presume it may have done, I think there would be a good deal of
propriety in a biography of the man. Is there sufficient material
for such a purpose, and could he be made to appear as anything
more than a deluded prophet who led a little band of men
armed with scythes and broad axes?

Du Bois: In my opinion no single man before 1850 had a greater
influence on Southern legislation & feeling than Nat Turner
and in the North it disfranchised the Negroes of Penn. &
strengthened the black laws. There is abundant material for his
life & times. I should however not be satisfied to have you depend entirely on my opinion in this matter, but would be glad
to have you get the opinion of men like Professor MacMaster
and Professor Hart.

Oberholtzer: I fear you will think me very hard to suit, but I
should prefer, if you can see your way clear to do it, that you
should make John Brown the centre of your volume. That, I
think, will enable you to give such an account as you outline
of the Southampton and other insurrections, and the changing economic system in the South which may have been the
result of that affair.[76]

Du Bois agreed, in the end, to write a biography of John Brown for the
series. Nevertheless, he made clear to his readers that the courageous
efforts of Nat Turner and his followers inspired Brown to launch his
daring raid on Harpers Ferry.[77]

The modern-day freedom struggle, like the abolitionist movement, demanded heroes and martyrs of both races in order to succeed, according to Du Bois. Time and again as a scholar-activist, he commemorated the spirit of rebellion symbolized by Nat Turner and John Brown. He invoked both icons as founder of the Niagara Movement, a national organization of African-American elites who openly declared their opposition to Washington and his Tuskegee Machine. In July 1905, twenty-nine delegates from fourteen states answered a call from Du Bois to meet on the Canadian side of Niagara Falls. There they declared their commitment to free speech, equal rights, and ceaseless agitation. One year later, the group met in Harpers Ferry, West Virginia — the site of John Brown's raid — and reaffirmed its reformist agenda. "We do not believe in violence, neither in the despised violence of the raid nor the lauded violence of the soldier, nor the barbarous violence of the mob," Du Bois read from the group's Address to the Nation, "but we do believe in John Brown, in that incarnate spirit of justice, that hatred of a lie, that willingness to sacrifice money, reputation, and life itself on the altar of right. And here, on the scene of John Brown's martyrdom we reconsecrate ourselves, our honor, our property to the final emancipation of the race which John Brown died to make free." Du Bois went on to recite the honor roll of antislavery heroes and martyrs whose leadership, though scorned by many at the time, had been vindicated by history. "Thank God for John Brown! Thank God for Garrison and Douglass! Sumner and Phillips, Nat Turner and Robert Gould Shaw, and all the hallowed dead who died for freedom! Thank God for all those today, few though their voices may be, who have not forgotten the divine brotherhood of all men, white and black, rich and poor, fortunate and unfortunate." Thus was Turner transformed from a race warrior intent on exterminating his white enemies into an icon of interracial cooperation.[78]

As the all-black Niagara Movement waned, Du Bois joined forces with white radicals and progressives to found the National Association for the Advancement of Colored People. The organization grew out of a 1909 conference held in response to deadly mob violence against blacks in Springfield, Illinois, the birthplace of Abraham Lincoln. Sympathetic whites, invoking "the spirit of the abolitionists," invited Du Bois and other veterans of the Niagara Movement to join them in the "discussion of present evils, the voicing of protests, and the renewal of the struggle for civil and political liberty." Though Du

Bois joined a black contingent that included Monroe Trotter, Mary Terrell, Ida Wells-Barnett, Kelly Miller, and other prominent leaders, he alone assumed a leadership post in the organization that emerged from the conference. Established in May 1910, the NAACP set out to make African Americans "politically free from disfranchisement, legally free from caste, and socially free from insult." With the exception of Du Bois, who was named director of publicity and research, all of the founding officers of the NAACP were white. As editor of the NAACP house organ, the *Crisis,* Du Bois publicized the violent persecution of African Americans and disseminated his views on questions of race and class. Within eight years, the magazine boasted a circulation of more than one hundred thousand.

Du Bois sought to reach the masses with more popular forms of education while building an elite following through the NAACP's journal. He wrote two historical pageants featuring Nat Turner as one of freedom's martyrs. *The Star of Ethiopia* dramatized "the history and development of the black race" in five scenes. The first production at the 1913 Emancipation Exposition in New York City used 350 colored actors and drew 14,000 people. A subsequent production in Philadelphia placed special emphasis on "the religious development of the Negro," with Nat Turner "prominently featured" as one of "the twelve apostles of Negro Christianity." Du Bois brought Turner to the stage again in *The People of Peoples and Their Gifts to Men* (1913). The rebel leader made his appearance after the revolt of the Maroons in Jamaica, the revolution in Haiti, and the brave charge of American troops against the British, led by Crispus Attucks. Du Bois exulted at the public response to his dramatic productions. "The Pageant is the thing," he wrote. "This is what the people want and long for. This is the gown and paraphernalia in which the messages of education and reasonable race pride can deck itself."[79]

Du Bois's efforts to publicize the great achievements of "the Negro race" had little, if any, impact on mainstream popular culture. D. W. Griffith's twelve-reel silent film *The Birth of a Nation* (1915) translated the overtly racist imagery and pro-Southern historiography of Thomas Dixon's best-selling novels *The Clansman* and *The Leopard's Spots* into the new medium of moving pictures. A private showing of the film in the East Room of the White House prompted President Woodrow Wilson, a native Southerner, to exclaim, "It is like writing history with lightning. And my only regret is that it is all so terribly true." Reviving the hoary charge that Reconstruction unleashed the "black beast rapist" on a prone white South, the film included a sensational scene in which a white woman (played by Lillian Gish) leapt to her death to avoid being ravaged by a lascivious black man (played by a white actor in blackface).

Du Bois and his colleagues argued that the film, particularly two scenes depicting the Negro as a "vicious rapist," served as an incitement to antiblack violence. Houston audiences, they noted, responded to the attempted rape scenes in *Birth of a Nation* with shouts of "Lynch him!" — no idle threat to black people of that era. The *Crisis* reported that the "Lynching Industry" of the Jim Crow South produced sixty-nine colored victims in 1914, bringing the thirty-year death toll to more than 2,700. Unable to persuade the National Board of Censors to act, Du Bois and "five hundred of the most prominent white and colored people" in New York City took their complaints directly to the mayor, who agreed to have the rape scenes cut in the interest of "public peace and decency." Mass protests and civil unrest in Boston brought similar results, demonstrating both the rising assertiveness of African Americans and the benefits of an interracial civil rights movement. Still, the protests did little to keep white audiences away from the film; more than a million people, some undoubtedly drawn by the controversy, watched *The Birth of a Nation* in theaters across the country. Griffith's film, which made heroes of the robed and hooded Ku Klux Klan, contributed to the reconstitution of the secret organization that very same year.[80]

Du Bois promoted the great northward migration of African Americans, which began accelerating around 1914 and continued for more than a decade, as a rebellion of sorts against persistent antiblack violence and oppression in the Jim Crow South. He first took note of the "recent migration of colored people" in the June 1917 issue of the *Crisis*. By then, nearly a quarter of a million black workers had participated in this mass movement, with hundreds of thousands more to follow. Du Bois cited severe flooding and the infestation of the boll weevil, which left many farmers destitute and homeless, as two of the most immediate causes. Meanwhile, the outbreak of war in Europe stemmed the flow of ethnic white immigrants to the North, creating a severe shortage of "common labor" and new opportunities for black workers. Railroad companies, packing houses, foundries, factories, and automobile plants of the North and Midwest looked southward to fill their labor needs. Behind these "immediate causes" of the migration, Du Bois noted, lay a "general dissatisfaction with the conditions in the South," as documented in interviews with numerous migrants and community leaders. The deadly race riots in East St. Louis (at least thirty-nine confirmed dead, some six thousand left homeless) and other destination cities did little to quell his enthusiasm for migration. "The North is no paradise," Du Bois would write, but its cities were "safer and better" for African Americans. "We can vote in the North. We can hold office in the North. As workers in northern establishments, we are getting good wages, decent treatment, healthful homes and schools for our children. Can we hesitate? COME NORTH!"[81]

The entry of the United States into the Great War in 1917 tested the loyalties of African Americans. The failure of the government to protect the constitutional rights of its black citizens at home led some to oppose participation in what they called a "white man's war." Instead of embarking on a crusade to "make the world safe for democracy," the militant Boston editor William Monroe Trotter argued, the United States should concentrate on "making the South safe for the Negroes." Leading black newspapers — the *Baltimore Afro-American*, the *Chicago Defender*, and the *Cleveland Gazette* — expressed similar sentiments. Yet civil rights leaders countered that African Americans must support the war effort in order to secure for themselves "the rights and privileges of true and loyal citizens." Not to participate, they added, would only inflame the antiblack prejudices of white Americans.

Nearly 370,000 African Americans served in the armed forces under strict policies of racial segregation. Of that number, 42,000 served in all-black combat units. African Americans were barred from service in the marines; they were permitted to serve in the navy, but only in menial capacities. Army regulations prohibited African Americans from offices above the rank of captain, and many black officers were subjected to arbitrary transfers and court-martials. Despite the intense prejudice they encountered, hundreds of black officers and enlisted men earned commendations for meritorious service and valor from the U.S. and French governments.

Du Bois surprised and outraged many when he urged African Americans to suspend their agitation for civil rights for the duration of the war. In a July 1918 editorial in the *Crisis*, he wrote: "Let us, while this war lasts, forget our special grievances and close ranks shoulder to shoulder with our white fellow citizens and the allied nations that are fighting for democracy." With the end of the war in 1919, Du Bois called for renewed action on civil rights: "This country of ours, despite all its better souls have done and dreamed, is yet a shameful land. It *lynches*. . . . It *disfranchises* its own citizens. . . . It encourages *ignorance*. . . . It *steals* from us. . . . It *insults* us. . . ." Du Bois made no apologies for having supported the war. "It was right for us to fight. The faults of *our* country are *our* faults. Under similar circumstances we would fight again. But by the God of heaven we are cowards and jackasses if now that the war is over, we do not marshal every ounce of our brain and brawn to fight a sterner, longer, more unbending battle against the forces of hell in our own land. We *return*. We *return from fighting*. We *return fighting*."[82]

African Americans, who hoped the war would serve as a catalyst for social change at home, soon discovered that their position had actually deteriorated. In the "Red Summer" of 1919, antiblack riots in twenty-five towns and cities across the nation left nearly two hundred African Americans dead. Du Bois heralded the rising assertiveness of African Americans, ready and willing to fight back against those who would physically attack them. "For three centuries we have suffered and cowered. No race ever gave Passive Resistance and Submission to Evil longer, more piteous trial." The trial, Du Bois declared, was over. "Today we raise the terrible weapon of Self-Defense. When the murderer comes, he shall not longer strike us in the back. When the armed lynchers gather, we too must gather armed. When the mob moves, we propose to meet it with bricks and clubs and guns." Du Bois took pains to distinguish between "justifiable self-defense against individuals" and "blind and lawless offense against all white folk." He rejected the "old ideas of revolt and revenge," exemplified by Nat Turner, no less than the accommodationism of Booker T. Washington. "We must not seek reform by violence. We must not seek Vengeance." The New Negro would draw a clear line between "just resistance and angry retaliation."[83]

The "Back-to-Africa" movement of Jamaica-born Marcus Garvey offered a radical alternative for disillusioned blacks who had lost faith in transforming American society. Inspired to race leadership by Washington's *Up from Slavery*, Garvey organized the Universal Negro Improvement Association to promote race pride and unity. In 1916, Garvey moved to New York City from Jamaica, where he established the first American branch of the UNIA and began publishing a weekly newspaper, the *Negro World*. The mass migration of African

Americans from the rural South to the urban North and Midwest provided Garvey with a blue-collar constituency that rejected the middle-class agenda of the NAACP and other civil rights groups. Garvey fired their imaginations with visions of a redeemed African homeland, liberated from the thralldom of white European colonial rule by native Africans and repatriated blacks marching under the flag of the UNIA. In 1919 he launched an international shipping and transport company, the Black Star Line, which came to symbolize the UNIA program of black self-determination and economic independence. Huge parades attested to his popularity among black Harlemites, many of whom invested in his various black nationalist enterprises.

A great admirer of Toussaint L'Ouverture, Garvey imagined himself the leader of a slave rebellion. He traced his own ancestry to the famous Jamaican Maroons who rebelled against British rule in the eighteenth century.

> I wish I were born in slavery days. I would have taught someone a lesson then. If I were born eighty-four years ago in the West Indies, in the island of Jamaica, where, fortunately or unfortunately, I was born, tonight Jamaica would not have been a province of England. Jamaica would be a free and independent republic in the Caribbean Islands. But since I was not born then and I am born now, and they own that land out there, and since I am born at a time when Africa is not free, then my life, my blood will be given to Africa's redemption, Africa's freedom and Africa's liberty.

Garvey predicted that the next world war would be a "war of races," pitting the forces of Europe, led by England or France, against the "ninety million yellow and brown peoples of Asia, led by Japan." "Methinks I hear that clash, and methinks I hear the white man call: 'Brother Sambo, come over and help us.' (Laughter). Methinks I hear Sambo answering in the language of Dr. Eason: 'Call me Sambo no more. I am the new Toussa[i]nt L'Ouverture of the Negro race, and I am coming 400 million strong to carve an African imperialism and an African nationalism.'" Garvey established the Universal African Legion, a paramilitary unit, to drive the white colonialists out of Africa; in 1921, without having waged a single battle, he proclaimed himself provisional president of the Empire of Africa.[84]

Though Garvey sang the praises of Negro heroes and martyrs on numerous occasions, he rarely — if ever — placed Nat Turner in their company. Still, Garvey contributed mightily to the popularization of black history and the cultural revitalization that found expression in the Harlem Renaissance and New Negro movement of the 1920s. Like nineteenth-century advocates of black uplift, Garvey urged his black followers to build monuments to builders and heroes of the race. "We must treat our heroes, saints and martyrs and great men and women just the same as other races treat theirs; we must elevate them to the same loftiness as others have done." Where white people worshiped St. Joan of Arc, black people "should look up to St. Sojourne[r] Truth as their pattern." Where white people admired George Washington as the greatest hero of the American Revolution, black people could look with admiration on "one equally as great," "a black man by the name of Crispus Attucks, who on Boston Common shed the first drop of blood for American Independence." Where white men considered Napoleon the ablest and most brilliant leader in "the Military Field," Negroes could point to Toussaint L'Ouverture, "the great Negro General who in the plains of Santo Domingo defeated the combined armies of France, England and Spain and made his country free and independent." Black heroes of the American and Haitian revolutions provided more compelling icons for Garvey's movement than the leaders of thwarted slave conspiracies and rebellions, such as Gabriel, Denmark Vesey, and Nat Turner.[85]

Garvey's vision of an Africa redeemed from white colonial rule by armies of black people never materialized; membership in the UNIA declined precipitously after the U.S. government indicted him on charges of mail fraud related to his stock promotion scheme for the Black Star Line. The UNIA suffered another major setback when it was revealed that Garvey had met secretly with the acting imperial wizard of the Ku Klux Klan in Atlanta, Georgia, to explore their broad areas of agreement on race policy. Convicted of mail fraud in 1923, Garvey served thirty-three months in the Atlanta federal penitentiary before he was released and deported, never to return.

"The Negro Digs Up His Past"

The fighting spirit of the rebellious slave found expression in the New Negro Movement/Harlem Renaissance of the 1920s, a literary-cultural awakening that heralded the "spiritual" emancipation of black

America. No longer would African Americans allow the mythical figure of the faithful "Old Negro," manufactured by white Americans, to define them. As the literary critic Alain Locke declared in *The New Negro* anthology (1925), "The day of 'aunties,' 'uncles' and 'mammies'" was long gone; "Uncle Tom and Sambo" had "passed on." The New Negro Movement, as defined by Locke and others, promised to bring whites and blacks alike a greater appreciation for the native genius of the Negro race through its "artistic endowments and cultural contributions, past and prospective." Crucial to this enterprise was the reclamation of African-American history and folk culture as a source of race pride. The black bibliophile Arthur A. Schomburg stated the mission succinctly in his contribution to *The New Negro* anthology: "The American Negro must remake his past in order to make his future."[86]

No scholar-activist of the New Negro era did more to popularize the study of African-American history than Carter G. Woodson. He channeled his own enthusiasm for "digging up the past" into scholarly journals, history clubs, commemorative activities, and textbooks. Unlike Du Bois, he remained aloof from political activity, focusing his energies instead on the production and distribution of educational materials that would complement the efforts of mainstream black protest organizations.[87]

Woodson's path to success resembled that of Booker T. Washington, whom he admired. Born in rural Buckingham County, Virginia, in 1875, he moved with his family to West Virginia, where his work in the coal mines prevented him from entering high school until the age of twenty. He later earned his bachelor's degree at Berea College in Kentucky and became the second African American after Du Bois to receive his Ph.D. in history at Harvard.

Woodson was nearly forty years old when he founded the Association for the Study of Negro Life and History (ASNLH) with the dual aims of building self-esteem among blacks and reducing racial prejudice among whites. He secured backing for his new organization from black moderates and conservatives associated with the Tuskegee Institute, the YMCA, and the National Urban League; conspicuously absent from the board of directors were Du Bois and other "radicals" associated with the NAACP.

To promote the "scientific" study of the Negro, free from racial bias, and to disseminate the work of young black scholars denied access to mainstream professional journals, Woodson established *The Journal of Negro History* the following year. Under his editorial direction, the journal published a number of pathbreaking articles on slave resistance, including "The Aftermath of Nat Turner's Insurrection" (1920) and "The Struggle of the Negro Slaves for Physical Freedom" (1928); "The Participation of White Men in Virginia Negro Insurrections" (1931); "American Slave Insurrections Before 1861" (1937); and "Day to Day Resistance to Slavery" (1942).

The ASNLH also published textbooks, literary anthologies, and scholarly monographs through its own publishing company, the Associated Publishers. Woodson devoted considerable attention to "Negro insurrectionists" in his widely used and oft-reprinted college textbook *The Negro in Our History,* adapted for use in senior high schools as *The Story of the Negro Retold* and in elementary schools as *Negro Makers of History.* "During the years of the enslavement of Negroes," he wrote, "they were not always quiet and submissive." Woodson went on to describe the efforts of runaways and rebellious slaves to free themselves "in spite of the apparent hopelessness of their efforts." At the end of the chapter, which included a segment on Turner's Rebellion, students were asked: "Has resistance helped or hindered the Negro in America?" They would have to find the answer, of course, for themselves.[88]

In 1926, Woodson inaugurated the annual celebration of Negro History Week to "impress the thought of Negro achievement upon the public mind" within an interracial framework. The ASNLH distributed official guidelines for the celebration among schools, churches, and societies throughout the country. Among those "heroes and heroines" singled out as deserving "a high place of honor" was Nat Turner, "who lived up to the ideal of Jesus that, 'greater love hath no man than this, that a man lay down his life for his friends.'" Though Woodson sought to raise the profile of black Americans, he made it clear that Negro History Week should honor brave and noble white men too. His list of white "reformers" whom "we must not forget" included Thomas Jefferson, William Lloyd Garrison, Charles Sumner, Elijah Lovejoy, and Abraham Lincoln. "And John Brown, inspired by the example of Nat Turner, would close the chapter with that moral courage and martyrdom, which made him one of the saints of God." For Woodson, Negro history was "not a history of selected races or nations, but the history of the world void of national bias, race hate, and religious prejudice."[89]

Of all the activities sponsored by the ASNLH, historian and member Luther Porter Jackson declared in the mid-1930s, Negro History Week had "done most in reaching the people." He found it particularly significant that Southampton — "the county of Nat Turner" — was "a beehive for Negro history activity." The ASNLH applauded Mrs. Maud Weaver Winston, a schoolteacher from Southampton County, for her tireless efforts to promote Negro history, particularly in the rural areas. Yet Jackson recognized the limitations of the ASNLH as a voluntary organization that catered to a black middle-class audience and reached only a small fraction of public school teachers. "In using the term 'the people,' we can not mean all the people," Jackson wrote. "No organization, except the civil state, ever reaches such an end."[90]

Indeed, state and local officials throughout the Jim Crow South tightly controlled official textbooks and other historical narratives to promote their conservative agenda. In 1930, the rural supervisor of schools for the Commonwealth of Virginia prepared a geography supplement for use in Southampton County. Nowhere in her brief account of "the famous Nat Turner Insurrection" did she mention the fact that Turner and his followers were slaves; instead, she presented the uprising as the work of black desperadoes who launched an unprovoked attack on a peaceful white community similar to the Indian raids of frontier days. A similar proslavery synopsis of Turner's Rebellion appeared on two Southampton County highway markers, erected by the State Commission on Conservation and Development in the late 1920s. One noted the collapse of the uprising at the first sign of "resistance"; the other paid tribute to the "faithful slaves" who fought alongside their masters and defeated the rebel forces.[91]

"Bumptious Negroes" and "Rebel Daughters"

The efforts of white Southerners to memorialize the faithful slave outside the Jim Crow South generated a torrent of criticism from civil rights leaders in 1931, the one hundredth anniversary of Nat Turner's Rebellion. The United Daughters of the Confederacy precipitated the conflict when it unveiled plans to build a "Faithful Slave Memorial" at Harpers Ferry, long an African-American shrine to John Brown and the abolitionist movement. The UDC proposed to honor the memory of Heyward Shepherd, "a faithful slave murdered by Brown" during his famous raid. That Shepherd died a free man mattered little to the Confederate Daughters. They simply recast the luckless Shepherd as "an industrious and respected colored man" who, while bravely performing his duties as a night watchman for the B & O Railroad, "became the first victim of the attempted insurrection." To them Shepherd exemplified the "character and faithfulness" of all those Negroes who turned their backs on John Brown and who later refused to join the invading armies of the North during the era of the Civil War.[92]

The UDC quickly discovered that abolitionist sympathies ran deep in Harpers Ferry. On the outskirts of town stood Storer College, founded in 1867 by a Massachusetts philanthropist as one of the first institutions of higher education for African Americans. "People at the locality of the college describe the students as being very 'Bumptious,'" that is, offensively self-assertive, the Faithful Slave Memorial Committee reported. UDC members discovered, to their horror, that Storer College had taken possession of the disassembled and reconstructed John Brown Fort and transformed it into an abolitionist museum. "In it are ridiculous examples of spiked collars, handcuffs, and other freak collections exploited as the cruel relics of slavery methods." UDC members hoped that the Faithful Slave Memorial would counter these abolitionist libels and "remove a sensational means of spreading false propaganda."[93]

Town officials, for their part, feared that erection of the pro-Confederate monument might offend the Storer College students and "occasion unpleasant racial feeling in a community where we are so entirely free of it." In 1931, after more than ten years of negotiations, the UDC received permission from the mayor and town council — "the mayor at this time being the son of a Confederate veteran" — to erect the Heyward Shepherd memorial on private property. The UDC agreed, in the spirit of compromise, to remove inflammatory references from the memorial text. There would be no mention of Brown arming his followers with "pikes and staves," no reference to the "bloody massacre" that might have ensued had the slaves rallied behind Brown as planned. While the editing of the inscription on the memorial mollified local white authorities, it did little to address the concerns of African Americans who had been all but excluded from the negotiations. The black press lampooned the UDC's memorial as an insult to the memory of Brown and the brave black men who fought alongside him. "Confederates to Dedicate 'Uncle Tom' Monument," read a banner headline in the *Afro-American,* a large weekly newspaper published in Baltimore and widely circulated throughout the mid-Atlantic states.[94]

An estimated three hundred white and one hundred "colored" farmers and citizens of Harpers Ferry attended the dedication of the Faithful Slave Memorial at Harpers Ferry on October 10, 1931. Like most interracial gatherings of the day, it was a highly choreographed affair. The UDC arranged for a welcoming address by the white president of Storer College and a benediction by a prominent black minister, the Reverend George F. Bragg of Baltimore. It also designated two African Americans, a nephew of Heyward Shepherd and a man who held Shepherd's old job as the B & O Railroad's night watchman, as special guests.[95]

UDC president general Laura M. Bashinsky made clear in her keynote address that the Faithful Slave Memorial stood as a rebuke to abolitionists and their modern-day sympathizers. She noted that Frederick Douglass, upon learning of Brown's plan to arm the slaves, "shrank with horror from the proposal and predicted that any such effort would end in failure." Like most white abolitionists, she maintained, Brown was oblivious to the interests of themselves. His ill-conceived raid on Harpers Ferry did far more harm than good — a lesson symbolized in the death of the faithful night watchman, Heyward Shepherd. Bashinsky's plantation South had no place for rebellious slaves like Nat Turner. For her, the exemplary figure was the "black mammy," who cared for "her white 'chilluns'" as if they were her own. "Now I ask you," Bashinsky said, "how, under such conditions and with such existing relationships, could the sons of these 'mammies' be prevailed upon to use 'spikes and staves' against their white masters and friends? Fred Douglass was right. It could not be done."[96]

After Bashinsky had finished her speech and taken her seat, the director of the Storer College choir — an African-American woman by the name of Pearl Tattem — engaged in her own small act of rebellion. Instead of introducing the choir as scheduled, Tattem addressed herself to the crowd: "I am the daughter of a Connecticut volunteer, who wore the blue, who fought for the freedom of my people, for which John Brown struck the first blow. Today we are looking forward to the future, forgetting those things of the past. We are pushing forward to a larger freedom, not in the spirit of the black mammy but in the spirit of new freedom and rising youth." A "strange silence" fell over the audience, and several moments passed before Tattem directed the Storer College choir to begin singing "Standing in Need of a Prayer." Tattem's unscripted remarks made a mockery of the UDC's carefully staged tribute to the Faithful Slave as a symbol of interracial goodwill. At the conclusion of the dedication ceremonies, an outraged member of the UDC handed Tattem a note that read: "I wonder at your temerity. Your untimely remarks were out of place, in poor spirit, and most discourteous. Such ignorance is colossal."[97]

For the UDC, the incident illustrated the disorderly conduct of the "modern negro" and "the need for safeguarding the problem of racial adjustment." The Faithful Slave Memorial Committee noted the unwelcome presence of African Americans, "some entertaining race antagonism," at the dedication ceremonies. "Any number of sharp ears were attuned for an inciting word that could be ordered to the Masthead." There might well have been more "outbreaks" during the dedication ceremony, the committee reported, if not for "the presence of so many relatives of the Washingtons, the Allstadts, and other well-known citizens, who were seized upon that tragic night seventy-five years ago."[98]

African Americans reveled in the news that the Daughters of the Confederacy had been upstaged by the daughter of a black Union soldier. A front-page story in the *Baltimore Afro-American* — "Yankee Woman Steals Rebel Girls' Show; Confederate Daughters Gape As She Lauds John Brown" — commended the courage of "the little brown woman" whose words "cut the very vitals out of every speech that had been made." In the weeks that followed, the *Afro-American* published numerous letters and articles condemning the UDC's "Uncle Tom/Pappy Memorial" as a monument to perpetual black servitude and an insult to black manhood.[99]

One of the most powerful critiques came from the pen of J. Max Barber, director of a Philadelphia branch of the NAACP and president of the John Brown Memorial Association. Barber accused the UDC of using the monument to Heyward Shepherd as "a pretext to lie" about John Brown. "This poor Negro didn't do a single thing to merit a monument by the wildest stretch of the imagination. He ran when one of John Brown's men ordered him to halt. He certainly could not have worshipped slavery. It is a bet that he did not know what John Brown's men came for." Barber suggested that the rebel

Daughters stop "grovelling in the embers for the old ash cake of bondage" and erect a monument to real martyrs — the victims of lynching and mob violence in the Jim Crow South. Other civil rights leaders concurred. NAACP field director William Pickens called the UDC's Faithful Slave project "the sort of monument which Southerners always decide on when they want to 'honor' the Negro; a monument to a servant, a subordinate, a slave — a faithful human dog. They are not interested in monuments to Negro manhood, courage, and self-respect."[100]

The dedication of the UDC's Faithful Slave Memorial prompted calls for the erection of a countermemorial to honor the rebellious slave. In a letter dated November 11, 1931, the one hundredth anniversary of Turner's execution, the historian Rayford W. Logan invited W.E.B. Du Bois to serve on the Board of Trustees of the newly established Nat Turner Memorial Association. "While this decision had been reached before the United Daughters of the Confederacy erected a monument to the Faithful Slave at Harper's Ferry," Logan wrote, "their act makes our purpose all the more necessary." The Nat Turner Memorial Association would be led by a Board of Trustees "composed of leaders of Negro thought and action all over the country." The group's letterhead bore the names of four officers, all with Richmond addresses. Du Bois politely declined to serve on the board. "I have seen so many memorial associations come to a bad end," he wrote, "that I have made it a rule not to join them. I am sorry." Though the Nat Turner Memorial Association folded without leaving a mark on the commemorative landscape, its establishment prefigured efforts to challenge the iconography of white supremacy in the heart of the Jim Crow South.[101]

The Nat Turner Centenary of 1931

The one hundredth anniversary of Nat Turner's Rebellion in 1931, in the depths of the Great Depression and at the dawn of the New Deal era, provided an occasion for reflection on the state of race relations and the efficacy of mainstream civil rights leadership in the United States. The stock market crash of October 1929 and the economic crisis that followed produced mass unemployment among black domestic and industrial workers in the cities and left black sharecroppers and tenant farmers destitute. The black business and professional classes, which catered to segregated black communities, suffered accordingly. Racial discrimination in the distribution of relief funds and a sharp escalation in lynchings (from twenty-seven in 1929 to forty in 1930) compounded the anger and frustration of black America.

Mainstream civil rights organizations, with their focus on political and civil rights, had no answer for the economic plight of African Americans. While the black middle class continued to support the NAACP and the National Urban League, particularly at the local chapter and branch levels, a small cadre of black workers and intellectuals embraced more radical solutions. The international Communist movement, which gained a foothold among Northern black radicals after World War I, turned its attention to the American South as a locus of revolutionary struggle in the late 1920s. Communist leaders declared that black peasants and workers in the so-called Black Belt constituted a nation within a nation, with a right to self-determination. For black Southern radicals, the appeal of the party lay not in its Marxist-Leninist dogma but in its willingness to organize for racial justice and better living conditions. Black farmers in rural Alabama, assisted by Communist Party organizers, founded the Alabama Sharecroppers Union in 1931; some union members, like Ned Cobb, took up arms in self-defense and engaged in violent showdowns with union-busting planters and local white authorities. Black party membership rose rapidly, from about two hundred in 1929 to fifteen hundred in 1930, encouraging more aggressive efforts by party organizers to recruit in the South.[102]

The one hundredth anniversary of Turner's Rebellion served as a rallying point for Communist Party organizers, eager to cast their appeal to black Southern workers within the idiom of black folk culture and black history. The Turner centenary coincided with the Communist Party's legal defense of "the Scottsboro Boys," a landmark civil rights case that began in March 1931 and dragged on for more than fifteen years. The case involved nine Negro youths accused of raping two white women aboard a freight train near Scottsboro, Alabama. To thwart mob violence against the defendants, local authorities posted National Guardsmen at the jail where the "boys" — ranging in age from thirteen to nineteen — were held. Yet a weak defense by an ill-prepared lawyer and the speedy convictions of the Scottsboro Boys by an all-white jury led many to accuse the government of a "legal lynching." The judge sentenced eight of the youths to death, sparing only the thirteen-year-old because of his age.

As the date of execution approached, the Communist Party's International League of Defense (ILD) intervened on behalf of the plaintiffs. The NAACP, which rarely involved itself in local court cases, entered the fray belatedly. A bitter struggle for control of the case — and the hearts and minds of black Southerners — ensued. The Communists assailed NAACP officials as "Negro bourgeois reformers" who had betrayed "the Negro masses" and "the Negro liberation struggle." NAACP officials, in turn, accused the Communists of exploiting the Scottsboro case for the purpose of spreading "communistic propaganda" among the "colored people of the South."[103]

Black communists seized on the concurrence of "the Scottsboro Case and the Nat Turner Centenary" to criticize the mainstream civil rights organizations and rally support for the defendants. Writing in the *Liberator,* published by the Communist Party's League of Struggle for Negro Rights and inspired by the nineteenth-century abolitionist newspaper of the same name, editor Cyril V. Briggs accused the NAACP, the National Urban League, and other "reformist organizations" of collaborating with "the American bosses" in "wiping out of the consciousness of the Negro masses all memory of their glorious revolutionary traditions." The bosses, Briggs wrote, feared that such "traditions of revolt and struggle" might inspire the "Negro masses" and "stiffen their resistance to present-day sharecropper slavery, lynching, etc." And so, with the help of "prostitute bourgeois historians" and "Negro Uncle Tom reformists," they replaced the "heroic figures" of Nat Turner, Frederick Douglass, and Denmark Vesey with such "servile figures" as Booker T. Washington and his successor at Tuskegee, Robert Russa Moton.[104]

Civil rights activists, apparently stung by the criticism, responded with editorial tributes that portrayed Turner as a symbol of the revolutionary discontent that had been brewing in black America for more than a century. In "Nat Turner, A Hundred Years Afterwards," published in the NAACP's journal the *Crisis,* the Baptist minister and historian Miles Mark Fisher explored the implications of the bloody uprising for African Americans still chafing under the yoke of racial oppression in the twentieth century. "The life of Nat Turner," he opined, "is both a warning and an encouragement — a warning in showing the utter futility of armed resistance as a final settlement of a great issue; an encouragement in showing a typical Negro willing to seal his covenant of beliefs with his own blood." Fisher presented Turner as a revolutionary hero for the ages. "General Nat," he argued, deserved an honored place alongside "General Washington" in the American pantheon. Both men "essayed militantly to lead an oppressed people." Indeed, Turner was "one of the few men in the world," Fisher wrote, "whose daring vision has anticipated the ultimate course of history."[105]

The National Urban League, the other "bourgeois" civil rights group derided by the Communists, turned to Rayford W. Logan, founder of the Nat Turner Memorial Association, for its centennial tribute. A World War I veteran, Logan noted that the November 11 anniversary of Turner's execution coincided with Armistice Day, a national holiday that marked the end of "the greatest holocaust of the modern age." Logan suggested that African Americans celebrate the national holiday with Turner in mind. "To 12,000,000 black folk it should be a day of pride — for on that day one hundred years ago a black man kept his 'Rendezvous with Death' rather than live a bondsman. His simple courage surpassed the comprehension of his executioners as did that of the Man of Galilee." Logan acknowledged that African Americans faced a new set of challenges in the twentieth century. "The South no longer shackles black bodies — that is, in general. It has, however, enslaved the minds of black folk just as surely as it once did their bodies. What a glorious task on this, the one hundredth anniversary of Nat Turner's Insurrection, to dedicate ourselves to the emancipation of the minds of twelve million black folk." Logan held out hope that the "white master minds" would recognize the legitimate aspirations of the Negro to freedom and equality and respond with intelligence. "If not, who will dare predict that there will never be another Nat Turner?"[106]

The Communist Party's aggressive legal defense of the Scottsboro Boys, whose convictions were overturned by the U.S. Supreme Court on appeal, improved the party's standing among the black masses and expanded its influence among black artists and intellectuals. In 1936, after years of bashing mainstream civil rights organizations as tools of the bosses, the Communists adopted a new strategy of cooperation and cooptation known as the Popular Front. The Communist-sponsored National Negro Congress embodied the new strategy. President A. Philip Randolph, a black labor leader, announced that the group would address "the problems of black America" through the "formal integrating and coordinating of the various Negro organizations, church, fraternal, civil, trade union, farm, professional, college, and whatnot, into the framework of a united front." In an obligatory nod to the black revolutionary tradition, Randolph invoked "the spirit of Frederick Douglass and Nat Turner, of Gabriel and Denmark Vesey, of Harriet Tubman and Sojourner Truth — those noble rebels who struck out in the dark days of slavery that Negro men and women might be free."[107]

Throughout the 1930s, Communist Party propagandists mined the history of slave rebellion in America to educate, inspire, and mobilize the "New Masses." Transforming Nat Turner's apocalyptic visions of race war into an inspirational tale of working-class solidarity across the color line required a radical spin. In a 1936 article for the *New York Daily Worker*, a Communist Party newspaper, Elizabeth Lawson credited Turner's revolt with inspiring poor white farmers of western Virginia to stand up for their rights and speak out against slavery. The legislative debates that followed the revolt, she argued, marked the first stirrings of antislavery agitation among the yeomanry, a movement that culminated in the separation of West Virginia on the eve of the Civil War. "For half a century," she wrote, "the poor whites of the South had been voiceless. The slavocracy heaped degradations upon them; drove them from the last foot of fertile soil; deprived them of every civil and political right. The poor whites hated the slaveholders; they could not and dared not speak that hatred. It was the representatives of these hill-people who formed the vanguard of the attack against slavery in the 1831 debates." Proslavery legislators crushed the political insurgency by preventing "a vote on Abolition from being taken to the people." Yet they could not keep the world from learning about the impoverished condition of the South under slavery. "With the floodgates of inquiry opened, the Virginia delegates drew for the world to see the true and terrible picture of a State ruined by slavery, farms abandoned, resources wasted, industry stifled, and a white population without land, without work, without education, without rights."[108]

Red, White, and Black:
The Rebellious Slave in Art and Literature

By the mid-1930s, Americans had several stock images of Nat Turner from which to choose. There was the working-class hero and proto-Marxist revolutionary embraced by Communists. There was the religious fanatic and cold-blooded murderer of white Southern tradition. And there was the American patriot and Christian martyr celebrated by Carter G. Woodson and the Negro history movement. The publication of Benjamin Brawley's *Negro Builders and Heroes* (1937) and the scathing reviews that followed cast these three traditions in high relief. A professor of English at Howard University and the author of several popular books on Negro history, Brawley emphasized the genius of the race and its contributions to American history and culture. His seemingly indiscriminate choice of subjects, as well as his blurring of ideological distinctions among them, drew criticism from right and left.[109]

Bell Irvin Wiley, a white Southern historian who reviewed Brawley's book for the *Journal of Southern History,* questioned "the propriety of including in the roster of 'Negro Builders and Heroes' such pillaging and murdering insurrectionists as Cato and [Nat] Turner, and such murder bent characters as Gabriel and [Denmark] Vesey."

> Even more questionable is the author's devotion of more space to these insurrectionists than to men about the constructiveness of whose work there can be no doubt. What justification can there be for devoting half a page to Cato's insurrection and a half sentence to Paul Robeson's singing and acting? Why should two and one half pages be consumed in narrating the plots of Gabriel and Vesey when Countee Cullen and Langston Hughes together are dismissed with a lone short paragraph? What reason can there be for giving in a book bearing the title *Negro Builders and Heroes* six times as much space to criminal Nat Turner as to one of the nation's most eminent scientists of all time, George Washington Carver?[110]

From the other end of the ideological spectrum, Benjamin Stolberg, a white radical writing in the *Nation,* took Brawley to task for blindly embracing the "Negro insurrectionists" without any recognition of their relevance to contemporary Negro thought. "Since most of these trouble-makers are all now dead, Mr. Brawley is inordinately proud of them, without in the least understanding their revolutionary role and their lasting impact on the psychology of the American

Negro. Didn't they all get in the history books? That's enough for Mr. Brawley." Stolberg complained that conservative "race men" like Brawley who lauded black radicals and revolutionaries of the antebellum era would have nothing to do with black radicals and revolutionaries of their own day.[111]

Black writers of the Harlem Renaissance/New Negro generation leapt to the defense of Brawley and the older "Negro race history" tradition he represented. Poet Claude McKay expressed his impatience with white radicals who insisted that African Americans follow the party line in their choice of heroes. "The trouble with intellectuals like Mr. Stolberg," McKay wrote, "is that they often become so immersed in social theories that they ignore social facts. For example, it is fine old-fashioned rhetoric to name labor leaders as the only leaders of the workers. But many American workers, white and colored, are good churchgoers and also acknowledge their church leaders. There are other leaders too. Some Socialist theorists may ignore them. Hard-headed politicians don't." McKay suggested that celebrating the accomplishments of "Negro Builders and Heroes," however marginal to the revolutionary struggle, played an important role in sustaining the morale of a people long denied recognition as historical actors.[112]

The New Negro literary critic Alain Locke reminded Stolberg that compensatory racialism, in the right doses, could provide a healthy antidote to white racism. "I am not defending fanaticism, Nordic or Negro, or condoning chauvinism, black or white; nor even calling 'stalemate' because the same rot can be discovered in both the majority and the minority baskets," Locke wrote. "I merely want to point out that minority expression has its healthy as well as its unhealthy growths." Locke noted that several books published during the previous year had countered the arguments of white racial chauvinists without stooping to chauvinism themselves. Some of these literary "counter-arguments" had been written from the "racial angle," others from the "class angle." Locke declared both approaches valid so long as they produced "sound science" and "good art." He urged literary critics — Stolberg included — to evaluate the literature of the Negro on its artistic and scholarly merits rather than its point of view.[113]

African-American writers and artists who embraced the figure of the rebellious slave in the 1930s had no single motive, no single image, and no single audience in mind. Randolph Edmonds, a professor of English and drama at historically black Morgan College in Baltimore, wrote a one-act dialect play, *Nat Turner,* that was performed in Negro Little Theaters and historically black colleges and universities throughout the Jim Crow South. Though Edmonds cast Turner in the traditional black messiah/Christian martyr role, he raised the possibility that the rebel leader misread the sign from God: "Ma hands is full o' blood, too. Will dey ever be clean? Was Ah wrong, Lawd, tuh fight dat black men mout be free?"

The novelist Arna Bontemps, who rose to prominence as a poet in the Harlem Renaissance of the 1920s, secured a mainstream publisher and a national audience for his two novels dealing with slave rebellion: *Black Thunder* (1936), based on Gabriel's conspiracy, and *Drums at Dusk* (1939), based on the Haitian Revolution. Bontemps rejected Turner as the protagonist of *Black Thunder* because he could not relate to the mystical figure portrayed in "The Confessions." He was put off by "Nat's 'visions' and 'dreams'" and the "trance-like mumbo-jumbo" attributed to him by Thomas R. Gray. Gabriel's "less complicated" desire for freedom, Bontemps explained, was "a more unmistakable equivalent of the yearning I felt and which I imagined to be general."[115]

The rebellious slave attracted the attention of black visual artists and their patrons as well. In 1938, Jacob Lawrence displayed a series of forty-one small paintings on Toussaint L'Ouverture and the Haitian revolution. "I choose Haiti as my theme," Lawrence told the *New York Amsterdam News,* "because of the similarity of his status in the world today in his fight for economic freedom." Hale Woodruff painted a three-panel mural marking the one hundredth anniversary of the *Amistad* mutiny in 1939. Buell G. Gallagher, the president of Talledega College in Alabama, writing in the *Crisis,* explained why his school commissioned the *Amistad* murals for its new library. "A century ago," he wrote, "the alternative before the Negro was acquiescence or revolt. Despite much real progress in some areas, the situation has not really changed." Gallagher called on Americans "to find a third way out for the Negro — the way of constructive citizenship."[116]

The experience of artist Charles White, who featured Nat Turner and thirteen other historical figures in his social-realist mural *The Contributions of the Negro to American Democracy* (1942), illustrates the interplay of art, history, and politics in the New Deal and World War II eras. White first developed an interest in African-American history and culture as a child growing up in Chicago. After reading *The New Negro* anthology in the public library, he found himself in open rebellion against the ignorance and obstinacy of his white instructors. "I would ask my teachers why they never mentioned a Negro in history. I would bring up the name of Crispus Attucks, the first martyr of the American Revolution of 1776, or of Denmark Vesey, Nat Turner, and Frederick Douglass." His teachers "smugly" dismissed his complaints. "The histories from which we were taught, they would say, were written by competent people, and whatever they did not mention was simply not important enough to mention."[117]

Lonely and disenchanted with school, White turned to art as an outlet for his intellectual and creative energies. At the age of nineteen, he won a statewide competition for a full scholarship to the prestigious Art Institute of Chicago. Like so many African-American artists at the height of the Depression, however, he soon found himself without steady work. The federal Work Projects Administration offered relief to unemployed artists by putting them to work on public arts projects, but the director of the Illinois Arts Project "did not think that Negro people could be artists" and excluded them. White joined an artists' union that fought such discriminatory practices. "We picketed the projects," he recalled. "Finally we won. And so my first lesson on the project dealt not so much with paint as with the role of the unions in fighting for the rights of working people."[118]

A two-thousand-dollar fellowship from the Julius Rosenwald Foundation in the early 1940s allowed White to begin work on *The Contributions of the Negro to American Democracy.* He and his wife, an accomplished sculptor, set out on a tour of the Southern states for inspiration. "These two years in the South were one of the deeply shaking and educative experiences of my life," he recalled. "I was in the real home of my people, where the vast majority had lived and worked from the days when they were brutally brought in the slave ships. In many places Negro people were almost the entire population. Yet, without the right to vote, without elementary civil rights, denied any protection of courts or government, they were domineered over by a corrupt ruling clique, who had the guns, and had the reins of the police, courts, and politics in their hands." White experienced the indignities and brutality of life under Jim Crow firsthand. "In New Orleans, once, I walked into a tavern, and was brutally beaten, for Negroes were not allowed to enter such public places. In Hampton, Virginia, a streetcar conductor pulled a gun on me and could with impunity have pulled the trigger." White decided to make the struggle against such "anti-democratic forces" the theme of his mural.[119]

The *New York Times* covered the unveiling of White's mural at the Hampton Institute. "Negro Paints Story of Race in America," read the headline. The *Times* correspondent wrote approvingly of the Negro artist and his patriotic theme. "The mural, a vigorous protest against anti-democratic forces, depicts among other heroes of Negro history Crispus Attucks, first American to die in the Boston massacre; Peter Salem, who killed Major Pitcairn at Bunker Hill; Nat Turner and Denmark Vesey, who led open revolts against slavery before Emancipation." Whether the students, faculty, and visitors who gazed on the mural as they passed through the Hampton Institute's Clarke Hall recognized "the figure with the torch pointing" as Nat Turner is impossible to say. White himself expressed confidence in the ability of "the people" to read the message of the work. "Easel paintings hang in museums and galleries where they are apt to be seen only by the privileged few," he said. "But art is not for artists and connoisseurs alone. It should be for the people. A mural on the wall of a commonly used building is there for anyone to see and read its message."[120]

The Folklore of Resistance and Rebellion

The infusion of federal funds into Southern states under New Deal relief programs produced the first major attempt to document oral traditions of slavery and slave rebellion in the South. White officials in Jim Crow Virginia commissioned the Negro Studies Project, staffed and directed by African Americans and housed at the historically black Hampton Institute, to produce a state-sponsored guide called *The Negro in Virginia*, based on interviews with ex-slaves and more general scholarly research.

Field researchers interviewed as many as three hundred ex-slaves, several of whom recalled scenes from Nat Turner's insurrection as if they had witnessed the event themselves. A guide issued by the national office of the Federal Writers' Project listed more than three hundred potential questions that might be put to the ex-slaves, including this one at No. 281: "Did you ever hear of Nat Turner?" Roscoe

C. Lewis, a chemistry professor at the Hampton Institute who directed the Negro Studies Project, described the questionnaire as an effort "to secure recurring uniformity of response in order that a reasonably accurate pattern of remembrance could be established." He noted, however, that interviewers were under no obligation to use the questionnaire, and most abandoned it in favor of more open-ended interviews.[121]

Only a small fraction of the ex-slaves interviewed by African-American researchers for the Negro Studies Project made explicit references to Nat Turner or the Southampton insurrection in their recollections. Susie R. C. Byrd, a native of Virginia and a graduate of the Hampton Institute, interviewed some fifty ex-slaves in the Tidewater area. Her February 1937 interview with Mrs. Fannie Berry of Petersburg produced this recollection:

> Back 'fore the sixties I can remember my mistress, Miss Sara Ann, coming to de window an' hollering, "De niggers is arisin', De niggers is arisin', De niggers is killin' all de white folks — killin' all de babies in de cradle!" It must have been Nat Turner's Insurrection which wuz some time 'fo' de breakin' of de Civil War. I wuz waitin' on table in dinin' room an' dis day dey had finished eatin' early an' I wuz cleaning off table. Don't you know? Must have been a good size gal.

If Fannie Berry was a "good size gal" old enough to wait on tables in 1831, she would have been at least one hundred and ten years old at the time of her 1937 interview with Byrd. It seems more likely, given the inscription on her WPA photograph ("86 yrs. old") and other circumstantial evidence, that Berry recalled a later insurrection scare and confused it with Turner's Rebellion.

When Byrd interviewed Ella Williams, another elderly ex-slave from Petersburg, she heard a similar story about the excitement that prevailed as word of an insurrection in Southampton spread through the region:

> I was gittin' water fum de well fo' mammy to wash with when all a sudden Missus come drivin' up in de carriage jus' screamin' to beat de ban'. "De niggers is riz," she yelled. "De niggers is resurrrected, an' dey's killin' all de white folks." Marsa Charlie

come runnin' out wid his gun an' he say, "where is dey?" Den she say, "Down in Southampton County." An' he say, "Aw, I thought dey was in dis county," and he took his gun on back in de house 'cause Southampton County must been hundreds miles fum us.

Once again, the age of the informant — whose birth date was listed as 1836 — suggests that the scare occurred sometime after Nat Turner's Rebellion.[122]

Turner apparently lived on in African-American folk culture as a legendary figure, famous for having outfoxed the white soldiers and bounty hunters who pursued him for more than two months before his capture. Cornelia Carney of Williamsburg, Virginia, recalled that many slaves — her father included — ran away and hid in the woods, never to be found by their masters. "Niggers was too smart fo' white folks to git ketched," she said. "White folks was sharp too, but not sharp enough to git by old Nat." The reference to "Nat" caught the attention of the interviewer, who asked Carney to elaborate. "Nat?" she said. "I don't know who he was. Ole folks used to say it all de time. De meanin' I git is dat de niggers could always out-smart de white folks. What you git fum it?"[123]

The most revealing account of Turner's Rebellion to emerge from the interviews of ex-slaves came from centenarian Allen Crawford of North Emporia, Virginia. Born in Southampton County, just three miles from where the uprising began, Crawford crafted his narrative out of oral traditions rooted in an intimate local knowledge of people and places associated with the rebellion. He knew the names of the Southampton County militia units ("Blues and Reds") and the two female house servants ("Lucy and Charlotte") who divided the clothes of their presumed-dead mistress ("Miss Venie Frances"). Crawford did not shrink from the gut-wrenching violence of the uprising and its suppression as so many bourgeois historians did. His narrative, as written down by Susie R. C. Byrd, featured the most gripping scenes: Turner reluctantly killing his mistress's baby (an act attributed to fellow insurgents Henry and Will in Turner's "Confessions"); the brief reign of the slaves over the Francis household; and Turner's own dramatic escape, capture, and execution. The narrative, as recorded by Byrd, captured the "voice" of the ex-slave, complete with mocking laughter ("ha, ha, ha"). Crawford did not say — and his interviewer probably did not ask — how he came to know what he knew about the insurrection. His credibility as a storyteller rested on his family ties to those who had witnessed the event and lived to tell the story.[124]

With the interviewing of ex-slaves completed by the summer of 1937, the publication phase of the Negro Studies Project began. Project director Roscoe C. Lewis drew heavily on the ex-slave narratives in drafting the text for *The Negro in Virginia,* a historical travelogue that covered the three-hundred-year journey of "the Negro race" from indentured servitude and slavery to second-class citizenship. Excerpts from the slave narratives, quoted liberally throughout the book, challenged the plantation legend of faithful slaves and kindly masters. The manuscript went through at least four revisions before it was published in 1940 to rave reviews.[125]

The heavy editing of *The Negro in Virginia* by the white supervisor of the Virginia Writers' Project — who declared herself "entirely sympathetic with the Negro's desire for equality of opportunity" — did little to blunt the antislavery/prodemocracy thrust of the book and its implicit critique of the plantation legend. Chapters on slave punishment ("Thirty and Nine") and the domestic slave trade ("Sold to Georgia") immediately preceded the chapter on slave revolts ("Slave No More"), suggesting that the mistreatment of slaves and the harsh conditions of slavery led to rebellion. The authors further legitimized antislavery violence by comparing rebellious slaves to the American revolutionaries who fought at Bunker Hill and Yorktown. The "spirit of freedom" that filled the air during the American Revolution, they noted, had "rekindled in Negroes the hope of liberty." That spirit continued to burn within the slaves long after the nation had achieved its independence. A series of "deliverers," from Gabriel to Nat Turner, arose from among the enslaved masses. "While his fellow slaves danced," they wrote, "young Nat Turner brooded in silence on July 4, 1826, the fiftieth anniversary of American independence." The authors portrayed Turner as a mystic who, guided by voices from heaven and passages from his "well-worn Bible," followed in the footsteps of "the great man Jesus Christ, to whom also visions had appeared and spirits talked." The account of Turner's Rebellion that followed left no doubt that the authors considered the rebel leader a hero and martyr, worthy of veneration. "And on November 11, Armistice Day now — commemorative of a million others who died for freedom — Nat swung from an old tree in Jerusalem."[126]

A far less flattering picture of Turner and his followers emerged from the other side of the color line that divided the Virginia Writers' Project into Negro and white units. Here is how the white unit that produced *Virginia: A Guide to the Old Dominion* (1940) character-ized the rebellion for those considering a leisurely drive through Southampton County along State Highway 35:

> Plantations bordering this road from Boykins to Courtland (at that time called Jerusalem) were in August 1831 the scene of the greatest slave uprising in the history of the United States. Leader of the uprising was one Nat Turner, who had taught himself to read the Bible and had impressed upon his followers that he had Divine guidance to free the slaves of the neighborhood and "go into Jerusalem." The county seat was the only Jerusalem known to Turner. Negroes at a Sunday camp meeting, exhorted to frenzy by Turner, armed themselves with corn knives, axes, and scythes and followed him in an orgy of butchery.

The brief historical sketch gave a precise tally of whites killed by the insurgents, "including 12 pupils of a girls' school," but made no men-tion of reprisals against blacks, noting only that "many slaves were killed by the soldiers." Where the black authors of *The Negro in Virginia* portrayed Turner as a Christian martyr and American patriot in the tradition of the Founding Fathers, the white authors of *Virginia: A Guide to the Old Dominion* saw only ignorance and religious fanaticism at work in the "orgy of butchery" orchestrated by the rebel leader. Virginia would retain a divided historical conscience. [127]

Revolt Among the Academics

Demographic changes within the historical profession and the steady demise of scientific racism (discredited, in part, by the racial theoriz-ing of Adolf Hitler) contributed to a revisionist assault on the South-ern citadel of proslavery historiography in the late 1930s and early 1940s. A small cadre of white dissidents — several of them Jewish — joined African-American scholars in challenging the pro-Southern view of slavery as an efficient system of labor and a model system of racial control. Their work set the stage for a major paradigm shift in slavery studies after World War II, when liberal scholars forged a new consensus emphasizing slave resistance and slave rebellion.[128]

A flurry of revisionist scholarship emerged from the graduate seminar of Northwestern University anthropologist Melville Herskovits. Once an advocate of assimilation, Herskovits began to see the value of a distinctively African-American cultural heritage, with roots in Africa, to the African-American freedom struggle. If American Negroes were to "fight back" against discrimination, he reasoned, they needed a source of inspiration that lay outside the mainstream of American culture. Herskovits encouraged his graduate students to study the records of slave revolts and slave resistance in the United States for the roots of African-American resistance. Several of their articles appeared in leading academic journals of Negro and Southern history and, before long, influenced the work of other scholars.[129]

The first of several articles on slave insurrections by Herskovits student Harvey Wish, "American Slave Insurrections Before 1861," appeared in the July 1937 volume of the *Journal of Negro History*. Wish argued that the "romantic portrayal of ante-bellum society on the southern plantation," with its images of "contented slaves and kindly masters," obscured the "true picture" of slave unrest and domestic insecurity revealed in private letters, trial records, slave codes, and other historical documents. Wish revisited the theme of slave discontent in an article titled "Slave Disloyalty in the Confederacy," published in the *Journal of Negro History* in October 1938. Once again, he dismissed Southern planters' accounts of "faithful slaves" as antiabolitionist propaganda and a "psychological escape" from reality. Wish cited the enduring legacy of "Turner's bloody insurrection" in "The Slave Insurrection Panic of 1856," published in the *Journal of Southern History* in May 1939. Tales of the Southampton revolt "were yet unforgotten," he wrote, when "wild rumors of an all-embracing slave plot extending from Delaware to Texas" swept across the Southern states that election year.[130]

Herskovits students Raymond A. Bauer and Alice H. Bauer extended the concept of slave resistance beyond the more "spectacular" episodes of slave revolt in "Day to Day Resistance to Slavery," published in the *Journal of Negro History* in October 1942. The Bauers found evidence of covert resistance to slavery in the overt behavior of slaves, such as the "accidental" breaking of tools or the "careless" mistreatment of livestock. "There is, indeed, a strong possibility that this behavior was a form of indirect aggression," they wrote. Hardly the "cheerful, efficient worker" described by proslavery historians, the American Negro slave was "frequently rebellious, and almost always sullen, as any person faced with a disagreeable situation from which he cannot escape will normally be."[131]

Herskovits himself used the revisionist scholarship on slave revolts to debunk racist theories of black inferiority in his book *The Myth of the Negro Past* (1941). The idea that Negroes acquiesced to slavery, he argued, was an "integral part" of a myth that provided "one of the principal supports of race prejudice" in the United States. "Unrecognized in its efficacy, it rationalizes discrimination in everyday contact between Negroes and whites, influences the shaping of public policy where Negroes are concerned, and affects the trends of research by scholars whose theoretical approach, methods, and systems of thought presented to students are in harmony with it." Anxious to demonstrate the more general character of slave discontent, Herskovits chose not to recount the details of the "famous" slave revolts led by Gabriel, Denmark Vesey, and Nat Turner. Yet he did find one biographical detail worthy of note. "It is not without interest to learn that Nat Turner, the leader of one of the most important slave revolts, was almost a victim of his mother's frantic refusal to bring another slave into the world. Herself African born, she is said 'to have been so wild that at Nat's birth she had to be tied to prevent her from murdering him.'" In this anecdote, Herskovits found evidence of slave resistance as a cultural survival, transmitted from African-born mother to American-born son.[132]

The most influential scholar of slave rebellions to emerge from the growing cadre of revisionists in the mainstream academy was Herbert Aptheker, whose magesterial *American Negro Slave Revolts* remains a standard work in the field. Aptheker was born in Brooklyn, New York, in 1915. His father was a manufacturer; his mother, a union organizer. Aptheker became radicalized as a high school student during the Great Depression. "The most flagrant injustice in the 1930s," he recalled, "was the oppression of Black people, which was open, naked, blatant, institutionalized, and in many areas legalized. This naturally attracted my attention." Aptheker accompanied his father on a trip from New York to Alexander City, Alabama, in the 1930s. "This was during the depths of the Depression when it was bad in the North and bad for white people, but it was starvation in the South for Black people, absolute starvation. I had never seen this." After five weeks on the road, Aptheker returned home and wrote a series of columns called "The Dark Side of the South" for his high school newspaper. "I never stopped studying the question after that."[133]

As a graduate student in the history department at Columbia, Aptheker found little interest in black history among his colleagues. "History in those days was almost unbelievably racist," he recalled. "People like U. B. Phillips were the authority on what it meant to be a Black slave. I just knew these things were not true, could not have been true. So that sort of gave me a lifetime work in history, an effort to investigate this and to find out what really happened." Aptheker eventually would develop close professional ties with black historians, such as Carter G. Woodson and W.E.B. Du Bois, but he did not know their work well at the time. "When you went to school in those days, you didn't learn that."[134]

Aptheker chose Nat Turner's Rebellion as the topic for his master's thesis. As a budding Marxist historian, he believed that the application of scientific, humanist, antiracist principles would change the way history judged Turner. "One need not find himself in the dilemma of acclaiming one man as a martyr because he is white, and calling another man a wretch because of some degree of coloration." Aptheker hoped that the Negro masses of the twentieth century would see their own revolutionary potential in the courageous deeds of the slave insurrectionist. "Nat Turner was one who refused to 'be reasonable,' and it is believed that as the present-day stirrings of the American Negro people grow, the significance of the Turner Revolt as a tradition of progressive struggle will increase."[135]

Aptheker took William Sidney Drewry's study of Turner's Rebellion, with its racist assumptions and proslavery conclusions, and turned it on its head. Drewry stated that Southampton County was enjoying great prosperity at the time of the uprising; Aptheker described a region in the throes of economic depression. Drewry claimed that the slaves in Southampton County had shown no inclination to rebel; Aptheker pointed to evidence of general slave unrest in Virginia and North Carolina shortly before the uprising. Drewry emphasized the lax supervision of slaves in Southampton County; Aptheker described the passage of "new repressive legislation" in Virginia just five months before the uprising. Drewry noted that Turner, by his own admission, belonged to a kind master at the time of the uprising;

Aptheker pointed out that Turner had been owned previously by other masters and that he had run away from one of them "after a change in overseers." Drewry attributed the uprising, in part, to the influence of abolitionist propaganda; Aptheker found no evidence that abolitionist propaganda of any type "had any connection whatsoever with bringing on the Turner Revolt." Drewry downplayed the lynching of Negroes in the aftermath of the uprising, saying "as many guilty negroes escaped as innocent ones perished"; Aptheker reversed the moral calculus, saying "at least as many Negroes were killed without a trial as whites had perished due to the Revolt." Aptheker took a parting shot at Drewry in his bibliographical entry for *The Southampton Insurrection:* "The book is valuable for the rumors and reminiscences it presents. It is notable for exceedingly poor documentation and often very uncritical and contradictory statements. The pictures are the best part of the book."[136]

In 1938, Aptheker headed south and began the archival research for his dissertation. He found clandestine support for his project among the black laboring classes of the South. "During one memorable search, a janitor led Herbert into an archival collection in the dead of night, and found the materials he had otherwise been unable to obtain." Aptheker combined scholarly activity with social and political activism during his stay in the South. He worked with such radical groups as the Food and Tobacco Workers Union, the Abolish Peonage Committee, and the Southern Negro Youth Congress. He joined the Communist Party in 1939 and never repudiated it, as so many radical scholars and intellectuals later did. Aptheker enlisted in the army in 1942, two months after the United States entered World War II, and continued to work on his dissertation while training as an officer. He completed the manuscript the following year, just months before shipping out for active duty in the European theater.[137]

In *American Negro Slave Revolts,* Aptheker boldly proclaimed his revisionist thesis that "discontent and rebelliousness were not only exceedingly common, but, indeed, characteristic of American Negro slaves." More startling, perhaps, was his claim to have found "records of two hundred and fifty revolts and conspiracies in the history of American Negro slavery." Aptheker defined an "insurrection or conspiracy" as having "a minimum of ten slaves involved; freedom as the apparent aim of the disaffected slaves; [and] contemporary references labeling the event as an uprising, plot, insurrection, or the equivalent of these terms." In using sketchy, unverifiable reports of insurrectionary activity among the slaves as the basis for his scientific survey, Aptheker left himself open to legitimate scholarly criticism of his methodology. Nevertheless, his book documented the widespread fear of rebellion that kept the slave regime on edge and spurred the development of "complex and thorough systems of control."[138]

To some historians, Aptheker succeeded brilliantly in documenting unrest among the slaves and anxiety among the masters. The author of *American Negro Slave Revolts* had "done much to destroy the legend that the slaves, as a whole, accepted their situation," wrote a reviewer for the *English Historical Review.* "The concept of slavery as a kind of idyll, in which gracious white masters mingled genially with their dusky serviots and white folks sat on high-columned plantation porches with mint juleps in hand, to enjoy the singing of happy field workers, fades away in the light of an impressive chronicle of events." Other historians complained that Aptheker accepted abolitionist propaganda at face value and ignored evidence that flatly contradicted his thesis. J. G. de Roulhac Hamilton, writing in the *American Historical Review,* dismissed the book as a Garrisonian libel against the masters. Aptheker "exaggerates the rebellious character of the slaves quite as much as most writers have magnified their docility. He apparently accepts every rumor as fact, and most of the study deals with rumor, much of it of doubtful origin and most of it unverified."[139]

Prominent mainstream historians soon joined Aptheker in the revisionist assault on proslavery historiography and the plantation legend. In 1944, Richard Hofstadter — one of the leading scholars of the post–World War II era — published an article in the *Journal of Negro History* that signaled the changing of the guard within the historical profession. Hofstadter described U. B. Phillips, the Georgia-born author of *American Negro Slavery* (1918) and *Life and Labor in the Old South* (1929), as a shameless propagandist for the planter class, with a "characteristically Southern" bias against the Negro. "His books can best be placed in the course of our intellectual history when it is realized that they represent a latter-day phase of the pro-slavery argument." Hofstadter concluded that the time had come for historians who shared the "limitations" of Phillips's view to step aside in favor of others who would "realize that any history of slavery must be written in large part from the standpoint of the slave."[140]

· · ·

In the decade between the Great Depression and World War II, a loose coalition of antiracist scholars, writers, artists, and activists placed the rebellious slave in the vanguard of the twentieth-century movement for civil rights and democracy. Not since the days of Reconstruction had African Americans and their radical white allies joined forces in such a bold display of common purpose and collective memory. Their efforts to breach the color line and desegregate historical consciousness prefigured the work of novelists James Baldwin and William Styron in the civil rights era.

The growing demand for popular literature that spoke to the roots of black rage and the agony of race relations in America was confirmed by the critical and commercial success of Richard Wright's novel *Native Son*. Its protagonist, Bigger Thomas, driven to madness by racial oppression, murders a white woman and burns her body. Published in 1940, the book sold 200,000 copies within three weeks of its publication and became the first book by an African-American writer to be featured in the Book-of-the-Month Club. Yet the nostalgic appeal of the plantation legend and the mythology of the "Lost Cause" remained strong. That same year, 25 million moviegoers flocked to see *Gone With the Wind*, the Hollywood version of Margaret Mitchell's novel about a Southern family's travails during the Civil War and Reconstruction. Shorn of offensive scenes by the producer and vetted by civil rights groups, the movie featured strong black characters in traditional roles of maids and butlers. Hattie McDaniel's performance as "Mammy" won her an Oscar for best supporting actress, the first such honor bestowed on an African American. Progress?[141]

Sterling Brown, a poet and literary critic at Howard University who coordinated the collection of ex-slave narratives for the Federal Writers' Project, probed the cultural synapses of memory and amnesia in "Remembering Nat Turner." The poem, which occupied a full page in the February 1939 issue of the *Crisis*, described a modern-day pilgrimage to Southampton County, where "Old Nat" made "his angry stab for freedom a hundred years ago." The unidentified pilgrims, who travel by automobile, find the scene of the rebellion "quiet," the night air "still"; only the mist "rising" now. The local residents they encounter, white and black, seem almost willfully ignorant of Nat Turner and the cataclysmic events of 1831. As they drive back to Courtland, "along the way that Nat came down upon Jerusalem," the pilgrims reflect on Turner's legacy for the freedom struggles of the twentieth century.

> We wondered if his troubled spirit still roamed the Nottaway,
> Or if it fled with the cock-crow at daylight,
> Or lay at peace with the bones in Jerusalem.[142]

5

COMMEMORATIONS

T HE REBELLIOUS SLAVE so openly embraced by artists, writers, and scholars in the radical thirties became something of a fugitive in the two decades that followed. The nationalism of World War II discouraged all but the most patriotic expressions of dissent, while the conservative climate of early cold war America proved inhospitable to radicals, past or present, who dealt in moral absolutes and refused to work within the system. Mainstream civil rights leaders argued that African Americans desired nothing more than peaceful assimilation into the mainstream of American life. "Old Prophet Nat" made a poor spokesman for the patient legal strategy pursued by the NAACP in its landmark school desegregation cases of the 1940s and 1950s; his call to rise and slay clashed with the philosophy of nonviolent protest espoused by the Reverend Martin Luther King, Jr., the nationally recognized leader of the post-1954 movement. While Turner remained a revered figure in African-American oral tradition and Negro history educational materials, his memory played no significant role in the King-led campaign for civil rights, social justice, and racial equality in America.

The stature of the rebellious slave began to rise in the 1960s as the civil rights movement, energized by student leadership, took to the streets. Media coverage of nonviolent protest and civil disobedience — sit-ins, "Freedom Rides," marches, and mass demonstrations — stirred public interest in slavery and the historical roots of the modern-day "Negro revolt." In his famous "I Have a Dream" speech at the 1963 March on Washington, King reassured white America of the movement's commitment to nonviolence and interracial harmony. Yet some black activists, repeatedly assaulted by white segregationist mobs, began to question the efficacy of nonviolence as a means of social change. Radical voices from outside the civil rights movement made themselves heard as well. Malcolm X, who rose to prominence as spokesman for Elijah Muhammad's Nation of Islam and later founded the Organization of Afro-American Unity, urged black people to liberate themselves "by any means necessary." Integration, he argued, was a trap; black people needed to control their own institutions, write their own history, chart their own destiny. By 1965, many black actiwvists who once followed King looked to the late Malcolm X and his idol, Nat Turner, for inspiration.

The October 1967 publication of William Styron's novel *The Confessions of Nat Turner* returned the rebellious slave to broad public consciousness and spurred the most intense debate over Turner's memory since the era of Reconstruction. The first wave of book reviews highlighted the parallels between the slave uprising of 1831 and the race riots of 1967; the writers, included some of the best-known historians and literary critics in the country, praised Styron for accurately depicting the horror and degradation of slavery and its legacy of racial hatred and racial violence in contemporary America. Black critics, invoking key principles of Black Power, accused Styron of defaming their ancestors and distorting their history. They charged that the white Southern author, aided and abetted by the white-controlled media, perpetuated racist stereotypes about black men lusting after white women. The black backlash against the novel, culminating in a volume of essays (*William Styron's Confessions of Nat Turner: Ten Black Writers Respond*), overshadowed the protests of white Southern partisans who complained that Styron had defamed *their* ancestors and distorted *their* history. Styron's efforts to create a common history, merging the perspectives of slave and slaveholder, satisfied the descendants of neither. To this day, the Styron controversy remains a focal point for historians and literary critics interested in race, memory, and the cultural politics of the civil rights and Black Power eras.

The Rise of the Modern Civil Rights Movement

Membership in mainstream civil rights organizations, which languished during the economic crises of the 1930s, surged during World

War II. Adolf Hitler's goal of world domination by the so-called Aryan master race discredited scientific racism in the United States and provided civil rights activists with new ammunition for an assault on Jim Crow laws and customs. Their patriotic "Double V" campaign called for victory over racism at home and fascism abroad. African-American labor organizer A. Philip Randolph joined with civil rights leaders to push for the desegregation of the military and defense-related industries. The threat of a peaceful march on Washington prompted President Franklin Roosevelt to establish the Committee on Fair Employment Practices to investigate complaints of racial discrimination. Wartime demand for labor created new opportunities for rural black Southerners to enter the industrial economy. Two million African Americans found work in newly desegregated defense plants; black membership in labor unions doubled by the war's end.

While the war reinvigorated mainstream civil rights groups and accelerated social and cultural trends crucial to mass mobilization, wartime nationalism stifled radical dissent and drove the rebellious slave, as a symbol of black militancy, into hiding. Alarmed by race riots in Harlem and Detroit and rumored uprisings in the South, civil rights leaders sponsored "Good Conduct" campaigns that discouraged assertive behavior. Black radical membership in Communist Party organizations declined as the Soviet Union, closing ranks with its American allies, abandoned its aggressive support of the black freedom struggle during the war. African Americans saw far more to be gained by stressing their wartime patriotism, symbolized by the contributions of black defense workers and more than a million black soldiers, than by invoking the insurgent spirit of the rebellious slave.

The civil rights successes and economic gains of African Americans during World War II, modest though they were, heightened expectations of more substantial reforms after the war. The continuing migration of African Americans into the cities of the North and Midwest, meanwhile, expanded the numbers and enhanced the political clout of black voters. The Democratic Party, once dominated by white segregationists from the "Solid South," fractured as African Americans and their liberal white allies placed civil rights on the national agenda. In 1947, President Harry Truman's Committee on Civil Rights issued a landmark report calling for "the elimination of segregation based on race, color, creed, or national origin from American life." When the national Democratic Party included a pro–civil rights plank in its 1948 platform, white Southern Democrats walked out of the convention and formed their own States' Rights Party. The Dixiecrats, as they became known, nominated the segregationist governor of South Carolina, Strom Thurmond, for president. The Dixiecrat ticket carried four Southern states — South Carolina, Alabama, Mississippi, and Louisiana — but Truman and the Democrats won the election, thanks in large part to black voters in closely contested California, Illinois, and Ohio.

The conservative cultural politics of the cold war years ensured that Nat Turner would not enjoy a Popular Front revival in arts and literature. As the Truman administration committed the United States to the worldwide containment of Soviet expansion and Communist influence, a new "Red Scare" swept the United States. American fears of subversion by card-carrying Communists and Communist sympathizers ("pinkos") were easily manipulated by demagogues seeking to discredit their reform-minded foes. Mainstream civil rights organizations, the frequent targets of anti-Communist propaganda and harassment, severed their ties with radical groups and denied any revolutionary intent. Turning anti-Communist rhetoric to their own purposes, they argued that the extension of civil rights to African Americans would deprive the Communists of a powerful source of anti-American propaganda, particularly in the nonaligned nations of the Third World.

Oddly enough, the best evidence for the irrelevancy of the rebellious slave to mainstream African-American social and political thought in the late forties comes from a scholarly study that concluded just the opposite. Peter Rodgers Brown, a master's degree candidate at the Oberlin Graduate School of Theology, detected a significant rise of Turner in historical consciousness, linked to a growing restiveness among those who felt "hampered and restricted" by Jim Crow laws and other discriminatory practices. Brown drew heavily on his own personal experience in developing his thesis. Born and raised in the Southampton County village of Newsoms, "ten miles from the spot of the death of Turner," he was schooled in an African-American oral tradition that celebrated the faith, courage, and intelligence of the rebel leader. "I was constantly thrown into contact with persons who used Turner to sanction their many deeds and actions," he recalled. "Parents used him to show their children that only courage would indeed help them. They often said, 'After Old Nat's fray the masters were afraid of the slaves, so they kept them fooled.'" It was this oral tradition that inspired Brown to investigate Turner's Rebellion as an enduring influence in African-American life.[1]

As part of his thesis research, Brown set out "to secure from prominent contemporary thinkers their ideas concerning the Nat Turner insurrection" and its place in Negro thought. Among those who received surveys were Father M. J. Divine, the leader of a religious sect with a large interracial following based in Philadelphia; Luther P. Jackson, a historian and voting-rights activist at Virginia State College; John Hope Franklin, a historian at Fisk University and author of the widely used textbook *From Slavery to Freedom;* and W.E.B. Du Bois, the *éminence grise* of black scholars. Question one dealt with the immediate impact of the rebellion, circa 1831–32; questions two through five dealt with the place of Nat Turner in popular culture and professional historiography, circa 1948.[2]

Brown's survey piqued the interest of Father Divine, who confessed that he had "not thought" of Nat Turner's Rebellion "for quite some time." What he knew of Turner, he said, came not from the "literary historical record" but from oral tradition — or "natural history," as he called it. Once, while traveling through Southampton County, he stopped for the night at a farmhouse in the Cross Keys, not far from where the uprising began. The local residents informed him — erroneously, perhaps for dramatic effect — that Turner and his pregnant wife were tied to a tree, stripped, and shot to death not far from the house where he was staying. "One man was telling ME how his old master was the one who helped do the killing." The master, a small man with a soft voice, spoke with bluster and bravado in the presence of the lynch mob: "Let me get there!" he roared. "Let me shoot him! Let me have a chance at him!" The scene, as reenacted by Father Divine, delighted everyone in the room. "It is wonderful," Father Divine agreed. History seemed so much "more real," he noted, when narrated in this way.[3]

Father Divine attributed Turner's relative obscurity to a dearth of historical documentation. "We don't have as much literary historical record of him as we do John Brown." He also speculated that Turner's efforts to free himself and his fellow slaves were seen by many as self-serving and, thus, less worthy of commemoration. "That is why I say that if anyone can do anything unselfishly, internationally and interracially, it would be considered more as of some count than that which could be done selfishly or personally or racially or nationally or from any other point of view pertaining to self, that self would motivate it." When one of his secretaries suggested that Nat Turner's Rebellion "started the emancipation" of the slaves, Father Divine agreed. "But evidence shows that by what you see and by what you know, CRIME DOES NOT PAY, and it is not advantageous to use violence and destruction, for I did say: 'He that fighteth by the sword, shall by the sword perish.' It may sound foolish, but yet it is true."[4]

Du Bois, then in his seventy-ninth year, answered Brown's survey in a brusque and dismissive note.

> *Brown:* How important a part does the Nat Turner insurrection play in current Negro thought — that is, in religion, journalism, political propaganda, contemporary philosophy of American history, prejudices, etc.?
>
> *Du Bois:* The insurrection has practically no influence at present because it is forgotten.
>
> *Brown:* What ideas, if any, are there peculiar to Negro thought of today which stem directly from the insurrection?
>
> *Du Bois:* None that I know of.

Du Bois had little reason to believe that the rebellious spirit of Nat Turner lived on in African-American thought of the post–World War II era. His radical politics clashed with the liberal anti-Communism of the mainstream civil rights organizations. Rehired by the NAACP as director of special research in 1945, Du Bois quickly alienated himself from the leadership. In 1946, he addressed a meeting of the Southern Negro Youth Congress, an arm of the Communist-sponsored National Negro Congress. In 1947, he coordinated an appeal to the U.N. Commission on Human Rights on behalf of African Americans. In 1948, he supported the Progressive Party presidential campaign of Henry Wallace, a Socialist. For these and other transgressions, Du Bois was fired by the NAACP. His continued work with radical organizations led to his indictment in 1950 as an alleged agent of a foreign government.[5]

For Du Bois, once a towering figure in the civil rights movement, to declare Turner's Rebellion entirely "forgotten" must have surprised and disappointed Brown. The young scholar made no mention of his correspondence with the professor emeritus in his footnotes or bibliography. Ignoring the results of his own survey, Brown steadfastly maintained that interest in Nat Turner was on the rise. He cited two "recent articles" as evidence: the published transcript of Father Divine's office talk, prompted by his survey, and a single-panel Negro history cartoon called "They'll Never Die" published in the *Norfolk Journal and Guide*. From these scant sources, it appears that the Turner revival was largely of Brown's own making. Nevertheless, Brown believed that Turner offered African Americans a powerful source of inspiration in the fight against Jim Crow. "He will one day be called blessed, not only by his own people, but by the descendants of the 'masters.'"[6]

By the late 1940s, the legal scaffolding that undergirded the segregation and disfranchisement of African Americans in the Jim Crow South had begun to buckle. In 1946, the U.S. Supreme Court overturned a Virginia law that required all passenger motor vehicle carriers to separate their white and colored passengers. Two years later, the Court declared racially restrictive housing covenants unconstitutional. Victories in two major court cases challenging segregation in professional and graduate schools — *Sweatt v. Painter* (1950) and *McLaurin v. Oklahoma Board of Regents* (1950) — convinced Thurgood Marshall, chief counsel for the NAACP Legal Defense Fund, that the time had come to challenge *Plessy v. Ferguson* and its "separate but equal" doctrine head-on.

In 1952, a divided U.S. Supreme Court agreed to hear oral arguments in five NAACP-sponsored cases from across the country — South Carolina, Virginia, the District of Columbia, Delaware, and Kansas — combined and docketed as *Brown v. Board of Education of Topeka*. A vote to have the cases reargued, with input from the Eisenhower administration, bought time for the Court to build a consensus under newly appointed Chief Justice Earl Warren. It also allowed the NAACP to introduce social scientific evidence showing that racial segregation stamped black children with a "badge of inferiority" and damaged their self-esteem. On May 17, 1954, the Supreme Court announced its unanimous decision: "We conclude that, in the field of public education, the doctrine of 'separate but equal' has no place. Separate educational facilities are inherently unequal." Though the *Brown* decision applied only to public education, Jim Crow had been dealt a mortal blow. The Court did not say how it intended to enforce the ruling; instead, it invited all of the parties involved, as well as the U.S. attorney general, to submit briefs on how the ruling might be implemented.

The ruling met with stiff resistance, bordering on open defiance, from white Southern officials. Georgia governor Herman Talmadge proclaimed that enforcement of the court ruling would "create chaos not seen since Reconstruction days." The U.S. senator Harry F. Byrd, Sr., of Virginia warned that the decision would "bring implications and dangers of the greatest consequence." Race-baiting politicians drowned out the voices of white Southern moderates and liberals who urged compliance. Hoping to avoid a violent showdown, the U.S. Supreme Court ordered local school boards to devise desegregation plans "with all deliberate speed." The ruling granted federal district court judges — most of them native white Southerners — wide latitude in deciding whether local school districts were in compliance. Some districts adopted policies of token integration; others voted to close their public schools rather than desegregate.[7]

A wave of violence against black Southerners in the wake of the *Brown* decision sent a clear message that open challenges to white supremacy would not be tolerated. In August 1955, two white men kidnapped and murdered Emmett Till, a Chicago teen visiting relatives in Money, Mississippi, after the Northern visitor — unschooled in Southern racial etiquette — allegedly "insulted" the wife of one of the men. Till was beaten and shot, his lifeless body dumped in the Tallahatchie River. The case attracted national attention when Till's mother insisted on a public, open-casket funeral. A photograph of the mangled corpse, printed in *Jet* magazine, sent a message that a generation of black activists never forgot. For many, Emmett Till became the first great martyr of the modern civil rights movement.[8]

As the push for desegregation met with "massive resistance" from white Southern authorities, a peculiar drama involving Nat Turner played out on Virginia's public stage. The Jamestown Corporation, a state-chartered theater production company, awarded first prize in its nationwide Write-A-Play contest to an African-American playwright, Thomas D. Pawley, Jr., whose winning entry depicted the rebel leader as a self-deluded messiah. The sponsors hoped this gesture of interracial goodwill would show the world that the Commonwealth of Virginia — its vigorous defense of Jim Crow notwithstanding — recognized and appreciated the contributions of Negroes to "The Common Glory."

Pawley had a keen understanding of Southern racial etiquette. He was born in Jackson, Mississippi, and raised on the campus of Virginia State College, a historically black institution. He left the South to pursue his graduate studies in drama at the University of Iowa; among his classmates were NBC television director Norman Felton and playwright Tennessee Williams. Pawley taught at two historically black institutions — Prairie View A&M in Texas and Lincoln University of Jefferson City, Missouri — before returning to Iowa for his Ph.D. During that span he taught, acted, and directed in the Atlanta University Summer School of Theatre and staged more than fifty productions at various schools and colleges.

Pawley's *Messiah*, written as part of his doctoral dissertation, depicted Nat Turner as a religious zealot who led himself and his followers astray.

> In the play, which is written in eight scenes, Nat convinces the slaves that he has been divinely appointed to free them from slavery by causing a paralytic to walk. An eclipse of the sun is interpreted by him to mean that God is ready for him to begin his mission. For several days the uprising proceeds according to plan until the "patyroller" begins to track them down. One by one they are killed until several months later Nat, a chastened man, realizes that he has been deluded and dies from hunger, shock and exhaustion.

Pawley himself joined the "all-Negro cast" in a 1948 University of Iowa production, playing the part of Will Francis, a disciple of Turner's.[9] In an interview with the student newspaper, Pawley explained that the "messiah" of the title referred to both Christ and Moses. "But there is more of the old testament feel to it," he said. "The hero, Turner, must justify his bloodshed, and that would be impossible if he followed Christ too closely."[10]

In 1953, Pawley decided to enter *Messiah* in the nationwide playwriting contest sponsored by the Jamestown Corporation. The state-chartered theater company, which produced the long-running outdoor drama *The Common Glory*, was offering cash awards of up to a thousand dollars for plays dealing with "a portion of the history of Virginia, or with a Virginia historical figure or figures."[11] The contest drew twenty-four inquiries and fifteen submissions — seven from Virginia, three from New York, two from North Carolina, one from Tennessee, one from California, and one from Missouri.[12] Jamestown Corporation employees divided the scripts among themselves and nominated four finalists. A panel of three independent judges then read the plays and ranked them on the basis of historical accuracy and dramatic content.[13]

The Virginia Historical Society director John Melville Jennings, who judged the historical accuracy of the plays, was not terribly impressed with the finalists. "Not a single one of the plays is entirely free from historical inaccuracies," he wrote. Jennings saved his most extensive critique for Pawley's *Messiah*. The play, "insofar as it goes and insofar as the facts are known, is fairly solid," he wrote. "But only a few people today have heard of the Nat Turner Insurrection. Mr. Pawley resurrects the incident, gives it undue significance in the light of later developments, and leaves his reader completely unaware of the fact that the insurrection dealt a death blow to the manumission societies and the organized emancipation movement which had gotten underway in the South." Jennings detected an abolitionist bias in the script. There was, he felt, "a vindictiveness in Mr. Pawley's one-sided approach that [displayed] a singular lack of feeling for the rounded tragedy of the whole slavery issue."[14] The other judges — the theater critic John Gassner and the dramatist Kermit Hunter — ranked *Messiah* first on the basis of its dramatic qualities. Gassner found nothing celebratory in Pawley's depiction of the rebellious slave. "Wisely, if not fully and deeply enough, the author of this play has concentrated his attention on the *failure* of Nat Turner; and this is the universally interesting theme of a *false* Messiah."[15]

The Jamestown Corporation executive vice president Allan R. Matthews exulted over the selection of "a Negro writer" by the contest's judges. "Although the Corporation — and I, personally — made no effort to influence the judging of these dramas, I can think of no happier fact than that a Southern organization will be able at this particular time to recognize the creative work of a Negro writer."[16] The Jamestown Corporation identified Pawley as "a Negro" in press releases announcing the contest winner, hoping that its enlightened racial policies would produce favorable publicity.[17]

Matthews envisioned the drama department of the Hampton Institute staging the award-winning play. He must have been shocked when the president of the historically black college reviewed the script and found it unacceptable. "Personally," Dr. Alonzo Moron wrote, "I would be reluctant to sponsor for our students such a play in which the role of religion has been so misconceived."[18]

Unable to arrange a production of *Messiah* at the Hampton Institute, Matthews invited Pawley to accept his award during a performance of *The Common Glory* on July 3, 1955. By law and custom, the award-winning Negro playwright would be eating in a segregated inn, sleeping in a segregated hotel room, and sitting in a segregated section of The Common Glory amphitheater before coming on stage to accept his award before a segregated audience.[19]

The Jamestown Corporation's adherence to Jim Crow law and custom made a mockery of its self-professed egalitarianism in awarding first prize to "a Negro" in the Write-A-Play contest. Matthews sympathized with white cast members who considered segregation an affront to the democratic ideals celebrated in *The Common Glory* but insisted that he was constrained by Virginia law. "The matter of segregation in connection with a drama which, as ours does, preaches the equality of men is, to me, a degrading one," he wrote. "It is not maintained here, however, as a matter of personal or corporate policy." Matthews attached a copy of the 1950 Code of Virginia, spelling out the penalties for noncompliance. He indicated that the Jamestown Corporation routinely subverted the law by allowing individuals and small groups of Negroes to sit where they pleased. This flexible seating policy, he suggested, mitigated the impact of Jim Crow on black theatergoers and made *The Common Glory* accessible to all.[20]

African Americans, emboldened by the Supreme Court's ruling in the school desegregation cases, were growing tired of such compromises and half-measures. On December 1, 1955, on a city bus in Montgomery, Alabama, a forty-three-year-old seamstress named Rosa Parks initiated a mass movement when she refused to give up her seat so that a white person could sit down, as required by law. Her arrest prompted local black activists to organize a one-day boycott of city buses in protest. The success of the boycott led to the founding of the Montgomery Improvement Association (MIA), under the leadership of the Reverend Martin Luther King, Jr. The group did not initially ask for an end to segregation on city buses; rather, it requested more courteous treatment of black passengers, a more equitable system of allocating seats, and the hiring of black bus drivers on black bus routes. When the bus company rejected these moderate proposals, MIA leaders vowed to continue the boycott indefinitely. Despite an intense campaign of harassment and violence, the African-American community stayed off the buses for more than a year. The boycott finally came to an end in December 1956 when the U.S. Supreme Court upheld a lower-court ruling outlawing segregation on city buses.

The Montgomery Bus Boycott thrust the Reverend Martin Luther King, Jr., a twenty-six-year-old native of Atlanta with a Ph.D. from Boston University, into the leadership of a mass movement. In Montgomery, King declared, African Americans had discovered "a new and powerful weapon" against discrimination and injustice: the technique of "nonviolent resistance." The nonviolent protestor, he explained, sought to uplift and redeem his opponent through the "regulating ideal" of love. King pointed to the recent success of the Indian independence movement led by Mahatma Gandhi, who had confronted the "physical force" of the British army with the "soul force" of his people. King rejected the use of violence as "both impractical and immoral. If this method becomes widespread, it will lead to terrible bloodshed, and that aftermath will be a bitterness that will last for generations." King put the philosophy of nonviolent resistance into practice as head of the Southern Christian Leadership Conference (SCLC), founded in 1957 to extend the Montgomery movement throughout the South. Judging from his collected papers, King made few if any references to the rebellious slave as a heroic figure in his public oratory.[21]

The few public tributes to Nat Turner in the mainstream black press of the late 1950s submerged the armed rebellion within a narrative of nonviolent protest. Lucy Mae Turner, an African-American poet and schoolteacher from East St. Louis who identified herself as Nat Turner's granddaughter, stressed the themes of Christian faith and endurance in her two-part history, "The Family of Nat Turner, 1831 to 1954," published in Carter G. Woodson's *Negro History Bulletin*.[22] Turner's "family history" doubled as "Negro history," written from an integrationist perspective. The trials and tribulations of the family, in slavery and freedom, mirrored those of the race as a whole. The author glossed over the gory details of the rebellion, saying only that Nat Turner was "driven to desperation by the terrible beatings that were given to his people, when the fury of the master class was let loose on helpless men, women and children alike." Rather, she emphasized the ennobling characteristics — courage, perseverance, faith in God — that sustained her family through good times and bad. In the spirit of interracial goodwill, the author acknowledged the patronage and protection extended to her father, Gilbert Turner, by the "better classes" of white people while condemning the virulent prejudice among the white working class. At the same time, she decried the social divisions among African Americans in the post-emancipation era and looked to the church as a unifying force within the black community.[23]

Turner drew heavily on the oral traditions passed down to her by her father, who resettled in Ohio after the Civil War. "He was such a wonderful conversationalist," she wrote, "that his reminiscences were more fascinating than the accounts of past events as given in the history books." Her father and other ex-slaves "would sit by the open fire-place of evenings, and go through the story of slavery from Nat Turner's insurrection to the assassination of President Abraham Lincoln." Their "quaint anecdotes" of life under slavery, "though true, never found their way into the polite United States history," she lamented. "Negro History, in those days, was a profane subject, only to be whispered in chimney corners and never discussed in open or in polite society." "Miss Lucy" (as her friends in the Negro History Home Study Club called her) was untroubled by the absence of any records linking Nat Turner to a wife named Fannie or children named Gilbert, John, and Melissa. She maintained that her father concealed his identity as Turner's son until after emancipation. The editors of the *Bulletin* accepted her royal lineage at face value, a testimonial to the authority accorded oral tradition in African-American culture.[24]

The narrative concluded with an autobiographical sketch that revealed Turner's bitter frustrations as an African-American woman in a society that favored white over black, male over female. After graduating from an "integrated" high school with the highest average in the class, she thought some of the local civic organizations might help send her to college, as they "had assisted in sending some ambitious local colored boys to Ohio State." But the offers never came. Turner quickly realized that she had "two strikes" against her: "I was black and I was a woman." Knowing she "could master the higher intellectual subjects" as well as her "more-favored" classmates, she laid her "plan of attack." She would work hard, save her money, and pay her own way to college. She went on to earn a bachelor's degree from Ohio State in 1934 and a master's degree from the University of Illinois in 1942. When St. Louis University opened its law school to "colored students" in 1946, she entered the evening school and graduated with the Bachelor of Law degree in 1950 — the "first colored woman" to do so. She soon discovered, however, that a degree alone did not guarantee admission to the legal profession. "For, though I made a perfect attendance record, and finished all the courses with credit, I have never yet been admitted to the Bar to practice law." Only her enduring Christian faith kept her from despair. In troubled times, she remembered "the inspiring motto of the Turner family, as sung by Nat Turner in the Gethsemane of his suffering and sacrifice: 'Trust in the Lord, And you'll overcome, Somehow, Somewhere, Someday!'"[25]

By the late 1950s, the white South had rallied behind a program of "massive resistance" to court-ordered desegregation. The refusal of President Dwight D. Eisenhower to endorse the *Brown* decision emboldened white authorities to obstruct integration at every turn. The most brazen act of defiance occurred in Arkansas, where Governor Orval Faubus posted National Guardsmen at Little Rock's Central High School to prevent nine black students from entering. Faubus argued that it would "not be possible to restore or maintain order and protect the lives and property of citizens if forcible integration" were carried out as ordered. A federal judge rejected the claim and ordered desegregation to proceed. Almost by invitation, a white mob formed to harass the black students if they attempted to enter the school. When students, under police guard, entered unnoticed by a side entrance, the crowd became enraged. Concerned for the safety of the students, Eisenhower federalized the Arkansas National Guard and sent a thousand troops from the 101st Airborne Division to Little Rock. The next morning, the paratroopers dispersed the crowd and escorted the black students safely into the school. Armed guards patrolled the hallways for the rest of the year.

Such was the atmosphere in 1957 when Virginia's State Board of Education adopted a new history and government textbook, *Cavalier Commonwealth,* for use in high schools across the state. A set of principles consistent with a defense of white supremacy and states' rights undergirded the historical narrative. While the authors paid tribute to the "inherent dignity of every human being," they remained silent on the matter of racial equality. And while they noted the "inestimable value of freedom," they sang the virtues of "stability" in government and "moderate reforms as opposed to violent revolution."[26]

The authors presented Nat Turner's Rebellion as the work of misguided fanatics who unwittingly destroyed the Jeffersonian tradition

of antislavery reform in Virginia. Taking a strange appearance of the
sun as the sign to attack, Turner led his six disciples and their "mad-
dened" followers on a rampage that left fifty-five white Virginians
dead. "It was the worst slaughter ever committed in the United States
by Negro slaves," the authors noted. Turner and eighteen of his co-
conspirators were tried, convicted, and hanged. To prevent future outbursts, the General Assembly passed strict new laws banning the unsupervised assembly of Negroes and increasing the punishment for
various crimes. "Other slave states made their codes even more severe
upon the Negro," the authors noted. "Judged in that light, Nat Turner
did a distinct disservice to his race." Here was a pointed lesson for
restless young Negroes whose leaders, well-versed in the history and
government of the Commonwealth of Virginia, were busily plotting
the demise of the Jim Crow system.[27]

Civil rights groups that monitored primary and secondary school
textbooks of the late 1950s and early 1960s found a similar bias
against antislavery agitation among the slaves. James O. Lewis, a
graduate student at Danbury State Teachers College in Connecticut,
presented the NAACP with a copy of his 1960 master's thesis, "Treatment of the 'Negro' in a Selected Group of Social Studies Middle
Grade Textbooks." According to Lewis, most of the nineteen American history textbooks "completely ignored or seriously distorted" the
efforts of slaves "to free themselves or to otherwise change their status
in the American slave system."

> It is interesting to note here that most of the textbooks mention
> one famous slave revolt, that is characterized as a murderous rebel-
> lion which generated fear in the Southern community. The slave
> rebellion of Nat Turner is recorded in most of the seventh and
> eighth grade textbooks. However, it must be pointed out that in
> only one book is this event characterized as an expression of slave
> dissatisfaction with their status and a legitimate reaction of human
> beings determined to attain their freedom.

Despite such findings, civil rights activists could take heart in the
growing body of revisionist scholarship on slavery and the public
commitment of leading professional historians to the black freedom
struggle. By the mid-1950s, a liberal consensus prevailed among the
leading practitioners of Southern and Negro history. Several promi-

nent historians — most notably C. Vann Woodward at Johns Hopkins and John Hope Franklin at Howard University — contributed to the NAACP's *Brown v. Board of Education* brief, and many others expressed their moral commitment to racial equality through their scholarship.[28]

Kenneth M. Stampp's *The Peculiar Institution: Slavery in the Antebellum South* (1956), a synthesis of more than two decades of revisionist scholarship, represented the liberal consensus in the postwar academy. Stampp argued that new findings "from the natural and social sciences about the Negro's potentialities and about the basic irrelevance of race" had rendered previous interpretations of slavery, based on assumptions of Negro inferiority, obsolete. "I have assumed," he wrote in the preface, "that the slaves were merely ordinary human beings, that innately Negroes *are*, after all, only white men with black skins, nothing more, nothing less." In other words, Stampp believed that Negroes responded to slavery no differently than whites would have responded under the same conditions. Human nature, not race or culture, was the key determinant. By learning "what slavery meant to the Negro and how he reacted to it," Stampp argued, white Americans might better understand "his more recent tribulations" in the struggle for civil rights. Indeed, there was "a peculiar urgency" to the study of slavery, Stampp noted, "because American Negroes still await the full fruition of their emancipation — still strive to break what remains of the caste barriers first imposed on them in slavery."[29]

Stampp presented Nat Turner as the embodiment of a rebellious spirit that lurked, sight unseen, within the psyche of every Negro slave. Turner "was a pious man, a Baptist exhorter by vocation, apparently as humble and docile as a slave was expected to be. There is no evidence that he was underfed, overworked, or treated with special cruelty. If Nat Turner could not be trusted, what slave could?" Stampp attributed the dearth of armed uprisings after 1831 not to any lack of desire on the part of the slaves but to a rational assessment of the chances for success and the consequences of failure. "They now realized that they would face a united white community, well armed and quite willing to annihilate as much of the black population as might seem necessary." Only the "boldest and most discontented slaves," Stampp argued, dared resort to violence against their masters. Most slaves hid their true selves behind masks of obedience. Some even "flattered the whites, affected complete subservience, and behaved like buffoons." These slaves, in Stampp's view, were merely acting the part of "Sambo." Under the right circumstances, he suggested, they might act the part of Nat Turner with no less enthusiasm.[30]

The historian Stanley Elkins lampooned the neo-abolitionist infatuation with the rebellious slave in *Slavery: A Problem in American Institutional and Intellectual Life* (1959). "The picture of the ideal slave," Elkins wrote in the preface, "is that of a man who has fully resisted all the effects on personality of a social system as coercive as any yet known. Special attention is called to examples of Negro courage, Negro rebelliousness, Negro hatred for the slave system, and so on — all the characteristics one might expect of white men who knew nothing of what it meant to be reared in slavery." There was no place in this politically correct but historically flawed portrait, Elkins noted, for the characteristics of "submissiveness, cheerfulness, and childishness" so widely observed among antebellum plantation Negroes. In their zeal to "prove master and slave equal before their Maker," neo-abolitionist historians "automatically discredited" these personality traits as demeaning "stereotypes" with no basis in reality or as figments of the white Southern racist imagination. "These features could not be accepted as typical and normal," Elkins noted, "not for a white man, and therefore not for anyone."[31]

A Boston native of Eastern European Jewish descent, Elkins approached the plantation South from the perspective of an outsider seeking to understand the region's place in American culture. Elkins was "a bit of a disillusioned radical" by the time he entered graduate school at Columbia University. He took an iconoclastic view of the new liberal consensus on slavery exemplified by Stampp's work. Historians of the post–World War II era, he argued, remained trapped in an age-old debate over the rightness and wrongness of slavery. While the "moral center of gravity" had shifted from the "pro-slavery sympathies" of U. B. Phillips and his followers to the "strong antislavery position" articulated by Stampp, the terms of the debate had remained essentially unchanged for more than a hundred years. Elkins concluded that it was time for a more detached approach, one that would take for granted the "evils" of slavery and pose new questions for scholarly investigation.[32]

Elkins would posit his own theory as to why enslaved black men might have demonstrated these submissive qualities, so embarrassing to liberal white historians, and it had nothing to do with racial inheritance. Breaking ranks with his neo-abolitionist colleagues, he proposed to treat the "Sambo" figure of Southern lore not as a racial "stereotype" but as a "personality type" produced under unique historical conditions. Elkins argued, in a nutshell, that the absence of institutional buffers between master and slave in American society created a uniquely oppressive system — roughly analogous to a German concentration camp — that severely damaged the psyche of the slave and produced the childlike "Sambo" personality. In making this analogy, Elkins drew on the work of social psychologist Bruno Bettelheim, an ex-inmate of Dachau and Buchenwald who had studied the adjustment of prisoners in the concentration camps. Bettelheim had observed a childlike quality to the behavior of the prisoners; many came to view their SS guards as father figures. "If the concentration camp could produce in two or three years the results that it did," Elkins mused, imagine the impact that two hundred years of slavery had on the "attitudes, expectations, and values" of the enslaved.[33]

Elkins acknowledged that American slavery could produce a rebellious personality type under the right conditions. Nat Turner, for example, belonged to that small but "significant" subset of slaves who managed "to escape the full impact of the system and its coercions upon personality." This group included house servants, urban mechanics, and slaves allowed to hire themselves out. "It is of great interest to note," Elkins wrote, "that although the danger of slave revolts (like Communist conspiracies in our own day) was much overrated by touchy Southerners, the revolts that actually did occur were in no instance planned by plantation laborers but rather by Negroes whose qualities of leadership were developed well outside the full coercions of the plantation authority-system." Here Elkins cited the examples of Gabriel, "a blacksmith who lived a few miles outside Richmond"; Denmark Vesey, "a freed Negro artisan who was born in Africa and served several years aboard a slave-trading vessel"; and Nat Turner, "a literate preacher of recognized intelligence." Yet Elkins pointed to the conspicuous failure of these rebel leaders to mount sustained, effective attacks on the slave regime. "The best organized of such 'revolts,' those of Vesey and Gabriel, were easily suppressed, while the most dramatic of them — the Nat Turner Rebellion — was characterized by little more than aimless butchery." Elkins concluded that the devastating impact of American slavery on the typical slave personality rendered organized rebellion futile.[34]

Several leading historians noted that the Elkins thesis, for all its conceptual boldness and originality, lacked an empirical foundation.

"The reading of secondary materials, a broad-ranging interest in other disciplines, and an extended use of comparisons and analogies do not compensate for the want of basic research," reviewer David Donald wrote in the flagship *American Historical Review*.[35] Oscar Handlin was no less blunt: "The disaster of this book is not due to the use of either concepts drawn from the social sciences or of imaginative analogies, but to a much older and simpler deficiency — the misuse of evidence." Handlin took Elkins to task for accepting the "Sambo" figure, so extravagantly drawn by white slaveholders, at face value. "Above all," Handlin wrote, "there is no evidence that the Sambo stereotype described all or a significant proportion of the plantation Negroes, any more than the nineteenth-century Ike or Pat stereotype described the American Jew or Irishman."[36]

The stature of the rebellious slave rose dramatically in the years between 1960 and 1965 as the civil rights movement, energized by student participation and leadership, took to the streets. Black and white activists engaged in various forms of nonviolent protest and civil disobedience — sit-ins, "Freedom Rides," marches, and mass demonstrations — to provoke confrontation with white segregationists, attract national media attention, and generate pressure for passage and enforcement of federal civil and voting-rights laws.

The sit-in movement signaled both a generational shift within the civil rights movement and a turn toward a grass-roots, "direct action" protest. In February 1960, four black freshmen from North Carolina Agricultural and Technical College staged a sit-in after they were denied service at a segregated Woolworth's lunch counter in Greensboro, North Carolina. As word of the protest spread, other students joined in. By the end of the month, the *New York Times* reported that the sit-in movement had "spread from North Carolina, Virginia, Florida, South Carolina, and Tennessee and involved 15 cities." To coordinate their protest activities and maintain their independence from the mainstream civil rights leadership, student activists established a new group, the Student Non-Violent Coordinating Committee (SNCC). The youth movement infused veteran civil rights organizations with new life. In 1961, an interracial group of thirteen "Freedom Riders," sponsored by the Congress of Racial Equality (CORE), traveled by bus into the Deep South in order to challenge the continued segregation of interstate transportation. White mobs in Alabama, unrestrained by local police, stormed the buses and assaulted the Freedom Riders; the bloody clash attracted national media attention and forced the Kennedy administration to intervene.

A loosely coordinated 1961–62 desegregation campaign in Albany, Georgia, exposed rifts among the various civil rights groups and called Martin Luther King's effectiveness as a leader into question. White authorities jailed dozens of protesters, including King, and prevented the open confrontation that civil rights leaders desired. Determined to organize a more effective campaign, King and his lieutenants chose Birmingham, Alabama, as their next target. Cameras rolled as Birmingham police arrested King on April 12, 1963 — Good Friday — for defying a court order against sit-ins and demonstrations. King defended his strategy of nonviolent protest in his famous "Letter from a Birmingham Jail":

> You may well ask, "Why direct action? Why sit-ins, marches, and so forth? Isn't negotiation a better path?" You are quite right in calling for negotiations. Indeed, this is the very purpose of direct action. Nonviolent direct action seeks to create such a crisis and foster such a tension that a community is forced to confront the issue. It seeks so to dramatize the issue that it can no longer be ignored.

The crisis King and his fellow activists sought to provoke came in May 1963, when the Birmingham police chief Eugene "Bull" Connor used dogs and fire hoses to disperse a peaceful march by more than one thousand children, ages six to eighteen. Media coverage of the violent police crackdown, transmitted across the nation and throughout the world, generated enormous sympathy for the protesters. Under pressure to act, the Kennedy administration brokered a settlement in which local merchants agreed to desegregate the lunch counters and hire black sales clerks. White supremacists, hoping to scuttle the agreement, bombed the home of King's brother and the motel where King had been staying. As riots broke out, President Kennedy threatened to send in federal troops. Less than a month later, Alabama governor George C. Wallace stood in a doorway at the University of Alabama and vowed to prevent black students from entering the school; federal marshals had to escort the students to their dorms. Citing rising "tensions" and the "threat of violence," Kennedy seized the moment to propose civil rights legislation "giving all Americans the right to be served in facilities which are open to the public — hotels, restaurants, theatres, retail stores, and similar establishments."

A coalition of civil rights activists, church groups, and labor leaders organized a massive march on Washington in August 1963 to demonstrate public support for the bill and to push for a wider range of social and economic reforms. Nearly a quarter of a million people, black and white, gathered on the Mall to witness a carefully choreographed display of interracial harmony and organizational unity. "I have a dream," the Reverend Martin Luther King, Jr., declared in a speech that encapsulated the integrationist ideals of the movement under his leadership.

> I have a dream that one day on the red hills of Georgia, the sons of former slaves and the sons of former slave owners will be able to sit down together at the table of brotherhood. I have a dream that one day even the state of Mississippi, a state sweltering with the heat of injustice, sweltering with the heat of oppression, will be transformed into an oasis of freedom and justice. I have a dream that my four little children will one day live in a nation where they will not be judged by the color of their skin but by the content of their character.

Though King warned that the "whirlwinds of revolt" would "continue to shake the foundations of our nation until the bright day of justice [emerged]," his speech breathed the spirit of hope, Christian faith, and brotherly love.

Even as King spoke, more militant voices from within black America had begun to challenge his leadership. Malcolm X, the spokesman for Elijah Muhammad's Nation of Islam, scoffed at what he called the Farce on Washington. "Yes, I was there. I observed that circus. Who ever heard of angry revolutionists all harmonizing, 'We Shall Overcome . . . Suum Day . . .' while tripping and swaying along arm-in-arm with the very people they were supposed to be angrily revolting against? Who ever heard of angry revolutionists swinging their bare feet together with their oppressor in lily-pad park pools, with gospels and guitars and 'I Have a Dream' speeches?" Malcolm saw nothing revolutionary in the so-called Negro revolution led by King. "You don't have a turn-the-other-cheek revolution. There's no such thing as a non-violent revolution."[37] By 1964, Malcolm's name had become synonymous in the white press with the advocacy of armed revolt, a position he attempted to clarify. "I'm not for wanton violence," he told reporters. "I'm for justice." Malcolm argued that black people had a legal right and a moral responsibility to take up arms in self-defense against white racists. "I believe it's a crime for anyone who is being brutalized without doing something to defend himself." Many battle-scarred veterans of the civil rights movement's direct-action campaigns in the South concurred.[38]

The show of unity at the 1963 March on Washington obscured growing ideological divisions between King and more radical civil rights activists over the principles of interracialism and nonviolence. Plans for a massive voting-rights project, called Mississippi Freedom Summer, produced intense debate within the SNCC and CORE over the role of white volunteers. Some black activists, noting the tendency of whites to assume leadership roles, argued that black people should seize control of their own freedom struggle. Others countered that the participation of whites in direct-action campaigns drew national media attention and enhanced the likelihood of federal protection. The integrationists, led by Freedom Summer organizer Bob Moses, carried the day.

In June 1964, shortly after the first of eight hundred summer volunteers arrived in Mississippi, three civil rights workers disappeared. Six weeks later, FBI agents discovered the bodies of James Chaney, Andrew Goodman, and Michael Schwerner, who had been abducted and killed by local Klansmen, including the sheriff and deputy sheriff. The wave of violence against the Mississippi Freedom Summer volunteers left many civil rights activists traumatized and further eroded their faith in nonviolence as a tactic or a principle of reform. "I'm sick and tired of going to the funerals of black men who have been murdered by white men," SNCC's David Dennis declared at the funeral of James Chaney. "We've defended our country. To do what? To live like slaves?" A spirit of rebellion infused the Mississippi campaign. SNCC-sponsored Freedom Schools, established as alternatives to white-controlled public schools, sought to gird black Mississippians for battle through the teaching of black history. After a lesson on slave rebellion, for example, a teacher might ask: "Who do you know that is like Nat Turner?"[39]

Mainstream civil rights leaders continued to press for passage of federal legislation that would cut the vitals out of Jim Crow. The Civil Rights Act of 1964, signed into law by President Lyndon B. Johnson, outlawed discrimination in hotels, motels, restaurants, theaters, and other public accommodations engaged in interstate commerce; authorized the U.S. attorney general to file suits to force desegregation of public schools; and banned discrimination by businesses that employed more than twenty-five people. Johnson expected grateful Negroes to give him their full support at the Democratic National Convention in August 1964. When delegates to the racially integrated Mississippi Freedom Democratic Party (MFDP) threatened to disrupt the convention by challenging the credentials of the official Mississippi delegation, Johnson instructed his operatives to crush the insurgency. The party's willingness to seat avowed segregationists while accepting just two democratically elected MFDP members as at-large delegates left many black activists disillusioned with white liberals and more determined than ever to plot their own course.

A massive voting-rights campaign in Selma, Alabama, highlighted tensions between the mainstream civil rights coalition and younger, more radical organizers affiliated with SNCC and CORE. In January 1965, Martin Luther King, Jr. — just back from Norway, where he had received the Nobel Peace Prize — traveled to Selma and announced plans to register black citizens "by the thousands." Mass arrests and mob violence ensued. When Alabama state troopers killed a black demonstrator in the nearby town of Marion, King called for a fifty-mile march from Selma to the state capital in Montgomery, where civil rights leaders would present their grievances to Governor George Wallace. As the six hundred demonstrators crossed the Edmund Pettus Bridge leading out of Selma on Sunday, March 7, they were met by a phalanx of state troopers, who ordered them to turn back. Before the marchers could disperse, the police descended on them, tear-gassing and clubbing them. Media coverage of "Bloody Sunday," as it became known, heightened racial tensions and drew more demonstrators to Selma. King himself led a second march across the Pettus Bridge, but his decision to turn back to Selma rather than risk a bloody confrontation surprised and angered many. Finally, in late March, with a small army of federal troops to protect them, twenty-five thousand civil rights demonstrators made the historic march from Selma to Montgomery. Five months after the Selma campaign, Congress passed the 1965 Voting Rights Act, which transformed Southern politics by drawing newly enfranchised African Americans into the Democratic Party and driving conservative white Southerners out.

As King and other civil rights leaders plotted their next step, discontent brewed in America's ghettoes. A deadly riot in the Watts district of Los Angeles in August 1965 called attention to the economic disparities produced by racial oppression in America. The "long, hot summers" of urban uprisings that followed in 1966 and 1967 coincided with the purge of white volunteers and the open endorsement of revolutionary violence by SNCC and CORE. Chants of "Freedom Now" were drowned out by a new slogan: "Black Power." "We been saying freedom for six years and we ain't got nothing," SNCC's Stokely Carmichael declared at a 1966 rally in Greenwood, Mississippi. "What we gonna start saying now is Black Power." The news media buzzed; white America trembled. "Black Power!" What did it mean? The phrase, with its connotations of black guerrilla armies, helped to catapult SNCC's Stokely Carmichael and his successor, H. Rap Brown, into the national limelight. They were "The Angry Children of Malcolm X," to quote Julius Lester, and they were now in charge of the movement.

The Literature of Negro Revolt

The rebellious slave, as a symbol of rising black militancy, stirred the Southern white liberal imagination of novelist William Styron, whose literary excursion into the mind of Nat Turner put the celebrated author and the black rebel leader on the cover of *Newsweek* magazine in 1967. A native of Tidewater Virginia, Styron traced his interest in slavery to the stories his grandmother — whose family owned slaves — told him as a child. Yet his relationship with his native region was that of an expatriate. He left Virginia shortly after graduating from college, never to make his home in the South again. As an adult, his values were shaped by a more or less rootless community of intellectuals — writers and editors and historians — who viewed the South as a microcosm of the United States, a bastion of racial prejudice and simmering class conflict. Styron befriended other Southern exiles — the novelist Robert Penn Warren, the historian C. Vann Woodward, the essayist Willie Morris — who felt the "burden" of Southern history and sought to interpret its significance for the nation at large. They spoke with the authority of native white Southerners who had rebelled against the folkways of the region and embraced the insights of moral philosophers and modern science.

Styron first gave serious thought to writing a novel about Turner in the early fifties, before the *Brown* decision and the Montgomery boycott launched the modern civil rights movement. His first book, *Lie Down in Darkness* (1951), earned him the coveted Prix de Rome, which included a yearlong sabbatical at the Academy of Arts and Letters in Rome. Styron began laying the groundwork for what he hoped would become his second book — "a novel based on Nat Turner's rebellion" — while in Paris, en route to Rome. "The subject fascinates me," he wrote to his father back in Newport News, "and I think I could make a real character out of old Nat."[40] Turner, he said, "is on the surface pretty much a bastard through and through. However I subscribe to the theory that all people, no matter how bad, have a scrap of nobility in them." Styron suggested that the Nat Turner of his creation would be more complex than the demon vilified by white slaveholders or the saint exalted by Communists and other modern-day revolutionaries.

> I hope that when I'm through with Nat Turner (and God, I know it's going to be a long, hard job) he will not be either a Great Leader of the Masses — as the stupid, vicious Jackass of a Communist writer might make him out — or a perfectly satanic demagogue, as the surface historical facts present him, but a living human being of great power and great potential who somewhere, in his struggle for freedom and for immortality, lost his way.

Styron prevailed on his father to send him a packet of books on the subject, some of them borrowed from the Hampton University professor J. Saunders Redding. Once in Rome, however, Styron abandoned the project, concluding that he was not quite ready to tackle a subject of such magnitude.[41]

In early 1961, as the bloody wars for black independence in Africa and the "Negro revolt" in America gave the subject new urgency, Styron informed his father of his plans to revive the Nat Turner project. He envisioned writing an original screenplay for a serious film — "not one of these Hollywood flashy colored numbers" — based on Turner's Rebellion. "Heaven knows the subject is pertinent now as it never was — the black man raging against the white — and if done properly (meaning done as I see it in my mind's eye) it would make a violent, moving film." Styron cited the assassination of the Congolese prime minister Patrice Lumumba in January 1961, just seven months after the African nation won its independence from Belgium, as an example of looming racial conflict throughout the world. "All you have to do is read about Lumumba and what's happening in the Congo," Styron told his father, "to see how significant Nat's story is, how contemporaneous and universal."[42]

Styron quickly jettisoned the film project, however, and rededicated himself to writing a historical novel. In May 1961, he arranged to visit Southampton County to conduct both archival and field research. "I have always wanted to trace the route of Nat's warpath — at least that part of it that can be traced — and, moreover, see whatever original houses and buildings are left standing," he informed his father. His daylong visit, which included a trip to the courthouse and a guided tour of the county, formed the centerpiece of his autobiographical essay, "This Quiet Dust," published four years later.

Styron drew inspiration for the figure of Nat Turner from James Baldwin, the celebrated black essayist and novelist (*Go Tell It on the Mountain, Notes of a Native Son, Giovanni's Room*) who had begun to emerge as the literary spokesman for the "Negro revolt." The two men conversed regularly during the winter of 1961–62, when Baldwin stayed with the Styrons as a houseguest. Styron told *Newsweek* magazine that knowing Baldwin "broke down the last shred of whatever final hangup of Southern prejudice I might have had which was trying to tell me that a Negro was never really intelligent. . . . Perhaps it was his diamond-bright intelligence which allowed me to say, 'When I plunge into Nat Turner, it will be with no holds barred, and he will respond with as much intelligence as I can bring to his voice.'" Baldwin was flattered by the comparison. "Yes, I think there's some of me in Nat Turner," he said. "If I were an actor, I could play the part."[43]

For scholarly guidance, Styron turned to Herbert Aptheker, the Marxist historian whose radically revisionist *American Negro Slave Revolts* presaged the liberal, antiracist historiography of the post–World War II era. Aptheker agreed to let Styron borrow a copy of his unpublished master's thesis on Nat Turner's Rebellion, which Styron found to be "a most persuasive and meaningful work." By September 1963, however, Styron was ready to consign Aptheker's work to the dustbin of historiography. Aptheker deserved credit, Styron wrote in the *New York Review of Books,* for demolishing the "theory of universal content and docility among the slaves" and demonstrating that "unrest and discontent were considerably more widespread than previous historians would grant." Had the Marxist historian named his book *Signs of Slave Unrest* and limited his thesis accordingly, Styron would have found nothing objectionable. Instead, Aptheker took the "extremist" position that "discontent and rebelliousness were not only exceedingly common, but, indeed, characteristic of American Negro slaves." Styron dismissed this claim as "a product of the white man's fantasy." The historical record showed that "there was only one sustained effective revolt in the entire annals of slavery: the cataclysmic uprising of Nat Turner in Virginia in 1831." To deny this fact, Styron said, was to distort the truth about American Negro slavery and demean the humanity of the Negro slave.[44]

Styron had discovered a new scholar-mentor in Stanley Elkins, whose theory of slave docility and the damaged black psyche resonated with liberals eager to explain the dearth of slave rebellions. "The character (not characterization) of 'Sambo,' wallowing happily in the dust," Styron wrote, "was no cruel figment of the imagination, Southern or Northern, but did in truth exist." Plantation slaves "*were* often observably docile, *were* childish, *were* irresponsible and incapable of real resistance." The recognition of such facts was "no significant commentary on the character of the Negro," Styron argued, "but rather a tribute to a capitalist super-machine which swiftly managed to cow and humble an entire people with a ruthless efficiency unparalleled in history." Like Elkins, Styron viewed Nat Turner as an exceptional figure, "a literate preacher and a slave of the Upper South" who "lived outside the thralldom of organized plantation slavery." Styron stressed the unique conditions that allowed Turner to develop a revolutionary mentality when so many of his fellow slaves had been reduced to shuffling Sambos. For one thing, there was his "native genius," which encouraged his owners to teach him to read. For another, there was "the relative latitude of freedom he had been granted" as a slave. Styron saw Turner as a heroic figure, a slave who struggled mightily against the determinism of history and, in doing so, asserted his humanity. "The many millions of other slaves, reduced to the status of children, illiterate, tranquillized, totally defenseless, ciphers and ants, could only accept their existence or be damned, and be damned anyway, like the victims of a concentration camp." Styron admired the boldness and originality of the Elkins thesis no less than its explanatory power. To him, it made the character of Nat Turner all the more extraordinary, all the more worthy of literary investigation.[45]

The Third World liberation movements of the day weighed heavily on Styron as he worked on his Nat Turner novel. He raised the subject in an interview with friend and fellow writer James Jones, published in the July 1963 issue of *Esquire* magazine. When Jones suggested that the global "stream of history" threatened to destroy the "algae" of American ideals, Styron responded: "Well, we have never recognized until recently that the obvious stream of history could be in a great measure what happens when X million Africans rise up and assert themselves. The story of Nat Turner is a little microcosmic — a thing which took place *here*, but which represents to me the whole continent of Africa." For Styron, the rising tide of race consciousness among people of color worldwide presented a significant threat to the liberal ideal of an integrated, colorblind society.

> *Styron:* Well, it seems quite apparent that the coming conflict's going to be one of color, to my mind. I think this is the tragedy of the era.
> *Jones:* I don't think it makes any difference.
> *Styron:* Well, perhaps it makes no difference, but it's going to happen.
> *Jones:* Do you think of the Chinese as colored?
> *Styron:* Well, I think the Chinese *are* going to be colored, yellow, plus black, plus brown, against what we call white.
> *Jones:* There'll probably be a conflict of that sort, but what's to keep the Chinese from thinking black is colored, and yellow isn't?

In exploring the contemporary "reverberations" of Nat Turner's Rebellion, Styron made no mention of the so-called Negro revolt in America. He supported the King-led civil rights movement, with its integrationist agenda and its philosophy of nonviolent direct action. If the more militant black voices being raised within — and against — the movement concerned him, he did not say.[46]

Styron's evolving depiction of Nat Turner as a tragic figure reflected his own ambivalence, as a white liberal, toward black revolutionary violence of the mid-1960s. In reading Turner's "Confessions," he noticed that the rebellion seemed to collapse after the rebel leader committed his first and only murder. "To my mind it was his dealing with violence that led him into a hopeless trap. He found out that he couldn't deal with the violence that he himself had ordained." Styron described this theme as "very central" to his book — "the idea of what happens when a man boldly proposes a course of total annihilation and starts to carry it out and finds to his dismay it's not working for him." This was hardly the image of Nat Turner that so inspired Malcolm X and other black revolutionaries of the day.[47]

Styron offered his first extended meditation on the history and memory of Nat Turner's Rebellion in "This Quiet Dust," an essay published in the April 1965 issue of *Harper's*. He portrayed the slave uprising as a "wild and daring" act, born of desperation and "doomed to catastrophe" for blacks and whites alike. "Had Nat lived to see the consequences of his rebellion, surely it would have been for him the cruelest irony that his bold and desperate bid for liberty had caused only the most tyrannical new controls to be imposed on Negroes everywhere — the establishment of patrols, further restrictions upon movement, education, assembly, and the beginning of other severe and crippling restraints which persisted throughout the slaveholding states until the Civil War." Politically, Turner's Rebellion produced a conservative backlash among white Virginians that killed the last best hope of emancipation without war.[48]

Styron traced his fascination with Nat Turner back to his boyhood in Tidewater Virginia. Like most native white Southerners, he was raised to believe that "Negroes were in every respect inferior to white people and should be made to stay in their proper order in the scheme of things." And, like most of his white schoolmates, he used the word "nigger" freely and often. Yet this hostile and condescending attitude toward Negroes "was based almost entirely on hearsay," he recalled, thanks to Jim Crow laws and customs designed to keep the races at a safe social distance. Styron suspected that his literary search for Nat Turner — "my own private attempt as a novelist to recreate and bring alive that dim and prodigious black man" — represented an effort to "break down the old law" of segregation and fulfill what he saw as the "moral imperative" of every white Southerner — "to 'know' the Negro."[49]

Styron contrasted his own prodigious knowledge of Turner's Rebellion with his nation's profound ignorance of the event. Even in

Southampton County, the epicenter of the revolt, Styron found that memories of Nat Turner's Rebellion had been suppressed as thoroughly as the insurrection itself. Several years earlier, he had arranged through his father to visit the county, hoping to find "some of the historic sites connected with the insurrection." Yet his local guide — an affable white farmer in his forties — could not think of a single surviving landmark associated with the event. "Had I really been so ingenuous," Styron asked, "as to believe that I would unearth some shrine, some home preserved after the manner of Colonial Williamsburg?" Styron's host had arranged with the white county sheriff to drive them around in search of landmarks, using William Sidney Drewry's "hopelessly outdated" map, blurry photographs, and descriptions as guides. The sheriff seemed to take pleasure in exposing the ignorance of the "country people" they met along the way. "You heard about old Nat Turner, ain't you?" he would ask them. "But few of them had," Styron noted. "As effectively as a monstrous and unbearable dream, Nat had been erased from memory."

Just as Styron was about to give up, he spotted a familiar landscape — a "monumental" oak tree and a "crumbling" house that he recognized, from one of Drewry's blurry photographs, as the home of Mrs. Catherine Whitehead. There, Nat Turner had chased down eighteen-year-old Margaret Whitehead and killed her. In the stillness of the rotting house, Styron ruminated on the significance of this "apocalyptic" scene, so briefly recounted in "The Confessions." "What happened to Nat in this place?" Styron asked. "Did he discover his humanity here, or lose it?"[50]

Styron completed his much-anticipated novel in 1967, the height of the Black Power era. Asked how he thought Negroes would react to his book, Styron responded: "I hope they read it as I wrote it: as an effort to produce a work of art, and to tell the truth about the institution of slavery. It's not to be read as propaganda, or pleading, or distortion of the truth, but as an attempt at a work of art. It might offend Negroes that I as a white man have presumed to intrude on the consciousness of a Negro. But James Baldwin has the right to intrude on the consciousness of a white man."[51] Styron had good reason to anticipate trouble: Black Power advocates were demanding black authorship of black history. "Throughout this country," Stokely Carmichael and Charles V. Hamilton wrote in *Black Power: The Politics of Liberation in America* (1967), "vast segments of black communities are beginning to recognize the need to assert their own definitions, to reclaim their history, their culture." Even Styron's use of the word "Negro" was taboo. "Many blacks are now calling themselves African-Americans, or Afro-Americans because that is *our* image of ourselves."[52]

In an author's note, Styron proclaimed his fidelity to the historical record of the event while insisting on his right, as an artist, to explore the undocumented moral universe of the rebellious slave. The novel opens with the captured rebel leader in jail, awaiting trial. There he is visited by Thomas R. Gray, who reads aloud from "The Confessions," which will be introduced as evidence at his trial. In a series of flashbacks, Styron's Turner presents an autobiographical history that bears only a superficial relationship to "The Confessions" as recorded by Gray.

In his most audacious display of literary license, Styron imagined a sexually charged relationship between Nat Turner and Margaret Whitehead, the young white woman whom Turner confessed to killing "by a blow on the head with a fence rail." Styron inferred the relationship from the fact, documented in the original 1831 "Confessions," that Whitehead was the only one of the fifty-five white victims that Turner killed with his own hands. "How come you only slew one?" Styron's Gray asks Turner. "How come, of all them people, this here particular young girl?" Styron also took liberties in his characterization of slaveholders identified as owners and intended victims of the rebellious slaves. Styron made no pretense of literal accuracy in concocting these scenes; his self-styled "meditation on history" required only that the novel remain faithful to larger "truths."[53]

Styron's unflinching portrait of slavery as a brutal, dehumanizing institution owed much to the revisionist historiography of the postwar era, particularly the work of Stanley Elkins. He imbued Turner's fellow slave and eventual co-conspirator Hark with the personality traits of the psychologically damaged "Sambo." Born on a large tobacco plantation in neighboring Sussex County, routinely abused by his white mistresses and masters, Hark exhibits the slavish behavior that so annoys Styron's Turner — "the unspeakable bootlicking Sambo, all giggles and smirks and oily, sniveling servility." Though Styron's Turner berates Hark — "you ain't a *man* when you act like that" — he does so out of love, not hate, for a misguided brother. Turner observes that the big-hearted, childlike, docile Hark must be taught to hate the white people who sold his wife and children and kept an entire race in bondage. "Although I had not yet told him of my great plans, it was my purpose that when the day came to obliterate the white people, Hark would be my right arm, my sword and shield." Awakened to the reality of his oppression, even the Sambo-like Hark could become an axe-wielding rebel.[54]

The Confessions of Nat Turner burst on the American literary scene at the end of a long, hot summer of urban rioting. Two of the deadliest riots took place in late July 1967. In Newark, the arrest and beating of a black cab driver triggered a series of confrontations between police and angry residents that ended in the deaths of twenty-three people. In Detroit, a police raid on a private social club exacerbated racial tensions over the recent killing of a black army veteran by a gang of white youths. Mobs formed, flames erupted, and the area was sealed off by the police. As reports of casualties mounted, the governor declared a state of "insurrection" and asked President Johnson to federalize the Michigan National Guard. On July 27, a national wire service reported that "Detroit's racial riot" had "set a modern record for bloodshed. The death toll soared to 36, topping the Watts bloodbath of 1965 and making Detroit's insurrection the most deadly racial riot in modern U.S. history." When the smoke cleared, forty-three persons lay dead — thirty-three of them black, ten of them white.[55]

The nation's leading newspapers turned to Styron, as a recognized authority on slave rebellion, for insights into the causes of the riots. Styron analyzed the riots from the perspective of a sympathetic white liberal who believed violence begat violence. He acknowledged the social and psychological wellsprings of black rage but feared that the riots would produce a backlash from whites, similar to the "harsh restrictions" imposed on "Negroes all over the South" after Nat Turner's Rebellion. He expressed his own fatalistic belief that little could be done to prevent the rioting and the "tragic destruction" of human lives. "It is the working out of a historical process," he explained, "for at the core of Negro unrest is a demand for intertwined economic and psychological recognition." Styron urged white Americans to gain a better "understanding of the Negro people" through the study of black history and psychology. He suggested that his own book might be the place to start. "I hope the book creates an interest in the American Negro past," he said. "It certainly wasn't planned to coincide with today's rioting, but it could lead to an understanding of the outbursts."[56]

Styron warned against viewing Nat Turner's Rebellion as a "prototype or a metaphor" for the black militancy of 1967. "The Negroes have political power now, and consciousness," Styron was quoted as saying, "whereas then they had none." Yet Styron saw parallels in the psychology of the rebellious slave and the Black Power militant. Asked if he thought the concept of Black Power was "necessary, or right, or good," Styron paraphrased the black revolutionary psychologist Frantz Fanon, author of *The Wretched of the Earth:* "It's not right or good. It's necessary. It's cathartic. It's a purgation for them . . . to burn things. When violence is a form of the assertion of one's identity it allows the participants to reach a sense of dignity and self. I think that's what Nat was doing, asserting his sense of self and the reality of his self." Styron made no special pleas for leniency or forgiveness on behalf of white people. "We deserve the violence," he said, "in that we cannot oppress a race for four hundred years without getting our just deserts."[57]

The media eagerly seized on Styron's novel, released in October 1967, as a commentary on modern-day racial unrest in the United States. *Life* magazine, one of the most widely read periodicals of the day, introduced a lavishly illustrated prepublication excerpt by noting the novel's relevance to contemporary events: "By a purely accidental timeliness, it will be published in the same year that saw the 'insurrections' of Detroit, Newark, and scores of other American cities."[58] *Time* magazine treated publication of the book as a news event: "Readers will not fail to recognize that the shadow of Nat Turner darkened the streets of Newark and Detroit in the summer of 1967 — and hovers still."[59]

Newsweek drew an explicit analogy between Nat Turner and Black Power militants in its cover story, "The Negro As Rebel." The magazine began its "special report" with a brief, explosive excerpt from the novel, the scene in which Turner and his followers plot the rebellion: "Us gotta *kill* all dem white sonsabitches. Ain't dat what de Lawd done told you? Ain't dat right, Nat?" Turner reflects on what he has heard: "It was as if by those words we were committed. *Us gotta kill . . .*" *Newsweek* found such dialogue strikingly familiar: "That's not Rap Brown talking about a black-power meeting in 1967. The scene is the tidewater county of southern Virginia in 1831, and the man so coolly hell-bent after Whitey is Nat Turner, an educated black preacher who led the only carefully planned and effective slave revolt in American history." *Newsweek* described Styron as "extremely reluctant to draw any parallels about 'backlash' between Nat Turner's revolt and the current ghetto riots." Yet his comments made clear that he viewed the militant rhetoric of Black Power advocates as socially and politically counterproductive. "I certainly don't mean to glorify the figure of the Negro rebel against society today. You can see Nat Turner as an archetypal American tragic hero, but this doesn't make Rap Brown an archetypal American hero, nor does it make what he is preaching capable of anything but disaster."[60]

Most early reviewers agreed that the book had something important to say about race relations in 1967. Edmund Fuller of the *Wall Street Journal* observed that the book "has bearing, historically and psychologically, on the tragic stresses between the races today."[61] Alfred Kazin, in the *Washington Post Book World,* agreed: "The book is more a psychological narrative for 1967 than it is a social narrative of 1831, and will undoubtedly be read by many people in the interest of 'Negro-White Understanding.'"[62] Such pronouncements were rarely followed by any sustained effort to articulate the lessons that readers, white or black, might draw from the novel.

John Thompson, who reviewed the book for *Commentary* magazine, went further than most critics in exploring the implications of the novel for contemporary race relations. He praised Styron for having the "courage" to deal with "the almost impossible question, that of the justification of murder." Styron implicated his white readers in the violent deeds of Nat Turner, Thompson suggested, by creating empathy for his black protagonist. Having shared his sufferings vicariously, readers could not deny his right to assert his humanity by rising against his oppressors. "By the time Nat Turner's project begins to form, we cannot wait for the heads to roll," Thompson wrote. "Then what of Newark and Detroit? What of burning stores and stealing television sets, or shooting a fireman in the back, supposing it was not the police or the National Guardsmen who did the shooting? Is this really required to make Negroes worth something?" Thompson had no easy answers. White people of good will might hope that the circumstances that gave rise to the riots in 1967 could be alleviated with "due process," with "natural decency," and without further bloodshed. "But all we know for certain, considering now the truths of art rather than the blessings of politics or religion, is that from time to time men will rise and slay, if not the oppressor, then whosoever lies at hand in the oppressor's likeness."[63]

Several reviewers complained that the news media had obscured the literary merits of the book by reading it as a commentary on the riots. "The novel seems to be receiving more critical acclaim for its supposed timeliness and commentary than for its aesthetic qualities," Edward Sklepowich wrote in the *Virginia Weekly,* a newspaper published by the Southern Student Organizing Committee, an interracial civil rights group. "This is inevitable, and most likely only with the passage of time will the work be placed in its proper perspective."[64] Gerald Wade of the *Omaha World-Herald* argued that coverage of the book as a "news event" made "any attempt to judge the book on its literary merits difficult." Wade acknowledged that "an echo of the riots last summer in Detroit and Newark and elsewhere" ran through the narrative. Yet he concluded that "there is no connection between the novel and what happened in American cities last summer. It is neither a primer nor a report." Styron had simply explored the universal theme of men striving "to break out of what binds them."[65]

For months after the publication of his book, Styron rode a wave of critical acclaim and commercial success that placed him in the top rank of American novelists. Historians, literary critics, and book reviewers, writing in newspapers and magazines across the country, hailed the book as a milestone in the literature of American race relations. They applauded Styron for transcending his identity as a white Southerner and creating an authentic, historically accurate portrayal of American slavery from "inside the mind" of a Negro slave. Most found the book a revelation, a work of art that told the truth about slavery and its degradation of whites and blacks alike, a work of history that would help Americans understand the roots of their contemporary racial problems.

Prominent white liberal historians, writing in popular magazines and literary journals, affirmed the general accuracy of Styron's "meditation on history." C. Vann Woodward, the nation's leading scholar of the American South, found Styron's fictionalized portrait of Nat Turner "not inconsistent with anything historians know. It is informed by a respect for history, a sure feeling for the period, and a deep and precise sense of place and time." The presidential historian Arthur Schlesinger, Jr., praised Styron for his "superb and responsible use of the artistic imagination." Martin Duberman, a historian of the antebellum South who doubled as a playwright, declared himself "astonished at Styron's mastery of both the details and the interpretive themes of the period." If anything, Duberman observed, Styron adhered too closely to the original "Confessions" in his depiction of Turner. The novelist chose "to put aside his subjective vision, his own truth, in order to serve those 20-odd scraps of paper we call the Nat Turner 'confessions,' a document, ironically, which almost certainly distorts what actually happened."[66]

Some of the best-known black scholars in the nation applauded Styron's work. The historian John Hope Franklin lauded *The Confessions* as "a skillful and engrossing book" that conveyed a "profound understanding of the institution of slavery." For Franklin, the novel effectively conveyed the horrors of slavery — the "barbarism," the "deception," the degradation of blacks and whites alike. More important, the book challenged simplistic assumptions about slave personality by showing that even the pampered slave (Nat Turner) felt a sense of responsibility toward his fellow slaves and that even the "comical Sambo" (Hark Travis) could become deadly serious when it came time to act. The essayist and literary critic J. Saunders Redding, who helped Styron locate sources on Turner's Rebellion back in the early 1950s, considered the novel a triumph. It "ruins — utterly destroys — many long-cherished and defensively held myths about American slavery and slaves."[67]

Signs of a growing "black backlash" against Styron's *Confessions* began to appear in late November and early December 1967, after the book had been favorably reviewed in many national publications. Some black critics expressed disappointment with Styron's "failure of sensibility" as a writer; others called him a racist. Still others directed their anger at the "white-controlled" mass media for relying on a white man to interpret the experience of black people. All agreed that the overwhelmingly positive response to the book in the national press demonstrated a blatant disregard for the opinions, recorded history, and folk traditions of blacks.

Writing in the *Nation*, the poet June Jordan (then known as June Meyer) complained that "the phenomenon of Nat Turner *alias* William Styron" reflected a media bias toward whites as "spokesmen for the blacks." Jordan argued that the "white-controlled media" denied the black man living in "white America" an opportunity to express "his own voice, his own desires, his own rage. In fact, the preferred form of communication, black to white, is through a white intermediary — be he sociologist or William Styron." There was a difference between black and white perspectives on history, the claims of colorblind liberals notwithstanding. Until the general public heard from black people, speaking as black people, it would not know "the human meaning of that difference."[68]

The essayist and novelist Albert Murray argued that Styron's *Confessions of Nat Turner* revealed "much the same old failure of sensibility that plagues most other fiction about black people." Styron had created "a Nat Turner whom many white people may accept at a safe distance, but hardly one with whom Negroes will easily identify." If Styron had looked to Negro folklore for inspiration, he would have found a Homeric figure "ready-made" for literature. "The Nat Turner Southern Negro children used to celebrate in pageants during Negro History Week was a magnificent forefather enshrined in the National Pantheon beside the greatest heroes of the Republic." This noble figure "nourished the hopes of Negroes" by "symbolizing the human spirit victorious in defeat." Instead, Styron fell back on a white tradition that viewed black experience as something alien and pathological. His version of Nat Turner had its origins in the "pro-slavery imagery of white brutality and black docility," incorporated into a "Marxist-Freudian or psychopolitical theory of black castration." The Nat Turner who emerged from the novel was barely recognizable to Murray. In attempting to convey the black experience from the perspective of a black man, Murray concluded, Styron had shown little respect for the black cultural traditions that shaped the real-life Nat Turner and sustained his memory.[69]

Cecil Brown, a budding playwright and novelist, criticized the book from the more radical perspective of a black cultural nationalist. Writing in the *Negro Digest*, Brown argued that Styron portrayed "not a black Nat, but a white Nat (at best a 'colored' one), in a white world." Styron's Nat Turner was a "superconformist," an integrationist and assimilationist. "Not only does he adopt white mannerisms and parrot their linguistic rhythms, but (truth be told) he wishes he were white." White middle-class readers empathized with Styron's Turner, Brown maintained, because he spoke their language and embraced their values as his own. Styron failed to show his readers the "darker side" of Nat Turner, "the emotional, irrational, schizophrenic, charismatic powers of a man who for all who knew him was a witch doctor, magician, shaman, and prophet." This Nat Turner was a product of the "tribal (pre-literate)" society of black Africa and the "No-man's land" of black America, not the shared cultural landscape of the

American South that both Styron and Murray claimed as common ground.[70]

By February 1968, the backlash against Styron's novel had become loud enough to attract the attention of the national press. The *New York Times* addressed the "bitter controversy" in two news stories and a brief news item, published within a span of ten days. "Some Negroes Accuse Styron of Distorting Nat Turner's Life," read the headline over the first. The *Times* stressed the gulf between mainstream critical opinion and the minority views of the black protesters. "The novel has been hailed as a literary triumph by most critics and is considered a leading contender for the National Book Award and the Pulitzer Prize," the newspaper reported. "Yet several Negro leaders and intellectuals argue that the Virginia-born Mr. Styron distorted the historical record and promoted racial stereotypes." *New York Times* readers, many of whom had heard nothing but praise for the book, got an earful of black rage. "It's the worst thing that's happened to Nat Turner since he was hanged," the Harlem writer William Strickland was quoted as saying. "It's a racist book designed to titillate the fantasies of white America." The *Times* indicated that black critics, while few in number, were mobilizing protests against the book and any motion picture screenplay that might be based on the book. The NAACP was planning to make a "presentation" to Wolper Pictures, which owned the movie rights to the novel, and John Henrik Clarke of the journal *Freedomways* was editing "a collection of essays by Negroes critical of the novel."[71]

The white literary establishment, sensitive to "minority criticism" of the novel, began to distance itself from Styron. The National Book Awards provided the first test. In February 1968, the judges announced the five "leading nominees" for the thousand-dollar prize in fiction: Styron's *The Confessions of Nat Turner,* Norman Mailer's *Why Are We in Vietnam?,* Joyce Carol Oates's *A Garden of Earthly Delights,* Chaim Potok's *The Chosen,* and Thornton Wilder's *The Eighth Day.* Three judges — Josephine Herbst, Granville Hicks, and John Updike — would select the winner.[72] The critical acclaim that greeted Styron's novel made his the odds-on favorite. The results, as reported in the *New York Times,* came as something of a surprise: "Wilder's 'Eighth Day' Tops Styron's 'Nat Turner' and Three Others for National Book Award." Both the headline and the article highlighted the snubbing of Styron, yet the reporter ventured no explanation for the unexpected outcome.[73]

Styron enjoyed a measure of vindication when his novel won the Pulitzer Prize for fiction in May 1968. Yet, unbeknownst to the public, the Columbia University Board of Trustees, which administered the prize, had overruled its own jury in making the selection. Two of the three jurors — Maxwell Geismar and Melvin Maddocks — voted to give the prize to Isaac Bashevis Singer's *The Manor,* citing "strong minority criticism of Styron's use of historical material and his central view of slavery."[74]

The *New York Amsterdam News* responded to news of the award with a vitriolic screed from the pen of Gertrude Wilson — the same white columnist who had once praised Styron for his literary efforts. "I Spit on the Pulitzer Prize!" read the headline over her column. Wilson took "the white establishment" at Columbia to task for giving the award to "a white Southerner who made a Negro revolutionist look like a 'nigger.'" Wilson described how she had first become disillusioned with the awards two years earlier when the Board of Trustees rejected a unanimous recommendation by its advisory board to give Duke Ellington a special citation. That decision "smelled to high heaven, and it still does," she wrote, "but I'm writing it now because of this smellier award by the PULL-IT-Zer committee which has chosen to overlook the outraged reaction of the Negro community to this book; disregarding verified testimony to its historical dishonesty, and its cruel image of Nat Turner as a black buck lusting after white flesh." Wilson argued that the decision of the Columbia trustees reflected a more general insensitivity toward black students and the local black community. During the previous month, white and black students at Columbia had occupied several buildings to protest the decision to build a gym in Morningside Park against the wishes of community groups. The awarding of a prize to Styron reflected the general "ineptitude" of the Columbia administration, whose actions had sparked "a student rebellion without parallel in this country."[75]

Nat Turner in Hollywood

As the black and white intelligentsia slugged it out in the pages of the *New York Times,* the *New York Review of Books, Freedomways,* and *Dissent,* black activists on the West Coast waged a grassroots effort to stop the making of a major Hollywood film based on Styron's book. To replicate the false and distorted view of Nat Turner presented in the novel, they charged, would be socially irresponsible. They insisted that the filmmakers eliminate objectionable scenes and draw on other sources to create "a positive image of Nat Turner as a black revolutionary." Key principles of Black Power — self-definition and community control — shaped the demands of the protesters. Yet the public strategy they employed — a statement of grievances, the threat of a boycott, followed by a negotiated settlement — owed far more to the nonviolent civil rights movement than it did to the incendiary street-level politics of Black Power.

As a young writer, Styron made no secret of his ambition to reach a mass audience via film adaptations of his work. In a 1955 roundtable discussion entitled "What's Wrong with the American Novel?" Styron observed that novelists faced stiff competition from the mass media. He noted that his own desire to reach a larger audience was motivated by an egotism common to serious fiction writers: "this feeling . . . that all these tremendous, fantastic, marvelous things that he has to say do not reach nearly the number that they might."[76]

Several people with connections to the Hollywood film industry read *The Confessions of Nat Turner* shortly before its release in October 1967 and commented on the possibility of a motion picture adaptation. Garson Kanin, a writer, director, and producer with a long list of Hollywood screenplays to his credit, told Styron that he had read the novel three times and had no doubt it would make a great film. George Stevens Jr., a producer of documentary films (including "Nine at Little Rock"), apologized to Styron for "writing about the motion picture possibilities of your book before it has had a chance to breathe as a novel. I only do so because I feel strongly about it and fear that others less reticent than I might lunge in with some conclusive proposal." Stevens prevailed on his father, who had directed such film classics as *A Place in the Sun, Shane,* and *Giant,* to read the book. "He thinks it is magnificent. Whether it should be a film, whether the integrity of the idea can be preserved in an art so beholden to the marketplace, whether the book, so complete in itself, should not rest its case without a motion picture, whether or not he should do it if it is done — he raises all of these questions. I don't know all the answers. I just think it could be one of the great films."[77]

In November 1967, the *New York Times* reported that Styron had sold the motion picture rights to his novel to Wolper Pictures for $600,000, plus a percentage of the distributor's gross. Three months

later, Twentieth Century Fox announced that it had completed negotiations with David L. Wolper and Norman Jewison to finance and
distribute the motion picture adaptation of *The Confessions* "throughout the world." The Hollywood studio called the distribution deal
"one of the most significant agreements in its history." At the time of
the announcement, *The Confessions* was "the nation's Number One
best-selling novel," having "topped the best-seller lists for the past 13
weeks."[78]

Director Norman Jewison had a reputation as a friend of the civil
rights movement. In 1967, he produced and directed *In the Heat of the
Night,* which focused on the relationship between a black New York
City detective, played by Sidney Poitier, and a white Southern sheriff,
played by Rod Steiger, as they worked together to solve a murder mystery. "It was the first film I can think of in which the black man hit the
white man," Steiger later recalled. "Sidney Poitier and I used to sneak
into theatres just to watch the audience's reaction." The film went on
to win five Oscars, including best picture and best screenplay.[79]

Several black actors and writers with connections to the Hollywood film industry seethed over the announcement that the book
would be made into a movie. They began to talk among themselves
about the possibility of organizing a campaign against the movie
project. The catalyst behind the grassroots campaign was Louise
Meriwether, a forty-three-year-old fiction writer who had recently
quit her job as a story analyst at Universal Studios so that she could
work full-time on her first novel. Born in New York and raised under "mean" circumstances in Harlem, Meriwether moved around the
country before settling in Los Angeles in the 1950s. She worked at a
variety of jobs while earning a bachelor's degree in English from New
York University and a master's degree in journalism from the University of California at Los Angeles.[80]

Meriwether had experience as a participant in organized protest
movements. In the summer of 1965, she and hundreds of CORE volunteers traveled to Bogalusa, Louisiana, to support local black residents. There, she sometimes carried guns for the local chapter of the
Deacons for Defense and Justice, whose members armed themselves
in self-defense against the Ku Klux Klan. In August 1965, Meriwether
returned to Los Angeles, "right in time for the Watts riot." She suspected that the riots led to her hiring as the first black Hollywood
story analyst. "I had gone to Universal Studios maybe ten years before,

trying to get a job, and I was told I was overqualified to be in the steno pool." In both Watts and Bogalusa, Meriwether had seen that organized protest produced results. She had also seen how different strategies for social change — radical and reformist, militant and pacifist — complemented one another.

Meriwether and her co-organizer, the actor and Hollywood set designer Vantile Whitfield, decided to call their group the Black Anti-Defamation Association (BADA). They began their organizational campaign by soliciting the endorsements of prominent black figures in the field of arts and entertainment. The first endorsements came from Godfrey Cambridge, the actor and comedian; Ossie Davis, the actor and playwright; and LeRoi Jones, the playwright, poet, and militant advocate of Black Power.[81] Jones described Styron's "meditation on history" as a product of a distorted white consciousness, incapable of perceiving "the black reality of Nat Turner." He attributed the protest against the movie to the lack of black community control over black cultural commodities. "The real drag," he wrote, is "that we Black People have not got a film industry of our own, have not got the power to project our own strong images of Blackness. How pitiable are we that we cannot even tell our children our own story, but must instead protest the devilishness of the devil. A wearisome task at best." Cambridge complained that most whites remained ignorant of black history. When they finally did take an interest in the subject, they relied on "a repentant southern racist" to tell the story. Nat Turner was a black hero, "our black hero," Cambridge wrote; Styron had no right to tamper with that heroic figure, no matter how "deductive and creative" his meditation on history might be.[82]

The Hollywood protesters secured the endorsements of several prominent political figures whose names were synonymous with Black Power. Stokely Carmichael and Rap Brown issued a joint statement from SNCC headquarters in Atlanta. "*The Confessions of Nat Turner* is a joke to us as black people," they wrote. "Nat Turner is a black hero who belongs to our people, and hunkies such as William Styron do not have the right or authority from black people to speak for us or interpret our heroes. We don't even have to waste time on the distorted contents of Styron's book, because lies, deception, and distortion is the only thing we can expect from hunkies." Adam Clayton Powell, the former congressman from Harlem, signed on to the protest with a statement from the island of Bimini. He called on "all black people to

stand together against this latest effort of Hollywood to spew its sub-
tle race hatred and open white supremacy through alleged entertainment. 'The Confessions of Nat Turner' must not be filmed. It will be a
testing ground for black power and all of its ennobling manifestations
to prevent this latest brutality against black people." Powell's letter was
forwarded to Meriwether by Chuck Stone, author of *Tell It Like It Is:
Black Political Power in America* and a participant in the National Conference on Black Power. Stone characterized the making of the movie
as a step toward the annihilation of black people. "I think we should
declare to the world that we see no difference between the filming of
'The Confessions of Nat Turner' and the education campaign that
Goebbels and Hitler undertook to prepare the way for the slaughter of
6,000,000 Jews. If the film is made, it will amount to a declaration of
war against black people of the world by David Wolper and Norman
Jewison and, as such, the black community should be prepared to react
accordingly."[83]

The Hollywood protesters found their most eloquent celebrity
spokesman in Ossie Davis, the well-known actor and playwright who
upset many white liberals when he delivered a eulogy at the funeral of
Malcolm X.[84] Davis issued an angry public statement charging that
Styron's depiction of Nat Turner fed white racist fantasies of black
men lusting after white women. "Certainly, to feed this inflammatory
lie to angered white racism on a mass scale is the height of social irre-
sponsibility." In a panel discussion with Styron, moderated by their
mutual friend James Baldwin, Davis indicated that "it was not beyond
the realm of possibility" for Nat Turner to have loved Margaret
Whitehead.

> What I am disturbed about is that this is one of the areas about
> which I fear my country can be most immediately psychotic and
> destructive. I have only to think back in the last hundred years to
> the more than 3,500 black men lynched in the South, the rationale
> of such activities being that these men constituted a threat to
> white womanhood . . . Are we that clear of our horror at the
> thought of a black male lusting after white flesh?

In arguing that the film would incite violence against black people,
Davis echoed the position set forth more than fifty years earlier by
W.E.B. Du Bois in his campaign to prevent the screening of *The Birth*

of a Nation. "I am not against Hollywood making the book into a movie," Davis wrote to the BADA, "provided they take one of their greatest box office giants — and put blacking on his face! That way we will all know what the industry really thinks about black sensibilities in our country . . . that way Hollywood would confess its own racism."[85]

Meriwether did not limit her appeals to black militants. She approached the Reverend Martin Luther King, Jr., during one of his visits to Los Angeles and asked for his support.

> Whenever anybody came to town I would go to meet them and greet them and give them this information and ask them to give us a letter of support. So when Dr. King was in town, I went up to him with something in hand, whatever information I had, and told him that we had endorsements from the NAACP, churches, Ossie Davis, and the Urban League — the local ones, I'm not talking about national. And Dr. King said, "I have heard about this and I am going to Kansas and I will read the book and let you know." And when he was killed, he had a copy of the book with him.[86]

With endorsements in hand, the BADA officially announced its objections to the film in a five-page letter to Wolper and Jewison. "Gentlemen," the letter began. "You are murdering the spirit of Nat Turner, one of the great ethnic heroes of black Americans. You are distorting and falsifying the history of black people in this country, and by extension, defaming the entire black race. You are pandering to white racism and deepening the gulf of alienation between the races."[87] The letter writers proceeded to cite numerous scenes from the book that they considered both historically inaccurate and defamatory. For example:

> Styron's Turner never consummates a sexual relationship with a woman, masturbating instead in a woodshed while fantasizing about copulating with the white goddess, Margaret Whitehead. He has a homosexual orgy with a young boy in the woods, and even finds relief rubbing himself up against a tree. Only once does Turner indulge in sexual fantasies with a black woman and even then, at the moment of climax, she turns white. In reality, Nat Turner was married to a black slave woman. His masturbatory

fantasies, homosexuality and Margaret Whitehead are all figments of Styron's imagination.

In Styron's book . . . Nat's mother is a slut who enjoys being raped by the drunken Irish overseer. Another pure fiction. In reality it has been reported that she tried to kill Nat when he was born because she didn't want to bring a child into slavery. This is some very weird interpreting by Styron.

Styron's Will . . . is bestial to the point of being inhuman. A runaway slave, hungry and bruised, and with the dogs practically yapping at his heels, Will is not seeking sanctuary, but in Styron's own words, "some white pussy." Compare this with Will's quiet rejoinder to Turner that he only sought liberty at the cost of his life. Even the most prejudiced accounts of the Turner insurrection reported no cases of rape. Turner has been credited with insisting that they kill without torture and without violating the women. Yet, in Styron's account, Will, beast that he is, mounts a white woman he has just murdered while Turner cowers in fear in a corner.

The group concluded its letter with two demands. First, the film must be based on "the historical facts of Nat Turner, or no picture be made at all." Second, the film must "not bear the title of William Styron's book lest it lend validity to his falsification of history." The protesters did not say what action they would take if their demands were not met. They simply noted that the BADA represented a broad cross-section of the black community — a pointed reminder of the pressure that could be brought to bear on the filmmakers.[88]

Jewison vigorously defended his right, as an artist, to bring Styron's vision of Nat Turner to the big screen. In a sympathetic story titled "Civil Rights and a Producer's Dilemma," the Los Angeles Times portrayed Jewison as a friend of the civil rights movement who suddenly found himself under attack from a small but vocal group of black militants. "When Norman Jewison first became interested in civil rights," the article began, "he lent his activist directorial energies to the filming of 'In the Heat of the Night,' which he considers 'a plea for interracial understanding and respect.'" Now, as the director of a film based on Styron's Confessions — "a book many people consider more civil wrong than right" — Jewison faced a dilemma. How could he demonstrate his enduring commitment to the black freedom struggle without compromising his convictions or sacrificing his artistic freedom? The writer described Jewison as "the 41-year-old symbol of the New Hollywood," a man who melded "showbiz tradition" with the principled politics of the New Left. His previous success at the box office had given him "the privilege of complete control over his films." Jewison was not about to cede that control without a fight. "I'll make the film my way," he said, "and nobody is going to tell me how to do it. I'll listen to all the people involved, but it will be done my way, and my way alone. That goes for the studio as well as the protest groups." Jewison, the "capitalist-hippie," defended his artistic freedom while looking to the box office for vindication. "The film will be mine, and I'll stand by it," he repeated later in the article. "I stood by 'Cincinnati Kid,' 'The Russians Are Coming,' and 'Heat of the Night.' Every one of them contained an idea and they were successful."[89]

Jewison dismissed the claims of the Black Anti-Defamation Association as unfounded and somewhat hysterical. He accused the group of misreading Styron's novel, mischaracterizing fictionalized scenes as historical inaccuracies. "They blew some of the incidents in the book way out of proportion," he said. Quoting from Styron's introduction, Jewison argued that the book should be read as a "meditation on history," not as a collection of discrete facts culled from the documentary record. For him, the appeal of the book lay in its larger truths about race relations in the United States, its "excellent examination of the relationship between Southern landholders and slaves during the 1830s." Jewison attempted to turn the tables on his black critics by accusing them of racial prejudice. "They claim that a white man like Styron shouldn't write a novel about a black slave," he said. "Well, I am not concerned about the color of Mr. Styron's skin. I am, however, impressed that he spent six years on his book and that his knowledge of slavery is better than almost anyone else's, black or white."[90]

Incensed by Jewison's public comments, Meriwether fired off a letter of rebuttal. She charged that Jewison had misrepresented the BADA as sharing the extreme antiwhite position of some of its Black Power supporters. "The most serious misstatement," she wrote, "is that we claim a white man like Styron shouldn't write a novel about a black slave. We never made such a statement." The BADA did not object to a white man like Styron writing a novel about a black slave, she said, so long as he did not falsify black history or defame black people. Meriwether also took issue with Jewison's assertion that the

BADA was "in the minority" within the black community. "How does he know?" she asked. "We represent organizations that cut across every economic and political line, ranging from the grass roots level to college professors, from black nationalists to the churches."[91]

Meriwether had the signatures to prove it. The assassination of Martin Luther King, Jr., in April of 1968 generated an unprecedented show of unity among black groups in the Los Angeles area. The Black Congress, an umbrella group representing more than forty organizations from across the political spectrum, coordinated memorial activities and channeled anger into activism. The BADA took advantage of the institutional framework provided by the Black Congress to solicit endorsements from local leaders of the NAACP, the Southern Christian Leadership Conference, SNCC, Maulana Karenga's black nationalist group US, the Black Panther Party, and the Malcolm X Foundation. The BADA also secured the support of black churches, black student unions, black newspapers, and black political groups from throughout the Los Angeles area. A request for letters of support, published in black newspapers across the nation, produced an "avalanche" of replies. "It is evident," Meriwether wrote, "that this is the kind of project which can unify black people on all levels; they all can participate."[92]

In mid-April of 1968, the BADA took out a full-page ad in the *Hollywood Reporter* urging black actors to boycott the film. The ad, Meriwether recalled, "blew Hollywood away." Meriwether sent press releases to black newspapers across the country — some two hundred media outlets in all — describing the escalating protest campaign and soliciting letters of support. Her quotes appeared in the *New York Amsterdam News*, the largest black newspaper on the East Coast: "We are ignoring director Norman Jewison's newspaper statement that we can't tell him what to do. We don't have to depend upon the whim of producers. If the black actors refuse to accept roles in this picture Hollywood will have to abandon it or play it in blackface."[93] Just how many black actors agreed to observe the boycott is impossible to gauge. Sidney Poitier, the leading black actor of the day, refused to take sides in the public debate. He bristled when reporters asked his opinion of the Nat Turner film project. "I prefer not to comment," he responded curtly. "In any case I'm not interested in doing a period piece."[94]

As a public relations gambit, Wolper and Jewison moved quickly to hire a black screenwriter. Less than two weeks after the BADA announced its protest, Jewison told the *Los Angeles Times* that he hoped — "rather remotely because he's very busy" — that James Baldwin would write the screenplay for Styron's book. When Baldwin declined, the filmmakers secured the services of Louis Peterson, a black screenwriter who had written a screen adaptation of Styron's previous novel, *Set This House on Fire*. The filmmakers apparently hoped that having a black screenwriter would shield them against charges of racial insensitivity and give the script a veneer of black authorship. Moreover, at a time when civil rights organizations were pushing for racial diversity in the Hollywood film industry, the hiring of a black screenwriter made good publicity. "Negro Will Screenplay 'Turner,' Slave Revolt," read the headline in *Variety*. The article noted, pointedly, that Peterson attended Morehouse College in Atlanta, "the alma mater of the late Dr. Martin Luther King Jr."[95]

The radical black critique of Styron's book culminated in the publication of *William Styron's Nat Turner: Ten Black Writers Respond*. Published by Beacon Press, the volume became the political and cultural manifesto for the grass-roots movement against the movie. The BADA hailed the "ten brilliant essays attacking Styron's falsification of history and racist dogma."[96] The collection of essays repeated many of the points that had been made elsewhere. What gave the book its power was its use of the collective voice. It was one thing for an individual black critic, writing in a small-circulation periodical, to call Styron a racist and accuse him of willfully distorting history to serve his own reactionary agenda; it was quite another for a major press to assemble ten such essays in a bound volume and publish it as the manifesto of a larger social and cultural movement. The contributors spoke for a "black intellectual community" united in protest against the bestselling novel and its uncritical reception by white historians, white literary critics, and the white-controlled news media. "No event has touched and stirred the black intellectual community more than this book," editor John Henrik Clarke wrote in his introduction to the volume. "They are of the opinion, with a few notable exceptions, that the Nat Turner created by William Styron has little resemblance to the slave insurrectionist who is a hero to his people." Clarke presented the individual essays assembled in the volume as an expression of black solidarity in the face of white cultural aggression. Critical acclaim for the novel in the "national press" reflected the hegemonic power of the "white literary establishment" and the marginalization of black intellectuals with more intimate knowledge of black history and black life.[97]

Supporters of Styron viewed the charges lodged by the "Ten Black Writers" as not merely groundless but symptomatic of a growing intolerance, bordering on "hysteria," among black revolutionary ideologues. "I think it is obscene," Martin Duberman wrote, "to say that Styron is 'an unreconstructed Southern rebel' and that his purposes in writing the 'Confessions' were to confirm white racists in their view that Negroes are ingrates and incompetents and to defuse black militancy by suggesting that all rebellions are acts of futility. Styron's chief crime, it appears, is his refusal to reduce any man to caricature, whether as Hero or Oppressor."[98] The Marxist historian Eugene Genovese argued that *Ten Black Writers* revealed more about "the thinking of intellectuals in the Black Power movement" than Styron's flaws as a writer. Genovese cited the "political affinities" between the "Ten Black Writers" and "the Black Power movement, which increasingly demands conformity, myth-making, and historical fabrication" in the name of black liberation. "I should respectfully suggest," he wrote, "that although the oppressed may need history for identity and inspiration, they need it above all for the truth of what the world has made of them and of what they have helped make of the world."[99]

Styron, for his part, dismissed the "Ten Black Writers" as "hysterical in the extreme. Responsible critics, black and white, have refuted them." Styron attributed the black backlash against his book to the racial chauvinism of the Black Power movement. "There's a sense on the part of some black critics that I have invaded their world, that I as a white man have entered privileged territory." When an interviewer suggested that "much of the so-called Black Revolution occurs in the form of emotion and rhetoric and slogans," Styron agreed. "I'm impatient with irrationality. The argument that we must use irrationality as a club is shameful. It's time that Negroes, confronting historical crisis, stop being infantile."[100]

The threat of a black actors' boycott and picket lines at the opening convinced the Hollywood filmmakers that they could not make the movie without the support of the black community. In December 1968, the filmmakers offered to meet with the BADA representatives to discuss a settlement. Meriwether made no effort to hide her disdain at the belated peace offering. "Wolper should have come to the black community for approval before he paid $600,000 for the

movie rights," she wrote. "There was enough protest at the time to indicate black displeasure, but he chose to ignore it."[101]

Meriwether kept a detailed record of the meeting, documenting
each concession made by Wolper and Jewison. The filmmakers assured the group that "such things as lusting after white women, rape,
black slaves putting down the rebellion, homosexuality, were not included in Lew Peterson's screenplay." Wolper and Jewison promised
to present a "positive image" of Nat Turner, whom they envisioned as
"a black revolutionary fighting for his freedom." The filmmakers apparently balked at the demand to change the title of the film to distinguish it from the book; Wolper had paid for the rights to Styron's best-
selling novel and the publicity that went with the name. In the end,
however, he agreed to shorten the title to *Nat Turner*. He also agreed
to the demand that the historian Herbert Aptheker, a vocal critic of
Styron's book, be hired as an advisor. Meriwether promised that she
would "call off the troops" as soon as Wolper signed the agreement.
Six months later, after a series of minor disputes over the wording,
Wolper signed.[102]

A skeptical mainstream press portrayed the settlement as a capitu-
lation to Black Power ideologues by a skittish white liberal Hollywood
producer. The *Los Angeles Times* reported that Wolper changed the
name of the film and "agreed to certain other demands" in response to
"prodding" by militant advocates of Black Power. The *New York Times*
quoted Wolper as saying he felt "uneasy" about yielding to pressure
from the black community. "But I tried to understand the pressure," he
said. "I was making not only a work of art but also a social work."
Wolper noted that the protest reflected the sentiments of black people from across the country. "Every legitimate black organization in
America came out against certain parts of the book, and I felt something had to be done. You don't go forward and make a film about a
black hero if the entire black community feels it is wrong, any more
than you'd make a film of 'Exodus' if the Jewish community felt it was
wrong."[103] Such arguments failed to assuage white liberal critics. The
New York Times columnist Tom Wicker argued that the value of a
work of art rested in the creative vision of its author, not the "social ac-
ceptance" of a particular community or group. While Styron's novel
might one day be considered a great work of art, the Hollywood film
adaptation would never achieve that status because its producers had
compromised their artistic integrity.[104]

In its coverage of the settlement, *Variety* reported the departure of

Norman Jewison as director of the film and the hiring of James Earl Jones to play Nat Turner. *Variety* explained that Jones, then appearing in the Broadway production of *The Great White Hope*, could not get free until the spring of 1970; the resulting delay created a conflict for Jewison, already committed to making *Fiddler on the Roof.* Sidney Lumet, whose credits included *Twelve Angry Men* (1957) and *The Pawnbroker* (1965), took over as director of *Nat Turner.*[105]

Conspicuously absent from press coverage of the negotiated settlement was any comment from William Styron. The *New York Times* reported that Styron, "who has frequently defended his book against attacks by Negroes," was in Africa on safari and unavailable for comment. Wolper spoke for him, saying that Styron was "completely aware of what's going on and has no objections." The *Times* added that Styron had "no official role in preparing the film"; the screenplay was being finished by "a Negro writer." In an interview with the *Boston Globe*, published several weeks after the settlement was announced, Styron spoke sympathetically of Wolper. "He's been forced to compromise." Styron gave no indication that he felt betrayed by the filmmakers. Apparently he had resigned himself to the necessity of such a compromise and, in effect, signed off on it.[106]

Nat Turner *on Location in Southampton County*

In the summer of 1969, with the Hollywood protest behind them, Wolper and Lumet began scouting locations for *Nat Turner.* They quickly settled on Southampton County — the original scene of the rebellion — as the ideal location. The advantages were obvious. Those who visited the rural county, with its open fields dotted by rotting wooden homesteads, could easily imagine themselves back in Nat Turner's time. There was just one problem: Styron's novel deeply offended many white residents of the area, particularly the descendants of slaveholders depicted unfavorably in the book. Like the black protesters in Hollywood, these white critics accused Styron of distorting their history and defaming their ancestors. Some feared that a movie based on Styron's book would incite modern-day Nat Turners to rise in arms against an entrenched white establishment. If they had their way, Turner's Rebellion would not be remembered at all.[107]

Styron knew that his book was despised by a strong contingent of white Southerners, despite the rave reviews in newspapers throughout the South. He told an interviewer that he occasionally received hate mail from the region.[108] A woman from Texas questioned his racial and regional loyalties. "I have been looking at the picture on the dust jacket of Nat Turner," she wrote, "and since you look light-skinned, I can only conclude that you are 'passing' as one of the worst degenerates of our time. I have one thing to be thankful for, you aren't a Texan. The people of Alabama should lynch you. (I hope they do.)"[109] Another white Southern partisan told the Book-of-the-Month Club that she was "disgusted" with its choice of Styron's book as its November selection. "Mr. Styron reportedly has Southern blood. But he should try to remember he is not Faulkner and only Faulkner could emphasize the shortcomings of the 'country within a country' — and still let his love for the South shine through."[110]

Anti-Styron sentiment among white Southern partisans attracted little attention from national media preoccupied with Black Power militancy and urban rioting in the North and West. The passage of landmark civil rights and voting-rights legislation heralded the dawn of yet another "New South." Yet the region remained a site of tense, frequently violent encounters between blacks and whites grappling with the changes wrought by the civil rights movement.

The production phase of the film project took place against a backdrop of racial turmoil in Nat Turner country. In September of 1967, the *Virginian-Pilot* reported that the "appearance" of forty-two robed Klansmen at a grocery store in an African-American residential area of Franklin had led to a "disturbance" involving "an estimated 300 Negroes." When police tried to disperse the black demonstrators, they "became unruly." Ten city policemen and twelve state troopers responded to the scene; police arrested two black men on charges of inciting a riot.[111] The following day, the newspaper published an article on the continuing presence of the Klan in Southside Virginia. Though active membership was low, the Klan attempted to keep a high profile by holding cross-burning rallies every Saturday night in farm fields throughout the Tidewater region. The rallies were "preceded by visits to communities near the fields," during which robed Klansmen "sometimes passed out Klan literature, George Wallace for president bumper stickers, or membership applications." The Grand Nighthawk of the Virginia Realm of the Knights of the Ku Klux Klan told the *Virginian-Pilot* that the group was trying to improve its "blood-spattered" image. "We're not a bunch of hooded bigots anymore. Our people wear coats and ties; they're neatly dressed. Take a good look at our robes; they're satin. We don't wear bedsheets."[112]

The Virginia Council on Human Relations, a branch of the Southern Regional Council, reported on the Klan-inspired Franklin "riot" in its monthly newsletter. "It was not a bloodbath," the authors wrote, "but it was an insurrection — an inspiration? — in its own way as surely as was Nat Turner's rebellion. And it can, and probably will, happen again, for the people of Franklin seem to have learned little of what the upheaval meant." The police chief reportedly blamed the uprising on a pair of outside agitators, Stokely Carmichael and H. Rap Brown; the "elite of the town" blamed the riot on "a useful scapegoat: the Kluxers." The authors of the article pointed to a more fundamental source of discontent: the separate and unequal status of blacks and whites in Southampton.[113] Indeed, despite the legal victories and legislative gains of the civil rights movement, the county remained rigidly segregated. In 1967, a federal examiner stripped the Southampton school system of all federal funds — nearly $400,000 — for violating the school desegregation provisions of the Civil Rights Act of 1964. Of the 3,400 black children enrolled in county schools, only eighty attended school with white children.[114]

To navigate these turbulent waters, Twentieth Century Fox hired local attorney Gilbert Francis as its liaison to Southampton County and neighboring locales. Francis prided himself on his ability to communicate with people of widely divergent social backgrounds and political views. "Practically speaking," he boasted to a member of the film production crew, "I believe I have the best relations with the Negro community of any other white person in the area, and, ironically, I am also tied by heritage to the old Southern families and to the political and governmental Establishment."[115] Francis convinced the filmmakers that he could get the entire community behind the film project so long as they made the movie "in accordance with the true history — and not like Styron said it."[116]

Gilbert Francis had become interested in the history of the insurrection at an early age. His father, who was old enough to hear the eyewitness accounts of aged survivors, passed along the family lore to his five children. Francis and other Southampton County schoolchildren were briefed on the insurrection by their teachers as well. "We were told that Nat Turner was a religious fanatic and a slave who decided he was going to kill all the white folks, and that's what happened," Francis recalled. "The blacks were taught the same thing because the white people wrote the history for the blacks." While practicing law in Richmond in the late 1940s, Francis lived around the corner from William Sidney Drewry. The two men were kin; their families were intermarried at three different places. Francis became a student and disciple of the retired historian, taking Drewry's book as the last word on the insurrection.[117] Francis established himself as an authority on Turner's Rebellion; local residents directed inquiring visitors to his Boykins law offices. His status as a direct descendant of several white victims greatly enhanced his credentials. "They knew that my family was one that lost almost as many as any of the rest of the families." Francis considered his depiction of Nat Turner unbiased. "I did not show him as a hero and I did not show him as a villain. I discussed history."[118]

Francis loathed Styron's novel, which depicted his slaveholding great-grandfather as a "gross, hairless man with a swinish squint" who took pleasure "by getting drunk at more or less regular intervals and beating his Negroes ruthlessly with a flexible wooden cane wrapped in alligator hide." To Francis, the motive was clear: "Styron was trying to make Nathaniel Francis the bad guy in order to make Nat Turner look good." Francis also objected to the way that Styron portrayed white people in general. "His novel showed all white people to be bad and stupid and all blacks to be children of God, almost."[119]

Contemporary observers commented on the intensity of anti-Styron sentiment in the Southampton County area. Bernice Kelly Harris, a newspaper columnist in Raleigh, North Carolina, located the epicenter among white county residents whose ancestors appeared as fictionalized characters in the book. "Some of the buzzing among these unprejudiced and sophisticated people is not due to any treatment of the book's hero or any heroic mold contrary to tradition, but rather to the use of names of living descendants whose forebears with the same names, are pictured as cruel slaveholders, when there are family records to the contrary."[120]

Francis detected a more general aversion to the subject of slave rebellion among white county residents. "A lot of white people said, 'We don't want a movie made about a Negro hero in Southampton County. And we think that the Nat Turner insurrection ought to be pushed under the rug and forgotten.' And they didn't want anybody talking about the damn thing, particularly making a movie about the insurrection. My position was that a movie's going to be made about the insurrection and we better have it made under circumstances that we've got some control over." In essence, Francis espoused a philosophy similar to the cultural nationalism of the Black Power movement. His strategy differed, however, in that he worked behind the scenes to secure editorial concessions from the filmmakers.[121]

As a key condition of his involvement in the project, Francis demanded the right to review the script for historical inaccuracies. He made no bones about his personal stake in the revisions. "Great Grandfather Nathaniel Francis would have an uneasy rest in his grave if he thought I was allowing him to be maligned in the film. I do not dread his ghostly manifestation so much as I respect the feelings of my mother, brother, sisters and all the family kin. From an ethical standpoint, if I am to live with myself, I must vindicate Styron's unjustifiable representation of Nathaniel Francis, and therefore, I am depending on you to correct this historical inaccuracy." Francis proceeded to highlight the offensive passages: "On pages 76 and 77 of the script, the scene in which Nathaniel Francis forces Sam and Will to fight does nothing to further the story or enhance the script. On pages 94 and 95 and 113 Nathaniel Francis is again mentioned in a derogatory manner and not one word is said about how his pregnant wife was hidden and protected from the insurgents by her faithful servant." Francis suggested no other substantial changes in the script.[122] Director Sidney Lumet promised Francis that "any *knowing* historical inaccuracy" — whether it involved the depiction of a person or the use of a place name — would be corrected.[123]

On September 25, 1969, the *Tidewater News* announced the coming film project under a double-deck banner headline: "Southampton County Most Likely Location for $4 Million Movie on Nat Turner Rebellion." Residents of the rural county eagerly anticipated the economic benefits of the film project. Nearly half of the film's budget would be spent in Southampton County. Most of that sum would be used "to rent land and erect a movie set replica of the original town of Jerusalem." A recreation center, including tennis courts, would be built "to allow the movie crew of approximately 100 actors and production workers to relax without affecting local living patterns." Local labor and materials would be used to build the exterior sets. A number of local residents, both "Negro and white," would be hired as extras, "some with small speaking parts, to round out the professional cast."[124]

Throughout the fall of 1969, Francis attempted to neutralize opposition to the film project within the white community. "This group," he later recalled, "was fearful that the filming of the movie here in this area would trigger new racial unrest and that each negro would try to be a 1970 Nat Turner. Such a fear was even voiced in our local historical society (of which I happen to be president), when some of the 'little old ladies with umbrellas' bitterly protested the proposed local filming." Styron met personally with various white civic and social clubs "to explain the situation and to answer any questions. This proved very helpful in getting white support."[125]

Like the black protesters in Hollywood, African-American residents of Southampton County wanted assurances that filmmakers would treat them — and Nat Turner — fairly. Francis sought to allay their concerns by inviting "Negroes of all types" to a series of public meetings and asking for their input.[126] "From the very beginning I could sense that the Black Community was fearful that it would be excluded from full and equal participation," Francis wrote at the time. "I did not want this to happen for Democratic reasons as well as the fact that it would not be good business for 20th Century-[Fox]."[127] The Assembly of Southampton, whom Francis described as "our most radical Negro group," formed a committee to study the script and to weigh the economic impact of the project on the black community. Francis responded enthusiastically. "I am delighted you are interested in being sure the movie is historically correct and that it in no way shows the Negro in a derogatory or disrespectful light."[128] Black residents who identified themselves as "heirs" of Nat Turner formed their own special interest group to ensure that they would reap economic benefits from the making of the movie.[129] Francis sought to appease the Turner heirs by informing them that he had recommended the use of their properties in the film. Francis urged the filmmakers to follow through on his recommendations as a show of "good faith."[130]

Some black residents of the area suspected that Francis had ulterior motives in his dealings with their community. In December of 1969, *Jet* magazine reported rumors that Francis, the white lawyer for Twentieth Century Fox, was "attempting to purchase as many of the old Nat Turner–connected historical sites as he can, such as Cross Keys, the spot where the revolt began and which Francis is believed to have bought." The article identified Francis as the leader of "the whites," who were said to be "well-organized." The article suggested that Francis hoped to profit from the making of the movie at the expense of black property owners.[131] Francis denied any effort to buy up properties and bristled at the "allegations in *JET* about [his] 'leading the whites.'" He characterized his relationship with the local black community as friendly, professional, and based on mutual trust — not, as *Jet* described it, adversarial or exploitative.[132]

In January 1970, after a two-hour meeting with black leaders, Francis reported that he had secured their full support and cooperation. "The Black Community was responsive and appreciative of our bringing them into the project as equal participants," he reported.[133] Just when Francis appeared to have everyone on board, Twentieth Century Fox announced a "feature film hiatus" that would close the studio for at least six months. *Nat Turner* and at least six other films, including *The Salzburg Connection, Portnoy's Complaint,* and *Play It Again, Sam,* were affected. The studio cited heavy production costs and other industry-wide financial woes as the primary reason for the shutdown.[134]

Reporters heard a more sensational explanation for the film's postponement when they asked Styron for his reaction to the news. "Black power protests," he declared, had forced the filmmakers to put the project on hold. "The protests were getting so loud I would say it was scaring them. I think they were worried." The film project, Styron recalled, had been "in trouble from the beginning." Styron said he started out as an advisor on the film but quit because he "became an embarrassment to them because of the black power protests." Styron acknowledged that "most Hollywood studios" were in financial trouble because of "a terrific clampdown from the banks." Nevertheless, he maintained that "the money situation was secondary" to "black power protests" as the cause of the film's delay.[135] Styron's speculative comments and off-the-cuff remarks fueled white liberal paranoia about Black Power radicals extorting concessions and subverting civil liberties.[136]

Francis was shocked to read that Black Power protests had forced Twentieth Century Fox to postpone the movie. He dashed off a note to the production manager, who assured him that "it was not 'Black Power,' but the money that caused this postponement." Francis concluded that Black Power has nothing to do with the demise of *Nat Turner.* "In fact," he wrote, "we could not have asked for any more support and cooperation" from the black community. Though Francis held out hope that the project would be revived, it was not to be.[137]

In 1975, long after the press had lost interest in the subject, Styron retreated from his earlier claim that "Black Power" protests killed the Nat Turner film project. "It was partly the Black protest that buggered the works badly," he told the *Mississippi Quarterly*, "but they were going to go ahead and do it anyway." Styron blamed the demise of the film on *Dr. Dolittle* and *Hello, Dolly!*, two big-budget films that cost Twentieth Century Fox millions of dollars. "Both of them flopped," Styron explained, "and *Nat Turner* was the casualty. They simply didn't have the money at the moment, so it was shelved and they never made it." As Styron spoke those words, he sensed that Black Power had run its course. Perhaps the time was ripe, he suggested, for Twentieth Century Fox to revive the Nat Turner project. "There's a much better chance now that the movie will be a good one than there was at the time," he mused, "because they were going to turn it into some terrible piece of propaganda, you know, a lot of heroic blather." Still, Styron was not about to invest any emotional capital in the project. "I don't honestly care," he said. "I've seen so many bad movies made of people's works that I am just as happy if it is forgotten." And, until very recently, it was.[138]

Styron failed to realize that the political struggles of the sixties, including the controversy over his novel, had profoundly transformed mainstream academic writing and popular culture by the mid-seventies. Portrayals of black people as damaged by slavery, once standard liberal fare, now appeared racist and conservative. A new wave of scholarship highlighted the vitality and autonomy of black community life under slavery. Unlike the damaged victims of white totalitarian oppression described by Elkins and Styron, the black people of these studies lived in a world of their own making and resisted white encroachment at every turn.[139]

This new direction in scholarship undergirded popular depictions of slave family life, such as Alex Haley's *Roots* (1976), the saga of an African-American family's harrowing yet triumphant odyssey from slavery to freedom. Not long after the demise of his Nat Turner film project, producer David Wolper teamed up with Haley to transform *Roots* into a television extravaganza. An estimated 85 million people — some 40 percent of the American population — watched the story of Kunta Kinte and his descendants unfold over eight consecutive nights in January 1977.[140] Critics viewed the miniseries, like Styron's novel, as liberal social commentary on the roots of racial conflict in contemporary America. Vernon Jordan, executive director of the National Urban League, called it "the single most spectacular educational experience in race relations in America." David Duke, grand wizard of the Ku Klux Klan, dismissed it as "a vicious malignment of the white population." The Socialist Workers Party newspaper proclaimed *Roots* a spur to "Black Pride and militancy." Nancy Reagan, wife of conservative Republican presidential candidate Ronald Reagan, accused the producers of inflaming antiwhite sentiment among blacks in Los Angeles.[141]

Black radical scholars who participated in a forum on TV's *Roots* bemoaned the absence of Nat Turner's rebellious spirit from the Hollywood production. Robert Chrisman observed that the televised saga represented "a regression to a less heroic, less dignified, black image than we saw and projected in the 1960s." The black characters depicted in the miniseries, he wrote, responded to each calamity and atrocity with a mood of resignation and submission rather than a spirit of defiance.[142] Other contributors to the forum concurred. It was no accident, Chinzweizu argued, that Hollywood chose to tell the story of "Chicken George" (one of Haley's opportunistic ancestors) and not the story of Nat Turner. "Imagine a film, *Nat Turner,* made with even so mild a treatment as that in the movie *Spartacus.* Would any network pick it up and risk having all those young and impressionable all-American kids who rooted for Chicken George root instead for Nat Turner?"[143]

Wolper scoffed at complaints that the black characters in *Roots* were insufficiently rebellious. "If Alex Haley's particular family didn't fight back, so be it. However, I thought there was plenty of black resistance on the ship, and by Kunta Kinte and Tom, Kunta beaten into being named Toby, losing his foot trying to escape." Wolper argued that the "image of a black family held together in love, honor, and courage," so skillfully portrayed by Alex Haley in the book and miniseries, did far more to advance the cause of racial equality in America than the "image of blacks fighting on the streets."[144]

Styron, for his part, dismissed *Roots* as "crude mass culture." He took an elitist view of efforts to popularize the topic of slavery, citing the moral complexity of the subject and his own bruising experience as author of *The Confessions of Nat Turner.* In 1993, he joined a campaign against Disney's America, a proposed three-thousand-acre historical theme park near Washington, D.C. Styron seized on the comment, uttered by Disney's "chief imagineer" Robert Weis, that the proposed theme park would include "painful, disturbing, and agonizing" exhibits that would make visitors "feel what it was like" to be a slave. In an op-ed column, he wrote:

> I was fascinated by Mr. Weis's statement, because 27 years ago I published a novel called "The Confessions of Nat Turner," which was partly intended to make the reader feel what it was like to be a slave. Whether I succeeded or not was a matter of hot debate, and the book still provokes controversy. But as one who has plunged into the murky waters where the Imagineers wish to venture, I have doubts whether the technical wizardry that so entrances children and grown-ups at other Disney parks can do anything but mock a theme as momentous as slavery, the great transforming circumstance of American history.

The *Washington Post* columnist Richard Cohen took Styron to task for suggesting that certain topics — such as slavery and the Civil War — were too serious, too complex for anyone but historians and novelists to interpret for the public.

"Of course, Disney cannot capture the totality of the slavery era in the United States," Cohen wrote. "But to countless millions who do not read Styron (their loss) and who do not, really, read anything, is a Disney trek along the Underground Railroad such a bad thing?" Cohen reminded Styron that the controversies surrounding his most famous novels, *The Confessions of Nat Turner* and *Sophie's Choice,* stemmed from his insistence on writing about historical experiences that his most vociferous critics — "blacks, Jews, literary people, historians" — claimed as their own.[145]

For all his elitism, Styron did more to popularize the history and memory of Nat Turner's Rebellion than any other writer of the twentieth century. Tens of thousands of Americans have come to know the event through the interpretive lens of Styron's novel or the critical responses to it. The controversy has had a profound impact on scholarship as well, inspiring an outpouring of books, articles, and document collections that stress the multiplicity of perspectives on the event.

Perhaps the most traditional line of research has led back to the historical document that served as Styron's primary source of inspiration — the original 1831 "Confessions of Nat Turner, As Told to Thomas R. Gray." Historians and literary critics have subjected the pamphlet to close scrutiny and, in several provocative and pathbreaking studies, suggested radically new possibilities for interpretation.

In a 1971 essay titled "Styron and His Sources," the historian Henry Irving Tragle theorized that Gray outlined the narrative of "The Confessions" months before his jail cell interview with Nat Turner. Tragle pointed to "striking similarities" in style and content between an anonymous letter to the editor of the *Richmond Whig* dated September 17, 1831, and Gray's introduction to "The Confessions of Nat Turner," published two months later. Tragle theorized that Gray, "a clever lawyer, and a shrewd entrepreneur," arranged the jail cell interview with Turner to confirm conclusions he had already reached weeks before, thus enabling him to "produce a salable manuscript" within an extraordinarily brief time span. "And if there is any truth at all in this chain of speculation, then who can say, with reference to *The Original Confessions*, where Gray stops and Nat begins?"[146]

Like many historians before him, Tragle assumed that the sixty- to seventy-year-old "Thomas Gray" who appeared in the 1830 census for Southampton County and the "Thomas R. Gray" who published "The Confessions" were one and the same. It took the painstaking research of a county historian to set the record straight. In *Southampton County, Virginia* (1978), Thomas C. Parramore revealed that the two Grays were actually father and son, Capt. Thomas Gray and Thomas Ruffin Gray. The elder Gray died three weeks after the Southampton uprising and left his son Thomas — a thirty-one-year-old planter-turned-lawyer — almost entirely out of his will. "At the nadir of his troubles in the fall of 1831," Parramore wrote, "fortune thrust before Thomas R. Gray a sudden and dazzling prospect of salvation." The capture of Turner presented the enterprising attorney with an opportunity to record the "confessions" of the rebel leader and sell them in pamphlet form at twenty-five cents a copy. Perhaps Gray saw a kindred spirit in the rebellious slave, Parramore mused. "The same blind destiny that cast Nat into a life of slavery had robbed Gray of his patrimony, his wife, the affection of his father, his standing in the community." In effect, Parramore made co-conspirators of Gray and Turner, thus diffusing "the specter of racial antipathy" that had haunted Southampton County residents ever since the rebellion.[147]

The literary critic Eric Sundquist characterized "The Confessions" as more of a literary "collaboration" that — like slavery itself — could

be read from the dominant perspective of the master or from the sub-
versive perspective of the slave. In *To Wake the Nation: Race in the
Making of American Literature* (1993), Sundquist argued for "the possibility that Nat Turner's voice — and hence his thought, his vision,
and his leadership — remains strongly present in the historical 'text.'"
With Turner firmly reestablished as author of "The Confessions," his
radical commentary on race and American democracy fully expli-
cated, the text could assume its rightful place in the literary canon
of the American Renaissance. "Indeed," Sundquist wrote, "given its
formative role in the course of African American cultural history
and both anti- and pro-slavery argument, it is hard to imagine why
Turner's 'Confessions' should not be accorded the same attention
granted, say, Emerson's 'Self-Reliance' or Thoreau's 'Civil Disobedience.'"[148]

Sundquist's emphasis on Turner's agency in authoring "The Confessions" drew a sharp rebuke from the legal historian Daniel S. Fabricant, who read the document as a legal and literary instrument of
repression. Any suggestion of a voluntary "collaboration" between
Turner, a black slave accused of insurrection, and Gray, a white lawyer
with "a keen interest in maintaining the Southern social order," struck
Fabricant as naive and dangerously misleading. In an essay titled
"Thomas R. Gray and William Styron: Finally, a Critical Look at the
1831 *Confessions of Nat Turner*," published in the *American Journal of
Legal History* (1993), Fabricant theorized that most scholars accepted
"The Confessions" at face value because they had an enormous professional stake in its authenticity. "Reluctance to probe Gray's work," he
wrote, "may reflect belief that criticism would necessarily call into
question the veracity of the narrative he attributes to Nat, and the validity of much of what has come to be accepted as Nat's life story and
his legacy as one of the earliest and most important black-American
revolutionary figures." Fabricant viewed "The Confessions" as the
work of a "white Southern racist" dedicated to "the political, social,
and economic interests of the Southern slaveocracy." He concluded
that Gray's pamphlet revealed a great deal more about "the systematic
victimization of blacks that was carried out under the guise of law and
justice in early nineteenth-century Virginia" than it revealed about
the enigmatic figure of Nat Turner.[149]

In a recent essay marking the twenty-fifth anniversary edition of
his novel, Styron argued that the original "Confessions" could never

be made to yield the historical truth about Nat Turner. Perhaps we, like him, should feel liberated by that knowledge. Perhaps we know all we will ever need to know about Turner and his motives. Perhaps the time has come for scholars to question whether the tight narrative framework of "The Confessions" has foreclosed inquiry into alternative scenarios too dangerous to contemplate in 1831.[150]

EPILOGUE:

THE CONTINUING SAGA

O N NOVEMBER 11, 1831, Southampton County authorities hanged Nat Turner by the neck until dead, then dismembered his body and dispersed its parts among the living as curios and relics. Today, more than 170 years later, Americans continue to argue over what to make of Turner's life and what to do with his uninterred remains. The strange saga of Turner's skull illuminates the changing image of the rebellious slave and the complex cultural transactions involved in the transmission of memory from generation to generation.

The earliest published references to Nat Turner's remains reveal the sharply divergent perspectives of slavery's white apologists, who had nothing but disdain for "negro cut-throats," and the small but growing band of radical dissenters known as abolitionists. A correspondent for the *Norfolk Herald* portrayed "*General* Nat" as a pathetic figure who "sold his body for dissection, and spent the money on gingercakes," which he feasted on before his own execution. The claim that Turner "sold" himself struck William Lloyd Garrison and his fellow abolitionists as preposterous. "In the first place, he was a slave, and by the laws of Virginia a slave cannot make a bargain or own anything. In the next place it is the policy of the Southern press to make the black race appear despicable. In the third place the fact is totally inconsistent with the heroism with which he met death." Abolitionists viewed the dissection of Turner's body as further evidence of Southern slaveholders' depravity. An item in the *Liberator*, published two weeks after Turner's execution, condemned the Southern medical school practice of dissecting the bodies of slaves without their consent or any consideration for their families and communities. "They have no feelings to be respected or offended!! You may cut up and mangle them as you please: but they are blacks, and no more to be regarded than any *other* beasts of the field."[1]

Gruesome reminders of Turner's fate, preserved as human relics and oral traditions, haunted the black people of Southampton County long after the suppression of Turner's Rebellion. Historian William Sidney Drewry, a white Southampton County native who interviewed dozens of local residents on this topic in the late nineteenth century, chronicled the disposition of Turner's corpse as a chilling footnote to the insurrection. Immediately after his execution, Drewry wrote, Turner's body was "delivered to the doctors, who skinned it and made grease of the flesh. Mr. R. S. Barham's father owned a money purse made of his hide." Turner's skeleton "was for many years in the possession of Dr. Massenburg, but has since been misplaced." As for Turner's skull, there were "many citizens still living" who had seen it. "It was very peculiarly shaped, resembling the head of a sheep, and at least three-quarters of an inch thick." Drewry cited a nineteenth-century folk belief as evidence of the fear instilled in slaves by the rendering of Nat Turner's body. "The famous remedy of doctors of antebellum days — castor oil — was long dreaded for fear it was 'old Nat's grease,' and it is doubtful if the old prejudice has entirely died out among the older darkies."[2]

Drewry's willingness, in 1900, to identify the owners of Turner's skeleton and the wallet supposedly made of Turner's skin suggests that the white people of his day took considerable pride in their association with such artifacts. An unabashed apologist for the slaveholders and their descendants, Drewry noted that Western tradition offered numerous examples of victors displaying the remains of their vanquished enemies. "During the French Revolution," he observed, "books are said to have been bound in the skin of victims of the guillotine, and now in the British Museum books are exhibited bound in tanned human skin. Our newspapers have recorded frequently that in other States are preserved many memorials of like morbid and depraved taste." Perhaps, viewed in the context of world history, the public display of Turner's remains was unexceptional. Yet, by 1900, the lynching of black people and the public display of their charred, mutilated, and dismembered bodies had become a distinctively white Southern practice. These rituals reinforced the written and unwritten codes of white supremacy and reminded African Americans of their subordinate place in a post-emancipation, post-Reconstruction society. One could hardly gaze on the skull of Nat Turner or hear the gruesome tale of a wallet made of his skin without considering the fate of countless other black men accused of breaching the Southern racial code.

The strange chronicle of Nat Turner's skull highlights the circuitous path of Turner's Rebellion in history and memory: both reappear frequently in sometimes unexpected places. According to Southampton County native Frances Lawrence Webb, Turner's head "was found in possession of a local physician at the close of the War Between the States, became the property of the Provost Marshall who dominated the county in the days of reconstruction, and was given by him, as a precious relic, to one of the Northern Universities."[3] The skull reportedly arrived at Wooster College in Ohio in 1866 with a certificate of authenticity signed by Dr. James R. Parker and other prominent Southampton County residents. It sat for several years in the office of Dr. Leander Firestone, "where it was regarded as a rare object-lesson by his medical students, to view the phrenological skull developments of a man who had made an indelible mark in the annals of Virginia during the old slavery days." At some point, the skull was "placed in University Museum for safe keeping, as an historical relic of the Old Dominion." There it remained until the "great fire" of December 11, 1901, which destroyed the university building that housed the museum. The day after the fire, a student discovered Turner's skull among the debris, "serenely reposing there in the best condition, as if at home." The editors of the local newspaper saw a legend in the making. Perhaps, they mused, the rescue of Turner's skull was a mystery for "theologians," not scientists or historians, to solve. "It may be that Nat Turner is, like John Brown, 'his soul marching on,' and that he is the personal custodian of his own skull, and himself, saved it for the University of Wooster and the State of Virginia. Who knows?"[4]

The skull remained on display in the biology building at the College of Wooster well into the twentieth century. A San Diego dentist, writing to William Styron in 1967, remembered seeing it there as a small child. ("This is the skull of Nate [sic] Turner," read a label pasted to the forehead, "a Negro Slave who led an unsuccessful revolt against the white owners in 1831.") Yet college archivists, contacted in the mid-1990s, could find no record of its presence or its removal.

Then, in December 2002, columnist Donna Britt of the *Wash-*

ington Post reported that the Indiana NAACP president Franklin Breckenridge had purchased the skull and donated it to the proposed Civil Rights Hall of Fame in Gary, Indiana. Richard Hatcher, director of the Hall of Fame project and the first black mayor of Gary, welcomed this addition to the collection and confidently told Britt that the identity of the skull had been authenticated by an Indiana University historian. The organizers hoped that the display of the skull at the new "high-tech institution" could educate young people "who have no real understanding or memory" of the slave insurrection. Within their sphere of popular-culture worship, according to Hatcher, the youngsters might not have realized that "thousands who never got on television made very important contributions."

Publication of the item prompted an angry letter to the editor from Rudolph Lewis, editor of *ChickenBones: A Journal,* an Internet resource for "Literary and Artistic African-American themes" (www.nathanielturner.com). "For a former black consciousness leader to plan the display of the remains of a historical figure in order to raise money is more than just a travesty but quite outrageous," he wrote. "If Mr. Hatcher has indeed received and authenticated the skull, he should return it to Southampton County, Va., for the proper burial it did not receive in 1831. . . . I am sure he does not want to be counted among those purveyors of black flesh — profiteers of black bodies." In his online reply to a letter on the subject, Lewis explained that he held "no great animus" against Hatcher, citing as his only motive the restoration of dignity and integrity of "the prophet of Southampton." In this regard, historians remained as culpable as the public: "A century or more of writing and earnest scholarship have yet to sustain his holiness, his intellectual acumen, and his earnest revelatory experience. He has been reduced continually, as the poor and the powerless usually are, to a political and useful object of opportunists, that is, to satisfy their selfish and narrow ends."[5]

Back in Virginia, news that Turner's skull had turned up in Indiana prompted this question from a local newspaper: "Shouldn't his skull come home?" Elizabeth Nabors, reported as Turner's great-great-granddaughter, recalled her ancestral legacy and the fear that "those with bloodlines connected to Turner" carried for decades after the event. Nonetheless, the passage of time — and the fading sting of history — required that his remains "be afforded some dignity." Several Southampton County residents, black and white, agreed that the skull should be returned for burial in an appropriately marked grave, providing a "focal point" for commemoration. Yet some citizens in Turner country feared the prospect of another bruising battle in an area where, nearly two centuries later, the issue remained raw. "Now, golly day, I can see the battle over what to put on his gravestone," exclaimed Rick Francis, son of the late Gilbert Francis and an emerging local authority on the subject of Turner's Rebellion. Francis suggested a simple, if naive solution to the problem: choose an inscription with facts that everyone could agree on. "It should be simple: Nat Turner, 1800–1831. That's it. Leave the commentary out."[6]

THE

CONFESSIONS

OF

NAT TURNER,

THE LEADER OF THE LATE

INSURRECTION IN SOUTHAMPTON, VA.

As fully and voluntarily made to

THOMAS R. GRAY,

In the prison where he was confined, and acknowledged by
him to be such when read before the Court of Southampton; with the certificate, under seal of
the Court convened at Jerusalem,
Nov. 5, 1831, for his trial.

ALSO, AN AUTHENTIC

ACCOUNT OF THE WHOLE INSURRECTION,

WITH LISTS OF THE WHITES WHO WERE MURDERED,

AND OF THE NEGROES BROUGHT BEFORE THE COURT OF
SOUTHAMPTON, AND THERE SENTENCED, &C.

———

Baltimore:
PUBLISHED BY THOMAS R. GRAY.
Lucas & Deaver, print.
1831.

DISTRICT OF COLUMBIA, TO WIT:

Be it remembered, That on this tenth day of November, Anno Domini, eighteen hundred and thirty-one, Thomas R. Gray of the said District, deposited in this office the title of a book, which is in the words as following:

"The Confessions of Nat Turner, the leader of the late insurrection in Southampton, Virginia, as fully and voluntarily made to Thomas R. Gray, in the prison where he was confined, and acknowledged by him to be such when read before the Court of Southampton; with the certificate, under seal, of the Court convened at Jerusalem, November 5, 1831, for his trial. Also, an authentic account of the whole insurrection, with lists of the whites who were murdered, and of the negroes brought before the Court of Southampton, and there sentenced, &c. the right whereof he claims as proprietor, in conformity with an Act of Congress, entitled "An act to amend the several acts respecting Copy Rights."

                    EDMUND J. LEE, Clerk of the District.

                    In testimony that the above is a true copy,
                    from the record of the District Court for
(Seal.)   the District of Columbia, I, Edmund J.
                    Lee, the Clerk thereof, have hereunto
                    set my hand and affixed the seal of my
                    office, this 10th day of November, 1831.

                    EDMUND J. LEE, C.D.C.

TO THE PUBLIC.

The late insurrection in Southampton has greatly excited the public mind, and led to a thousand idle, exaggerated and mischievous reports. It is the first instance in our history of an open rebellion of the slaves, and attended with such atrocious circumstances of cruelty and destruction, as could not fail to leave a deep impression, not only upon the minds of the community where this fearful tragedy was wrought, but throughout every portion of our country, in which this population is to be found. Public curiosity has been on the stretch to understand the origin and progress of this dreadful conspiracy, and the motives which influences its diabolical actors. The insurgent slaves had all been destroyed, or apprehended, tried and executed, (with the exception of the leader,) without revealing any thing at all satisfactory, as to the motives which governed them, or the means by which they expected to accomplish their object. Every thing connected with this sad affair was wrapt in mystery, until Nat Turner, the leader of this ferocious band, whose name has resounded throughout our widely extended empire, was captured. This "great Bandit" was taken by a single individual, in a cave near the residence of his late owner, on Sunday, the thirtieth of October, without attempting to make the slightest resistance, and on the following day safely lodged in the jail of the County. His captor was Benjamin Phipps, armed with a shot gun well charged. Nat's only weapon was a small light sword which he immediately surrendered, and begged that his life might be spared. Since his confinement, by permission of the Jailor, I have had ready access to him, and finding that he was willing to make a full and free confession of the origin, progress and consummation of the insurrectory movements of the slaves of which he was the contriver and head; I determined for the gratification of public curiosity to commit his statements to writing, and publish them, with little or no variation, from his own words. That this is a faithful record of his confessions, the annexed certificate of the County Court of Southampton, will attest. They certainly bear one stamp of truth and sincerity. He makes no attempt (as all the other insurgents who were examined did,) to exculpate himself, but frankly acknowledges his full participation in all the guilt of the transaction. He was not only the contriver of the conspiracy, but gave the first blow towards its execution.

It will thus appear, that whilst every thing upon the surface of society wore a calm and peaceful aspect; whilst not one note of preparation was heard to warn the devoted inhabitants of woe and death, a gloomy fanatic was revolving in the recesses of his own dark, bewildered, and overwrought mind, schemes of indiscriminate massacre to the whites. Schemes too fearfully executed as far as his fiendish band proceeded in their desolating march. No cry for mercy penetrated their flinty bosoms. No acts of remembered kindness made the least impression upon these remorseless murderers. Men, women and children, from hoary age to helpless infancy were involved in the same cruel fate. Never did a band of savages do their work of death more unsparingly. Apprehension for their own personal safety seems to have been the only principle of restraint in the whole course of their bloody proceedings. And it is not the least remarkable feature in this horrid transaction, that a band actuated by such hellish purposes, should have resisted so feebly, when met by the whites in arms. Desperation alone, one would think, might have led to greater efforts. More than twenty of them attacked Dr. Blunt's house on Tuesday morning, a little before day-break, defended by two men and three boys. They fled precipitately at the first fire; and their future plans of mischief, were entirely disconcerted and broken up. Escaping thence, each individual sought his own safety either in concealment, or by returning home, with the hope that his participation might escape detection, and all were shot down in the course of a few days, or captured and brought to trial and punishment. Nat has survived all his followers, and the gallows will speedily close his career. His own account of the conspiracy is submitted to the public, without comment. It reads an awful, and it is hoped, a useful lesson, as to the operations of a mind like his, endeavoring to grapple with things beyond its reach. How it first became bewildered and confounded, and finally corrupted and led to the conception and perpetration of the most atrocious and heart-rending deeds. It is calculated also to demonstrate the policy of our laws in restraint of this class of our population, and to induce all those entrusted with their execution, as well as our citizens generally, to see that they are strictly and rigidly enforced. Each particular community should look to its own safety, whilst the general guardians of the laws, keep a watchful eye over all. If Nat's statements can be relied on, the insurrection in this county was entirely local, and his designs confided but to a few, and these in his immediate vicinity. It was not instigated by motives of revenge or sudden anger, but the results of long deliberation, and a settled purpose of mind. The offspring of gloomy fanaticism, acting upon materials but too well prepared for such impressions. It will be long remembered in the annals of our country, and many a mother as she presses her infant darling to her bosom, will shudder at the recollection of Nat Turner, and his band of ferocious miscreants.

Believing the following narrative, by removing doubts and conjectures from the public mind which otherwise must have remained, would give general satisfaction, it is respectfully submitted to the public by their ob't serv't,

T. R. GRAY.

———

Jerusalem, Southampton, Va. Nov. 5, 1831.

We the undersigned, members of the Court convened at Jerusalem, on Saturday, the 5th day of Nov. 1831, for the trial of Nat, *alias* Nat Turner, a negro slave, late the property of Putnam Moore, deceased, do hereby certify, that the confessions of Nat, to Thomas R. Gray, was read to him in our presence, and that Nat acknowledged the same to be full, free, and voluntary; and that furthermore, when called upon by the presiding Magistrate of the Court, to state if he had any thing to say, why sentence of death should not be passed upon him, replied he had nothing further than he had communicated to Mr. Gray. Given under our hands and seals at Jerusalem, this 5th day of November, 1831.

JEREMIAH COBB, *Seal.*
THOMAS PRETLOW, *Seal.*
JAMES W. PARKER, *Seal.*
CARR BOWERS, *Seal.*
SAMUEL B. HINES, *Seal.*
ORRIS A. BROWNE, *Seal.*

———

State of Virginia, Southampton County, to wit:

I, James Rochelle, Clerk of the County Court of Southampton in the State of Virginia, do hereby certify, that Jeremiah Cobb, Thomas Pretlow, James W. Parker, Carr Bowers, Samuel B. Hines, and Orris A. Browne, esqr's are acting Justices of the Peace, in and for the County aforesaid, and were members of the Court which convened at Jerusalem, on Saturday the 5th day of November, 1831, for the trial of Nat *alias* Nat Turner, a negro slave, late the property of Putnam Moore, deceased, who was tried and convicted, as an insurgent in the late insurrection in the county of Southampton aforesaid, and that full faith and credit are due, and ought to be given to their acts as Justices of the peace aforesaid.

In testimony whereof, I have hereunto set my hand and caused the seal of the Court aforesaid, to be affixed this 5th day of November, 1831.

(Seal.) **JAMES ROCHELLE, C.S.C.C.**

CONFESSION

Agreeable to his own appointment, on the evening he was committed to prison, with permission of the jailer, I visited NAT on Tuesday the 1st November, when, without being questioned at all, he commenced his narrative in the following words: —

Sir, — You have asked me to give a history of the motives which induced me to undertake the late insurrection, as you call it — To do so I must go back to the days of my infancy, and even before I was born. I was thirty-one years of age the 2d of October last, and born the property of Benj. Turner, of this county. In my childhood a circumstance occurred which made an indelible impression on my mind, and laid the ground work of that enthusiasm, which has terminated so fatally to many, both white and black, and for which I am about to atone at the gallows. It is here necessary to relate this circumstance — trifling as it may seem, it was the commencement of that belief which has grown with time, and even now, sir, in this dungeon, helpless and forsaken as I am, I cannot divest myself of. Being at play with other children, when three or four years old, I was telling them something, which my mother overhearing, said it had happened before I was born — I stuck to my story, however, and related somethings which went, in her opinion, to confirm it — others being called on were greatly astonished, knowing that these things had happened, and caused them to say in my hearing, I surely would be a prophet, as the Lord had shewn me things that had happened before my birth. And my father and mother strengthened me in this my first impression, saying in my presence, I was intended for some great purpose, which they had always thought from certain marks on my head and breast — [a parcel of excrescences which I believe are not at all uncommon, particularly among negroes, as I have seen several with the same. In this case he has either cut them off or they have nearly disappeared] — My grandmother, who was very religious, and to whom I was much attached — my master, who belonged to the church, and other religious persons who visited the house, and whom I often saw at prayers, noticing the singularity of my manners, I suppose, and my uncommon intelligence for a child, remarked I had too much sense to be raised, and if I was, I would never be of any service to any one as a slave — To a mind like mine, restless, inquisitive and observant of every thing that was passing, it is easy to suppose that religion was the subject to which it would be directed, and although this subject principally occupied my thoughts — there was nothing that I saw or heard of to which my attention was not directed — The manner in which I learned to read and write, not only had great influence on my own mind, as I acquired it with the most perfect ease, so much so, that I have no recollection whatever of learning the alphabet — but to the astonishment of the family, one day, when a book was shewn me to keep me from crying, I began spelling the names of different objects — this was a source of wonder to all in the neighborhood, particularly the blacks — and this learning was constantly improved at all opportunities — when I got large enough to go to work, while employed, I was reflecting on many things that would present themselves to my imagination, and whenever an opportunity occurred of looking at a book, when the school children were getting their lessons, I would find many things that the fertility of my own imagination had depicted to me before; all my time, not devoted to my master's service, was spent either in prayer, or in making experiments in casting different things in moulds made of earth, in attempting to make paper, gunpowder, and many other experiments, that although I could not perfect, yet convinced me of its practicability if I had the means.* I was not addicted to stealing in my youth, nor have ever been — Yet such was the confidence of the negroes in the neighborhood, even at this early period of my life, in my superior judgment, that they would often carry me with them when they were going on any roguery, to plan for them. Growing up among them, with this confidence in my superior judgment, and when this, in their opinions, was perfected by Divine inspiration, from the circumstances already alluded to in my infancy, and which belief was ever afterwards zealously inculcated by the austerity of my life and manners, which became the subject of remark by white and black. — Having soon discovered to be great, I must appear so, and therefore studiously avoided mixing in society, and wrapped myself in mystery, devoting my time to fasting and prayer — By this time, having arrived to man's estate, and hearing the scriptures commented on at meetings, I was struck with that particular passage which says: "Seek ye the kingdom of Heaven and all things shall be added unto you." I reflected much on this passage, and prayed daily for light on this subject — As I was praying one day at my plough, the spirit spoke to me, saying "Seek ye the kingdom of Heaven and all things shall be added unto you." *Question* — what do you mean by the Spirit. *Ans.* The Spirit that spoke to the

---

* When questioned as to the manner of manufacturing those different articles, he was found well informed on the subject.

prophets in former days — and I was greatly astonished, and for two years prayed continually, whenever my duty would permit — and then again I had the same revelation, which fully confirmed me in the impression that I was ordained for some great purpose in the hands of the Almighty. Several years rolled round, in which many events occurred to strengthen me in this my belief. At this time I reverted in my mind to the remarks made of me in my childhood, and the things that had been shewn me — and as it had been said of me in my childhood by those by whom I had been taught to pray, both white and black, and in whom I had the greatest confidence, that I had too much sense to be raised, and if I was, I would never be of any use to any one as a slave. Now finding I had arrived to man's estate, and was a slave, and these revelations being made known to me, I began to direct my attention to this great object, to fulfil the purpose for which, by this time, I felt assured I was intended. Knowing the influence I had obtained over the minds of my fellow servants, (not by the means of conjuring and such like tricks — for to them I always spoke of such things with contempt) but by the communion of the Spirit whose revelations I often communicated to them, and they believed and said my wisdom came from God. I now began to prepare them for my purpose, by telling them something was about to happen that would terminate in fulfilling the great promise that had been made to me — About this time I was placed under an overseer, from whom I ran away — and after remaining in the woods thirty days, I returned, to the astonishment of the negroes on the plantation, who thought I had made my escape to some other part of the country, as my father had done before. But the reason of my return was, that the Spirit appeared to me and said I had my wishes directed to the things of this world, and not to the kingdom of Heaven, and that I should return to the service of my earthly master — "For he who knoweth his Master's will, and doeth it not, shall be beaten with many stripes, and thus have I chastened you." And the negroes found fault, and murmured against me, saying that if they had my sense they would not serve any master in the world. And about this time I had a vision — and I saw white spirits and black spirits engaged in battle, and the sun was darkened — the thunder rolled in the Heavens, and blood flowed in streams — and I heard a voice saying, "Such is your luck, such you are called to see, and let it come rough or smooth, you must surely bare it." I now withdrew myself as much as my situation would permit, from the intercourse of my fellow servants, for the avowed purpose of serving the Spirit more fully — and it appeared to me, and reminded me of the things it had already shown me, and that it would then reveal to me the knowledge of the elements, the revolution of the planets, the operation of tides, and changes of the seasons. After this revelation in the year 1825, and the knowledge of the elements being made known to me, I sought more than ever to obtain true holiness before the great day of judgment should appear, and then I began to receive the true knowledge of faith. And from the first steps of righteousness until the last, was I made perfect; and the Holy Ghost was with me, and said, "Behold me as I stand in the Heavens" — and I looked and saw the forms of men in different attitudes — and there were lights in the sky to which the children of darkness gave other names than what they really were — for they were the lights of the Saviour's hands, stretched forth from east to west, even as they were extended on the cross on Calvary for the redemption of sinners. And I wondered greatly at these miracles, and prayed to be informed of a certainty of the meaning thereof — and shortly afterwards, while laboring in the field, I discovered drops of blood on the corn as though it were dew from heaven — and I communicated it to many, both white and black, in the neighborhood — and I then found on the leaves in the woods hieroglyphic characters, and numbers, with the forms of men in different attitudes, portrayed in blood, and representing the figures I had seen before in the heavens. And now the Holy Ghost had revealed itself to me, and made plain the miracles it had shown me — For as the blood of Christ had been shed on this earth, and had ascended to heaven for the salvation of sinners, and was now returning to earth again in the form of dew — and as the leaves on the trees bore the impression of the figures I had seen in the heavens, it was plain to me that the Saviour was about to lay down the yoke he had borne for the sins of men, and the great day of judgment was at hand. About this time I told these things to a white man, (Etheldred T. Brantley) on whom it had a wonderful effect — and he ceased from his wickedness, and was attacked immediately with a cutaneous eruption, and blood ozed [*sic*] from the pores of his skin, and after praying and fasting nine days, he was healed, and the Spirit appeared to me again, and said, as the Saviour had been baptised so should we be also — and when the white people would not let us be baptised by the church, we went down into the water together, in the sight of many who reviled us, and were baptised by the Spirit — After this I rejoiced greatly, and gave thanks to God. And on the 12th of May, 1828, I heard a loud noise in the heavens, and the Spirit instantly appeared to me and said the Serpent was loosened, and Christ had laid down the yoke he had borne for the sins of men, and that I should take it on and fight against the Serpent, for the time was fast approaching when the first should be last and the last should be first. *Ques.* Do you not find yourself mistaken now? *Ans.* Was not Christ crucified. And by signs in the heavens that it would make known to me when I should commence the great work — and until the first sign appeared, I should conceal it from the knowledge of men — And on the appearance of the sign, (the eclipse of the sun last February) I should arise and prepare myself, and slay my enemies with their own weapons. And immediately on the sign appearing in the heavens, the seal was removed from my lips, and I communicated the great work laid out for me to do, to four in whom I had the greatest confidence. (Henry, Hark, Nelson, and Sam) — It was intended by us to have begun the work of death on the 4th July last — Many were the plans formed and rejected by us, and it affected my mind to such a degree, that I fell sick, and the time passed without our coming to any determination how to commence — Still forming new schemes and rejecting them, when the sign appeared again, which determined me not to wait longer.

Since the commencement of 1830, I had been living with Mr. Joseph Travis, who was to me a kind master, and placed the greatest confidence in me; in fact, I had no cause to complain of his treatment to me. On Saturday evening, the 20th of August, it was agreed between Henry, Hark and myself, to prepare a dinner the next day for the men we expected, and then to concert a plan, as we had not yet determined on any. Hark, on the following morning, brought a pig, and Henry brandy, and being joined by Sam, Nelson, Will and Jack, they prepared in the woods a dinner, where, about three o'clock, I joined them.

Q. Why were you so backward in joining them.

A. The same reason that had caused me not to mix with them for years before.

I saluted them on coming up, and asked Will how came he there, he answered, his life was worth no more than others, and his liberty as dear to him. I asked him if he thought to obtain it? He said he would, or loose his life. This was enough to put him in full confidence. Jack, I knew, was only a tool in the hands of Hark, it was quickly agreed we should commence at home (Mr. J. Travis') on that night, and until we had armed and equipped ourselves, and gathered sufficient force, neither age nor sex was to be spared, (which was invariably adhered to.) We remained at the feast, until about two hours in the night, when we went to the house and found Austin; they all went to the cider press and drank, except myself. On returning to the house, Hark went to the door with an axe, for the purpose of breaking it open, as we knew we were strong enough to murder the family, if they were awaked by the noise; but reflecting that it might create an alarm in the neighborhood, we determined to enter the house secretly, and murder them whilst sleeping. Hark got a ladder and set it against the chimney, on which I ascended, and hoisting a window, entered and came down stairs, unbarred the door, and removed the guns from their places. It was then observed that I must spill the first blood. On which, armed with a hatchet, and accompanied by Will, I entered my master's chamber, it being dark, I could not give a death blow, the hatchet glanced from his head, he sprang from the bed and called his wife, it was his last word, Will laid him dead, with a blow of his axe, and Mrs. Travis shared the same fate, as she lay in bed. The murder of this family, five in number, was the work of a moment, not one of them awoke; there was a little infant sleeping in a cradle, that was forgotten, until we had left the house and gone some distance, when

Henry and Will returned, and killed it; we got here, four guns that would shoot, and several old muskets, with a pound or two of powder. We remained some time at the barn, where we paraded; I formed them in a line as soldiers, and after carrying them through all the manœvres I was master of, marched them off to Mr. Salathul Francis', about six hundred yards distant. Sam and Will went to the door and knocked. Mr. Francis asked who was there, Sam replied it was him, and he had a letter for him, on which he got up and came to the door; they immediately seized him, and dragging him out a little from the door, he was dispatched by repeated blows on the head; there was no other white person in the family. We started from there for Mrs. Reese's, maintaining the most perfect silence on our march, where finding the door unlocked, we entered, and murdered Mrs. Reese in her bed, while sleeping; her son awoke, but it was only to sleep the sleep of death, he had only time to say who is that, and he was no more. From Mrs. Reese's we went to Mrs. Turner's, a mile distant, which we reached about sunrise, on Monday morning. Henry, Austin, and Sam, went to the still, where, finding Mr. Peebles, Austin shot him, and the rest of us went to the house; as we approached, the family discovered us, and shut the door. Vain hope! Will, with one stroke of his axe, opened it, and we entered and found Mrs. Turner and Mrs. Newsome in the middle of a room, almost frightened to death. Will immediately killed Mrs. Turner, with one blow of his axe. I took Mrs. Newsome by the hand, and with the sword I had when I was apprehended, I struck her several blows over the head, but not being able to kill her, as the sword was dull. Will turning around and discovering it, despatched her also. A general destruction of property and search for money and ammunition, always succeeded the murders. By this time my company amounted to fifteen, and nine men mounted, who started for Mrs. Whitehead's, (the other six were to go through a by way to Mr. Bryant's, and rejoin us at Mrs. Whitehead's,) as we approached the house we discovered Mr. Richard Whitehead standing in the cotton patch, near the lane fence; we called him over into the lane, and Will, the executioner, was near at hand, with his fatal axe, to send him to an untimely grave. As we pushed on to the house, I discovered some one run round the garden, and thinking it was some of the white family, I pursued them, but finding it was a servant girl belonging to the house, I returned to commence the work of death, but they whom I left, had not been idle; all the family were already murdered, but Mrs. Whitehead and her daughter Margaret. As I came round to the door I saw Will pulling Mrs. Whitehead out of the house, and at the step he nearly severed her head from her body, with his broad axe. Miss Margaret, when I discovered her, had concealed herself in the corner, formed by the projection of the cellar cap from the house; on my approach she fled, but was soon overtaken, and after repeated blows with a sword, I killed her by a blow on the head, with a fence rail. By this time, the six who had gone by Mr.

Bryant's, rejoined us, and informed me they had done the work of death assigned them. We again divided, part going to Mr. Richard Porter's, and from thence to Nathaniel Francis', the others to Mr. Howell Harris', and Mr. T. Doyles. On my reaching Mr. Porter's, he had escaped with his family. I understood there, that the alarm had already spread, and I immediately returned to bring up those sent to Mr. Doyles, and Mr. Howell Harris'; the party I left going on to Mr. Francis', having told them I would join them in that neighborhood. I met these sent to Mr. Doyles' and Mr. Harris' returning, having met Mr. Doyle on the road and killed him; and learning from some who joined them, that Mr. Harris was from home, I immediately pursued the course taken by the party gone on before; but knowing they would complete the work of death and pillage, at Mr. Francis' before I could get there, I went to Mr. Peter Edwards', expecting to find them there, but they had been here also. I then went to Mr. John T. Barrow's, they had been here and murdered him. I pursued on their track to Capt. Newit Harris', where I found the greater part mounted, and ready to start; the men now amounting to about forty, shouted and hurraed as I rode up, some were in the yard, loading their guns, others drinking. They said Captain Harris and his family had escaped, the property in the house they destroyed, robbing him of money and other valuables. I ordered them to mount and march instantly, this was about nine or ten o'clock, Monday morning. I proceeded to Mr. Levi Waller's, two or three miles distant. I took my station in the rear, and as it 'twas my object to carry terror and devastation wherever we went, I placed fifteen or twenty of the best armed and most to be relied on, in front, who generally approached the house as fast as their horses could run; this was for two purposes, to prevent their escape and strike terror to the inhabitants — on this account I never got to the houses, after leaving Mrs. Whitehead's, until the murders were committed, except in one case. I sometimes got in sight in time to see the work of death completed, viewed the mangled bodies as they lay, in silent satisfaction, and immediately started in quest of other victims — Having murdered Mrs. Waller and ten children, we started for Mr. William Williams' — having killed him and two little boys that were there; while engaged in this, Mrs. Williams fled and got some distance from the house, but she was pursued, overtaken, and compelled to get up behind one of the company, who brought her back, and after showing her the mangled body of her lifeless husband, she was told to get down and lay by his side, where she was shot dead. I then started for Mr. Jacob Williams, where the family were murdered — Here we found a young man named Drury, who had come on business with Mr. Williams — he was pursued, overtaken and shot. Mrs. Vaughan was the next place we visited — and after murdering the family here, I determined on starting for Jerusalem — Our number amounted now to fifty or sixty, all mounted and armed with guns, axes, swords and clubs — On reaching Mr.

James W. Parkers' gate, immediately on the road leading to Jerusalem, and about three miles distant, it was proposed to me to call there, but I objected, as I knew he was gone to Jerusalem, and my object was to reach there as soon as possible; but some of the men having relations at Mr. Parker's it was agreed that they might call and get his people. I remained at the gate on the road, with seven or eight; the others going across the field to the house, about half a mile off. After waiting some time for them, I became impatient, and started to the house for them, and on our return we were met by a party of white men, who had pursued our blood-stained track, and who had fired on those at the gate, and dispersed them, which I new nothing of, not having been at that time rejoined by any of them — Immediately on discovering the whites, I ordered my men to halt and form, as they appeared to be alarmed — The white men, eighteen in number, approached us in about one hundred yards, when one of them fired, (this was against the positive orders of Captain Alexander P. Peete, who commanded, and who had directed the men to reserve their fire until within thirty paces). And I discovered about half of them retreating, I then ordered my men to fire and rush on them; the few remaining stood their ground until we approached within fifty yards, when they fired and retreated. We pursued and overtook some of them who we thought we left dead; (they were not killed) after pursuing them about two hundred yards, and rising a little hill, I discovered they were met by another party, and had haulted, and were re-loading their guns, (this was a small party from Jerusalem who knew the negroes were in the field, and had just tied their horses to await their return to the road, knowing that Mr. Parker and family were in Jerusalem, but knew nothing of the party that had gone in with Captain Peete; on hearing the firing they immediately rushed to the spot and arrived just in time to arrest the progress of these barbarous villians, and save the lives of their friends and fellow citizens.) Thinking that those who retreated first, and the party who fired on us at fifty or sixty yards distant, had all only fallen back to meet others with ammunition. As I saw them re-loading their guns, and more coming up than I saw at first, and several of my bravest men being wounded, the others became panick struck and squandered over the field; the white men pursued and fired on us several times. Hark had his horse shot under him, and I caught another for him as it was running by me; five or six of my men were wounded, but none left on the field; finding myself defeated here I instantly determined to go through a private way, and cross the Nottoway river at the Cypress Bridge, three miles below Jerusalem, and attack that place in the rear, as I expected they would look for me on the other road, and I had a great desire to get there to procure arms and ammunition. After going a short distance in this private way, accompanied by about twenty men, I overtook two or three who told me the others were dispersed in every direction. After tyring [sic] in vain to collect a sufficient force to proceed to Jerusalem, I determined to return, as I was sure they would make back to their old neighborhood, where they would rejoin me, make new recruits, and come down again. On my way back, I called at Mrs. Thomas's, Mrs. Spencer's, and several other places, the white families having fled, we found no more victims to gratify our thirst for blood, we stopped at Majr. Ridley's quarter for the night, and being joined by four of his men, with the recruits made since my defeat, we mustered now about forty strong. After placing out sentinels, I laid down to sleep, but was quickly roused by a great racket; starting up, I found some mounted, and others in great confusion; one of the sentinels having given the alarm that we were about to be attacked, I ordered some to ride round and reconnoitre, and on their return the others being more alarmed, not knowing who they were, fled in different ways, so that I was reduced to about twenty again; with this I determined to attempt to recruit, and proceed on to rally in the neighborhood, I had left. Dr. Blunt's was the nearest house, which we reached just before day; on riding up the yard, Hark fired a gun. We expected Dr. Blunt and his family were at Maj. Ridley's, as I knew there was a company of men there; the gun was fired to ascertain if any of the family were at home; we were immediately fired upon and retreated, leaving several of my men. I do not know what became of them, as I never saw them afterwards. Pursuing our course back and coming in sight of Captain Harris', where we had been the day before, we discovered a party of white men at the house, on which all deserted me but two, (Jacob and Nat,) we concealed ourselves in the woods until near night, when I sent them in search of Henry, Sam, Nelson, and Hark, and directed them to rally all they could, at the place we had had our dinner the Sunday before, where they would find me, and I accordingly returned there as soon as it was dark and remained until Wednesday evening, when discovering white men riding around the place as though they were looking for some one, and none of my men joining me, I concluded Jacob and Nat had been taken, and compelled to betray me. On this I gave up all hope for the present; and on Thursday night after having supplied myself with provisions from Mr. Travis's, I scratched a hole under a pile of fence rails in a field, where I concealed myself for six weeks, never leaving my hiding place but for a few minutes in the dead of night to get water which was very near; thinking by this time I could venture out, I began to go about in the night and eaves drop the houses in the neighborhood; pursuing this course for about a fortnight and gathering little or no intelligence, afraid of speaking to any human being, and returning every morning to my cave before the dawn of day. I know not how long I might have led this life, if accident had not betrayed me, a dog in the neighborhood passing by my hiding place one night while I was out, was attracted by some meat I had in my cave, and crawled in and stole it, and was coming out just as I returned. A few nights after, two negroes having started to go hunting with the same dog, and passed that way, the dog came again to the place, and having just gone out to walk about, discovered me and barked, on which thinking myself discovered, I spoke to them to beg concealment. On making myself known they fled from me. Knowing then they would betray me, I immediately left my hiding place, and was pursued almost incessantly until I was taken a fortnight afterwards by Mr. Benjamin Phipps, in a little hole I had dug out with my sword, for the purpose of concealment, under the top of a fallen tree. On Mr. Phipps' discovering the place of my concealment, he cocked his gun and aimed at me. I requested him not to shoot and I would give up, upon which he demanded my sword. I delivered it to him, and he brought me to prison. During the time I was pursued, I had many hair breadth escapes, which your time will not permit you to relate. I am here loaded with chains, and willing to suffer the fate that awaits me.

I here proceeded to make some inquiries of him, after assuring him of the certain death that awaited him, and that concealment would only bring destruction on the innocent as well as guilty, of his own color, if he knew of any extensive or concerted plan. His answer was, I do not. When I questioned him as to the insurrection in North Carolina happening about the same time, he denied any knowledge of it; and when I looked him in the face as though I would search his inmost thoughts, he replied, "I see sir, you doubt my word; but can you not think the same ideas, and strange appearances about this time in the heaven's might prompt others, as well as myself, to this undertaking." I now had much conversation with and asked him many questions, having forborne to do so previously, except in the cases noted in parenthesis; but during his statement, I had, unnoticed by him, taken notes as to some particular circumstances, and having the advantage of his statement before me in writing, on the evening of the third day that I had been with him, I began a cross examination, and found his statement corroborated by every circumstance coming within my own knowledge or the confessions of others whom had been either killed or executed, and whom he had not seen nor had any knowledge since 22d of August last, he expressed himself fully satisfied as to the impracticability of his attempt. It has been said he was ignorant and cowardly, and that his object was to murder and rob for the purpose of obtaining money to make his escape. It is notorious, that he was never known to have a dollar in his life; to swear an oath, or drink a drop of spirits. As to his ignorance, he certainly never had the advantages of education, but he can read and write, (it was taught him by his parents,) and for natural intelligence and quickness of apprehension, is surpassed by few men I have ever seen. As to his being a coward, his reason as given for not resisting Mr. Phipps, shews the decision of his character. When he saw Mr. Phipps present his gun, he said he knew it was impossible for him to escape as the woods were full of men; he therefore thought it was better to surrender, and trust to fortune for his escape. He is a complete fanatic, or plays his part most admirably. On other subjects he possesses an uncommon share of intelligence, with a mind capable of attaining any thing; but warped and perverted by the influence of early impressions. He is below the ordinary stature, though strong and active, having the true negro face, every feature of which is strongly marked. I shall not attempt to describe the effect of his narrative, as told and commented on by himself, in the condemned hole of the prison. The calm, deliberate composure with which he spoke of his late deeds and intentions, the expression of his fiend-like face when excited by enthusiasm, still bearing the stains of the blood of helpless innocence about him; clothed with rags and covered with chains; yet daring to raise his manacled hands to heaven, with a spirit soaring above the attributes of man; I looked on him and my blood curdled in my veins.

I will not shock the feelings of humanity, nor wound afresh the bosoms of the disconsolate sufferers in this unparalleled and inhuman massacre, by detailing the deeds of their fiend-like barbarity. There were two or three who were in the power of these wretches, had they known it, and who escaped in the most providential manner. There were two whom they thought they left dead on the field at Mr. Parker's, but who were only stunned by the blows of their guns, as they did not take time to re-load when they charged on them. The escape of a little girl who went to school at Mr. Waller's, and where the children were collecting for that purpose, excited general sympathy. As their teacher had not arrived, they were at play in the yard, and seeing the negroes approach, she ran up on a dirt chimney, (such as are common to log houses,) and remained there unnoticed during the massacre of the eleven that were killed at this place. She remained on her hiding place till just before the arrival of a party, who were in pursuit of the murderers, when she came down and fled to a swamp, where, a mere child as she was, with the horrors of the late scene before her, she lay concealed until the next day, when seeing a party go up to the house, she came up, and on being asked how she escaped, replied with the utmost simplicity, "The Lord helped her." She was taken up behind a gentleman of the party, and returned to the arms of her weeping mother. Miss Whitehead concealed herself between the bed and the mat that supported it, while they murdered her sister in the same room, without discovering her. She was afterwards carried off, and concealed for protection by a slave of the family, who gave evidence against several of them on their trial. Mrs. Nathaniel Francis, while concealed in a closet heard their blows, and the shrieks of the victims of these ruthless savages; they then entered the closet where she was concealed, and went out without discovering her. While in this hiding place, she heard two of her women in a quarrel about the division of her clothes. Mr. John T. Baron, discovering them approaching his house, told his wife to make her escape, and scorning to fly, fell fighting on his own threshold. After firing his rifle, he discharged his gun at them, and then broke it over the villain who first approached him, but he was overpowered, and slain. His bravery, however, saved from the hands of these monsters, his lovely and amiable wife, who will long lament a husband so deserving of her love. As directed by him, she attempted to escape through the garden, when she was caught and held by one of her servant girls, but another coming to her rescue, she fled to the woods, and concealed herself. Few indeed, were those who escaped their work of death. But fortunate for society, the hand of retributive justice has overtaken them; and not one that was known to be concerned has escaped.

The Commonwealth, } Charged with making insurrection, and
       vs.   } plotting to take away the lives of divers free
   Nat Turner.   } white persons, &c. on the 22d of August, 1831.

The court composed of — , having met for the trial of Nat Turner, the prisoner was brought in and arraigned, and upon his arraignment pleaded *Not guilty;* saying to his counsel, that he did not feel so.

On the part of the Commonwealth, Levi Waller was introduced, who being sworn, deposed as follows: (*agreeably to Nat's own Confession.*) Col. Trezvant* was then introduced, who being sworn, narrated Nat's Confession to him, as follows: (*his Confession as given to Mr. Gray.*) The prisoner introduced no evidence, and the case was submitted without argument to the court, who having found him guilty, Jeremiah Cobb, Esq. Chairman, pronounced the sentence of the court, in the following words: "Nat Turner! Stand up. Have you any thing to say why sentence of death should not be pronounced against you?

Ans. I have not. I have made a full confession to Mr. Gray, and I have nothing more to say.

Attend then to the sentence of the Court. You have been arraigned and tried before this court, and convicted of one of the highest crimes in our criminal code. You have been convicted of plotting in cold blood, the indiscriminate destruction of men, of helpless women, and of infant children. The evidence before us leaves not a shadow of doubt, but that your hands were often imbrued in the blood of the innocent; and your own confession tells us that they were stained with the blood of a master; in your own language, "too indulgent." Could I stop here, your crime would be sufficiently aggravated. But the original contriver of a plan, deep and deadly, one that never can be effected, you managed so far to put it into execution, as to deprive us of many of

* The committing Magistrate.

our most valuable citizens; and this was done when they were asleep, and defenceless; under circumstances shocking to humanity. And while upon this part of the subject, I cannot but call your attention to the poor misguided wretches who have gone before you. They are not few in number — they were your bosom associates; and the blood of all cries aloud, and calls upon you, as the author of their misfortune. Yes! You forced them unprepared, from Time to Eternity. Borne down by this load of guilt, your only justification is, that you were led away by fanaticism. If this be true, from my soul I pity you; and while you have my sympathies, I am, nevertheless called upon to pass the sentence of the court. The time between this and your execution, will necessarily be very short; and your only hope must be in another world. The judgment of the court is, that you be taken hence to the jail from whence you came, thence to the place of execution, and on Friday next, between the hours of 10 A.M. and 2 P.M. be hung by the neck until you are dead! dead! dead and may the Lord have mercy upon your soul.

A list of persons murdered in the Insurrection, on the 21st and 22d of August, 1831.

Joseph Travers and wife and three children, Mrs. Elizabeth Turner, Hartwell Prebles, Sarah Newsome, Mrs. P. Reese and son William, Trajan Doyle, Henry Bryant and wife and child, and wife's mother, Mrs. Catharine Whitehead, son Richard and four daughters and grand-child, Salathiel Francis, Nathaniel Francis' overseer and two children, John T. Barrow, George Vaughan, Mrs. Levi Waller and ten children, William Williams, wife and two boys, Mrs. Caswell Worrell and child, Mrs. Rebecca Vaughan, Ann Eliza Vaughan, and son Arthur, Mrs. John K. Williams and child, Mrs. Jacob Williams and three children, and Edwin Drury — amounting to fifty-five.

A List of Negroes brought before the Court of Southampton, with their owners' names, and sentence.

Daniel,	Richard Porter,	Convicted.
Moses,	J. T. Barrow,	Do.
Tom,	Caty Whitehead,	Discharged.
Jack and Andrew,	Caty Whitehead,	Con. and transported.
Jacob,	Geo. H. Charlton,	Disch'd without trial.
Isaac,	Ditto,	Convi. and transported.
Jack,	Everett Bryant,	Discharged.
Nathan,	Benj. Blunt's estate,	Convicted.
Nathan, Tom, and Davy, (boys,)	Nathaniel Francis,	Convicted and transported.
Davy,	Elizabeth Turner,	Convicted.
Curtis,	Thomas Ridley,	Do.
Stephen,	Do.	Do.
Hardy and Isham,	Benjamin Edwards,	Convicted and transp'd.
Sam,	Nathaniel Francis,	Convicted.
Hark,	Joseph Travis' estate.	Do.
Moses, (a boy,)	Do.	Do. and transported
Davy,	Levi Waller,	Convicted.
Nelson,	Jacob Williams,	Do.
Nat,	Edm'd Turner's estate,	Do.
Jack,	Wm. Reese's estate,	Do.
Dred,	Nathaniel Francis,	Do.
Arnold, Artist, (free)		Discharged.
Sam,	J. W. Parker,	Acquitted.
Ferry and Archer,	J. W. Parker,	Disch'd without trial.
Jim,	William Vaughan,	Acquitted.
Bob,	Temperance Parker,	Do.
Davy,	Joseph Parker,	
Daniel,	Solomon D. Parker,	Disch'd without trial.
Thomas Haithcock, (free,)		Sent on for further trial.
Joe,	John C. Turner,	Convicted.
Lucy,	John T. Barrow,	Do.
Matt,	Thomas Ridley,	Acquitted.
Jim,	Richard Porter,	Do.
Exum Artes, (free,)		Sent on for further trial.
Joe,	Richard P. Briggs,	Disch'd without trial.
Bury Newsome, (free,)		Sent on for further trial.
Stephen,	James Bell,	Acquitted.
Jim and Isaac,	Samuel Champion,	Convicted and trans'd.

Proston,	Hannah Williamson,	Acquitted.
Frank,	Solomon D. Parker,	Convi'd and transp'd.
Jack and Shadrach,	Nathaniel Simmons,	Acquitted.
Nelson,	Benj. Blunt's estate,	Do.
Sam,	Peter Edwards,	Convicted.
Archer,	Arthur G. Reese,	Acquitted.
Isham Turner, (free,)		Sent on for further trial.
Nat Turner,	Putnam Moore, dec'd,	Convicted.

Notes

Rare Books, Manuscripts, and Special Collections

The following manuscript sources were used, by permission, in the research of this book. They are denoted by the given abbreviations.

University of Virginia Library, Charlottesville, Virginia
- BFP   Barbour Family Papers
- HBSP   Harriet Beecher Stowe Papers
- VCHRR   Virginia Council on Human Relations Records

Archives of American Art, Smithsonian Institution, Washington, D.C.
- CWP   Charles Wilbert White Papers (microfilm)

Duke University Library, Durham, North Carolina
- WSP   William Styron Papers

Houghton Library, Harvard University, Cambridge, Massachusetts
- TWHP   Thomas Wentworth Higginson Papers

Library of Congress, Washington, D.C.
- TJP   Thomas Jefferson Papers

Library of Virginia, Richmond, Virginia
- EC   Executive Communications, John Floyd Slave and Free Negro Letterbook, 1831
- EP   Executive Papers, March 1835
- SCJ   Southampton County Court Judgments, Box 93
- SCL   Southampton County Land Tax Books, 1822–1832A
- SCO   Sussex County Order Book, 1827–1835
- SCP   Southampton County Personal Property, 1818–1824, 1825–1830

Schomburg Center for Research in Black Culture, New York Public Library
- ACP   Alexander Crummell Papers (microfilm)
- ODRD   Ossie Davis and Ruby Dee Papers

Southampton County Historical Society, Rochelle-Prime House, Courtland, Virginia

Earl Gregg Swem Library, College of William and Mary, Williamsburg, Virginia
    JCR Jamestown Corporation Records
    JTP John Tyler, Jr., Papers

Virginia Baptist Historical Society, Richmond, Virginia
    ABC Records of Antioch Baptist Church (Raccoon Swamp), Sussex
        County, 1772–1837
    PBA Minutes of the Virginia Portsmouth Baptist Association, 1831–35

Virginia Historical Society, Richmond, Virginia
    LFP Lee Family Papers
    TFP Tyler Family Papers

Yale University
    HBSm Harriet Beecher Stowe Letters (microfilm)

Louise Meriwether, Private Collection, New York, New York
    BADAP Black Anti-Defamation Association Papers

Descendants of Gilbert Francis, Private Collection, Boykins, Virginia
    GFP Gilbert Francis Papers

Introduction

1. Extract from diary of Gov. John Floyd, 23 August 1831; reprinted in Tragle, *Southampton Slave Revolt*, 251–52; *Raleigh (N.C.) Register*, 1 September 1831.

2. *Petersburg Intelligencer*, 26 August 1831; *Norfolk American Beacon*, 29 August 1831; *Richmond Constitutional Whig*, 29 August 1831; *Fayetteville (N.C.) Journal*, 31 August 1831.

3. *Fayetteville Journal*, 31 August 1831; extract of a letter dated 25 August 1831, Winton, N.C.; *Richmond Constitutional Whig*, 3 September 1831; *(Lynchburg) Virginian*, 1 September 1831. *Raleigh Register*, 1 September 1831.

4. For use of the term "neighborhood" to describe the location of the "disturbance," see *Petersburg Intelligencer*, 26 August 1831. For reference to "the infected district, if District it can be called," see *Richmond Compiler*, 24 August 1831. For reference to the spontaneity of the uprising, see *Richmond Constitutional Whig*, 29 August 1831. For revised estimates of black troop strength, see *Richmond Constitutional Whig*, 29 August 1831, and *Richmond Compiler*, 3 September 1831. For references to Billy Artis as one of the leaders or "principals" of the uprising, see *Richmond Compiler*, 27 August 1831 and 3 September 1831, and *Norfolk American Beacon*, 9 September

1831. For references to the "celebrated Nelson, called by the blacks, 'Gen. Nelson,'" see *Norfolk American Beacon,* 29 August 1831; troops from Norfolk claimed to have killed Nelson and sent his head back to Norfolk. All newspaper articles cited above reprinted in Tragle, *Southampton Slave Revolt.*

5. *Richmond Enquirer,* 30 August 1831; *Richmond Compiler,* 3 September 1831 and 27 August 1831; all reprinted in Tragle, *Southampton Slave Revolt.*

6. On the history, theory, and methodology of social/collective memory, see Thelen, *Memory and American History;* James Fentress and Chris Wickham, *Social Memory* (Cambridge, Mass.: Blackwell, 1992); and Confino, "Collective Memory and Cultural History." I offer my own reading of this concept in "What Is Social Memory?" *Southern Cultures* 2 (Fall 1995): 9–18.

7. Scot A. French and Edward L. Ayers, "The Strange Career of Thomas Jefferson: Race and Slavery in American Memory, 1943–1993," in Onuf, *Jeffersonian Legacies,* 418–56.

8. In the wake of the Styron controversy, historians and literary critics published several document collections that testified to the enduring memory of Nat Turner. Melvin J. Friedman and Irving Malin included several "poetic, journalistic, and fictional portrayals" of Turner in their edited volume *William Styron's The Confessions of Nat Turner: A Critical Handbook* (Belmont, Calif.: Wadsworth, 1970). Eric Foner featured the recurring theme "Nat Turner Remembered" in *Nat Turner.* Henry Irving Tragle devoted a quarter of his document collection *The Southampton Slave Revolt of 1831: A Compilation of Source Material* to "previously printed accounts," beginning with Thomas R. Gray's "The Confessions of Nat Turner" and ending with his own essay "Styron and His Sources." More recently, cultural historian Albert E. Stone surveyed selected nineteenth- and twentieth-century representations of Turner in *The Return of Nat Turner: History, Literature, and Cultural Politics in Sixties America.* Likewise, literary critic Mary Kemp Davis analyzed six "fictional treatments" of the Southampton slave uprising in *Nat Turner Before the Bar of Judgment: Fictional Treatments of the Southampton Slave Insurrection.*

1. Prophecy

1. For a history of the jeremiad as "America's first distinctive literary genre," see Bercovitch, *The American Jeremiad.* The classic study is Perry Miller, *Errand into the Wilderness* (Cambridge: Belknap Press of Harvard University Press, 1956).

2. Moses, *Black Messiahs and Uncle Toms,* 31. See also David Howard-Pitney, "Wars, White America, and the Afro-American Jeremiad: Frederick

Douglass and Martin Luther King, Jr.," *Journal of Negro History* 71 (Winter-Autumn, 1986): 23–37.

3. Henry S. Randall, *The Life of Thomas Jefferson*, vol. 1 (New York: Derby and Jackson, 1858), 11. Merrill D. Peterson, *Thomas Jefferson and the New Nation* (New York: Oxford University Press, 1970), 9, 27–28.

4. Jefferson to Edward Coles, 25 August 1814, TJP.

5. This argument is set forth by Peter S. Onuf in *Jefferson's Empire*.

6. On colonial Virginia's 1692 act establishing courts of oyer and terminer, see Schwarz, *Twice Condemned*, 17.

7. Lord Dunmore's Proclamation is reprinted in Michael Mullin, ed., *American Negro Slavery: A Documentary History* (Columbia: University of South Carolina Press, 1976), 118–19. Benjamin Quarles, "Lord Dunmore As Liberator," *William and Mary Quarterly*, 3rd series, 15 (Oct. 1958): 494–507.

8. Sidney Kaplan, "The 'Domestic Insurrections' of the Declaration of Independence," *Journal of Negro History* 61 (July 1976): 243–55. Likewise, a draft constitution for Virginia, written by Jefferson in June 1776, accused the king of "prompting . . . negroes to rise in arms among us." See draft text in Merrill D. Peterson, ed., *Writings: Thomas Jefferson* (New York: Viking Press, 1984), 336.

9. Jefferson, *Notes on the State of Virginia*, Query XIV, "Laws," in Merrill D. Peterson, ed., *The Portable Thomas Jefferson* (New York: Penguin Books, 1977), 185–86.

10. Jefferson, *Notes*, Advertisement, 25, 29–30, fn. 1; Douglas L. Wilson, "Jefferson and the Republic of Letters," in Onuf, ed., *Jeffersonian Legacies*, 53–58.

11. Jefferson, *Notes*, Query XIV, "Laws," in Peterson, *Portable Thomas Jefferson*, 186–93.

12. Jefferson, *Notes*, Query XVII, "Manners," in Peterson, *Portable Thomas Jefferson*, 214–15. Public debates over Jefferson's paternity of Hemings's children continue to this day. See Jan Ellen Lewis and Peter S. Onuf, eds., *Sally Hemings and Thomas Jefferson: History, Memory, and Civic Culture* (Charlottesville: University Press of Virginia, 1999); Annette Gordon-Reed, *Thomas Jefferson and Sally Hemings: An American Controversy* (Charlottesville: University Press of Virginia, 1997); and Scot A. French and Edward L. Ayers, "The Strange Career of Thomas Jefferson: Race and Slavery in American Memory, 1943–1993," in Peter S. Onuf, *Jeffersonian Legacies*, 418–56.

13. Banneker to J, Baltimore County, Md., 19 August 1791, TJP.

14. J to James Madison, Paris, 30 January 1787, TJP. Likewise, to Abigail Adams, he wrote: "The spirit of resistance to government is so valuable on certain occasions, that I wish it to be always kept alive. It will often be exer-

cised when wrong, but better so than not to be exercised at all. I like a little rebellion now and then. It is like a storm in the Atmosphere" (Paris, 22 February 1787). J to William Short, Philadelphia, 3 January 1793, TJP. Likewise, to François D'Ivernois, he wrote: "It is unfortunate, that the efforts of mankind to recover the freedom of which they have been so long deprived, will be accompanied with violence, with errors, & even with crimes. But while we weep over the means, we must pray for the end" (Monticello, 6 February 1795).

15. J to William Short, 24 November 1791, and J to James Monroe, 14 July 1793, TJP. The term "black Jacobins" comes from C.L.R. James, *The Black Jacobins: Toussaint L'Ouverture and the San Domingo Revolution* (New York: Knopf, 1989).

16. J to St. George Tucker, 28 August 1797, TJP.

17. Callender to J, 17 October 1800, TJP. It was Callender who first published reports of Jefferson's alleged affair with Sally Hemings, beginning in September 1802. Once dismissed by historians as a scandalmonger with little or no credibility, Callender is now regarded as a muckraking journalist whose reports on the Hemings-Jefferson affair were remarkably accurate. See, for example, Joshua D. Rothman, *Notorious in the Neighborhood: Sex and Families Across the Color Line in Virginia, 1787–1861* (Chapel Hill: University of North Carolina Press, 2003).

18. Schwarz, *Twice Condemned*, 17–20. Monroe to J, 15 September 1800, J to Dr. Benjamin Rush, 23 September 1800, TJP.

19. Thomas Newton to Gov. James Monroe, Norfolk, Va., 24 September 1800, *Calendar of Virginia State Papers*, vol. 9. James Monroe to Col. Thomas Newton, 5 October 1800, reprinted in Hamilton, *Writings of James Monroe*, vol. 3, 213. A. Blair, Clerk of Council, Richmond, 28 September 1800; *Calendar of Virginia State Papers*, vol. 9. *U.S. Gazette*, 9 October 1800, quoted in [Higginson], "Gabriel's Defeat," 344.

20. J to Monroe, 20 September 1800, TJP.

21. Monroe to the Speakers of the General Assembly, 5 December 1800, reprinted in *Writings of James Monroe*, vol. 3, 243. Monroe to J, 15 June 1801, TJP. Monroe to the Speakers of the General Assembly, 16 January 1802, reprinted in *Writings of James Monroe*, vol. 3, 328–29. Monroe to J, 13 February 1802, TJP; reprinted in *Writings of James Monroe*, vol. 3, 336–38.

22. J to Monroe, 24 November 1801, TJP.

23. J to Rufus King, 13 July 1802; Monroe to J, 11 June 1802, TJP.

24. J to William A. Burwell, 28 January 1805; J to Edward Coles, 25 August 1814, TJP.

25. J to Edward Coles, 25 August 1814; Edward Coles to J, 26 September 1814, TJP.

26. J to James Heaton, 20 May 1826, TJP. See also J to Jared Sparks, 4 Febru-

ary 1824, TJP. Discussing his plan for the emancipation of all children born to slaves after a certain date, Jefferson wrote: "This was the result of my reflections on the subject five and forty years ago, and I have never yet been able to conceive any other practicable plan."

27. Advertisement quoted in Lucia Stanton, "'Those Who Labor for My Happiness': Thomas Jefferson and His Slaves," in Onuf, ed., *Jeffersonian Legacies*, 147–48.

28. Sean Wilentz, ed., *David Walker's Appeal* (New York: Hill and Wang, 1995), 14–15.

29. Ibid., 55.

30. For biographical details, see Wilentz, "The Mysteries of David Walker," in *Walker's Appeal*, vi–xxiii, and Peter P. Hinks, *To Awaken My Afflicted Brethren: David Walker and the Problem of Antebellum Slave Resistance* (University Park: Pennsylvania State University Press, 1997). For references to Walker's residence in Charleston and his knowledge of the Vesey affair, see Wilentz, op. cit., vii–xi, and Hinks, op. cit., 22–62. On Vesey and the slave conspiracy that bears his name, see Douglas R. Egerton, *He Shall Go Out Free: The Lives of Denmark Vesey* (Madison, Wis.: Madison House, 1999); David Robertson, *Denmark Vesey* (New York: Knopf, 1999); Edward A. Pearson, *The Trial Record of the Denmark Vesey Slave Conspiracy of 1822* (Chapel Hill: University of North Carolina Press, 1999); John Lofton, *Denmark Vesey's Revolt* (Kent, Ohio: Kent State University Press, 1983). For a critique of these works and a provocative counterthesis, see Michael P. Johnson, "Denmark Vesey and His Co-Conspirators," *William and Mary Quarterly* 58 (October 2001): XXX.

31. Text of Walker's speech to the Massachusetts General Colored Association, as printed in *Freedom's Journal*, 19 December 1828; reprinted in Wilentz, ed., *Walker's Appeal*, 89–93.

32. Wilentz, ed., *Walker's Appeal*, frontispiece, 21–22.

33. Ibid., 12.

34. Ibid., 11, 12, 20, 22, 25, 27.

35. Ibid., 10, 14–15.

36. These state-by-state accounts, drawn from several scholarly articles and theses, are synthesized and analyzed in Hinks, *My Afflicted Brethren*, 116–72. William H. Pease and Jane H. Pease, "Walker's Appeal Comes to Charleston: A Note and Documents," *Journal of Negro History* 59 (July 1974): 287–92.

37. *Baltimore Niles' Register*, 27 March 1830. The Georgia bill, according to the Savannah papers, "render[ed] capital the circulation of pamphlets of evil tendency among . . . domestics" and made "penal the teaching of free persons of color or slaves to read or write." Quotes drawn from "The Pamphlet," *Richmond Enquirer*, 28 January 1830. *Baltimore Niles' Register*, 27 March 1830. Acts Passed at a General Assembly of the Commonwealth of

Virginia (Richmond, 1831): 107–8. For a discussion of this "new repressive legislation," passed by anxious white legislators shortly before the Turner Revolt, see Aptheker, *Nat Turner's Slave Rebellion*, 27–32.

38. Wilentz, ed., *David Walker's Appeal*, 53, 72. Walker made specific reference to the legislative response to his pamphlet in Georgia and Virginia. "A law has recently passed the Legislature of this republican State (Georgia) prohibiting all free or slave persons of colour, from learning to read or write; another law has passed the republican House of Delegates, (but not the Senate) in Virginia, to prohibit all persons of colour, (free and slave) from learning to read, and even to hinder them from meeting together in order to worship our Maker! ! ! ! ! !"

39. See *Boston Liberator*, 22 January 1831. For a close reading of the evidence surrounding Walker's death, see Hinks, *My Afflicted Brethren*, 269–70.

40. *Boston Liberator*, 1 January 1831.

41. Wendell Phillips Garrison and Francis Jackson Garrison, *William Lloyd Garrison, 1805–1879: The Story of His Life Told by His Children, Vol. I, 1805–1835* (Boston: Houghton, Mifflin and Company, 1889), 64–66. Hereafter referred to as Garrison et al., *Story of His Life*.

42. For biographical information, see Henry Mayer, *All on Fire: William Lloyd Garrison and the Abolition of Slavery* (New York: St. Martin's Press, 1998); Merrill, *Against Wind and Tide*; and Thomas, *The Liberator*. Garrison et al., *Story of His Life*, 64–66, 127–37.

43. Park Street Church Address, 4 July 1829, reprinted in Garrison et al., *Story of His Life*, 127–37. An account of this event, attributed to "a traveller at the north" and signed "An Observer," appeared in the first issue of the *Baltimore Genius of Universal Emancipation* coedited by Garrison. Biographer Henry Mayer has argued, persuasively, that Garrison himself is the author of the piece. *Baltimore Genius of Universal Emancipation*, 2 September 1829.

44. *Baltimore Genius of Universal Emancipation*, 15 January, 26 February, 5 March 1830.

45. *Baltimore Genius of Universal Emancipation*, 2 September 1829.

46. *Boston Liberator*, 1 January 1831.

47. Ibid.

48. *Boston Liberator*, 15 January 1831.

49. *Boston Liberator*, 3 September 1831.

2. Inquisitions

1. *Richmond Constitutional Whig*, 3 September 1831; in Tragle, *Southampton Slave Revolt*, 66–72.

2. "Reminiscences of John Hampden Pleasants," undated, in BFP, MSS 1486; F. N. Boney, "Rivers of Ink, A Stream of Blood: The Tragic Career

of John Hampden Pleasants," *Virginia Cavalcade* 18 (Summer 1968): 33; Judge Robert W. Hughes, "Editors of the Past," lecture delivered at the annual meeting of the Virginia Press Association, Charlottesville, Va., 22 June 1897 (Richmond, Va.: W. E. Jones, Printer, 1897), 14; Lester J. Cappon, *Virginia Newspapers, 1821–1935* (New York: D. Appleton-Century, 1936), 123, 192.

3. *Richmond Constitutional Whig*, 29 August 1831, cited in Tragle, *Southampton Slave Revolt*, 50–52.

4. *Richmond Constitutional Whig*, 3 September 1831, cited in Tragle, *Southampton Slave Revolt*, 66–72.

5. *Richmond Constitutional Whig*, 29 August 1831, 3 September 1831, cited in Tragle, *Southampton Slave Revolt*, 50–53, 66–72.

6. *Richmond Constitutional Whig*, 3 September 1831, cited in Tragle, *Southampton Slave Revolt*, 70–71.

7. Ibid.

8. Robert E. Lee to Mary Lee Custis, undated "Sunday" (probably August 28, 1831, based on internal evidence) in LFP. *Boston Liberator,* 1 October 1831, cited in Tragle, *Southampton Slave Revolt*, 114–16.

9. *Richmond Enquirer,* 30 September 1831.

10. For reference to Beck as a "negro girl slave," see trial of Frank, 12 September 1831, SCO. James S. French to Gov. Littleton W. Tazewell, 14 February 1835, EP. *Richmond Enquirer,* 30 September 1831. See testimony of Beck at trial of Jim and Isaac, 21 September 1831, SCJ. Samuel A. Raines of Sussex County testified that "Mrs. Parker with her servant Beck was frequently at his house, on some occasions two or three weeks at a time." See trial of Solomon, Nicholas, and Booker, 13 September 1831, SCO, 249. In 1813 or 1823 (the date is illegible) the Raccoon Swamp Antioch Baptist Church listed four female Parkers as members: Mary, Elizabeth, Temperance, and Judith. That same year, the church counted 60 white members and 127 black members, for a total of 187 members. In 1831, the church listed 150 members in its annual report to the Virginia Portsmouth Baptist Association, with no breakdown by race. A year later, it listed 42 white members, with no report from the black congregation. See "Copy of the Records of the Church of Christ at Raccoon Swamp Meetinghouse in Sussex County Virginia," 47–49, and PBA, 1831–32.

11. See trial of Frank, 13 September 1831, SCO, 249. For a discussion of slave "disturbances" in the eighteen months preceding the Southampton uprising, see Aptheker, *Nat Turner's Slave Rebellion*, 19–22.

12. See trials of Frank and Boson, 12 September 1831, and trial of Solomon, Nicholas, and Booker, 13 September 1831, SCO, 249, 253–54.

13. See trial of Solomon, Nicholas, and Booker, 13 September 1831, SCO, 253–54.

14. Court records state that Beck overheard the conversation on August 15,

which would have been a full week before the uprising; yet Beck testified that she heard the conversation on "the day on which the insurrection broke out," which would have been August 22. See trials of Jim, Isaac, Preston, and Frank, 22 September 1831, SCJ.

15. Robert Key testified that "the two Mrs. Parkers came there for protection" on Monday evening. See trial of Shadrack, 13 September 1831, SCO, 255–56. At the time, rumor had the insurgents moving toward Sussex; Solomon Parker himself traveled to Sussex County "to get Col. Hargrave to order out the Cavalry, as he believed the negroes intended to cross the Creek. On his way he found his wife at Mrs. Keys where she had gone for safety." See trials of Squire, 12 September 1831, and Solomon, Nicholas, Booker, and Shadrack ("property of Ann Key of this County"), 13 September 1831, SCO, 251–52, 254, 255–56.

16. See trials of Frank and Boson, 12 September 1831, and Solomon, Nicholas, and Booker, 13 September 1831, SCO, 249, 253–54. See also trials of Jim and Isaac, 22 September 1831, SCJ.

17. See trial of Solomon, Nicholas, and Booker, 13 September 1831, SCO, 253–54.

18. Jim denied knowing Beck during his examination before the magistrate in Sussex County; see testimony of Beck at trial of Jim and Isaac, 22 September 1831, SCJ. For eyewitness accounts of denials by Solomon, Nicholas, and Booker, see testimony of William Thornton and David Potts at trial of Solomon, Nicholas, and Booker, 13 September 1831, SCO, 253–54.

19. See testimony of Solomon D. Parker at trials of Frank and Boson, 12 September 1831, and trial of Solomon, Nicholas, and Booker, 13 September 1831, SCO, 249, 253–54.

20. See trials of Bob, Davy, and Daniel, 8 September 1831, SCJ; and of Squire, Frank, Boson, Solomon, Nicholas, Booker, Fed, and Shadrack, 12 and 13 September 1831, SCO, 251–52, 253–54, 255–56.

21. *Richmond Enquirer*, 30 September 1831. Although the *Enquirer* correspondent entertained the possibility of a larger conspiracy, he did not reject the central role of Nat Turner in devising the plot and spreading word of it among the slaves. He simply allowed for the possibility that Turner traveled widely. "A dreamer of dreams and a would-be Prophet, he used all the arts familiar to such pretenders, to deceive, delude, and overawe their minds. — Whether these arts were practiced only in his own immediate neighborhood, or, as some say, were extended to a distance, I have not been able to ascertain, with any certainty. Some allege that he had never left the vicinity of his master's dwelling, whilst others think that he had even visited the Metropolis of the State in his character of Preacher and Prophet."

22. Letter from "a gentleman well conversant with the scenes he describes,"

dated 17 September at Jerusalem, published in *Richmond Constitutional Whig,* September 26, 1831, in Tragle, *Southampton Slave Revolt,* 90–99.

23. *Richmond Constitutional Whig,* 26 September 1831.

24. For reports of Turner's alleged capture in Baltimore, see *Baltimore Niles' Register,* 10 September 1831, and *Richmond Enquirer,* 20 September 1831. For reports of his alleged capture in Southampton and his alleged near capture in Botetourt County, Virginia, 180 miles from Southampton, see *Richmond Enquirer,* 4 and 18 October 1831. For a report of his alleged drowning while attempting to cross the New River, see *Baltimore Niles' Register,* 29 October 1831. For the Dismal Swamp theory, see Warner, "Authentic and Impartial Narrative," reprinted in Tragle, *Southampton Slave Revolt,* 281–300.

25. For the governor's proclamation, see *Richmond Enquirer,* 20 September 1831, 3, and 27 September 1831, 1. The proclamation identified Turner as "the contriver and leader of the late insurrection in Southampton." It urged "the good people of the Commonwealth, to use their best endeavors, to cause the said fugitive to be apprehended, that he may be dealt with as the law directs."

26. *Boston Liberator,* 1 October 1831. *Richmond Enquirer,* 21 October 1831.

27. *Edenton (N.C.) Gazette,* 19 October 1831.

28. "Extract of a letter received by a gentleman in Portsmouth, from another in Southampton County, who lives within 4 miles of the late bloody scene," quoted in the *Norfolk American Beacon,* 15 October 1831. *Richmond Constitutional Whig,* 24 October 1831. *Norfolk American Beacon,* 2 November 1831.

29. For the most detailed account of the interview, see *Norfolk American Beacon,* 2 November 1831. A correspondent from Jerusalem reported that the magistrates closely examined Turner for between ninety minutes and two hours before committing him to prison. According to the correspondent, Turner confessed that "the attempt originated entirely with himself, and was not known by any other Negroes, but those to whom he revealed it a few days before, and then only 5 or 6 in number!" Others verified the report. A correspondent for the *Richmond Enquirer* noted that Turner tended to "mystify" when questioned closely on his plan to emancipate the blacks. "He does not, however, pretend to conceal that he was the author of the design, and that he imparted it to five or six others, all of whom seemed prepared with ready minds and hands to engage in it." Another correspondent for the *Enquirer* added a new wrinkle: "Nat states that there was no concert of an insurrection; that he did mention the subject to two persons about the month of April or May, but that no other person knew anything about his plans until the day previous to the attack." The *Norfolk Herald* declared the confessions of little importance except in showing that Turner "was not

connected with any organized plan or conspiracy beyond the circle of the few ignorant wretches whom he had seduced by his artifices to join him." See the *Richmond Enquirer,* 8 and 15 November 1831, and the *Norfolk Herald,* 4 November 1831.

30. *Richmond Enquirer,* 8 November 1831, "Extracts of Letters."

31. I have found no official record of Gray's birth date, but his obituary in August 1845 listed him as "aged 45 years." See *Norfolk American Beacon* and *Norfolk and Portsmouth Daily Advertiser,* 26 August 1845; *Richmond Whig & Public Advertiser,* 29 August 1845. For Gray family genealogy, see "The Godwin Family, of Nansemond and Isle of Wight Counties, Va., with Notices of the Families of Holladay, Gray, Blunt &c.," *Virginia Magazine of History and Biography* 5 (June 1898): 201–2. The census-taker listed thirty-seven slaves in the Gray household in 1810: see U.S. Census, Southampton County, Va., National Archives Roll 252–71; SCL, positive reel 39; SCP.

32. The trial records give no indication that Gray put up a spirited defense, and all five suspects were found guilty and sentenced to hang: Davy (September 2), Sam (September 3), Jack (September 5), Nathan (September 6), and Moses (October 18). Gray may have pleaded for leniency on behalf of his clients, as the justices recommended that the governor commute the sentences of Nathan and Moses to sale and transportation out of state. Tragle, *Southampton Slave Revolt,* 191–92, 195–201, 220–21.

33. Extract of a letter dated at Southampton, 1 November 1831, in the *Richmond Compiler,* 5 November 1831.

34. For references to Gray's plans to print fifty thousand copies of "The Confessions," see *Norfolk American Beacon,* 11 November 1831; *Alexandria Gazette,* 14 November 1831. On the "accurate likeness" of Turner adorning the pamphlet, see the *Norfolk Herald,* 14 November 1831. For advertisements and sale prices, see the *Lynchburg Virginian,* 28 November 1831; *Baltimore American,* 29 November 1831; *U.S. Telegraph,* 9 December 1831; *Richmond Enquirer,* 3 January 1832.

35. "The Confessions," reprinted in Tragle, *Southampton Slave Revolt,* 318. Here is how Gray interpreted and articulated the social and political significance of the pamphlet: "It reads an awful and, it is hoped, a useful lesson, as to the operations of a mind like his, endeavoring to grapple with things beyond its reach. How it first became bewildered and confounded, and finally corrupted and led to the conception and perpetration of the most atrocious and heart-rending deeds. It is calculated also to demonstrate the policy of our laws in restraint of this class of our population, and to induce all those entrusted with their execution, as well as our citizens generally, to see that they are strictly and rigidly enforced."

36. "The Confessions," reprinted in Tragle, *Southampton Slave Revolt,* 316, 318.

37. Kenneth S. Greenberg, ed., *The Confessions of Nat Turner and Related Documents* (New York: Bedford Books, 1996), 56. Trial record for Nat Turner, Southampton County Court of Oyer and Terminer, 5 November 1831; reprinted in Tragle, *Southampton Slave Revolt*, 223.

38. *Norfolk Herald*, 14 November 1831, reprinted in Tragle, *Southampton Slave Revolt*, 140. *Petersburg Intelligencer*, 15 November 1831, cited in *Boston Liberator*, 26 November 1831.

39. *Richmond Enquirer*, 25 November 1831, reprinted in Tragle, *Southampton Slave Revolt*, 141–43.

40. *Boston Liberator*, 17 December 1831.

41. "The Confessions," reprinted in Tragle, *Southampton Slave Revolt*, 303–5.

42. Nat Turner himself may have had personal connections to Sussex. According to at least two newspaper accounts, Turner went by the name of "Gen. Cargill" during the uprising. The U.S. Census returns for 1830 do not list any Cargills as heads of households in Southampton County; the only Cargills listed in a statewide index of returns for that year lived in Sussex. Turner may have known the Cargills or the slaves who lived on their plantations. He may have been familiar with John Cargill as sheriff of the neighboring county. Or he may have borrowed his alias from the late Gen. Nathaniel Harrison Cargill of Sussex, who had served as quartermaster general of the Virginia forces during the War of 1812.

43. Williamson Mann to Ben Lee, 29 August 1831, EC.

44. "Joe" to "brother," no date, EC.

45. Jno. C. Harris to Gov. John Floyd, 25 September 1831, and L.N.Q. to Gov. John Floyd, 15 October 1831, EC. Ambler, ed., *Life and Diary of John Floyd*, 166–67.

46. All of these documents, too numerous to cite, can be found in EC.

47. Gov. John Floyd to Gov. James Hamilton, 19 November 1831, reprinted in Foner, *Nat Turner*, 58.

48. Ibid.

49. "Governor's Message and Accompanying Documents," dated 6 December 1831, reprinted in Tragle, *Southampton Slave Revolt*, 433–34. *Norfolk and Portsmouth Herald*, 9 December 1831, quoted in Freehling, *Drift Toward Dissolution*, 125. Virginia Gov. John Floyd to South Carolina Gov. James Hamilton, Jr., dated at Richmond, 19 November 1831, reprinted in Tragle, *Southampton Slave Revolt*, 275–76. Ambler, *The Life and Diary of John Floyd*, 172.

50. J. H. Johnston et al., "Antislavery Petitions Presented to the Virginia Legislature by Citizens of Various Counties," *Journal of Negro History* 12 (October 1927): 670–91.

51. *Richmond Constitutional Whig*, 16 December 1831.

52. *Richmond Constitutional Whig*, 13 January 1832.

53. "Speech of James McDowell, Jr. (of Rockbridge) in the House of Delegates of Virginia, on the Slave Question . . ." Richmond, 1832, excerpted in Foner, *Nat Turner*, 112–13.

54. Combined preamble and committee report, as quoted in Robert, *The Road from Monticello*, 32.

55. "Virginia Legislature. House of Delegates. Monday, February 6. Removal of Free Negroes." *Richmond Enquirer*, 14 February 1832.

56. Robert, *Road from Monticello*, 33–35.

57. Ch. XXII — an act to amend an act entitled "An act reducing into one the several acts concerning slaves, free negroes and mulattoes, and for other purposes," passed 15 March 1832. See *Acts Passed at a General Assembly of the Commonwealth of Virginia* (Richmond: Printed for the Commonwealth by Thomas Ritchie, 1832), 20–22. For historical background on Virginia's courts of oyer and terminer, see Schwarz, *Twice Condemned*, 17–20.

58. Conference reports dated 30 October 1831, 12 November 1831, 25 March 1832, and 22 April 1832, ABC, 63–64.

59. The Mill-Swamp Church reported that "since the insurrection in Southampton, which occurred in their neighborhood, their coloured members had become exceedingly refractory and ungovernable, refusing, in many instances, the rule of the Church and disobeying the injunctions of the Gospel. Several other Churches had also mentioned a similar state of affairs among them." Otter Dams Church, Surry County, Virginia, 26–28 May 1832, PBA, 25–26.

60. Tanner's Creek Church, Norfolk County, Virginia, 25–27 May 1833, PBA, 15. Such upbeat reports were not commonplace among members of the Portsmouth Baptist Association. Tucker's Swamp Church reported "nothing like a revival or excitement," just "regular monthly preaching and Sabbath prayer meetings." The Mill Swamp Church reported that "the word preached seems to profit but little the ungodly; having had no additions." The church at South Quay put it most succinctly: "We are in a cold and stupid state." Beaver Dams Church, Isle-of-Wight County, Virginia, 24–27 May 1834, PBA sess. 44, 10–11. Sappony Church, Sussex County, Virginia, 23–25 May 1835, PBA sess. 45, 10.

61. One of the three witnesses who identified Boson was his owner, William Peters, who testified that "he raised the prisoner Boson, and [knew] him to be the same person who was sentenced by the Court in September 1831 to be executed and escaped from Jail." Justices William Thornton, Henry J. Harrison, Cyrus Dillard, and Robert Key may have remembered Boson as well, having presided over his brief adjourned trial on 1 September 1831, or his full trial on 12 September 1831. Justice William Briggs Jr. did not participate in any of the earlier proceedings against Boson. See minutes of Sussex County Court for 1 September 1831, 12 September 1831, 21 February 1835, SCO, 248–49, 460.

62. Petition from residents of Sussex to the Governor and Council of the state of Virginia, EP. The willingness of the Sussex County petitioners to admit their error stands in sharp contrast to the actions of white officials involved in another slave conspiracy based on subsequently discredited testimony. In 1741, an indentured servant named Mary Burton created a panic in New York City after implicating slaves in a plot to burn the city and massacre the whites. Accusations led to more accusations. When Burton began to implicate prominent whites, prosecutors lost faith in their star witness and quietly dropped their investigation. Rather than admit their error, provincial authorities declared a day of thanksgiving "for deliverance from the conspiracy," gave Burton a reward, and thanked her "for the great service she [had] done." See Edgar J. McManus, *A History of Slavery in New York* (Syracuse: Syracuse University Press, 1966), 127–39.

63. Here is the new evidence as presented in full by the petitioners:

> Bear in mind, that the conversation is said to have taken place between several negroes at the Raccoon Meeting House, at the *May* meeting 1831, in which *Solomon* and Boatswain were the prominent conspirators. Solomon was condemned and executed under this testimony alone. Now, if any fact can be adduced to invalidate the truth of the witness's testimony, in any one point, surely we may justly & reasonably conclude that the witness might have erred on other points. Now, Mr. and Mrs. Laine, inhabitants of that immediate neighbourhood, both declare that on *this very meeting day,* viz. May Raccoon meeting in 1831, Solomon came out of the mill pond (contiguous to Mr. Laine's) where he had been fishing all morning; that he brought to them a fine string of fish, *just caught;* that he *remained* on the Plantation untill long after the meeting had broken up; that he had assisted Mr. Laine's servants in taking the horse of those who had rode from meeting to Mr. Laine's; that he Mr. Laine saw him, Solomon, there untill nearly or quite sun down; and that he did not leave there untill after that time, so as to render it *impossible* that he could have been at the meeting house during the time of the meeting on that day. To which facts they, Mr. & Mrs. Laine, are willing to make an affidavit if necessary.

Alexander N. Laine signed his name to the petition.

64. James S. French to Gov. Littleton W. Tazewell, 14 February 1835, EP.
65. Ibid.
66. SCO, 460.

3. Apotheosis

1. On philosophical debates within the movement, see Demos, "Problem of Violent 'Means,'" 501–26.

2. On the Confederate response to "insurrection anxiety," see Armstead L. Robinson, "In the Shadow of Old John Brown: Insurrection Anxiety and Confederate Mobilization, 1861–1863," *Journal of Negro History* 65 (Autumn 1980): 279–97.

3. "A Voice from Providence," dated at Providence, Rhode Island, 1 November 1832, reprinted in Garrison, *Thoughts on African Colonization*, under the section heading "Sentiments of the People of Color," 44–45; *Liberator* (Boston, Mass.), 5 November 1831, 21 January 1832.

4. Minutes and Proceedings of the Second Annual Convention for the Improvement of Free People of Color in these United States, Held By Adjournments, in the City of Philadelphia, From the 4th to the 13th of June inclusive, 1832, 15–20, reprinted in Howard Bell, *Proceedings*.

5. *Liberator*, 30 June 1832.

6. Declaration of Sentiments of the American Anti-Slavery Society, adopted at first convention in Philadelphia, December 1833; reprinted in Louis Ruchames, ed., *The Abolitionists* (New York: Putnam, 1963), 78–83.

7. *Liberator*, 11 April 1835, 18 April 1835.

8. Protest of the American Anti-Slavery Society, addressed to the President of the United States, dated at New York, 26 December 1835; reprinted in James G. Birney, ed., *A Collection of Valuable Documents* (Boston: Isaac Knapp, 1836), 41–53; Clement Eaton, *The Freedom-of-Thought Struggle in the Old South*, rev. ed. (New York: Harper & Row, 1964).

9. Demos, "Problem of Violent 'Means,'" 507–9; Mabee, *Black Freedom*, 27–37; Quarles, *Black Abolitionists*, 54–55.

10. Bell, "Expressions of Negro Militancy," 11; Leon Litwack, "The Emancipation of the Negro Abolitionist," in John H. Bracey, Jr., et al., eds., *Blacks in the Abolitionist Movement* (Belmont, Calif.: Wadsworth Publishing, 1971), 67–76.

11. For biographical details, see Ofari, *"Let Your Motto Be Resistance."*

12. Speech Delivered at the Liberty Party Convention, Massachusetts, 1842, reprinted in Ofari, *"Let Your Motto Be Resistance,"* 138–53.

13. Speech by Henry Highland Garnet, delivered before the National Convention of Colored Citizens, Buffalo, New York, 16 August 1843, in Ripley et al., *The Black Abolitionist Papers*, vol. 3, 403–12.

14. Ripley et al., *Black Abolitionist Papers*, vol. 3, 403–12.

15. "Minutes of the National Convention of Colored Citizens: Held at Buffalo, on the 15th, 16th, 17th, 18th and 19th of August, 1843. For the Purpose of Considering Their Moral and Political Condition as American Citizens" (New York: Piercy and Reed, 1843), 12–14, 18–19; reprinted in Bell, *Proceedings*.

16. Frederick Douglass, *Narrative of the Life of Frederick Douglass an American Slave* (New York: Penguin Books, 1968), 118.

17. For an account of Douglass's "first great public speech," see McFeely, *Frederick Douglass*, 86–90.

18. For a broad overview of this power struggle, see Schor, "The Rivalry," 30–38.

19. "Minutes of the National Convention of Colored Citizens: Held at Buffalo, on the 15th, 16th, 17th, 18th and 19th of August, 1843. For the Purpose of Considering Their Moral and Political Condition as American Citizens"; reprinted in Bell, *Proceedings*.

20. *Liberator*, 22 September 1843.

21. Schor, *Henry Highland Garnet*, 59–60.

22. Foner and Walker, *Proceedings*, vol. 1, 229. In January 1849, the State Convention of Colored Citizens of Ohio resolved that five hundred copies of Garnet's pamphlet "be obtained in the name of the Convention and gratuitously distributed." The conventioneers did not read the pamphlet as a call for slave insurrection; rather, they endorsed "the doctrine of urging the slave to leave immediately with his hoe on his shoulder, for a land of liberty." See Quarles, *Black Abolitionists*, 227–28.

23. In August 1848, Douglass once again alluded to Turner in a speech to more than four hundred people at the Ford Street Baptist Church in Rochester, New York. "About eighteen years ago," he recalled, "a man of noble courage rose among his brethren in Virginia." Douglass imagined the speech that Turner might have given to his followers: "We have long been subjected to slavery. The hour for our deliverance has come. Let us rise and strike for liberty. In the name of a God of justice let us stay our oppressors." Once again, Turner fell in a hail of "American bullets, fired by United States troops." Once again, Douglass urged white Northerners to repudiate the proslavery provisions of the Constitution as the first step toward the abolition of slavery. Blassingame, *Frederick Douglass Papers*, 130, 144–45.

24. Frederick Douglass, "The Heroic Slave," originally published in *Douglass' Paper* (Rochester, N.Y.), March 1853; reprinted in Takaki, *Violence in the Black Imagination*, 37–38.

25. Frederick Douglass, *Life and Times of Frederick Douglass* (Hartford, Conn.: Park Publishing, 1881), 279–80.

26. "Selections. From the Liberty Bell. Charity Bowery. By L. M. Child," *North Star* (Rochester, N.Y.), 3 March 1848.

27. Braxton writes: "The archetypal outraged mother travels alone through the darkness to impart a sense of identity and 'belongingness' to her child. She sacrifices and improvises to create the vehicles necessary for the survival of flesh and spirit. Implied in all her actions and fueling her heroic ones is abuse of her people and her person." Braxton, *Black Women Writing*, 21.

28. Excerpt from Lydia Maria Child, "Charity Bowery," *Liberty Bell* (Boston, 1839), 41–42; reprinted in Foner, *Nat Turner*, 66–67.

29. For chronology, see Jacobs, *Incidents in the Life of a Slave Girl*, 245.

30. Child to Jacobs, 13 August 1860, reprinted in Jacobs, *Incidents*, 266.

31. Jacobs, *Incidents*, 63–67.

32. Excerpt from *Narrative of Henry Box Brown* (Boston, 1849); reprinted in Foner, *Nat Turner*, 67–68.

33. Ibid. James L. Smith, who was an enslaved shoemaker living in Virginia at the time of the uprising, verified this picture of African-American resistance in his narrative. "When Nat. Turner's insurrection broke out, the colored people were forbidden to hold meetings among themselves. . . . Notwithstanding our difficulties, we used to steal away to some of the quarters to have our meetings." Excerpt from *Autobiography of James L. Smith* (Norwich, Conn., 1881), 26–30; reprinted in Foner, *Nat Turner*, 73–74.

34. For biographical details, see Hedrick, *Harriet Beecher Stowe*, 206.

35. Stowe to Henry Ward Beecher, 1 February 1851, HBSm.

36. Stowe to Gamaliel Bailey, 9 March 1851, quoted in Hedrick, *Harriet Beecher Stowe*, 209.

37. Harriet Beecher Stowe, *Uncle Tom's Cabin; or, Life Among the Lowly* (New York: Modern Library, 2001), 56, 78.

38. Stowe, *Uncle Tom's Cabin*, 380–83, 24–25, 27, 161, 533, 563.

39. Stowe to Duchess of Argyle, 17 June 1856, HBSP; Judie Newman, ed., introduction to Harriet Beecher Stowe, *Dred: A Tale of the Great Dismal Swamp* (Halifax, England: Ryburn Publishing, 1992): 11–12.

40. Stowe, *Dred*, 616, 622, 685.

41. Ibid., 268, 273, 615.

42. *Christian Examiner and Religious Miscellany* 60 (November 1856): 474. *Littell's Living Age* 53 (June 1857): 45. *Southern Literary Messenger* 27 (October 1858): 284.

43. *DeBow's Review* 26 (December 1856): 662.

44. *Christian Examiner and Religious Miscellany* 60 (November 1856): 474.

45. *Littell's Living Age* 53 (June 1857): 711.

46. Fields, *Life and Letters*, 216, 218, 221, 222.

47. Ibid., 222, 226.

48. Meehan, "The Solitary Horseman," 58–62.

49. See "Literary Notices," *National Era*, July 11, 1850, 110.

50. Anecdote is from Eyre Crowe, *With Thackeray in America*, as quoted in Ellis, *The Solitary Horseman*, 134, f. 1.

51. Ellis, *The Solitary Horseman*, 180.

52. G.P.R. James, *The Old Dominion* (London: George Routledge and Sons, 1903), 9–11. The subtitle has been changed from "The Southampton Massacre" to "A Tale of Virginia" in this London edition.

53. Ibid., 81–84.

54. Review of *The Old Dominion*, by James, in *Southern Literary Messenger* 22 (April 1856): 320.

55. "James's Last," *Liberator*, 4 April 1856, 56; reprinted from the *Philadelphia Bulletin*. This poem-review is not quoted in any of the biographical works on James.

56. Ellis, *The Solitary Horseman*, 199.

57. "Editor's Table," *Southern Literary Messenger* 31 (August 1860): 153.

58. For biographical sketches and interpretive essays, see "War upon the Whites: Black Rage in the Fiction of Martin R. Delany," in Takaki, *Violence in the Black Imagination*, 79–101; Theodore Draper, "The Father of American Black Nationalism," *New York Review of Books* 14 (May 1970): 33–41.

59. Martin R. Delany, "Blake; or, The Huts of America," serialized in *Anglo-African Magazine* (January–July 1859); reprinted in Takaki, *Violence in the Black Imagination*, 177–78.

60. Ibid., 179.

61. *California Press* (San Francisco), Oct. 20, 1959; *Louisville Journal*, undated clipping; *Press* (Philadelphia), Oct. 20, 1859; *Journal of Commerce* (New York), Oct. 26, 1859; *National Anti-Slavery Standard*, Nov. 19, 1859; *Evening Post* (Boston), undated clipping; TWHP.

62. Frederick Douglass, *Life and Times*, 278–79.

63. F. B. Sanborn, *The Life and Letters of John Brown, Liberator of Kansas and Martyr of Virginia* (Boston: Roberts Brothers, 1885), 421–22.

64. Sanborn later explained:

> We saw this lonely and obscure old man choosing poverty before wealth, renouncing his ties of affection, throwing away his ease, his reputation, and his life for the sake of a despised race and for "zeal to his country's ancient liberties." Moved by this example, shamed by this generosity, was it to be imagined that young men and devoted Abolitionists would examine cautiously the grounds of prudence, or timidly follow a scrupulous conservatism? Without accepting Brown's plans as reasonable, we were prepared to second them merely because they were his. (*Life and Letters of John Brown*, 424, 446)

65. Oates, *To Purge This Land*, 278–79.

66. Douglass, *Life and Times*, 323–25.

67. Oates, *To Purge This Land*, 290–302.

68. Interview with John Brown as reported by the *New York Herald*, 21 October 1859, reprinted in Oswald Garrison Villard, *John Brown: A Biography Fifty Years After* (Boston: Houghton Mifflin Company, 1911), 460; statement of John Brown as reported by the *New York Herald*, 3 November 1859, reprinted in Villard, op. cit., 498.

69. Quoted in Sanborn, *Life and Letters of John Brown*, 575.

70. John Brown's Last Speech (Nov. 2), reprinted in Sanborn, *Life and Letters of John Brown*, 584.

71. John Brown to Andrew Hunter, 22 November 1859; reprinted in Sanborn, *Life and Letters of John Brown*, 584, f. 1.

72. Villard, *John Brown*, 475.

73. Gov. Henry A. Wise, speech of Oct. 21, 1859; reprinted in Villard, *John Brown*, 468–69.

74. James Redpath, *The Public Life of Capt. John Brown* (Boston: Thayer and Eldridge, 1860), 45–46.

75. Frederick Douglass, "John Brown," speech at Harpers Ferry, 30 May 1881; reprinted in Louis Ruchames, ed., *John Brown: The Making of a Revolutionary* (New York: Grosset & Dunlap, 1969), 295.

76. W.E.B. Du Bois, *John Brown* (Philadelphia: George W. Jacobs, 1909), 97.

77. Abraham Lincoln, Address at Cooper Institute, New York, 27 February 1860, in Roy P. Basler, ed. *Abraham Lincoln: His Speeches and Writings, 1859–1865* (New York: World Publishing Co., 1946), 529–32.

78. Ibid., 124.

79. Ibid., 125.

80. "The Nat Turner Insurrection," *Weekly Anglo-African* (New York), 31 December 1859.

81. "Lecture on Nat. Turner, by a Former Slave," *National Anti-Slavery Standard,* 19 November 1859; reprinted from *Evening Post,* 3 November 1859.

82. Speech of Dr. John S. Rock, delivered in Boston on the ninetieth anniversary of the Boston Massacre, 5 March 1860; text published in the *Liberator,* 16 March 1860. William C. Nell, the Rev. J. Sella Martin, and William Lloyd Garrison also addressed the meeting.

83. *Louisville Journal,* undated clipping; TWHP.

84. "Servile Insurrections" and "The Southampton Tragedy-Negro Outbreak in 1831," *California Press,* 20 October 1959; TWHP.

85. "Insurrections at the South," *New York Journal of Commerce,* 26 October 1859; TWHP.

86. "Negro Insurrections at the South; False Alarms," *Evening Post,* undated clipping; TWHP.

87. "Slave Insurrections," *National Anti-Slavery Standard,* 19 November 1859, in TWHP.

88. Joshua Coffin to Amos A. Phelps, 23 November 1833, published as Appendix A in Amos A. Phelps, *Lectures on Slavery and Its Remedy* (Boston: New-England Anti-Slavery Society, 1834), 239–51.

89. "History of Slave Insurrections; Note from Joshua Coffin," letter to editor of the *National Anti-Slavery Standard,* dated 21 November 1859 at Newbury, Mass., with editor's note, from undated clipping; TWHP.

90. *An Account of Some of the Principal Slave Insurrections and Others, Which Have Occurred, Or Been Attempted, in the United States and Elsewhere, During the Last Two Centuries. With Various Remarks. Collected from Various Sources by Joshua Coffin* (New York: American Anti-Slavery Society, 1860; reprinted by the Negro History Press, Detroit, 1970), 3.

91. Phelps, *Lectures on Slavery,* 249–50; Coffin, *Slave Insurrections,* 24–33.

92. Renehan, *The Secret Six.*

93. For biographical details, see Edelstein, *Strange Enthusiasm.* For quote on "liberal" ministry, see Thomas Wentworth Higginson, *Cheerful Yesterdays* (Boston: Houghton, Mifflin, 1899), 98.

94. [Thomas Wentworth Higginson], "Physical Courage," *Atlantic Monthly* 2 (November 1858): 730–33.

95. T. W. Higginson to Louisa Higginson, 18 April 1860, TWHP.

96. [Thomas Wentworth Higginson], "The Maroons of Jamaica," *Atlantic Monthly* 5 (February 1860): 222.

97. [Thomas Wentworth Higginson], "The Maroons of Surinam," *Atlantic Monthly* 5 (May 1860): 553.

98. [Thomas Wentworth Higginson], "The Ordeal of Battle," *Atlantic Monthly* 8 (July 1861): 94.

99. Higginson to James T. Fields, 2 June 1861, TWHP.

100. [Higginson], "Nat Turner's Insurrection," 173, 175–76, 186.

101. Ibid., 174.

102. Ibid., 173, 187.

103. [Higginson], "Gabriel's Defeat," 337.

104. Metta V. Victor, *Maum Guinea and Her Plantation "Children"; or, Holiday Week on a Louisiana Estate. A Slave Romance* (New York: Beadle and Company, 1861); Orville J. Victor, *History of American Conspiracies: A Record of Treason, Insurrection, Rebellion, &c. in the United States of America, from 1760 to 1860* (New York: James D. Torrey, 1863).

105. Albert Johannsen, *The House of Beadle and Adams and Its Dime and Nickel Novels,* vol. 2 (Norman: University of Oklahoma Press, 1950), 279–80; 285–87.

106. Charles M. Harvey, "The Dime Novel in American Life," *Atlantic Monthly* 100 (1907): 37–38.

107. Ibid., 39.

108. Victor, *Maum Guinea,* iv.

109. Harvey, "The Dime Novel," 39. Johannsen writes: "I have been unable to trace the source of Harvey's information about Lincoln, but give it here because it has often been repeated." Johannsen, *House of Beadle and Adams,* vol. 1, 40–41.

110. William Everett, review of Beadle's Dime Books, *North American Review* 99 (July 1864): 307. Everett is identified as the author of this review in

Edmund Pearson, *Dime Novels, or, Following an Old Trail in Popular Literature* (Boston: Little, Brown, 1929), 271.

111. George M. Fredrickson, *The Black Image in the White Mind*, 118.

112. Victor, *Maum Guinea*.

113. Pearson, *Dime Novels*, 48–49.

114. Harvey, "The Dime Novel," 43.

115. Simmons, "Maum Guinea," 81.

116. Victor, *History of American Conspiracies*, xi–xii, 25–26.

117. Ibid., 397.

118. Ibid., 373.

119. Ibid., ix.

120. William Wells Brown, *The Black Man, His Antecedents, His Genius, and His Achievements* (New York: Thomas Hamilton, 1863). Brown is first introduced, with a biographical sketch, in the preceding chapter.

121. Ibid., 59–61.

122. Ibid., 73–75.

123. Carl Sandburg, *Abraham Lincoln, The War Years*, vol. 2 (New York: Harcourt, Brace, 1939), 14.

124. Franklin, *The Emancipation Proclamation*.

125. "Lincoln and His Proclamation," *Richmond Enquirer*, Oct. 1, 1862; reprinted in the *New York Herald*, 14 October 1862.

126. Ibid.

127. Ibid.

128. "The Situation," *New York Herald*, 4 October 1862.

129. "The Emancipation Proclamation — The Last Card of the Abolition Programme," *New York Herald*, 3 January 1863.

130. Herbert Aptheker, ed., *A Documentary History of the Negro People in the United States*, vol. 1 (New York: Citadel Press, 1969), 477–80.

131. Frederick Douglass, "How to End the War," *Douglass' Monthly*, May 1861; reprinted in Foner, *Life and Writings*, 94.

132. Frederick Douglass, "Black Regiments Proposed," *Douglass' Monthly*, May 1861; reprinted in Foner, *Life and Writings*, 97.

133. Frederick Douglass, "Fighting the Rebels with Only One Hand," *Douglass' Monthly*, September 1861; reprinted in Foner, *Life and Writings*, 97.

134. Frederick Douglass, "A Black Hero," *Douglass' Monthly*, August 1861; reprinted in Foner, *Life and Writings*, 132–34.

135. Franklin, *Emancipation Proclamation*, 25, 97, 104.

136. Aptheker, *A Documentary History*, 479.

137. Ibid.

138. Harriet Beecher Stowe, "The Chimney-Corner," *Atlantic Monthly* 15 (January 1865): 110.

139. Ibid.

140. Ibid., 114–15.
141. Ibid., 115.

4. Signposts

1. On the gendered construction of the "black public sphere," see Higginbotham, *Righteous Discontent*, and Brown, "Negotiating and Transforming the Public Sphere."

2. Foner, *A Short History of Reconstruction*, 71–72.

3. *Nation* 1 (23 November 1865): 651.

4. Carter, "The Anatomy of Fear," 348, f. 10.

5. Quoted in ibid., 362.

6. "The Colored Shiloh Regular Baptist Association of Virginia," *Richmond Daily Dispatch*, 9 August 1867. Minutes of the first and second day's proceedings were reported on p. 1. This episode is discussed in Crofts, *Old Southampton*, 243–44.

7. Ibid. On the black church as an "invisible institution" under slavery, see Albert Raboteau, *Slave Religion: The 'Invisible Institution' in the Antebellum South* (New York: Oxford University Press, 1978.) On the black church after emancipation, see William E. Montgomery, *Under Their Own Vine and Fig Tree: The African-American Church in the South, 1865–1900* (Baton Rouge: Louisiana University Press, 1993).

8. Lowe, *Republicans and Reconstruction in Virginia*, 90–92.

9. "The Position of the Dispatch," *Richmond Daily Dispatch*, 3 August 1867. "Nat Turner's Massacre," *Richmond Daily Dispatch*, 12 August 1867.

10. "Nat Turner's Massacre," *Richmond Daily Dispatch*, 12 August 1867.

11. "What Is Sauce for the Goose Is Sauce for the Gander," *Richmond Weekly New Nation*, 22 August 1867.

12. Crofts, *Old Southampton*, 239, 248, 255, 260, 263, 265. *Charlottesville Chronicle*, 1 April 1869. Thanks to Corey D. B. Walker for calling this item to my attention.

13. Quoted in *Petersburg Index*, 7 May 1870; reprinted in Tragle, *Southampton Slave Revolt*, 155–56.

14. On the "politics of race" and the Readjuster movement in Virginia, see Dailey, *Before Jim Crow*.

15. Dailey, "Deference and Violence in the Postbellum Urban South," 580. See also Charles E. Wynes, *Race Relations in Virginia, 1870–1902* (Charlottesville: University Press of Virginia, 1961), 16–38.

16. *Richmond Daily Whig*, 14 November 1883.

17. "Rumored Uprising of the Negroes of Southampton County," *Norfolk Virginian*, 9 November 1883; "The Southampton County Disturbance," *Norfolk Virginian*, 10 November 1883.

18. "The Responsibility of Virginians," editorial in the *New York Herald*, reprinted in *Petersburg Index-Appeal*, 12 November 1883, 1. The editors of the *New York Herald* called on both parties — the Democrats and the Readjusters, also known as "the Mahoneparty" after General William Mahone — to stop playing the race card. "The leaders of the democratic party, victorious there on Tuesday, will fail in patriotic duty if they do not take energetic measures instantly to dispel any fears colored people entertain that they are imperilled in person or property by the result of the election; and on the other side the Mahone partisans will equally fail in that duty if they do not scrupulously abstain from giving any unwarranted political color to riots and disturbances in which the two races happen to be engaged."

19. "Groundless Fears! Anxiety at an End in Southampton; No Disturbance Apprehended," *Norfolk Landmark*, 10 November 1883, 4.

20. For a penetrating analysis of black uplift ideology in the post-Reconstruction era, see Gaines, *Uplifting the Race*, 1–46.

21. William Wells Brown, *The Black Man, His Antecedents, His Genius, and His Achievements* (New York: Thomas Hamilton, 1863), 73–75. William Wells Brown, *The Negro in the American Rebellion: His Heroism and His Fidelity* (Boston: Lee & Shepard, 1867), 355–56. William Wells Brown, *The Rising Son; or, The Antecedents and Advancement of the Colored Race* (New York: Negro Universities Press, 1874), 303–18, 413–17.

22. William Wells Brown, *My Southern Home: The South and Its People*, 3d edition (Boston: A. G. Brown and Co., 1882), 243.

23. For a close study of the "early race historians" and their "denominationally-based historical production," see Maffly-Kipp, "Mapping the World," 610–26. See also Smith, *An Old Creed for the New South*, chap. 7, "A Different View of Slavery: Blacks Confront the New Proslavery Argument," 195–238.

24. John Hope Franklin, "George Washington Williams, Historian," *Journal of Negro History* 31 (January 1946): 61–64.

25. George Washington Williams, *History of the Negro Race in America, from 1619 to 1880*, vol. 1 (New York: G. P. Putnam's Sons, 1883), v–x.

26. Ibid., vol. 2, 82.

27. Ibid., vol. 2, 91.

28. "Although the vast majority of Negroes lived in the South," historian Emma Lou Thornbrough writes, "the most influential and enduring race papers were published in the cities of the North. Race was their raison d'etre. They were published by black men for black readers. With varying degrees of militancy, all protested against racism in their editorial pages and publicized racial achievements and acts of racial injustice in their news columns." Thornbrough, *T. Thomas Fortune*, 38.

29. Ibid., 44.

30. T. Thomas Fortune in the *Globe* (New York), 17 February 1883; excerpted in Dann, *The Black Press,* 165–66.

31. T. Thomas Fortune, "The Afro-American League," 2 June 1887; reprinted in Dann, *The Black Press,* 165–66. T. Thomas Fortune, "Nat Turner," *Cleveland Gazette,* 22 November 1884; reprinted in Foner, *Nat Turner,* 146–47.

32. T. Thomas Fortune, "John Brown and Nat. Turner," *New York Age,* 12 January 1889; reprinted in Foner, *Nat Turner,* 147–48.

33. Frederick Douglass, Jr., *National Leader* (Washington, D.C.), 19 January 1889; reprinted in Foner, *Nat Turner,* 148–49.

34. T. Thomas Fortune, *Age* (New York), 26 January 1889; reprinted in Foner, *Nat Turner,* 149–50.

35. "The Ten Greatest Negroes; A Few of the Many Guesses," *Indianapolis Freeman,* 17 May 1890, 7.

36. *Indianapolis Freeman,* 20 September 1890.

37. "Negro Greatness," *Indianapolis Freeman,* 27 September 1890, 4. "Negro Greatness Again," *Indianapolis Freeman,* 4 October 1890, 4.

38. For biographical sketches, see Margie H. Luckett, *Maryland Women* (Baltimore: King Bros., 1931), 478–79; Charles B. Tiernan, *The Tiernan Family of Maryland* (Baltimore: Gallery and McCan, 1898), 160–64. For literary readings, see Watson, "Mary Spear Tiernan's Unique Contribution to Post-Bellum Virginia Fiction," 100–107; Davis, *Nat Turner Before the Bar of Judgment,* 169–98.

39. Tiernan, *Homoselle,* 189, 348.

40. Ibid., 353.

41. Marion Harland, *Marion Harland's Autobiography: The Story of a Long Life* (New York: Harper & Brothers Publishers, 1910), 191.

42. Ibid., 191–93.

43. I have drawn this biographical data from two sources: *Who Was Who in America,* vol. 1, 1897–1942 (Chicago: Marquis Who's Who, 1968), 120, and John William Leonard, ed., *Woman's Who's Who of America,* 1914–1915 (New York: American Commonwealth Company, 1914), 117. I have deduced the year of her birth from her obituary: "Mrs. Pauline C. Bouvé Dies; Author of Children's Books Was in Her 68th Year," *New York Times,* 31 December 1928, 15. For studies of Bouvé's work, see Sadler, "The Figure of the Black Insurrectionist in Stowe, Bouvé, Bontemps, and Gaither," 21–24; and Grigsby, "Jesus, Judas, Job or 'Jes a Happy Ole Nigga,'" 51–62.

44. Pauline Carrington Bouvé, *Their Shadows Before: A Story of the Southampton Insurrection* (Boston: Small, Maynard & Company, 1899), 3, 5, 7–8, 23, 25, 30, 46, 91–92, 96.

45. Ibid., 104, 139–40, 198, 201.

46. Rokela, "A Page of History," *Godey's Magazine* 136 (March 1898): 289–91. An incomplete draft of the article, written in longhand, is preserved in

TFP; I have not located any correspondence between Tyler and her editors at *Godey's*.

47. Ulrich B. Phillips, "The Central Theme of Southern History," *American Historical Review* 34 (October 1928): 31.

48. For a critical analysis of the work produced by scholars of slavery at Johns Hopkins in this period, see Smith, *An Old Creed*, 137–61. A 1902 survey, *Studies in Historical and Political Science*, found that "fifty-three Southern members of the Department of History have written 748 monographs, books or articles, of which 316 have been specifically on the South, while non-Southern men have written 51 articles in addition upon the South." Stephenson, "Herbert B. Adams and Southern Historical Scholarship at the Johns Hopkins University," 8–9, 3–4, 14.

49. Stephen B. Weeks, "The Slave Insurrection in Virginia, 1831, Known As 'Old Nat's War,'" *Magazine of American History* (June 1891): 448–58; reprinted in Tragle, *Southampton Slave Revolt*, 358–69.

50. Drewry, *Southampton Insurrection*, 198.

51. Drewry to Martha Rochelle Tyler, Oct. 22, 1898, TFP.

52. Drewry, *Southampton Insurrection*, 106–8.

53. Ibid., 29, 108, 116.

54. Ibid., 118–23, 115–16, 149–50.

55. Ibid., 158, 49, 38, 40, 45, 46–47, 52, 56, 62, 71, 160.

56. Ibid., 194.

57. "The Literary South," *Confederate Veteran* 13 (October 1905): 469–70. *Virginia Magazine of History and Biography* 8 (July 1900): 221–22.

58. Hart, *Slavery and Abolition*, xv, 215–20.

59. William H. Ferris, "Alexander Crummell, An Apostle of Negro Culture," American Negro Academy Occasional Papers No. 20 (Washington, D.C., 1920), 8–9; reprinted in *The American Negro Academy Occasional Papers 1–22* (New York: Arno Press and the New York Times, 1969).

60. Archibald H. Grimke, "Right on the Scaffold; or, The Martyrs of 1822"; T. G. Steward, "How the Black St. Domingo Legion Saved the Patriot Army in the Siege of Savannah, 1779"; Theophilus G. Steward, "The Message of San Domingo to the African Race"; all reprinted in *The American Negro Academy Occasional Papers, 1–22*.

61. Cromwell, "The Aftermath of Nat Turner's Insurrection," 208, f. 1. For biographical details, see obituary for John Wesley Cromwell, *Journal of Negro History* 12 (July 1927): 563–66.

62. Alexander Crummell, undated review of Cromwell's lecture, ACP. John W. Cromwell, *The Negro in American History* (Washington, D.C.: American Negro Academy, 1914): 12–16.

63. For an analysis of the "image of the faithful slave" in Lost Cause ideology, see Blight, *Race and Reunion*, 284–91.

64. "Faithful Old Slaves, Degenerate Progeny," *Confederate Veteran* 11 (September 1903): 407.

65. "Honor for the Old-Time Negro," *Confederate Veteran* 20 (September 1912): 410.

66. For a state-by-state study of disfranchisement, see Michael Perman, *Struggle for Mastery: Disfranchisement in the South, 1888–1908* (Chapel Hill: University of North Carolina Press, 2001). For a brief overview, see Litwack, *Trouble in Mind,* 218–29.

67. Brook Thomas, ed., Plessy v. Ferguson: *A Brief History With Documents* (Boston: Bedford Books, 1997), 57–58. For a "situational" explanation of segregation, relating its emergence to "technological, demographic, economic, and political changes" in the New South, see Ayers, *Promise of the New South,* 136–46.

68. Booker T. Washington, *Up from Slavery,* in Franklin, *Three Negro Classics,* 30. See also Harlan, *Booker T. Washington: The Making of a Black Leader, 1856–1901* and *Booker T. Washington: The Wizard of Tuskegee, 1901–1915.*

69. Washington, *Up from Slavery,* reprinted in Franklin, *Three Negro Classics,* 147–48.

70. Ibid., 35–38, 32–33.

71. Booker T. Washington, *The Story of the Negro: The Rise of the Race from Slavery,* vol. 1 (New York: Doubleday, Page, 1909), 183, 173, 183–84, 177–78, 185–86.

72. Ibid., vol. 2, 213.

73. Washington and Fortune quotes and general background on Washington's response to the Brownsville affair and the Atlanta riot are drawn from Louis R. Harlan, *Booker T. Washington: The Wizard of Tuskegee,* 299–300.

74. W.E.B. Du Bois, "A Negro Student at Harvard at the End of the Nineteenth Century," *Massachusetts Review* 1 (Spring 1960): 439–58. For a brief biographical sketch of Du Bois, see entry in Rayford Logan and Michael R. Winston, eds., *Dictionary of American Negro Biography* (New York: Norton, 1982), 193–99.

75. W.E.B. Du Bois, "The Evolution of Black Leadership," *Dial* 31 (July 16, 1902): 53–55; reprinted in Louis R. Harlan and Raymond W. Smock, eds., *The Booker T. Washington Papers,* vol. 6, 1901–1902 (Chicago: University of Illinois Press, 1977), 175–78.

76. Ellis P. Oberholtzer to W. E. Burghardt Du Bois, 25 January 1904; Du Bois to Oberholtzer, 30 January 1904; Oberholtzer to Du Bois, 3 February 1904; Du Bois to Oberholtzer, n.d.; Oberholtzer to Du Bois, 16 February 1904; in Herbert Aptheker, ed., *The Correspondence of W.E.B. Du Bois,* vol. 1 (Amherst: University of Massachusetts Press, 1973), 63–65.

77. W.E.B. Du Bois, *John Brown* (Philadelphia: George W. Jacobs, 1909), 85–86, 97, 127.

78. "The Niagara Movement Address to the Nation," read by W.E.B. Du Bois at the second annual meeting of the Niagara Movement, 16 August 1906, Harpers Ferry, West Virginia; reprinted in Philip S. Foner, ed., *W.E.B. Du Bois Speaks: Speeches and Addresses, 1890–1919* (New York: Pathfinder Press, 1970), 170–73.

79. W.E.B. Du Bois, "The People of Peoples and Their Gifts to Men," *Crisis* 6 (November 1913), 339–41; reprinted in Herbert Aptheker, comp. and ed., *Creative Writings by W.E.B. Du Bois: A Pageant, Poems, Short Stories, and Playlets* (White Plains, N.Y.: Kraus-Thomson Organization, 1985): 1–5. Four-page folder describing "The Star of Ethiopia," circa 1915, in Herbert Aptheker, ed., *Pamphlets and Leaflets by W.E.B. Du Bois* (White Plains, N.Y.: Kraus-Thomson Organization, 1986), 161–65; W.E.B. Du Bois, "The Star of Ethiopia," *Crisis* 11 (December 1915): 91–93; reprinted in Herbert Aptheker, *Selections from the* Crisis, vol. 1 (Millwood, N.Y.: Kraus-Thomson Organization, 1983), 114–15.

80. Unsigned editorial, "The Lynching Industry," *Crisis* 9 (February 1915): 196, 198; reprinted in Aptheker, *Selections from the* Crisis, vol. 1, 88–90. For Wilson quote, see John Hope Franklin, "*The Birth of a Nation:* Propaganda As History" in Franklin, *Race and History: Selected Essays 1938–1988* (Baton Rouge: Louisiana State University Press, 1989), 16. Unsigned editorial, "The Clansman," *Crisis* 10 (May 1914): 33; reprinted in Aptheker, *Selections from the* Crisis, vol. 1, 98–99. Thomas R. Cripps, "The Reaction of the Negro to the Motion Picture *Birth of a Nation*," *Historian* 25 (May 1963): 349.

81. "The Migration of the Negroes," *Crisis,* 14 (June 1917): 63–66; reprinted in Aptheker, *Selections from the* Crisis, vol. 1, 139. "Brothers, Come North," *Crisis* 19 (January 1920): 105–6; reprinted in Aptheker, op. cit., 248–49.

82. "Close Ranks," *Crisis* 16 (July 1918): 111; reprinted in Aptheker, *Selections from the* Crisis, vol. 1, 159. "Returning Soldiers," *Crisis* 18 (May 1919): 13–14; reprinted in Aptheker, op. cit., 196–97.

83. "Let Us Reason Together," *Crisis* 18 (September 1919): 231; reprinted in Aptheker, *Selections from the* Crisis, vol. 1, 240.

84. Report of the UNIA Meeting, Liberty Hall, New York, 7 March 1920, in Robert A. Hill, ed., *The Marcus Garvey and Universal Negro Improvement Association Papers,* vol. 2 (Berkeley: University of California Press, 1983), 380, 383.

85. "African Fundamentalism: Fount of Inspiration," in Robert A. Hill, ed., *Marcus Garvey: Life and Lessons* (Berkeley: University of California Press, 1987), 7–25. Originally published in *Blackman* (Kingston, Jamaica), 11, 18, and 25 October and 1 November 1930.

86. Alain Locke, "The New Negro," from Locke, *The New Negro;* reprinted in Nathan Huggins, ed., *Voices from the Harlem Renaissance* (New York: Oxford University Press, 1976), 47–56. Arthur A. Schomburg, "The Negro

Digs Up His Past," in Locke, *The New Negro;* reprinted in Huggins, *Voices from the Harlem Renaissance*, 217–21.

87. Goggin, *Carter G. Woodson*, 140.

88. Carter G. Woodson, *Negro Makers of History*, 4th ed. (Washington, D.C.: Associated Publishers, 1945), 95.

89. Carter G. Woodson, "The Celebration of Negro History Week, 1927," *Journal of Negro History* 12 (April 1927): 104–5.

90. Proceedings of the Annual Meeting of the Association for the Study of Negro Life and History, Held at Virginia State College, Petersburg, Virginia, 25–28 October 1936, *Journal of Negro History* 22 (January 1937): 4. Luther P. Jackson, "The Work of the Association and Its People," *Journal of Negro History* 20 (October 1935): 391–93. Proceedings of the Annual Meeting, 4.

91. Florence Pierce Jackson, *Southampton County Geography Supplement* (Charlottesville, Va.: Southampton County School Board and University of Virginia, 1930). *Virginia Highway Historical Markers: The Tourist Guide Book of Virginia Featuring the Inscriptions on the Markers Along the Historical and Romantic Highways of the Mother State* (Strasburg, Va.: Shenandoah Publishing House, 1931), 166. For a discussion of "the revolution in automobile travel" and its relationship to tourism, see Michael Kammen, *Mystic Chords of Memory: The Transformation of Tradition in American Culture* (New York: Vintage Books, 1991), 304.

92. Recommendation by Mrs. Roy McKinney, president-general, to establish Faithful Slave Committee, November 1920, as reported in the Minutes of the Thirty-Eighth Annual Convention, United Daughters of the Confederacy, Jacksonville, Fla., 17–21 November 1931, 298. Minutes of the Twenty-Eighth Annual Convention, UDC, St. Louis, Mo., 8–12 November 1921, 207–10.

93. Minutes of the Thirty-Fourth Annual Convention, UDC, Charleston, S.C., 15–19 November 1927, 264–65. Minutes of the Twenty-Ninth Annual Convention, UDC, Birmingham, Ala., 14–18 November 1922, 216–18. Minutes of the Thirty-Third Annual Convention, UDC, Richmond, Va., 16–20 November 1926, 210.

94. Minutes of the Thirty-Eighth Annual Convention, UDC, 298–302. Mary Johnson, "An 'ever present bone of contention': The Heyward Shepherd Memorial," *West Virginia History* 56 (1997): 11. "To 'True' Slaves," *Afro-American* (Baltimore), 3 October 1931. "Confederates to Dedicate 'Uncle Tom' Monument," *Afro-American* (Baltimore), 10 October 1931.

95. For crowd estimate, see "Yankee Woman Steals Rebel Girls' Show: Confederate Daughters Gape As She Lauds John Brown," *Afro-American* (Baltimore), 17 October 1831. "The colored representation on the platform, besides Rev. Bragg, was James Walker, nephew of Heyward Shepherd, James Moton employed by the B. & O. Railroad in the position that was

held by Shepherd." Minutes of the Thirty-Eighth Annual Convention, UDC, 301.

96. "Heyward Shepherd," *Confederate Veteran* (Nashville, Tenn.) 39 (November 1931): 411.

97. "Yankee Woman Steals Rebel Girls' Show."

98. Minutes of the Thirty-Eighth Annual Convention, UDC, 298–302.

99. "Yankee Woman Steals Rebel Girls' Show."

100. Ibid. "Daughters of the Confederacy and John Brown: Max Barber Tears Down False World of Southern Folk," *Afro-American* (Baltimore), 24 October 1831. William Pickens, "Suggestions to Daughters of the Confederacy," *Afro-American* (Baltimore), 7 November 1831.

101. Rayford W. Logan to W.E.B. Du Bois, 11 November 1931, Du Bois Papers, Reel 35, Frame 887. Du Bois to Logan, 13 November 1831, Du Bois Papers, Reel 35, Frame 888.

102. On black party membership, see Nell Irvin Painter, *The Narrative of Hosea Hudson: His Life As a Negro Communist in the South* (Cambridge: Harvard University Press, 1979), 17–18.

103. Quotes from Carter, *Scottsboro*, 64, 61, 85. See also Goodman, *Stories of Scottsboro*. For a study of Communist Party activity in the South during this period, see Kelley, *Hammer and Hoe*.

104. Cyril Briggs, "The Scottsboro Case and the Nat Turner Centenary," *Liberator*, 6 June 1931; reprinted in Foner, *Nat Turner*, 158–60.

105. Miles Mark Fisher, "Nat Turner, A Hundred Years Afterwards," *Crisis* 40 (September 1931): 305.

106. Rayford W. Logan, "Nat Turner: Fiend or Martyr?" *Opportunity* 9 (November 1931): 338–39.

107. Egerton, *Speak Now Against the Day*, 170–71. A. Philip Randolph, Keynote Address to the National Negro Congress, 1936; reprinted in Herbert Aptheker, ed., *A Documentary History of the Negro People in the United States, 1933–1945* (Secaucus, N.J.: Citadel Press, 1974), 212–20.

108. Elizabeth Lawson, "After Nat Turner's Revolt: He Died, But Not in Vain: The Voice He Raised Was Never Again Silent," *Daily Worker* (New York), 21 August 1936, 7.

109. Benjamin Brawley, *Negro Builders and Heroes* (Chapel Hill: University of North Carolina Press, 1937).

110. Bell Irvin Wiley, review of *Negro Builders and Heroes*, by Benjamin Brawley, in *Journal of Southern History* 4 (August 1938): 405–6.

111. Benjamin Stolberg, "Minority Jingo," *Nation* 145 (23 October 1937): 437–39.

112. Claude McKay, "Heroes and Valets," *Nation* 145 (20 November 1937): 571–72.

113. Alain Locke, "Jingo, Counter-Jingo and Us," *Opportunity* 16 (January 1938): 8.

114. Randolph Edmonds, *Nat Turner,* in *Six Plays for a Negro Theater* (Boston: Walter H. Baker, 1934).

115. Arna Bontemps, *Black Thunder* (New York: Macmillan, 1936; Boston: Beacon Press, 1968); Arna Bontemps, *Drums at Dusk* (New York: Macmillan, 1939).

116. Buell G. Gallagher, "Talladega Library: Weapon Against Caste," *Crisis* 46 (April 1939): 110.

117. White, "Path of a Negro Artist," *Masses and Mainstream* 8 (April 1955): 35–36.

118. Ibid., 38.

119. Ibid., 39.

120. "Negro Paints Story of Race in America: Mural by C. W. White Unveiled at Hampton Institute," *New York Times,* 27 June 1943, 28. Charles White, quoted in "Art Today," *Daily Worker,* 28 August 1943; CWP.

121. For historical background on the Virginia Writers' Project ex-slave interviews, see Charles L. Perdue Jr.'s introduction to Charles L. Perdue, Jr., Thomas E. Barden, and Robert K. Phillips, eds., *Weevils in the Wheat: Interviews with Virginia Ex-Slaves* (Charlottesville: University Press of Virginia, 1976), xi–xlv. For reference to Turner in questionnaire, see Appendix 6, "Questionnaire for Ex-Slaves," question no. 281, Perdue et al., op. cit., 375.

122. See transcript of Susie R. C. Byrd's interview with Fannie Berry, dated 26 February 1937; reprinted in Perdue et al., *Weevils in the Wheat,* 35. On "confusion" surrounding Berry's age, see editorial commentary and photograph, Perdue et al., op. cit., 30–31. See transcript of Susie R. C. Byrd's interview with Ella Williams, undated; reprinted Perdue et al., op. cit., 313–14. For discussion of Williams's age, see editorial commentary in Perdue et al., op. cit., 314.

123. See transcript of Claude W. Anderson's interview with Cornelia Carney, date unknown; reprinted in Perdue et al., *Weevils in the Wheat,* 66–67.

124. See transcript of Susie R. C. Byrd's interview with Allen Crawford, 25 June 1937; reprinted in Perdue et al., *Weevils in the Wheat,* 74–76.

125. For publication history, including Eudora Ramsay Richardson quotation, see Perdue's Introduction to *Weevils in the Wheat,* xx–xxiv, and his Foreword to *The Negro in Virginia,* comp. by Workers of the Writers' Program of the Work Projects Administration in the State of Virginia (Winston-Salem, N.C.: John F. Blair, 1994), vii–xviii.

126. *The Negro in Virginia,* chap. 7, "Slave No More," 193–208.

127. *Virginia: A Guide to the Old Dominion,* comp. by Workers of the Writers' Program of the Work Projects Administration in the State of Virginia (New York: Oxford University Press, 1940), 472–73. The book was sponsored by Gov. James H. Price of Virginia.

128. Meier and Rudwick, *Black History and the Historical Profession,* 100, 101, 107.

129. Walter Jackson, "Melville Herskovits and the Search for Afro-American Culture," 103–4.

130. Wish, "American Negro Slave Revolts Before 1861," 299, 313, 320; Wish, "Slave Disloyalty in the Confederacy," 435; Wish, "The Slave Insurrection Panic of 1856," 206.

131. Bauer and Bauer, "Day to Day Resistance to Slavery," 388, 393, 419. In their acknowledgments, the authors wrote: "We wish to express our appreciation to Professor M. J. Herskovits, under whose direction this research has been carried on."

132. Herskovits, *The Myth of the Negro Past,* 1, 86, 103.

133. "Aptheker, Herbert," *Contemporary Authors,* New Revision Series, vol. 6, 28, 30. Walter W. Ross interviewed Aptheker at his office in San Jose, California, on 28 May 1981.

134. Ibid., 30.

135. Aptheker, *Nat Turner's Slave Rebellion,* 3–5, 107.

136. Ibid., 3–5, 14–15, 19–22, 27–31, 33–35, 41–42, 60–62, 120, 36, 46, 72, 51, 107.

137. Bettina Aptheker, "Bibliographical Comment," in Gary Y. Okihiro, ed., *In Resistance: Studies in African, Caribbean, and Afro-American History* (Amherst: University of Massachusetts Press, 1986), 210–11.

138. Aptheker, *American Negro Slave Revolts,* 373, 162, 153, 53.

139. G. G. van D., review of Aptheker's *American Negro Slave Revolts* in *English Historical Review* 63 (April 1948): 283.

140. Richard Hostadter, "U. B. Phillips and the Plantation Legend," *Journal of Negro History* 29 (April 1944): 109, 122–24. For an analysis of this historiographical shift, see David Brion Davis, "Slavery and the Post–World War II Historians," *Daedalus* 103 (Spring 1974): 1.

141. On the vetting of *Gone With the Wind,* see Cripps, *Making Movies Black,* 3–34.

142. Sterling Brown, "Remembering Nat Turner," *Crisis* 45 (February 1939): 49.

5. Commemorations

1. Brown, "The Theology of Nat Turner As Reflected in the Insurrection." See preface and pp. 49, f. 50, 157, 160. Biographical details are taken from the following news article and obituary: "Va. Seminary Dean Killed Instantly in Car Crash," *Norfolk Journal and Guide* (Virginia Edition), 4 February 1950, p. 1; "Final Rites Held for College Dean," *Norfolk Journal and*

Guide (National Edition, N.C.), 18 February 1950, p. 4. For quotes, see preface to Brown, "The Theology of Nat Turner."

2. Brown to Du Bois, 7 December 1948, in *Correspondence of W.E.B. Du Bois,* vol. 3, 227–28.

3. "Office Talk," *New Day,* 18 December 1948.

4. Ibid.

5. Brown to Du Bois, 7 December 1948; Du Bois to Brown, 15 December 1948; in *Correspondence of W.E.B. Du Bois,* vol. 3, 227–28. For an autobiographical account of Du Bois's purge by the anti-Communist leadership of the NAACP, see W.E.B. Du Bois, *The Autobiography of W.E.B. Du Bois: A Soliloquy on Viewing My Life from the Last Decade of Its First Century* (International Publishers, 1968), 331–39.

6. Brown, "The Theology of Nat Turner," 158–59, 55, 99, 155–57. Sadly, Brown did not live to see his prophecy fulfilled; he was killed in a car accident in Virginia in January 1950, less than a year after his graduation from Oberlin and just four months after his appointment as dean of the School of Religion at the Virginia Seminary and College in Lynchburg. "Va. Seminary Dean Killed Instantly in Crash," 1; "Final Rites Held for College Dean," 4.

7. Juan Williams, *Eyes on the Prize: America's Civil Rights Years, 1954–1965* (New York: Viking Penguin, 1987).

8. For a study of Till's murder in collective memory, see Christopher Metress, *The Lynching of Emmett Till: A Documentary Narrative* (Charlottesville: University of Virginia Press, 2002).

9. Thomas Désiré Pawley, Jr., *Messiah,* in "Experimental Productions of a Group of Original Plays," unpublished Ph.D. dissertation, Department of Speech and Dramatic Art, Graduate College of the State University of Iowa, 10 August 1949, 4, 181.

10. Jo Wright, "Playwright Thomas Pawley — Writes to Accomplish a Mission," *Daily Iowan,* 27 July 1948.

11. Allen R. Matthews to Lewis A. McMurran, 19 June 1954, JCR.

12. Write-A-Play Contest Inquiries, Write-A-Play Entries, Addresses of 1954 Write-A-Play Entries; JCR.

13. Allen R. Matthews to John Gassner, 1 September 1954, JCR.

14. John Melville Jennings to Allen R. Matthews, 16 September 1954, JCR.

15. John Gassner to Allen R. Matthews, 7 September 1954, JCR.

16. A. R. Matthews to John Gassner, 29 September 1954, JCR.

17. Ibid.

18. Alonzo G. Moron to Allen Marshall [Matthews], 30 September 1954, JCR.

19. Allen R. Matthews to Thomas D. Pawley, 16 June 1955, JCR.

20. Matthews to Frank Langone, 15 December 1954, JCR.

21. Martin Luther King, Jr., "Non-Aggression Procedures to Interracial Harmony," Address Delivered at the American Baptist Assembly and American Home Mission Agencies Conference, 23 July 1956; reprinted in *The Papers of Martin Luther King,* vol. 3 (Los Angeles: University of California Press), 321–28.

22. Lucy Mae Turner, "The Family of Nat Turner, 1831 to 1954," *Negro History Bulletin* 18 (March 1955): 127–32, 145; continued in *Negro History Bulletin* 18 (April 1955): 155–58. The authority accorded African-American oral tradition in African-American popular culture of the 1950s is also evident in *Ebony* magazine, which published an article titled "Thomas Jefferson's Negro Grandchildren" — based solely on oral tradition — that very same year. See *Ebony* 10 (November 1954).

23. Turner, "The Family of Nat Turner" (April), 155.

24. Ibid., 146, 155.

25. Ibid., 156–58.

26. William Edwin Hemphill, Mavin Wilson Schlegel, and Sadie Ethel Engelber, *Cavalier Commonwealth: History and Government of Virginia* (New York: McGraw-Hill Book Company, c1957, 1963), xiv–xv.

27. Ibid., iv–v, 220–26.

28. James O. Lewis, "Treatment of the 'Negro' in a Selected Group of Social Studies Middle School Textbooks," unpublished master's thesis, Danbury State Teachers College, August 1960; NAACP Papers.

29. Stampp, *The Peculiar Institution,* vii–viii.

30. Ibid., 132–33, 139–40, 379.

31. Elkins, *Slavery,* 23.

32. Ibid.

33. Ibid., 82–85, 224, 112–13, 128–30.

34. Ibid., 137–38, f. 112.

35. David Donald, review of *Slavery* by Stanley M. Elkins, in *American Historical Review* 65 (July 1960): 922.

36. Oscar Handlin, review of *Slavery,* in *New England Quarterly* 34 (June 1961): 255.

37. For Malcolm X's quotes on black revolution and black nationalism, see Clayborne Carson et al., eds., *The Eyes on the Prize Civil Rights Reader: Documents, Speeches, and Firsthand Accounts of the Black Freedom Struggle* (New York: Viking Penguin, 1991), 251–54.

38. *Autobiography of Malcolm X,* 366–68, 280–81.

39. On the Freedom Schools as "precursors of the Black Studies thrust in education," see William L. Van Deburg, *New Day in Babylon: The Black Power Movement in American Culture, 1965–1975* (Chicago: University of Chicago Press, 1992), 49–51.

40. William Styron, Jr., to William Styron, Sr., 1 May 1952, WSP.

41. Styron, Jr., to Styron, Sr., 20 May 1952, WSP.

42. Styron, Jr., to Styron, Sr., 24 February 1961, WSP.

43. William Styron, "Jimmy in the House," *New York Times Book Review,* 20 December 1987, 30; Raymond Sokolov, "Into the Mind of Nat Turner," *Newsweek* 70 (16 October 1967): 67.

44. William Styron, "Overcome," review of *American Negro Slave Revolts* by Herbert Aptheker, in *New York Review of Books* 1 (26 September 1963): 18–19.

45. Ibid., 19. Styron thought so highly of Elkins's book that he and Thomas Guinzburg, a founder of the *Paris Review,* proposed to reissue it in paperback. Elkins told Styron he was flattered. Unfortunately, the offer had come two months too late; the University of Chicago Press had just sold the paperback rights to Grosset and Dunlap. Stanley Elkins to Styron, 20 March 1963, WSP.

46. James Jones and William Styron, "Two Writers Talk It Over," *Esquire* 60 (July 1963): 57–59; reprinted in James L. W. West III, ed., *Conversations with William Styron* (Jackson: University Press of Mississippi, 1985), 41, 44–48.

47. Robert Canzoneri and Page Stegner, "An Interview with William Styron," *Per/Se* 1 (Summer 1966): 37–44; reprinted in West, *Conversations with William Styron,* 69.

48. Willie Morris, Foreword, "The South Today . . . 100 Years After Appomattox," special supplement to *Harper's* (April 1965).

49. William Styron, "This Quiet Dust," *Harper's.*

50. Ibid., 146.

51. "Speaking Volumes: The Confessions of William Styron," *Washington Post Book World,* 1 October 1967, 6.

52. Stokely Carmichael and Charles V. Hamilton, *Black Power: The Politics of Liberation in America* (New York: Vintage, 1967), 35.

53. Styron, *The Confessions of Nat Turner,* 37, 299–300.

54. Ibid., 55, 57, 334.

55. *Report of the National Advisory Commission on Civil Disorders* (New York: Bantam Books, 1968), 56–69, 84–108.

56. Alden Whitman, "William Styron Examines the Negro Upheaval," *New York Times,* 5 August 1967, 13.

57. Maria Clara Moyano, "Speaking Volumes: The Confessions of William Styron," *Washington Post Book World,* 1 October 1967, 6.

58. "Close-up: William Styron Goes Back to 1831 and the Soul of Nat Turner," *Life* 63 (13 October 1967): 51.

59. "The Idea of Hope," *Time* 90 (13 October 1967): 110, 113.

60. Raymond A. Sokolov, "Into the Mind of Nat Turner," *Newsweek* 70 (16 October 1967): 65–66.

61. Edmund Fuller, "Power and Eloquence in New Styron Novel," *Wall Street Journal* (4 October 1967): 16.

62. Alfred Kazin, "Instinct for Tragedy: A Message in Black and White," *Washington Post Book World* (8 October 1967): 1.

63. John Thompson, "Rise and Slay!" *Commentary* 44 (November 1967): 81, 85.

64. Ed Sklepowich, "Two Views of Styron's 'Confessions of Nat Turner,'" *Virginia Weekly*, 27 October 1831, 7; WSP.

65. Gerald Wade, "'The Only Effective U.S. Negro Revolt,'" *Omaha World-Herald*, 29 October 1967; WSP.

66. C. Vann Woodward, "Confessions of a Rebel: 1831," *New Republic* 157 (7 October 1967): 25; Arthur Schlesinger, Jr., "The Confessions of Nat Turner, 'Finest American Novel in Years,'" *Vogue* 150 (1 October 1967): 143; Martin Duberman, *Village Voice* 13 (14 December 1967): 8, 16.

67. John Hope Franklin, *Chicago Sunday Sun-Times Book Week*, 8 October 1967, 1, 11; Saunders Redding, "Revolving Bookstand: Recommended Summer Reading," *American Scholar* 37 (Summer 1968): 542; Saunders Redding, "A Fateful Lightning in the Southern Sky," *Providence Sunday Journal*, 29 October 1967, W-18.

68. June Meyer, "Spokesmen for the Blacks," *Nation* 205 (4 December 1967): 597.

69. Albert Murray, "A Troublesome Property," *New Leader*, 4 December 1967, 18.

70. Cecil M. Brown, "Books Noted," *Negro Digest* (February 1968): 51–52, 89–91.

71. John Leo, "Some Negroes Accuse Styron of Distorting Nat Turner's Life," *New York Times*, 1 February 1968, 34.

72. "National Book Committee Lists 31 Nominees for 1968 Awards," *New York Times*, 13 February 1968, 40.

73. Henry Raymont, "Wilder's 'Eighth Day' Tops Styron's 'Nat Turner' and Three Other Novels for National Book Award," *New York Times*, 5 March 1968, 33.

74. John Hohenberg, *The Pulitzer Prizes: A History of the Awards in Books, Drama, Music, and Journalism Based on the Private Files Over Six Decades* (New York: Columbia University Press, 1974), 319–20.

75. Gertrude Wilson, "I Spit on the Pulitzer Prize," *N.Y. Amsterdam News*, 18 May 1968, 17.

76. "What's Wrong with the American Novel?" *American Scholar* 24 (Autumn 1955): 476, 478, 484, 501–3.

77. George Stevens, Jr., to Styron, 19 September 1967, WSP.

78. "Nat Turner Saga to Be Filmed," *Cleveland Plain Dealer*, 18 February 1968, 5-G; WSP.

79. Wolper, *The Inside Story of TV's "Roots,"* 1–26.

80. Biographical details from Mary Helen Washington, ed., *Black-Eyed Susans:*

Classic Stories By and About Black Women (Garden City, N.J.: Anchor Books, 1975), 62–64.

81. For the statements of Cambridge and Jones eschewing nonviolence as a philosophy, see John A. Adams and Joan Martin Burke, *Civil Rights: A Current Guide to the People, Organizations, and Events* (New York: Bowker, 1970), 7–8, 23. Cambridge was quoted as saying: "You're not going to find me on any picket lines. In the first place, I'm not non-violent." Jones was quoted as saying: "I'm in favor of black people taking power by the quickest, easiest, most successful means they can employ. Malcolm X said 'the ballot or the bullet.'"

82. Godfrey Cambridge, prepared statement, undated (February 1968), BADAP.

83. Stokely Carmichael and Rap Brown, prepared statement sent by Ethel Minor of SNCC to Louise Meriwether, 20 February 1968. See statement of Adam Clayton Powell, attached to letter from Chuck Stone to Louise Meriwether, 13 May 1968, BADAP.

84. Ossie Davis, "Why I Eulogized Malcolm X," from *The Autobiography of Malcolm X;* reprinted in *Negro Digest* 15 (February 1966): 64–66.

85. Davis to Meriwether, 4 March 1968, BADAP.

86. Louise M. Meriwether, interview by author, April 1995, New York City, tape recording.

87. Meriwether to David Wolper and Norman Jewison, 26 March 1968, BADAP. Later reprinted as broadside in *Black Theatre* (1969).

88. Ibid.

89. "Civil Rights and a Producer's Dilemma," *Los Angeles Times,* Calendar section, 14 April 1968, 1, 19.

90. Ibid.

91. Meriwether to editor of the *Los Angeles Times,* 16 April 1968, BADAP.

92. Meriwether to Davis, 2 April 1968, ODRD. For contemporary coverage of the Black Congress as a vehicle of black unity, see "Dr. King's Murder Spurs Unity Display by L.A. Groups" and "L.A. Negro Leaders Call for Tribute to Dr. King," both in *Los Angeles Times,* 7 April 1968, sect. B, p. 1.

93. "Re: 'The Confessions of Nat Turner,'" full-page advertisement in *Hollywood Reporter,* 18 April 1968, 13; "Protests Mount on Filming of Nat Turner," *N.Y. Amsterdam News,* 4 May 1968, 19.

94. "'Lone Black Star' Poitier Rejects 'Good Guy' Role As Race Spokesman," *Variety,* 12 June 1968, 2; "Filming of 'Nat Turner' Opposed by Negroes," Newspaper Enterprise Association, 10 June 1968.

95. For Jewison's reference to Baldwin, see "Civil Rights and a Producer's Dilemma," 1. "Negro Will Screenplay 'Turner,' Slave Revolt," *Variety,* 29 May 1968, 2.

96. *N.Y. Amsterdam News,* 4 May 1968, 19.

97. Clarke, *William Styron's Nat Turner*, vii–x.

98. Martin Duberman, "Historical Fictions," *New York Times Book Review*, 11 August 1968, 27.

99. "William Styron Before the People's Court," in Eugene D. Genovese, *Red and Black: Marxian Explorations in Southern and Afro-American History* (New York: Pantheon Books, 1971), 201–2; originally published in the *New York Review of Books*, 12 September 1968, 34–38.

100. Robert Taylor, "The Contentions of William Styron the Novelist Responds to Critics of *Nat Turner*," *Boston Sunday Globe Magazine* (20 April 1969): 6, 10–13.

101. Meriwether to [no name], 5 December 1968, BADAP.

102. Minutes of "Nat Turner Meeting," 13 December 1968, BADAP.

103. Steven V. Roberts, "[Conflict] Over the 'Nat Turner' Screenplay Subsides," *New York Times*, 31 March 1969, 28.

104. Tom Wicker, "In the Nation: What Sense in Censorship?" *New York Times*, 3 April 1969, 42.

105. "Norman Jewison off 'Nat Turner'; Other Changes," *Variety*, 6 February 1969.

106. Taylor, "The Contentions of William Styron," 11.

107. Francis to Carole Kass, 20 February 1970, GFP.

108. Taylor, "The Contentions of William Styron," 11.

109. Mrs. Homer Pittman to Styron, October 1967, WSP.

110. Miscellaneous correspondence, September–October 1967, WSP.

111. "300 Unruly, 2 Charged in Franklin," *Virginian-Pilot* (Norfolk, Va.), 1 October 1967, sect. B, p. 1.

112. Ken Wheeler, "Sheets-to-Satin Rise Claimed by Klansmen," *Virginian-Pilot*, 9 October 1967, 17.

113. Frank T. Adams, Jr., and Wayne Woodlief, "A Man Named Nat, a Man Named Lemon," *VCHR Observer* 1 (January 1968): 1–3; VCHRR. I am indebted to Professor Paul Gaston, who sat on the board of the Virginia Council of Human Relations and belonged to a local chapter, for historical background on this group.

114. Allan Jones, "Two Counties to Lose U.S. School Funds," *Richmond Times-Dispatch*, 15 April 1967, 1, 7.

115. Francis to Francisco Day, 17 December 1969, GFP.

116. Gilbert W. Francis, interview by author, Boykins, Virginia, 18 April 1994, tape recording.

117. Ibid.

118. Ibid.

119. Ibid.

120. Bernice Kelly Harris, "Nat Turner to Replace John Brown As Our Best Known Insurrectionist?" *News & Observer* (Raleigh, N.C.), 26 November 1967, sect. C, p. 2.

121. Francis interview, 18 April 1994.
122. "On page 30, where Greenville County is mentioned, the correct name is Greensville. And of course, you mentioned the matter of Doyle's plantation being Parker's Field." Francis to Sidney Lumet, 4 December 1969, GFP.
123. Francis interview, 18 April 1994.
124. *Tidewater News*, 25 September 1969.
125. Francis to Carole Kass, 20 February 1970, GFP.
126. Ibid.
127. Francis to Allen L. Hopkins, 11 February 1970, GFP.
128. Francis to Charles B. Higgins, 26 November 1969, GFP.
129. Francis to Francisco Day, 15 December 1969, GFP.
130. Ibid.
131. Peter Bailey, "Nat Turner 'Heirs' Seek Share of Movie Millions" and "Whites Trying to Buy All Sites in Va. County Where He Roamed" in *Jet*, 18 December 1969, 14–17.
132. Francis to Day, 20 December 1969, GFP.
133. Francis to Day, 5 January 1970, GFP.
134. "20th Fox Plans Feature Hiatus," *Hollywood Reporter*, 14 January 1970; "Richard Zanuck Reports No Pics Until June, Says Fall Sked to Be Heavy," *Hollywood Reporter*, 16 January 1970.
135. "'Nat Turner' Postponed," *Virginian-Pilot* (Norfolk, Portsmouth, Virginia Beach, Chesapeake), 27 January 1970.
136. Associated Press, "'Nat Turner' Film Stalled, Views Differ," undated news clipping, unidentified source; United Press International, "'Revolt' Stops Nat Turner," published in *Washington Daily News*, 28 January 1970; "One Movie Styron Doesn't Want to See," *New York Post*, 27 January 1970; "Styron Charges Black Pressure on Turner Film," *New York Times*, 28 January 1970.
137. Francis to Carole Kass, 20 February 1970, GFP.
138. Ray Ownbey, "Discussions with William Styron," *Mississippi Quarterly* (Spring 1977): 294–95. The interview took place in April 1975.
139. On this paradigm shift in scholarly studies of slave life, see Meier and Rudwick, *Black History and the Historical Profession, 1915–1980*, 251–76.
140. Wolper and Troupe, *Inside Story*, 30–33. A 1999 article in *The New Yorker*, written by Tony Horwitz, reported renewed interest in the Nat Turner film project. The African-American filmmaker Spike Lee met with Styron, at the urging of Henry Louis Gates, Jr., head of the Afro-American Studies Department at Harvard University, to discuss the possibility of a film adaptation that would not shy away from the novel's controversial themes. Gates detected a sea change in the attitudes of black intellectuals toward the book. "Back then," he told Horwitz, "there was a tiny representation of blacks in academia and the media — the whole thing was a blanket of whiteness — and all black people could do was raise hell and throw

stones. Now we have much more input and control of the image of black people." See Horwitz, "Untrue Confessions," *The New Yorker* (13 December 1999): 66.

141. Wolper and Troupe, *Inside Story,* 250–74.

142. Robert Chrisman, "*Roots:* Rebirth of the Slave Mentality," *Black Scholar* (May 1977): 41–42.

143. Chinweizu, "*Roots:* Urban Renewal of the American Dream," *Black Scholar* (May 1977): 38–39.

144. Wolper and Troupe, *Inside Story,* 172–73.

145. Richard Cohen, "Disney Deserves a Chance," *Washington Post,* 9 August 1994, sect. A, p. 19.

146. Henry I. Tragle, "Styron and His Sources," in *Southampton Slave Revolt,* 401–9; first published in *Massachusetts Review* 11 (Winter 1970): 135–53.

147. Parramore, *Southampton County, Virginia,* 105–21, x.

148. Sundquist, *To Wake the Nation,* 10, 36–39.

149. Fabricant, "Thomas R. Gray and William Styron," 334–36, 341.

150. William Styron, "Nat Turner Revisited," afterword to the first Vintage edition, *The Confessions of Nat Turner* (New York: Vintage, 1993), 452.

Epilogue. The Continuing Saga

1. *Norfolk Herald,* 14 November 1831; *Boston Liberator,* 3 December 1831; *Boston Liberator,* 26 November 1831.

2. Drewry, *Southampton Insurrection,* 102, see text and footnotes.

3. Frances Lawrence Webb, *Recollections of Franklin and Historical Sketches of Southampton County,* ed. John C. Parker (Franklin, Va.: Franklin Library Association, 1963).

4. *Wayne County (Ohio) Democrat,* 27 August 1902, courtesy of Southampton County Historical Society.

5. Donna Britt, "Some Memories Are Too Vital to Let Slip Away," *Washington Post,* 6 December 2002; Rudolph Lewis, "Selling Nat Turner's Skull," *Washington Post,* 11 December 2002; Rudolph Lewis, *ChickenBones: A Journal,* on-line resource at www.nathanielturner.com/hatchersskullletter.htm.

6. "Nat Turner's Skull Turns Up Far from Site of His Revolt," *Virginian-Pilot,* 3 May 2002.

Bibliography

Abzug, Robert H. "The Influence of Garrisonian Abolitionists' Fears of Slave Violence on the Antislavery Argument, 1829–40." *Journal of Negro History* 55 (January 1970): 15–26.

Ambler, Charles H., ed. *The Life and Diary of John Floyd, Governor of Virginia, An Apostle of Secession, and the Father of the Oregon Country.* Richmond: Richmond Press, 1918.

Anderson, Benedict. *Imagined Communities: Reflections on the Origins and Spread of Nationalism.* New York: Verso, 1983.

Andrews, William L. *To Tell a Free Story: The First Century of Afro-American Autobiography, 1760–1865.* Urbana: University of Illinois Press, 1986.

Aptheker, Herbert. *American Negro Slave Revolts.* New York: International Publishers, 1943; reprinted 1974.

———. *Nat Turner's Slave Rebellion.* New York: Grove Press, by arrangement with Humanities Press, 1966.

Ayers, Edward L. *The Promise of the New South: Life After Reconstruction.* New York: Oxford University Press, 1992.

Bardolph, Richard. *The Negro Vanguard.* New York: Vintage Books, 1961.

Bauer, Raymond A., and Alice H. Bauer. "Day to Day Resistance to Slavery." *Journal of Negro History* 27 (October 1942): 388–419.

Bell, Howard H. "National Negro Conventions of the Middle 1840's: Moral Suasion vs. Political Action." *Journal of Negro History* 42 (October 1957): 247–60.

———. "Expressions of Negro Militancy in the North, 1840–1860." *Journal of Negro History* 45 (January 1960): 11–20.

———, ed. *Proceedings of the National Negro Conventions, 1830–1864.* New York: Arno Press & The New York Times, 1969.

Bercovitch, Sacvan. *The American Jeremiad.* Madison: University of Wisconsin Press, 1978.

Blackett, R.J.M. *Beating Against the Barriers: Biographical Essays in Nineteenth-Century Afro-American History.* Baton Rouge: Louisiana State University Press, 1986.

Blassingame, John W., ed. *The Frederick Douglass Papers.* Vols. 1–5. New Haven, Conn.: Yale University Press, 1979–92.

Blight, David W. *Frederick Douglass' Civil War: Keeping Faith in Jubilee.* Baton Rouge: Louisiana State University Press, 1989.

———. *Race and Reunion: The Civil War in American Memory.* Cambridge: Belknap Press of Harvard University Press, 2001.

Boney, F. N. "Rivers of Ink, Streams of Blood: The Tragic Career of John Hampden Pleasants." *Virginia Cavalcade* 18 (Summer 1968).

Bratton, Mary J. "Fields's Observations: The Slave Narrative of a Nineteenth-Century Virginian." *Virginia Magazine of History and Biography* 88 (January 1980): 75–93.

Braxton, Joanne M. *Black Women Writing Autobiography: A Tradition Within a Tradition.* Philadelphia: Temple University Press, 1989.

Brown, Elsa Barkley. "Negotiating and Transforming the Public Sphere: African American Political Life in the Transition from Slavery to Freedom." *Public Culture* 7 (February 1994): 107–46.

Brown, Peter Rodgers. "The Theology of Nat Turner As Reflected in the Insurrection." Master's thesis, Oberlin Graduate School of Theology, Oberlin, Ohio, 1949.

Carter, Dan T. "The Anatomy of Fear: The Christmas Day Insurrection Scare of 1865." *Journal of Southern History* 42 (August 1976).

———. *Scottsboro: A Tragedy of the American South,* rev. ed. Baton Rouge: Louisiana State University Press, 1979.

Casciato, Arthur D., and James L. W. West III. "William Styron and 'The Southampton Insurrection.'" *American Literature* 52 (January 1981): 564–77.

Chafe, William F. *The Unfinished Journey: America Since World War II.* 5th ed. New York: Oxford University Press, 2003.

Clarke, John Henrik, ed. *William Styron's Nat Turner: Ten Black Writers Respond.* Boston: Beacon Press, 1968.

———, ed. *The Second Crucifixion of Nat Turner.* Baltimore: Black Classic Press, 1997.

Confino, Alon. *The Nation As a Local Metaphor: Württemberg, Imperial Germany, and National Memory, 1871–1918.* Chapel Hill: University of North Carolina Press, 1997.

———. "Collective Memory and Cultural History: Problems of Method." *American Historical Review* 102 (1997): 1386–401.

Cripps, Thomas. *Making Movies Black: The Hollywood Message Movie from World War II to the Civil Rights Era.* New York: Oxford University Press, 1993.

Crofts, Daniel. *Old Southampton: Politics and Society in a Virginia County, 1834–1869.* Charlottesville: University Press of Virginia, 1992.

Cromwell, John W. "The Aftermath of Nat Turner's Insurrection." *Journal of Negro History* 5 (April 1920): 208–34.

Dailey, Jane. "Deference and Violence in the Postbellum Urban South: Manners and Massacres in Danville, Virginia." *Journal of Southern History* 63 (August 1997): 552–90.

———. *Before Jim Crow: The Politics of Race in Postemancipation Virginia.* Chapel Hill: University of North Carolina Press, 2000.

Dann, Martin E. *The Black Press, 1827–1890: The Quest for National Identity.* New York: G. P. Putnam's Sons, 1971.

Davis, David Brion. "Slavery and the Post–World War II Historians." *Daedalus* 103 (Spring 1974): 1–16.

Davis, Mary Kemp. *Nat Turner Before the Bar of Judgment: Fictional Treatments of the Southampton Slave Insurrection.* Baton Rouge: Louisiana State University Press, 1999.

Demos, John. "The Antislavery Movement and the Problem of Violent 'Means.'" *New England Quarterly* 37 (December 1964): 501–26.

Drewry, William Sidney. *The Southampton Insurrection.* Washington, D.C.: Neale Company, 1900; reprinted Murfreesboro, N.C.: Johnson Publishing, 1968.

Du Bois, W.E.B. *The Correspondence of W.E.B. Du Bois.* Edited by Herbert Aptheker. 3 vols. Amherst: University of Massachusetts Press, 1976.

———. *Writings by W.E.B. Du Bois in Periodicals Edited by Others.* Compiled and edited by Herbert Aptheker. Vol. 1, *1891–1909.* Millwood, N.Y.: Kraus Thomson Organization, 1982.

———. *Selections from* The Crisis. Vol. 1, *1911–1925.* Millwood, N.Y.: Kraus-Thomson Organization, 1983.

———. *Creative Writings by W.E.B. Du Bois: A Pageant, Poems, Short Stories, and Playlets.* Compiled and edited by Herbert Aptheker. White Plains, N.Y.: Kraus-Thomson Organization, 1985.

———. *Writings in Periodicals Edited by W.E.B. Du Bois: Selections from* The Horizon. Compiled and edited by Herbert Aptheker. White Plains, N.Y.: Kraus-Thomson Organization, 1985.

———. *Pamphlets and Leaflets by W.E.B. Du Bois.* Compiled and edited by Herbert Aptheker. White Plains, N.Y.: Kraus-Thomson Organization, 1986.

———. *Newspaper Columns by W.E.B. Du Bois.* Edited by Herbert Aptheker. Vol. 1, *1883–1944,* and vol. 2, *1945–1961.* White Plains, N.Y.: Kraus-Thomson Organization Limited, 1986.

Duff, John B., and Peter M. Mitchell, eds. *The Nat Turner Rebellion: The Historical Event and the Modern Controversy.* New York: Harper & Row, 1971.

Eaton, Clement. *The Freedom-of-Thought Struggle in the Old South,* rev. ed. New York: Harper & Row, 1964.

Edelstein, Tilden G. *Strange Enthusiasm: A Life of Thomas Wentworth Higginson.* New Haven: Yale University Press, 1968.

Egerton, Douglas R. *Gabriel's Rebellion: The Virginia Slave Conspiracies of 1800 and 1802.* Chapel Hill: University of North Carolina Press, 1993.

Egerton, John. *Speak Now Against the Day: The Generation Before the Civil Rights Movement in the South.* Chapel Hill: University of North Carolina Press, 1994.

Elkins, Stanley M. *Slavery: A Problem in American Institutional and Intellectual Life.* Chicago: University of Chicago Press, 1959.

Ellis, S. M., ed. *The Solitary Horseman.* London: Cayme Press, 1927.

Fabricant, Daniel S. "Thomas R. Gray and William Styron: Finally, a Critical Look at the 1831 Confessions of Nat Turner." *American Journal of Legal History* 37 (July 1993): 332–61.

Farrison, William Edward. *William Wells Brown, Author and Reformer.* Chicago: University of Chicago Press, 1969.

Fields, Annie, ed. *Life and Letters of Harriet Beecher Stowe.* Boston: Houghton, Mifflin and Company, 1897.

Foner, Eric. *A Short History of Reconstruction, 1863–1877.* New York: Harper & Row, 1990.

———, ed. *Nat Turner.* Englewood Cliffs, N.J.: Prentice-Hall, 1971.

Foner, Philip S., ed. *The Life and Writings of Frederick Douglass.* Vol. 3. New York: International Publishers, 1950.

Foner, Philip S., and George E. Walker, eds. *Proceedings of the Black State Conventions, 1840–1865.* Vol. 1. Philadelphia: Temple University Press, 1979.

Franklin, John Hope. *The Emancipation Proclamation.* Garden City, N.Y.: Doubleday, 1963.

———. *George Washington Williams: A Biography.* Chicago: University of Chicago Press, 1985.

———, ed. *Three Negro Classics.* New York: Avon Books, 1965.

Franklin, John Hope, and Alfred Moss. *From Slavery to Freedom: A History of African-Americans,* 8th ed. New York: Alfred A. Knopf, 2000.

Fredrickson, George M. *The Black Image in the White Mind: The Debate on Afro-American Character and Destiny, 1817–1914.* New York: Harper & Row, 1971.

Freehling, Alison Goodyear. *Drift Toward Dissolution: The Virginia Slavery Debate of 1831–1832.* Baton Rouge: Louisiana State University Press, 1982.

Friedman, Melvin J., and Irving Malin, eds. *William Styron's The Confessions of Nat Turner: A Critical Handbook.* Belmont, Calif.: Wadsworth Publishing Company, 1970.

Gaines, Kevin K. *Uplifting the Race: Black Leadership, Politics, and Culture in the Twentieth Century.* Chapel Hill: University of North Carolina Press, 1996.

Garrow, David J. *Bearing the Cross: Martin Luther King, Jr., and the Southern Christian Leadership Conference.* New York: Vintage Books, 1988.

Gatewood, Willard B., Jr. "Edward E. Cooper and '10 Greatest Negroes' of 1890." *Negro History Bulletin* 40 (May-June 1977): 708–10.

Genovese, Eugene D. *Roll, Jordan, Roll: The World the Slaves Made.* New York: Vintage Books, 1976.

———. *From Rebellion to Revolution: Afro-American Slave Revolts in the Making of the Modern World.* Baton Rouge: Louisiana State University Press, 1979.

Goggin, Jacqueline. *Carter G. Woodson: A Life in Black History.* Baton Rouge: Louisiana State University Press, 1993.

Goldstein, Leslie Friedman. "Violence As an Instrument for Social Change: The Views of Frederick Douglass (1817–1895)." *Journal of Negro History* 61 (January 1976): 61–72.

Goodman, James. *Stories of Scottsboro.* New York: Pantheon Books, 1994.

Greenberg, Kenneth S., ed. *The Confessions of Nat Turner and Related Documents.* New York: Bedford Books of St. Martin's Press, 1996.

Grigsby, John L. "Jesus, Judas, Job or 'Jes a Happy Ole Nigga'; or, Will the Real 'Uncle Tom' Please Step Forward." *Publications of the Mississippi Philological Association* (1986): 51–62.

Gross, Seymour L., and Eileen Bender. "History, Politics and Literature: The Myth of Nat Turner." *American Quarterly* 23 (October 1971): 487–518.

Hale, Grace Elizabeth. *Making Whiteness: The Culture of Segregation in the South, 1890–1940.* New York: Vintage Books, 1998.

Hamilton, Stanislaus Murray. *The Writings of James Monroe.* Vol. 3, 1796–1802. New York: G. P. Putnam's Sons, 1900.

Harding, Vincent. "Symptoms of Liberty and Blackhead Signposts: David Walker and Nat Turner." In *A Turbulent Voyage: Readings in African American Studies,* edited by Floyd W. Hayes III, 237–58. San Diego: Collegiate Press, 1992.

Harlan, Louis R. *Booker T. Washington: The Making of a Black Leader, 1856–1901.* New York: Oxford University Press, 1975.

———. *Booker T. Washington: The Wizard of Tuskegee, 1901–1915.* New York: Oxford University Press, 1983.

Harrold, Stanley. *The Abolitionists and the South.* Lexington: University Press of Kentucky, 1995.

Hart, Albert Bushnell. *Slavery and Abolition, 1831–1841.* New York: Harper & Brothers, 1906.

Hedrick, Joan D. *Harriet Beecher Stowe: A Life.* New York: Oxford University Press, 1994.

Herskovits, Melville. *The Myth of the Negro Past.* New York: Harper, 1941.

Hicks, Granville, et al., eds. *Proletarian Literature in the United States: An Anthology.* New York: International Publishers, 1935.

Higginbotham, Evelyn Brooks. *Righteous Discontent: The Women's Movement in the Black Baptist Church, 1880–1920.* Cambridge: Harvard University Press, 1993.

Higginson, Thomas Wentworth. "Denmark Vesey." *Atlantic Monthly* 8 (June 1861): 728–44.

———. "Nat Turner's Insurrection." *Atlantic Monthly* 8 (August 1861): 173–87.

———. "Gabriel's Defeat." *Atlantic Monthly* 10 (September 1862): 337–45.

Hildebrand, Reginald F. "'An Imperious Sense of Duty': Documents Illustrating an Episode in the Methodist Reaction to the Nat Turner Revolt." *Methodist History* 19 (April 1981): 155–74.

Hofstadter, Richard. "U. B. Phillips and the Plantation Legend." *Journal of Negro History* 29 (April 1944): 109–24.

Huggins, Nathan I. "W.E.B. Du Bois and Heroes." *American Studies* 34 (1989): 167–74.

Jackson, Walter. "Melville Herskovits and the Search for Afro-American Culture." In *Malinowski, Rivers, Benedict and Others: Essays on Culture and Personality,* ed. George W. Stocking. Madison: University of Wisconsin Press, 1986.

Jacobs, Harriet. *Incidents in the Life of a Slave Girl; Written by Herself,* ed. Jean Fagin Yellin. Cambridge: Harvard University Press, 2000.

Johnson, F. Roy. *The Nat Turner Slave Insurrection.* Murfreesboro, N.C.: Johnson Publishing Company, 1966.

———. *The Nat Turner Story.* Murfreesboro, N.C.: Johnson Publishing Company, 1970.

Jones, James Earl, and Penelope Niven. *Voices and Silences.* New York: Simon and Schuster, 1993.

Jordan, Winthrop D. *Tumult and Silence at Second Creek: An Inquiry into a Civil War Slave Conspiracy.* Baton Rouge: Louisiana State University Press, 1993.

Kelley, Robin D. G. *Hammer and Hoe: Alabama Communists During the Great Depression.* Chapel Hill: University of North Carolina Press, 1990.

King, Richard H. "Politics and Fictional Representation: The Case of the Civil Rights Movement." In *The Making of Martin Luther King and the Civil Rights Movement,* ed. Brian Ward and Tony Badger, 162–78. Washington Square, N.Y.: New York University Press, 1996.

Levine, Lawrence W. *Black Culture and Black Consciousness: Afro-American Folk Thought from Slavery to Freedom.* New York: Oxford University Press, 1977.

Lewis, David Levering. "The Politics of Art: The New Negro, 1920–1935." In *Prospects: An Annual of American Cultural Studies,* ed. Jack Salzman, 237–61. New York: Burt Franklin, 1977.

———. *W.E.B. Du Bois: Biography of a Race, 1868–1919.* New York: Henry Holt, 1993.

———. *W.E.B. Du Bois: The Fight for Equality and the American Century, 1919–1963.* New York: Henry Holt, 2000.

Littlefield, Daniel C. "Blacks, John Brown, and a Theory of Manhood." *His Soul Goes Marching On: Responses to John Brown and the Harpers Ferry Raid.* Edited by Paul Finkelman, 67–97. Charlottesville: University Press of Virginia, 1995.

Litwack, Leon F. *Trouble in Mind: Black Southerners in the Age of Jim Crow.* New York: Alfred A. Knopf, 1998.

Locke, Alain. *The New Negro.* New York: Atheneum, 1992.

Lowe, Richard. *Republicans and Reconstruction in Virginia, 1856–70.* Charlottesville: University Press of Virginia, 1991.

Mabee, Carleton. *Black Freedom: The Nonviolent Abolitionists from 1830 Through the Civil War.* New York: Macmillan Company, 1970.

Maffly-Kipp, Laurie F. "Mapping the World, Mapping the Race: The Negro Race History, 1874–1915." *Church History* 64 (December 1995): 610–26.

Marable, Manning. "Revolt and Faith: Nat Turner and Sisyphus." *Claflin College Review* 2 (1977): 30–37.

Martin, Waldo E., Jr. *The Mind of Frederick Douglass.* Chapel Hill: University of North Carolina Press, 1984.

———. "Images of Frederick Douglass in the Afro-American Mind: The Recent Black Freedom Struggle." In *Frederick Douglass: New Literary and Historical Essays,* ed. Eric J. Sundquist, 271–85. New York: Cambridge University Press, 1990.

Maxwell, William J. *New Negro, Old Left: African-American Writing and Communism Between the Wars.* New York: Columbia University Press, 1999.

McFeeley, William S. *Frederick Douglass.* New York: W. W. Norton, 1991.

McKivigan, John R., and Stanley Harrold. *Antislavery Violence: Sectional, Racial, and Cultural Conflict in Antebellum America.* Knoxville: University of Tennessee Press, 1999.

Meehan, James. "The Solitary Horseman in Virginia: G.P.R. James As British Consul, 1852–1858." *Virginia Cavalcade* 27 (Autumn 1977): 58–67.

Meier, August, and Elliott Rudwick. *Black History and the Historical Profession, 1915–1980.* Chicago: University of Illinois Press, 1986.

Merrill, Walter. *Against Wind and Tide: A Biography of Wm. Lloyd Garrison.* Cambridge: Harvard University Press, 1963.

Moses, Wilson Jeremiah. *Black Messiahs and Uncle Toms: Social and Literary Manipulations of a Religious Myth,* rev. ed. University Park: Pennsylvania State University Press, 1993.

Novick, Peter. *That Noble Dream: The "Objectivity Question" and the American Historical Profession.* New York: Cambridge University Press, 1988.

Oates, Stephen B. *To Purge This Land with Blood: A Biography of John Brown.* New York: Harper & Row, 1970.

———. *The Fires of Jubilee: Nat Turner's Fierce Rebellion.* New York: Harper & Row, 1975.

Ofari, Earl. *"Let Your Motto Be Resistance": The Life and Thought of Henry Highland Garnet.* Boston: Beacon Press, 1972.

Onuf, Peter S. *Jefferson's Empire: The Language of American Nationhood.* Charlottesville: University Press of Virginia, 2000.

———, ed. *Jeffersonian Legacies.* Charlottesville: University Press of Virginia, 1993.

Osofsky, Gilbert, ed. *Puttin' on Ole Mass: The Slave Narratives of Henry Bibb, William Wells Brown, and Solomon Northrup.* New York: Harper & Row, 1969.

Painter, Nell Irvin. "Sojourner Truth in Life and Memory: Writing the Biography of an American Exotic." *Gender & History* 2 (Spring 1990): 3–17.

———. "Representing Truth: Sojourner Truth's Knowing and Becoming Known." *Journal of American History* 81 (September 1994): 461–92.

———. *Sojourner Truth: A Life, a Symbol.* New York: W. W. Norton, 1996.

Parramore, Thomas C. *Southampton County, Virginia.* Charlottesville: University Press of Virginia for the Southampton County Historical Society, 1978.

Pearson, Edmund. *Dime Novels; or, Following an Old Trail in Popular Literature.* Boston: Little, Brown, 1929.

Pease, William H., and Jane H. Pease. "The Negro Convention Movement." *Key Issues in the Afro-American Experience,* ed. Nathan I. Huggins, Martin Kilson, and Daniel M. Fox, 191–205. New York: Harcourt Brace Jovanovich, 1971.

Peterson, Merrill D. *The Jefferson Image in the American Mind.* New York: Oxford University Press, 1960.

———. *Lincoln in American Memory.* Oxford: Oxford University Press, 1994.

Quarles, Benjamin. *Black Abolitionists.* New York: Oxford University Press, 1969.

———. *Allies for Freedom: Blacks and John Brown.* New York: Oxford University Press, 1974.

———, ed. *Blacks on John Brown.* Chicago: University of Illinois Press, 1972.

Renehan, Edward J., Jr. *The Secret Six: The True Tale of the Men Who Conspired with John Brown.* New York: Crown Publishers, 1995.

Report of the National Advisory Commission on Civil Disorders. New York: Bantam Books, 1968.

Richardson, Willis, and May Miller, eds. *Negro History in Thirteen Plays.* Washington, D.C.: Associated Publishers, 1935.

Ripley, C. Peter, ed. *The Black Abolitionist Papers,* vols. 1–5. Chapel Hill: University of North Carolina Press, 1985.

Robert, Joseph Clarke. *The Road from Monticello: A Study of the Virginia Slavery Debate of 1832.* Durham, N.C.: Duke University Press, 1941.

Robinson, Armstead L. "In the Shadow of Old John Brown: Insurrection Anxiety and Confederate Mobilization, 1861–1863." *Journal of Negro History* 65 (Autumn 1980): 279–97.

Sadler, Lynn Veach. "The Figure of the Black Insurrectionist in Stowe, Bouve, Bontemps, and Gaither: Universality of the Need for Freedom." *MAWA Review* 2 (June 1986).

Sandage, Scott A. "A Marble House Divided: The Lincoln Memorial, the Civil Rights Movement, and the Politics of Memory, 1939–1963." *Journal of American History* (June 1993): 135–67.

Savage, Kirk. *Standing Soldiers, Kneeling Slaves: Race, War, and Monument in Nineteenth-Century America.* Princeton, N.J.: Princeton University Press, 1997.

Schor, Joel. *Henry Highland Garnet: A Voice of Black Radicalism in the Nineteenth Century.* Westport, Conn.: Greenwood Press, 1977.

———. "The Rivalry Between Frederick Douglass and Henry Highland Garnet." *Journal of Negro History* 64 (Winter 1979): 30–38.

Schwarz, Philip J. *Twice Condemned: Slaves and the Criminal Laws of Virginia, 1705–1865.* Baton Rouge: Louisiana State University Press, 1988.

Scott, Daryl Michael. *Contempt and Pity: Social Policy and the Image of the Damaged Black Psyche, 1880–1996.* Chapel Hill: University of North Carolina Press, 1997.

Sidbury, James. *Ploughshares into Swords: Race, Rebellion, and Identity in Gabriel's Virginia, 1730–1810.* New York: Cambridge University Press, 1997.

Simmons, Michael K. "Maum Guinea; or, A Dime Novelist Looks at Abolition." *Journal of Popular Culture* 10 (Summer 1976): 81–87.

Sitkoff, Harvard. *The Struggle for Black Equality, 1954–1980.* New York: Hill and Wang, 1981.

Smith, John David. *An Old Creed for the New South: Proslavery Ideology and Historiography, 1865–1918.* Westport, Conn.: Greenwood Press, 1985.

Stampp, Kenneth. *The Peculiar Institution: Slavery in the Ante-bellum South.* New York: Vintage Books, 1956.

Staudenraus, P. J. *The African Colonization Movement, 1816–1865.* New York: Octagon Books, 1980.

Stephenson, Wendell H. "Herbert B. Adams and Southern Historical Scholarship at the Johns Hopkins University." *Maryland Historical Magazine* 42 (1947).

Stone, Albert E. *The Return of Nat Turner: History, Literature, and Cultural Politics in Sixties America.* Athens: University of Georgia Press, 1992.

Styron, William. *The Confessions of Nat Turner.* New York: Vintage, 1967; reprinted 1993.

Sundquist, Eric. *To Wake the Nation: Race in the Making of American Literature.* Cambridge: Belknap Press of Harvard University Press, 1993.

Takaki, Ronald T. *Violence in the Black Imagination.* New York: Oxford University Press, 1993.

Terrill, Tom E., and Jerrold Hirsch, eds. *Such As Us: Southern Voices of the Thirties.* Chapel Hill: University of North Carolina Press, 1978.

Thelen, David P., ed. *Memory and American History.* Bloomington: Indiana University Press, 1990.

Thomas, John L. *The Liberator: William Lloyd Garrison, a Biography.* Boston: Little, Brown, 1963.

Thornbrough, Emma Lou. *T. Thomas Fortune: Militant Journalist.* Chicago: University of Chicago Press, 1972.

Tiernan, Mary Spear. *Homoselle: A Virginia Novel.* New York: R. F. Fenno, 1899.

Tragle, Henry Irving. *The Southampton Slave Revolt: A Compilation of Source Material.* Amherst: University of Massachusetts Press, 1971.

Trotter, Joe William, Jr. *The African American Experience.* Boston: Houghton Mifflin, 2001.

Ullman, Victor. *Martin R. Delaney: The Beginnings of Black Nationalism.* Boston: Beacon Press, 1971.

Van Deburg, William L. *New Day in Babylon: The Black Power Movement and American Culture, 1965–1975.* Chicago: University of Chicago Press, 1992.

Watson, Ritchie D. "Mary Spear Tiernan's Unique Contribution to Post-Bellum Virginia Fiction." *Southern Literary Journal* 17 (Spring 1985): 100–107.

Watts, Jill M. *God, Harlem U.S.A.: The Father Divine Story.* Berkeley: University of California Press, 1992.

West, James L. W., III. *William Styron: A Life.* New York: Random House, 1998.

———, ed. *Conversations with William Styron.* Jackson: University Press of Mississippi, 1985.

White, Deborah Gray. *Ar'n't I a Woman? Female Slaves in the Plantation South.* New York: W. W. Norton, 1985.

Wish, Harvey. "American Slave Insurrections Before 1861." *Journal of Negro History* 22 (July 1937): 299–320.

———. "Slave Disloyalty in the Confederacy." *Journal of Negro History* 23 (October 1938): 435–50.

———. "The Slave Insurrection Panic of 1856." *Journal of Southern History* 5 (1939): 206–22.

Wolper, David L., with Quincy Troupe. *The Inside Story of TV's "Roots."* New York: Warner Books, 1978.

Yarborough, Richard. "Race, Violence, and Manhood: The Masculine Ideal in Frederick Douglass's 'The Heroic Slave.'" In *Frederick Douglass: New Literary and Historical Essays,* ed. Eric J. Sundquist, 166–88. New York: Cambridge University Press, 1990.

Index